Selected Writings
of
Sir Hilary Jenkinson

Sir Hilary Jenkinson

Selected Writings
of
Sir Hilary Jenkinson

Alan Sutton
1980

Alan Sutton Publishing Limited
17a Brunswick Road
Gloucester GL1 1HG

British Library Cataloguing in Publication Data

Jenkinson, *Sir* **Hilary**
  Selected Writings of Sir Hilary Jenkinson
  I. Archives
  025.17'1   CD950

ISBN 0 904387 52 6

Typesetting and origination by
Alan Sutton Publishing Limited

Set in Baskerville 10/11

Printed in Great Britain
by Redwood Burn Limited
Trowbridge & Esher

Contents

Foreword

No one man had more influence on the establishment of the profession of archivist in Great Britain than Sir Hilary Jenkinson. His working life covered a period of remarkable change and development and he, himself, wrote in the Preface to the second edition of the *Manual of Archive Administration* in 1937 that his 'personal experience had . . . chanced to coincide with a period . . . during which appreciation of the value of archives, and organised effort for their better control and maintenance have increased to an unparalleled extent both in Europe and America generally and in England in particular'. Indeed, before his death in 1961, he had seen a nationwide service develop within England and Wales; had witnessed the growth of a professional society of which he became first President; had assisted in the establishment of post-graduate schools for the training of archivists; and, on the international level, had played his part in the setting up of the International Council on Archives.

He was a great scholar, a great archivist and to those who knew him best, a sincere friend; a man of firm principle, who fought mightily for that which he regarded as right and a teacher who won the respect and affection of those whom he guided.

This volume of his writings is comprehensive in its coverage of professional thinking and of academic interests. It includes papers on classification, conservation and the changing ideas of the years after 1945; it also embraces his special delight in palaeography and seals. It covers his concern for Italian archives; his thoughts on the growing profession in England and his wish for the development of a service in America and elsewhere based on sound principles.

The influence of Jenkinson was outstanding during his life and, principally through the *Manual of Archive Administration*, first published in 1922, has remained a vital element in British archive thinking. Inevitably, some of his beliefs have been modified by his successors, but the challenge of his principles remains a touchstone for all.

In 1937 he could write, 'undoubtedly we are at the moment on a rising tide of popular appreciation and general understanding of the value of Archives and of the existence of a special branch of learning dedicated to them'. The British experience embodied in those words can now be reiterated in an international setting and this volume, which contains a distillation of thought and experience, is still valid for all those dedicated to the preservation and proper use of archives. It is in that belief that the Society of Archivists offers it as a further tribute to the memory of a very great man and as a stimulus to our profession the world over.

Editors' Preface

Sir Hilary Jenkinson's reputation as a writer rests securely upon his *Manual of Archive Administration*, which remains basic reading for all archivists. Throughout his life however Sir Hilary wrote copiously upon all aspects of archive work, and while the *Manual* embodies his philosophy and lays down his principles it is these other writings which record his own direct experience in particular fields and illustrate his precept from practice.

To these writings, covering a period of some fifty years, a guide is furnished by the *Bibliography of the Writings of Sir Hilary Jenkinson* which was published first in ARCHIVES (Vol. 2, no. 14, Michaelmas 1955, 329-343) and was later reprinted in the volume of *Essays presented to Sir Hilary Jenkinson* edited by Dr. J. Conway Davies (Oxford University Press, 1957). Every reader of this bibliography must be struck first by the extraordinary scope of Sir Hilary's archival experience and writing, and next by the variety of the places in which his writings have appeared — as individual volumes, in the daily press, in the learned journals of several countries, in the Transactions and Proceedings of learned societies national and local, in presentation volumes, in War Office publications, and in literary periodicals not normally concerned with archive administration such as the Athenaeum, the Times Literary Supplement and the London Mercury. The range is wide, and the difficulty of locating all the writings was — as the compilers of the bibliography recall — formidable and is probably even harder now. There are none which the archivist cannot read with profit, yet there is no library which contains them all.

To re-publish all Sir Hilary's writings would be, in these days of costly printing and production, impracticable. It would also be, on archival grounds, unjustifiable, for the corpus inevitably includes some *pièces d'occasion* and even in the essays of substance Sir Hilary, who knew the value of repetition in advertisement, did not hesitate to say again what he had said before. The editors of the present volume, compelled by reasons of cost and space to be extremely selective, have made their choice with two considerations chiefly in mind, viz. as biographers to indicate from his writings the development of Sir Hilary's thought and the range of his experience as an archivist, and as archivists to offer to their colleagues, collected and accessible, the best of those papers relating to archive practice which are still valid and basic to the archivist's equipment. Every one of them is founded on Sir Hilary's own first-hand experience and is set down with a classical scholar's command of literary English. And on the front cover of the volume readers may see the likeness, drawn from Sir Hilary's personal archive, of the man who wrote them as few can remember him now — not as the patriarch of his last years but as the handsome and vigorous man in the prime of life who, his *Manual* fresh from the press, was setting out to re-create archive principle and practice first in his own country and, by his influence, throughout the world.

ROGER H. ELLIS
PETER WALNE

Palaeography and the Practical Study of Court Hand

INTRODUCTION

Palaeography as an essential preliminary to Research on Medieval History.

In this paper I wish not so much to communicate the result of research as to put forward a profession of faith. It is hardly necessary to dwell on the paramount importance to-day of Documentary Historical Sources: and the Science of Palaeography claims everywhere, claims unchallenged, a very prominent position as an essential preliminary to the study of the medieval sections of these. The Treasures which we in England possess in the way of Documentary, and in particular of Record, sources have, it has been declared on the best authority, no rivals in the world: on the other hand we are frequently told — we have been told so very recently by critics within our own gates — that our willingness and ability to apply ourselves to the necessary preliminaries, and among them particularly Palaeography, leave much to be desired. I would speak, if I may say so, upon this matter in three capacities; as an Archivist, not only loving Records for their own sake but also called upon as it happens to deal daily with large quantities of medieval documents of continually varying dates; as one who has in a small way attempted, at Cambridge, during the last three years to solve the question of giving in an economical fashion to ordinary historical students some slight incentive to and some general preparation for possible research work in the future upon English medieval sources; and as one who has assisted in the compilation of a comprehensive text book[1] upon the handwriting side of the same purpose. From these points of view I will venture to touch upon one or two features in that wealth of English sources to which I have alluded; and to examine the work of Palaeography in the light of them and their importance. If the examination is of the nature of criticism I hope it will appear that I wish not merely to pull down but also, and more anxiously, to set up.

1. *Court Hand Illustrated* . . . , now in the Press. Many of the matters dealt with in the present paper are expansions of questions touched on in this Book.

COURT HAND

The various forms of writing in which English medieval documents (other than formal books) are preserved to us are all derived from an increasingly current writing of the same script which, remaining formal, gives us Book Hand; and are known to us collectively as Court Hand, that is the writing of the Courts. At the risk of saying what has been said before we must examine for a moment the meaning of this word and what it connotes, before we pass to our main subject.

The original Court or *Curia* is the personal Court or *entourage* of the Monarch. The English *Curia* after the Conquest is highly administrative and in the processes of administration it assumes various aspects: beneath them is always the one *Curia*; but its appearance varies with the functions it is momentarily performing. There is for example the Chancery function: here one Officer is pre-eminent — the Chancellor presiding over his scribes; other members of the Court act merely as witnesses to those instruments under the King's Great Seal which it is his duty to prepare and issue. Then we have the Court sitting as a board of finance, presiding over the Annual Audit; in this case the Treasurer takes the lead, but other Members nearly all assist — Constable, Marshal, Chamberlain, Justiciar all have their seats at the Board.

Both in the Chancery and in the Exchequer business increases both in bulk and in scope; and with this goes the natural accompaniment, an increase in the number of subordinates and in the number of deputies: the Chancery and Exchequer have more and more to do and grow more and more professional in character. It is in a third aspect of the Court, however, that professionalism shews itself earliest and most strongly — the judicial aspect. Very early indeed the legal activities of the King, his Justiciar and the members of his Court — the sessions *Coram Rege* — have to be supplemented by itinerant judges: soon even this is not enough; the centralising and solidifying genius of the early Norman Kings works so fruitfully that a second, permanent, Court must be created in London — a Court with whose operations the King and his own *Curia*, travellers over the Realm, can have little to do: we have definitely established the Justices of Common Pleas, a definitely professional administrative class.

Administration[2] is founded on precedent, that is on memory; and it grows with the adoption for its own uses of artificial memory, that is of writing. What we claim for England, what is perhaps stronger in this than in any other country, is the early, continual, universal, crystallisation — formalisation — of administrative processes in the minutest, the most remote departments of life: and, accompanying this, first a necessary accumulation

---

2. By Administration I understand the regulation of any side (social, industrial, legal, military, ecclesiastical) of the affairs of a person or community of persons by constituted authority.

of pieces of artificial memory, of writing, relating to each of these minute departments of life; and then an unnecessary but most fortunate conservation of these in quite extraordinary quantities long after the probability of their use as precedents has disappeared.

But it is not enough to say, as we may say from the foregoing, that the course of English medieval administration has left us an enormous collection of documents: the development of formalised administration carried with it, and the peculiarities of English history and English character have preserved to us, a wonderful collection of what we may call in the strictest sense Records: that is to say, that the writer of the Courts had not only to deal with originals, which issue and seldom return to be preserved in the Official Collections; that is a comparatively small part of his business: there are also the two immensely important and bulky varieties of Copies of originals which issued and Registers of proceedings which took place.[3] No country can shew such examples of them as can England, with its score of great continuous series running down from the 13th century almost to the present day[4], all of them officially produced, preserved throughout in official custody and for official reference. I suggest that the importance of these *full, regular, authentic, officially preserved Records* is one to which a greatly increased comparative attention is due. The Enrolment or Register is too often treated as a place where lost originals may by good fortune be retrieved: I should rather say that such Records have in England an importance beside which that of originals is almost insignificant. Their immediate importance in their present connection, however, is the early, continuous, and highly varied currency of handwriting which goes with them and is largely fostered and developed by the peculiar circumstances under which they were produced.[5]

We have mentioned two varieties of Record making; but there is a third besides those which I have labelled Copies and Registers — the great class of regularly filed Originals, the Ancient Miscellanea which at one time were preserved by every Court. I would dwell for a moment on the Record character of these. This does not depend on the officiality of their writing; for although many of them may have been official originals returned (such as

3. The word *Record* applies properly and originally only to process at law. I use it here, as it is generally used, to mean a document which forms part of the collections in the Public Record Office: and in order to cover all the contents of that building we must define a Record as a document forming part of an official administrative process and preserved, for the purposes of official reference, in official custody. In a large number of cases, including the two classes here under consideration, we may add that the documents are officially written.

4. They begin in the Exchequer, the *Curia Regis* (Judicial) and the Chancery in the reigns of Henry II, Richard I and John respectively.

5. To take only one instance, handwriting will very obviously be affected in the case of a scribe whose chief or sole duty is to copy a large number of documents, in the purpose and original writing of which he had probably no share, on to a long roll as quickly as possible.

writs), probably quite half of them cannot claim that character, being merely supplementary details for more important Records or casual Memoranda or even documents of private origin and meaning which have been drawn into the Public Collections by such an accident as (*e.g.*) the escheat of a property, with its muniments, to the Crown: it depends rather upon their being filed, at some time, in an official connection with other official documents and preserved for purposes of official reference.

Two further points may perhaps be mentioned in connection with these. First there is the fact that they exemplify, obviously, the earliest kind of Record keeping; series in the other two classes have been formed by the separation off and subsequent standardisation of bulky classes of Memoranda or Copies from these Miscellaneous Collections; cases are not wanting where the border line between the formal Enrolment or Register on the one hand and the file of Miscellanea on the other is very slightly defined; and the process of differentiation is always going on[6].

The second point is this. The handwriting of these originals among the Miscellanea is chiefly important for our present purpose because it is so largely non-official: but it must be remembered that in England the influence of the official model was on every side of administrative activity remarkably strong; great interest attaches to the unanimity and closeness with which even the instruments of private or semi-public administration — Court Rolls, for instance, the Registers of Corporate Bodies, original private deeds, or, if I may select an instance I have myself to a slight extent worked out, private tallies of receipt — conform themselves to their contemporary parallels in public life; this conformancy is seen in fashions of all kind, in shape, in phraseology and — equally — in writing.

It will be seen that two circumstances — on the one hand the habit of the Official Record maker of preserving among his Miscellaneous Memoranda all kinds of documents which were not official in origin but which by some official accident came into his hands and had for him an official interest, and on the other the imitative habits of the Record makers of lesser, private, administrations — these two circumstances have joined with other more normal influences to preserve for us in the Collections made by the King's Courts a remarkably catholic body of pieces of medieval writing. So much, for the moment, for the medieval Courts and the general characteristics of their Records.

---

6. A good instance of this is supplied by a comparison of the medieval common law jurisdiction of the Court of Common Pleas and that of the Chancery; and of their respective Records. The Records of the Court of Common Pleas are, of course, bulky rolls of uniform membranes: those of the Chancery's Common Law jurisdiction are in phraseology like them; but since this jurisdiction never attained to great importance they themselves never attained to a more dignified form than that of most un-uniform membranes of Memoranda scattered over the Chancery's Miscellaneous files.

It is when we arrive at the period of letter writing that Court Hand loses its character of omnipresence. Simultaneously, or very nearly so, with what is usually considered the end of the medieval period in England — the reign of Henry VII — we find reforms, sometimes revolutionary, instituted in various Courts; in the Exchequer of Receipt, for instance, new Officials come to the front and with them new Records: almost at the same time appears a new class of Administration and Administrator, an institution which English Archive practice distinguishes from the old *Courts* — *the Department*, the Office of the Secretary of State; whose Records are *State Papers*, with, very soon, a special home of their own in the State Paper Office. The very word *Paper* indicates a change of fashions and it is about this same time that we have imported into England the new Italic handwriting, which gradually — very gradually — ousted the decadent current forms of Court Hand and which was the ancestor of our modern script.

The Court Hand thus displaced was a very slovenly and decadent form indeed; but by this time the Courts had established in their more formal Records a limit of currency beyond which their handwritings did not go. The writing thus established, or modifications of it, they continued to employ long after the Italic hand had become almost universal in ordinary usage: they even developed among themselves distinct contemporary varieties of it, and from this practice of theirs comes the use of the words *Court Hand*. The name, however, has been applied retrospectively to cover all those classes of documents the existence of which previous to 1485 I have adumbrated.

Summarising, therefore, we may say that when we speak of *Court Hand* we are referring — if the medieval period is our mark — in the first place to all kinds of current writing whose first step in its development out of Book Hand may be seen in the volumes of Domesday. Further, we are referring (1) to the documentary remains, formal and informal, of the Courts of Exchequer, Chancery, Common Pleas and King's Bench, (2) to the documentary remains of all kinds of private and semi-private Administrations — the Administrations of the Palatinate, the Borough, the Guild, the Manor, or any agglomeration of property or rights which leads to the collection of deeds, letters and memoranda, of *titres*, of evidences of its privileges and its proceedings. Touching the first class of these we have suggested so far that its most formal manuscript remains — its Registers and Copies — are of immense bulk and of an importance very much undervalued for the subject we have in hand: touching the second, the Records of private or semi-private Administration, we may say that accidents of various kinds have resulted in numerous specimens of the Records produced by the various activities which it includes being preserved among the Public Records — mainly among the Miscellanea of our first class. The Public Records in fact, the Archives in the Chancery Lane Repository, include the bulk of some of the most important classes of medieval documents and representatives of practically all: and to the writings in which all these classes of documents are cast the general term *Court Hand* is applied. It is a loose but convenient name.

THE SCIENTIFIC STUDY OF COURT HAND

It is not to be supposed, of course, that there were not distinguishable styles of handwriting in the various Courts for some time before the words Court Hand could be correctly used in the sense I have described. From about the time of John the most formal Exchequer hand — that of the Pipe Roll, and, later, the Enrolled Accounts which split off from it — large, angular and carefully written, is generally distinguishable from all others employed in the English Courts: the most formal hand of original Grants, *i.e.* of Charters and Letters Patent, which most nearly resembles this Pipe Roll hand, is yet again distinct: while the Enrolment hands of the Chancery and the Registering hands of the Plea Rolls and the Exchequer Memoranda Rolls after going through phases of general currency settled down during the 15th century into conventional forms which differentiate them from other hands and even from each other: and apart from these there is a general residuum of highly current writings varying almost infinitely according to circumstances. It is however to a rather earlier period than this — roughly the 13th and the early 14th centuries — that I wish chiefly to direct attention; and during this period the distinction between the current hands of most Enrolments and Registers and that of Miscellaneous Deeds and Memoranda of all kinds is not marked.

Knowledge of the circumstances and persons responsible for a given series of Records may enable us at various times to detect the spreading of influences from one of the classes mentioned above into another, to place and account for certain familiarities and unfamiliarities, habits of thought, fashions of abbreviation, and so forth. Thus the knowledge that Stapleton was at the Exchequer or that the Tellers were, at a given time, supplanting the Deputy Chamberlains might well throw light upon the script peculiarities of a Receipt Roll: the discovery that at a certain period most of the items in the Pipe Roll were written up beforehand, gives us a criterion of the speed at which the Record was written: the information that Plea Roll and Inquisition *post mortem* particulars and even Original Letters Patent were often supplied, ready written out, by the parties concerned must have a strongly modifying influence upon our opinions concerning their hand-writings and concerning the relations of State clerks and public scriveners: the fact that the Justice's clerk at one time made up those lists of fines which we meet in the Exchequer may serve a similar purpose. Taking a slightly different standpoint we might suggest that by compiling a list of the clerks in any given Office we could establish something in the nature of a succession with a possible inheritance of characteristic tricks of handwriting in the series of documents which that office is known to have produced; that private deeds, or even such official documents as assessments for taxation, being written locally by the parish priest might be found to fall into divisions according to the different houses of Religious in whose gift various livings lay; or that the detailed history of scriveners' guilds, if it could be worked out, might enable us in another way to establish the existence of undoubted schools of handwriting in divers places.

But where in all this does the science of Palaeography come in? I have endeavoured to indicate above a few possibilities of what would be undoubtedly discoveries of palaeographical interest. I would submit, however, that in all these the starting point is supplied by history, generally by the history of that Administration which is directly responsible for the making of the Records. The story of the succession of scribes of the Exchequer is written in the Rolls which detail the payment of their wages; the particulars of Henry VII's reforms at the Receipt come to us through the papers of a law suit between the Clerk of the Pells and the *Scriptor Talliarum*; the intrusion of the family solicitor into public documents is a matter of occasional points of internal evidence; the activities of the Justice's clerk may be traced to an Exchequer order: everywhere the tale is the same — the History of Administration supplies the initial explanations of Palaeography.

Now Palaeography may be defined as a science which examines the forms of individual letters in every obtainable stage of their evolution from the earliest known form down to that of the present day, classifying them according to the origin and succession of their forms, the writing materials used, the way in which the pen or other instrument is held, and so forth. It follows, of course, that the student trained in Palaeography should first be able, though this is really an incidental matter, to say without question what any given form of letter represents — to detect for instance in what looks at a certain part of the medieval period like a capital *M* what is really a capital *S*; and secondly should make some pretensions to the assigning of any given form to a certain class, a certain date, and even a certain locality. From these two powers of the palaeographical student it is usually argued firstly that everyone who is to deal with ancient handwritings should be trained to read them by a course of Palaeography and secondly that a man so trained will be able to assist the historical student by assigning a date to his documents. It is by these arguments that Palaeography, as a practical aid to the practical student of History, must stand or fall.

So far as concerns documents not in Book Hand the science of Palaeography (medievally speaking) was invented (as indeed was also *Diplomatique*) to deal with documents of an early date, when writing was comparatively little applied to administration; a date from which, consequently, survivals are very few and those, from the point of view of the information they offer to the critic of their structure and date, not fully developed. But, once again, it must be considered in the present paper in a strictly practical light, the light of the claim which it makes, or which is made for it, to be of essential utility to historical research upon English medieval sources as a whole — a whole of which the early documents above described form a part so insignificant as to be almost negligible. What we have to ask ourselves is: how far is the overloaded student of History to be saddled with special preliminary studies before he is allowed to undertake research work? or, supposing that we grant the necessity of such preliminary studies, are we quite sure that Palaeography is an essential one of them?

Now for the purposes of mere reading, Palaeography cannot be considered necessary. Scores of students have indisputably learned to read adequately, even well, without ever troubling to memorise a palaeographical rule, without even knowing why a particular sign is called Tironian or how the earliest contractions were concerned with the name of God: in all the great workers of the past in England there is to be found no trace of palaeographical training. I would not, of course, deny for a moment that minute knowledge of the way in which a given letter was habitually formed (say for instance, the medieval *g*, with its three essential parts of upper bow, lower bow and final horizontal stroke) may upon occasion lead to a definite conclusion in reading when all other aids fail; nor that the palaeographer can, for example, tell the student reader that *tñ* means *tamen* and not *tantum*. But the vast majority of the difficulties which beset the reader of medieval English documents — such difficulties as the resolution of a large number of minims into *i's*, *m's*, *n's* and *u's*, the distinction between *O* and *E*, or the question of the meaning of a marginal *ex̃* or *p.e.*[7] — cannot be cleared up by the palaeographer; and on the other hand it is extraordinary how few are the cases where more than one sense is possible in a given passage. To know what must be there, what the document must mean, is, in fact, a much greater assistance than to know what, palaeographically, the letters appear to represent; and to the necessities of the context Palaeography is no guide.

It is necessary to observe that the purpose of this paper is not to decry the value of Palaeography as an independent study, far less its interest; nor to deny its necessity in any historical field save that of English Court Hand and English official documents with their adjuncts. I would emphasise, however, once again the essentially administrative character of all English Court Hand documents: in the comparatively rare cases — I wish that I had space to point out how singularly rare they are — where even private documents[8]

---

7. One might add — an even more obvious instance — that Palaeography is powerless to aid in extending any of those suspensions (so common in later Court Hands) which represent an inflexion.
8. Taking only the case of a private deed touching the transfer of land we may point out that if — as very frequently occurs — it is in the form of a fine or recovery there will be a mass of documents relating to the transaction preserved by the Court of Common Pleas; alternatively, if it takes another form, it will very often be enrolled, for safety, upon the

have no connection with Public Administration and where, consequently, the explanation of difficult points in them cannot be sought among Public Records, they have generally an administrative connection, equally sufficient for explanatory purposes, with others in the same collection as themselves.

It is not my business here to point further the conclusion which should have emerged inevitably from the foregoing remarks that not *Diplomatique*[9] but the history of Administration — Public Administration in all its branches and its most minute details, and Palatinate, Ecclesiastical, Borough, Manorial and all other kinds of Private and semi-Private Administration — is the one thing necessary for the explanation of our English documents; nor to give instances (there are many) where lack of this, not of *Diplomatique*, has led the most distinguished users of Public Records into false conclusions. But I may justly mention the fact that it does so emerge because, if I am right in the statements I have made with regard to it and if in addition the actual deciphering of that writing which we call Court Hand can be well and practically learned by, in effect, mere practice, then it may be true (the justification of this paper is that the writer believes it to be most urgently true) that we require in England a much larger number of students to work upon Records for the express purposes of Administrative History — that unwritten science; but it is not true that we want them preliminarily trained in *Diplomatique* in the sense in which that highly organised science is usually understood; and, though a previous study of facsimiles may save them much time, it is equally untrue that we want them trained in scientific Palaeography.

But we have still another point to deal with; for if Palaeography is not necessary in order to teach us to read it may yet be necessary in order that we may learn to date our documents: this is the second and, after an absolute essentiality, the highest merit which Palaeography can claim in the position of an adjunct to History. Let us examine then the further proposition that Palaeography as an exact science ceases, or becomes overwhelmingly

dorse of the Close Roll; it may often, again, be subsequently confirmed, in which case it will be transcribed on the Patent or Charter Roll; if it relates to land held in chief a licence to alienate will be a necessary preliminary (Patent Roll and probably an Inquisition *ad quod damnum*) and later it may be cited or even quoted in Inquisitions *post mortem*: there are further numerous possibilities of the property being involved in a law suit and the deed quoted on a Plea Roll or of the Exchequer becoming interested and preserving a copy of the document among its Memoranda: while if the land in question ever falls into the hands of the Crown the actual deed will come into the Public Records with the other muniments of title.

9. *Diplomatique* is the Science which studies all matters touching the form of documents and, particularly, their phraseology: it tells us, for instance, that Henry II referred to himself as *ego* and *me* in his Charters while Richard I said *nos*. Three things follow: (1) as its name implies it is interested in originals more than in copies; (2) if two documents are duplicates in form it takes no account of the fact that their position in administration makes their significance completely distinct: it will use indifferently a Chancery Inquisition or the

difficult, where English Records, as series of importance, begin. I should like to adduce a few of the more obvious considerations which contribute to this view.

Apart from the fact that during the whole of the finished, active Record keeping period, which begins about *1200*, a large majority of Records date themselves, the first and most important consideration I have to suggest is that of bulk. I will take at hazard the eleventh year of Edward II — a date when governmental activity, as reflected in Records, had not reached anything approaching its most prolific state — and examine the document-ary remains of its Administration[10]. I need hardly remind the reader that we are deliberately excluding here all Private Records, except such as now figure among the Public Records; and even those we can only mention.

I should preface this statement by remarking that a Chancery Roll may be taken as consisting of any number up to 25 or 30 large membranes. The Exchequer Rolls are, relatively, very small at this period and perhaps the same modest estimate may be applied to them; but their membranes — except in the case of the Receipt and Issue Rolls — are twice the size of the Chancery ones. The same may be said of the lesser Plea Rolls; but the Rolls of the great permanent Courts are getting near to the period of their full size, when their membranes may run into hundreds.

The Chancery, then, supplies us in this regnal year with a Charter Roll; two Rolls of Letters Patent; a Fine Roll; part each of Extract, Gascon, Roman, Scottish, and Treaty Rolls; a Close Roll; parts of two supplementary Close Rolls; and a Roll of Writs for Issue (*Liberate*): turning to the Warrants for the issue of these "Great Seals" (not always a complete series by any means) we find four files, each containing perhaps a hundred writs; among those Returns by Inquisition, with writs attached, which often formed a preliminary to the issue of Chancery letters we find three large files of Inquisitions *post mortem*, eight files of Inquisitions *ad quod damnum*, and three of Miscellaneous Inquisitions: there is besides a considerable residuum of Miscellanea of various kinds.

The Exchequer yields much material. In the Receipt department we have six Rolls of Receipt and Issue and a little *Jornalia* Roll (giving daily and weekly balances); the original Tallies of receipt have perished but there is a fragmentary series of original Writs of *Liberate*. In the Exchequer of Audit we have, of course, the well known and bulky Pipe Roll (a single roll of this would make a very large volume if printed) and its copy the Chancellor's Roll, while accounts other than those of the Sheriffs' (*i.e.* the enrolled

Exchequer duplicate, though one is the return to a writ and the other the voucher to an account. (3) it treats documents *per se*; the fact that a particular letter under the Privy Seal is the warrant for a letter under the Great Seal does not particularly concern it, unless the fact induces a change of phraseology.

10.   I am indebted to my wife for the compilation of these statistics.

accounts of the Keeper of the Wardrobe, the Escheators, and so forth) are represented in the membranes of the Foreign Accounts: when we come to the remains of those preliminary accounts and vouchers of all kinds which preceded audit we find, of course, a very large number of documents, each numbering as a rule anything up to ten membranes; thus the Wardrobe produces eleven such accounts; the Sheriffs' Administrative Accounts two; the Customs five; the Fines, Amercements and Estreats, relating to the proceeds of justice, one complete account and parts of nine others; and altogether we have over 60 of these accounts to deal with — this in a year when the most numerous kind (that relating to Subsidies) is entirely wanting; the current business of the Exchequer is reflected in two Memoranda Rolls and one *Originalia* Roll (extracts from its own Rolls sent over by the Chancery): and finally the Exchequer, like the Chancery, has also a residuum of Miscellanea to shew us.

There was a Parliament in this year and its activities are marked by a Roll: but the Writs and Returns of Members have survived for only two counties: here again we have also some (Parliament and Council) Miscellanea in both the Chancery and the Exchequer[11].

Turning to the side of Justice, we find that this year gives us four King's Bench Plea Rolls, five Common Pleas Plea Rolls and one Exchequer Plea Roll; a Marshalsea Roll; two Rolls of the Courts of Wales and Chester; and the whole or parts of 19 Rolls kept by Justices on commission: further we have the Feet of Fines (copies of the most common form of deed for the transference of land) to the extent of 44 whole or part files. There are no Judicial Miscellanea for this year and the Writs have perished.

To these have to be added a very considerable number of Private Records belonging to this year now in the Public Record Office — Ministers' Accounts, Court Rolls and original deeds; and the much larger number of documents of the same description in other Public and in Private Collections[12]. And we must conclude by emphasising the fact that, while many years before this date we should find a quantity of Records almost equally large, not many years later the number would be many times larger.

A second consideration induced by this first one is that of the very large number of scribes whose work has come down to us though, in a large majority of cases, we are ignorant of their personalities; not to mention the great number of those who do not even live for us by this anonymous survival of their work. To begin with there is the crowd of official scribes: the Chancery scribes, including not only those who wrote original letters patent,

11. The medieval Records of Parliament are distributed between the two Courts.
12. To realise the size to which the medieval collections of a Private or a semi-Public Administrative body may go one has only to give the slightest glance at one of the fuller Reports of the Historical Manuscripts Commission.

charters and so forth, but also the scribes of documents under the lesser seals, the scribes of the enrolments, the scribes who wrote the already vast number of original writs which issued in judicial proceedings: there are the Exchequer scribes in four important and busy departments: there are the Judicial scribes who have left us in the Plea Rolls testimony of their own and the Justices' activities and who besides had the writing of all the very numerous judicial writs (or writs of process) which issued out of their various Courts, not to mention the numerous memoranda of panels of jurors and so forth which, like the process writs, have generally perished. Then there are all the scribes who had to compile for the Chancery or Exchequer the reports or accounts of such Royal Officers as the Escheators[13]. Besides all these there is the vast class of local writers who wrote the private letters and deeds or the private Manor Rolls not a tithe of which has come down to us; or again the local collectors and writers (to mention only one class of documents) of accounts and assessments for Subsidies. It can be no exaggeration to say that so early as the beginning of the reign of Henry III there was scarcely a place of the smallest importance in England which had not a scribe of some sort living in it; and we may add that there is not one of these scribes whose handwriting may not have been in large or small quantities preserved to us among the Public Records or elsewhere.

Surely in the face of such facts it is idle to pretend that any science can either cover with minute exactitude so wide a range of documents or on the other hand supply us with any common factors necessarily applicable to writers so many in number, distributed over so wide a space of country, in an age when means of communication were definitely bad, and practically all of them unknown to us in the matter of their age, origin, habits and standing.

There are, however, many lesser, yet still considerable, difficulties in the way of the palaeographer with which I have not yet dealt. With regard to the question of age, for instance, it has to be remembered that of any two clerks writing at one time similar, or parts of the same, documents one might be 60 years of age, the other 20; and this in a period when handwriting was undergoing constant and definite change: instances are not unknown where two contiguous pages in a Register are written in styles so distinct as to belong in appearance to dates a generation apart. Environment or early upbringing suggests, again, obvious possibilities of the most remarkable peculiarities of writing. And we cannot leave out the probability of personal idiosyncracies of all kinds — any constant user of Records may collect hundreds of instances in a very short time.

Of more importance is the question of yet another unknown factor — the comparative ignorance or knowledge of a scribe. It is a safe maxim in Record

13.   There are many indications that the Sheriffs and Escheators must have maintained local offices which not only dealt with a considerable volume of business but also supported a considerable permanent staff.

work that ignorance on the part of a scribe must never be presumed, but the opposite of that statement is equally true: thus I give two instances of remarkably skilful work in the way of forgery by scribes of whom one at least appears to have been singularly ignorant of documentary matters other than actual writing: on the side of pure ignorance may be quoted the scribe who breaks off suddenly in his copy of an original, which is still preserved to us and is quite legible to the modern scholar, with the despairing remark *plus non legi potest*: and most of the mistakes made by modern beginners in reading — such for instance as the mistaken reading of the 14th century *W* as *lb*, or the 15th century *x* as *p* — seem to have been made at some time by a medieval scribe.

Curious instances of this kind might be multiplied, as might the collection of other facts relating to the medieval scribe tending all to the same purpose. The mention of copying, however, leads me to a remark upon one more factor of some importance. Copying at length was common in all classes of English medieval documents. Bishops' Registers, for instance, are often full not only of letters sufficiently drawn out but also of replies quoting the first letter in full and even of further replies quoting both the preceding; the formidable habit of the English Kings of quoting in their charters the full text of older deeds or charters which they confirmed is another manifestation of the same spirit; which, again, gives us wills quoted in full in Inquisitions *post mortem*, Royal Writs often most unnecessarily copied at full length in the notes of legal proceedings, and so forth. In fact the habit appears in every kind of document; and there are traces of very curious effects springing from it. Thus the scribe, unable to read, may endeavour to copy exactly, with disastrous results (particularly in the case of Saxon Charters); or, coming to a letter, a capital for instance, which is not so familiar as to be formed without thought in the established contemporary manner, he may unconsciously imitate the form he has before him in a deed perhaps fifty years old; or again he may (undoubted instances occur) deliberately archaise: from any one of these may result such a palaeographical anomaly as the *M*, or beavertailed, form of capital *S* in a Richard II Charter Roll, or the open-topped superior *a* reappearing in the 15th century.

CONCLUSION

I do not wish for a moment to maintain the absurd proposition that the reading of medieval Documents is best acquired purely by rule of thumb; that there are no rules of abbreviation, no facts with regard to the formation of a given letter in (let us say) the 12th and again the 15th centuries which an experienced teacher may profitably communicate to an inexperienced student, to the great saving of the latter's time. My aim is merely to suggest that when we say Palaeography we do not mean the mere teaching of a student to read medieval documents — that we must be prepared to abide by the real meaning of the word: and to shew that the importance of Palaeographical Science is at present overrated, while that of the History of Administration is dangerously undervalued, in relation to the solution of normal difficulties in the reading of Court Hand and to the training of students for the purposes of Historical research. The result of this is, of course, that a great deal of time is given unnecessarily to Palaeography, while (an even more serious matter) the student is cut off from that knowledge of Administrative History which is really vital to his work.

If I have seemed to dwell over much on what certainly should be an obvious point — that the methods of the conventional *Diplomatique* and Palaeography, invented to deal with early and sparse documents, break down when applied to the large mass of Records (so much later as these are in date and in character so insular) — it is because the trend of contemporary criticism in England leads to the supposition that this conclusion is not yet sufficiently plain to many scholars whose opinion upon the subject is a matter of great moment. Our Records are of so much value, and the proper working of them a need so pressing, that the presentment in an emphatic form of the views of the English school of Record workers seems to be of real importance. That school is one which can trace its history from Fanshawe and others in the 16th and early 17th centuries down through Madox to Maitland. It has never ceased to handle English Records, whether from the point of view of form or from that of handwriting, on the basis of an examination of administrative activities. In the matter of Palaeography its views might perhaps be summed up best in the statement that Court Hand documents can generally be read with certainty, but only in the light of their meaning; and that they can nearly always be dated with accuracy, but not by their handwriting.

Some Notes on the Preservation, Moulding and Casting of Seals

The task of card-indexing the enormous number of seals scattered over the various groups and classes of documents in the Public Record Office, originally undertaken by Sir William St. John Hope, but interrupted by his death and by the war, was resumed in 1922 by Mr. R.C. Fowler[1]. It was then decided to create a small special section within the Repairing Department, to deal with questions of packing, repairing, moulding and casting. When this work came to be started, it was discovered that the various processes had been hitherto regarded in this country rather as trade secrets; and although some works on the subject have been published abroad,[2] though also various archivists have been most generous in placing their experience at my disposal,[3] I found that some matters which interested us were still unexplained and that in practice we had to make almost every step the subject of more or less elaborate experiment. As we are now passing out of this experimental stage, and as many Fellows of the Society of Antiquaries and other persons in this country are possessors of seals and may be presumed to have some interest in the technical and mechanical processes[4] involved in their preservation, it has seemed worth while to record the result of our modest inquiries in this place.[5]

1. Mr Fowler's paper on these seals was read on the same evening as the present note and will be published in *Archaeoligia*, vol. lxxiv.
2. Auguste Coulon, *Le Service Sigillographique* . . . , Paris, 1916. Baron Harald Fleetwood, *Moulage et Conservation des Sceaux du Moyen Age* (in *Meddelanden från svenska Riksarkivet*, ser. I, 59): Stockholm, 1923.
3. Notably the authors of the two works cited and Mlle Nicodème, of the Archives Génrales du Royaume at Brussels.
4. When the present paper was read examples were shown of all the processes described.
5. The subject is, in a way, one proper to an archivist rather than to antiquaries in general. I have dealt with it only very briefly in my *Manual of Archive Administration*, because at the time when that book was written I had not yet made any of the experiments described here.

COMPOSITION

The very large proportion of seals of importance were made of a mixture of bees-wax and resin,[6] the latter probably in the form now known as Venice turpentine; with the addition of colouring matter, if desired, vermilion and verdigris being the most common. Certain types of seal in 'natural' wax are said to contain also an admixture of chalk, which is held responsible for their crumbling. They are certainly found in a dry and flaky condition much more often than coloured ones and it is possible that the makers found it difficult without the chalk to get the light tone they required; whereas scarlet and green seals can be obtained by mixing the colour with quite a dark natural wax. Analysis, however, has shown up to date no trace of chalk in English seals of natural wax, but has shown traces of mould; it is probable therefore that the laminated and fragile appearance of these seals is due to damp, perhaps from the wax being softened in hot water. In green seals the verdigris, which is a fungicide, would prevent this.[7] It was common also to coat the surface of the finished seal with varnish. The mixture was not (it seems probable) melted, as a rule, to running point for sealing purposes, but merely warmed; the impression, whether pendent or applied, being obtained by hard vertical pressure on the matrix.

Modern wax (so called) is composed chiefly of shellac, which, we may conjecture, became available in large quantities as a result of the activities of the East India Company. Accordingly we find shellac seals becoming common only in the seventeenth century. Seals of this material appear, as a rule, in the form of small, applied signet-seals. The use of the large pendent seal had, indeed, largely declined by now, as a result of the greatly increased use of authentication by signature. Where the pendent seal was used it was as a survival of an old practice on documents of certain old types — notably Royal Letters and Charters — and for these the old mixture probably continued to be employed, as indeed it is occasionally at the present day. No research has yet been made into the question when shellac sealing first appears, nor in what mixture, nor into the chemical changes (if any) produced in it by age. It is much to be hoped that these gaps in our knowledge will presently be filled; but for the purposes of this article shellac and wax seals (save for one or two slight modifications) may be treated together.

Papered seals (the impression being made on paper, generally with wax

---

6.   For the varying mixtures, see the analysis of seals of various dates from the thirteenth to the fifteenth century in an article by Sir James Dobbie and Dr. J.J. Fox in the *Transactions of the Chemical Society* (1914), vol 105, p. 797.
7.   Vermilion, if, as is likely, it included mercury compounds, would have the same effect.

underneath) are again a late device.[8] The making of leaden *bullae* was probably never (or, if at all, only very rarely) practised in this country. We shall have to say something about their preservation, however, since foreign examples are not uncommon in our collections. The so-called seals of goldsmith's work are not, of course, made by impression and are so rare that they do not call for observation here.

NOMENCLATURE

It may be worth while to mention in passing that an effort has been made recently to devise a standard nomenclature for the description of seals. This was printed in a *Report on the Editing of Historical Documents*, compiled by a Committee of the Anglo-American Conference of Historians and published in the *Bulletin of the Institute of Historical Research*.[9] I have used the terms there laid down throughout the present paper.

PACKING AND REPAIRING

Seals may suffer from cracking or breakage, from scratching, from collapse due to pressure or to heat, from staining and mould under circumstances of exceptional dampness, and from 'perishing', i.e. decay due to change in their constituent elements. On the other hand they do not seem to require air as much as, certainly not more than, parchment and paper do; and research[10] has proved that as a rule there is surprisingly little chemical alteration in their substance even when they date from quite early times. Moreover it is within the experience of many archivists that seals which have been bestowed, without any particular care, in the ordinary chests or cupboards of an ordinary muniment room, and have been subjected to very little examination or disturbance, are as a rule in a remarkably sound condition; provided, of course, that they have not experienced any abnormal conditions of heat or damp. The seals enclosed in tightly fitting 'skippets' of wood or

---

8. I have seen many early seals over which a parchment cover had been sewn, but never one in which the impression had been made on the wax through the parchment. It is probable that these parchment covers are, as a rule, an early archivist's addition: that is certainly the case in a file of fourteenth-century applied seals in Chester 1/1, where addressing tags have been cut off the documents themselves and used for this purpose. I am indebted to Mrs. Sharp for this example.
9. Number 1, June 1923.
10. Dobbie and Fox op.cit The fragments analysed were supplied by the Public Record Office and were quite casually selected.

metal[11] are also, as a rule, well preserved.[12] The inference is that the best course to pursue with seals would be to have skippets made for them individually or, better still, to house them in some kind of rack which would prevent them from touching each other or coming under any pressure and in which they would enjoy the normal conditions, as regards ventilation and protection from dirt, which are prescribed for the parchment or paper documents to which they are generally attached; and then to leave them strictly alone. We need not seriously discuss the plan of severing them from the documents and preserving them separately, a procedure almost universally and deservedly condemned.

Unfortunately, in any large collection the conditions suggested are impracticable; the rack and skippet systems would involve an expenditure of time, material and space, and an alteration of existing arrangement, which are prohibitive; and it is impossible to cease production to students. It becomes necessary, therefore, to find the safest means of packing at a reasonable cost and to avoid production, wherever possible, by providing casts for study, incidentally neutralizing the worst results of any possible damage by preserving permanent moulds.

Packing

In the first place it is desirable to prevent the seals from knocking against each other, or against the walls of a receptacle, by the use of some soft material; but the Swedish authorities maintain — and our own examination of wadding that has been used tends, at least in some cases, to confirm them — that any absorbent material draws the greasy nature out of the wax, making the seal friable; and certainly seals preserved in bags of linen, cloth, etc., have almost invariably perished. We are at present trying to meet this difficulty by means of a kind of quilt made of wadding wrapped in waxed tissue paper and fastened together with a stitch.

The question of the receptacle to be used varies with the nature of the document, and more particularly with the way in which the seal is affixed to it.

I take the *Pendent Seals* first, assuming for the moment that we are dealing with the class of deeds and charters to which the vast majority of such documents belong. As a rule these have been folded and this, or a fresh folding,[13] is generally preserved, each deed becoming a separate package

11. It is perhaps worth while to add a note here that many old skippets are of iron and rusty; if therefore they are left on great precautions should be taken to prevent their coming in contact with the paper or parchment of the document.
12. In the cases of single seals (generally foreign) the wax and tag were often placed in the skippet first and the impression then made. A good example is T.R. Diplomatic Documents 436 (dated 1430) where the skippet is of wood, turned in the grain of the log. A number of further examples will be found in this class.
13. Where the old creases show a tendency to damage the writing.

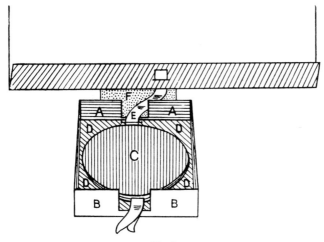

Fig. 1.

AA and BB Walls of box, cut away to take tag. C Seal. D Floor of box, lined and with (E) seal-tag sewn to it. F Strip of cloth fastened to bottom of box (outside) and sewn to document.

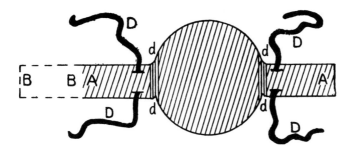

Fig. 2.

Millboard casing: plan of one side. AA Millboard and cloth. BB Cloth only. dd Board bent at this point. DD Tapes.

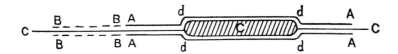

Fig. 3.

Millboard casing: section through both sides. AA Millboard and cloth, bent at dd. BB Cloth only. CCC Position of seal-tag and seal.

which is tied loosely with tape or (as at the Public Record Office) slipped into an open-topped envelope. If this method of packing has been adopted and if there are not more than two or three seals on a single document, and those small and relatively thick lumps of wax,[14] it will generally be safe to fold up the seals (protected with a 'quilt') inside the deed; this is particularly the case if the deeds thus folded are to be packed in a box on their edges, like the cards in a card-index,[15] so that there is comparatively little pressure.

If the seal is in the least frail, or much larger than an inch in diameter, the above method will not suffice; and indeed it should never be employed in the case of a really important seal. The next simplest plan may then be adopted — that of folding the seal in the deed as before but putting the whole package into a cardboard box with a loose, flanged lid.

More elaborate still (fig. 1), but often necessary, is the method by which the seal (c) alone, with suitable 'quilts', is placed in the cardboard box, in the sides of which (A, B) a hole is cut for the tab, tongue or cords by which it is suspended. When this is used it will be wise to secure the seal by a stitch (E) passing over the tab or cord and through the bottom of the box (D); and in some cases also to have an attachment to the box, of cloth or some other material (F), which may be fastened by a stitch to the document so as to take the weight.

A modification of this plan may be made by the use of two pieces of thin millboard, covered with binder's cloth (AA), of the shape shown in fig 2. Each of these, by means of two double scorings (dd), has a hollow formed in it for the seal (C) to lie in, as is shown in fig 3, and this hollow may be lined with the normal wood and tissue. The two pieces are laid one on each side of the seal and its tag, or cord, and strings or tapes (D) are tied[16] round the whole package immediately above and below the rounded part containing the seal. For extra strength the cloth may be produced (BB) beyond the millboard so as to reach the document itself, to which it may be stitched.

Exceptional cases, such as that of a document having a large number of seals pendent from it, must be treated each on its own merits. To take an example of the kind just mentioned, a document at the Public Record Office less than 30 inches in width, and having no less than twenty-five large seals pendent from its lower edge, has been attached to a card slightly larger than its own size plus that of the seals; and to the lower edge of this is hinged a box closing over the seals only and fastened in position by tapes. Within this the seals are separated into three layers by means of long 'quilts' slipped between them (plate I).

14. Such as the signet seals found normally on private deeds of all dates.
15. This is the Record Office practice.
16. Or wire clips may be used *provided they are made of brass*. The device described is itself a modification of one used by Dr. G.H. Fowler in the County Muniments at Bedford.

PLATE I: Deed with pendent seals, showing method of packing

The preservation of *Applied Seals* is a much more difficult matter to speak of; indeed most cases have to be treated on their merits. The documents are very frequently made up in bundles, files or even volumes.[17] In such cases the superimposed papers or parchments form to some extent a protection; for in made-up volumes and files the pages do not ever pack as closely to one another as they do in the case of the regular sheets of an ordinary printed book. Shellac seals in such a position, being harder but at the same time more fragile, resist the flattening action of the weight of paper laid upon them better than the wax ones, but have a greater tendency to break.

On the whole it will be wise always to give some added protection to applied seals if they are of any importance. A simple plan is to make a small 'quilt', strengthen one edge with a fold of linen, and through this sew it on to the document at the side of the seal, over which it forms a hinged flap. A more elaborate plan is to insert a stout guard in the volume or file and to fasten on to this a sheet of millboard having a hole cut in it to fit (with plenty of margin for possible shifting) over the seal. A loose single document having an applied seal it is best to put between two boards, the top one, with the hole as described, being hinged at the side to another, to which the document itself is fastened. It must be borne in mind in all cases, but particularly in that just mentioned, the applied seals, especially the small delicate wax ones of the fourteenth and fifteenth centuries, have very often become bent (carrying, of course, the parchment or paper with them) so that there is a hollow below them; and that in packing it is just as important to give support underneath this, by means of a pad, as to give protection to the upper surface. In the file shown in plate II certain small documents having delicate applied seals on them have been fastened at one end to larger pieces of millboard, which are themselves inserted like documents in the file: this ensures rigidity and makes it possible to pad the seals both at the back and at the front. Note the block at the right-hand (outer) edge of the lower file-board and the corresponding makeup of the back with pieces of board: this is, of course, a simple device to prevent pressure between the boards when closed.

It may perhaps be permissible, in concluding this section, to plead for a liberal interpretation of the word *important* in relation to small seals. Generally it is bestowed only on armorial ones or those having a curious or beautiful design. But the small rough private seals are often very interesting and, in particular, they are one of our chief sources for the study of a subject very little known at present but quite important — that of merchants' and other marks: which makes them well worth care in preservation. An important criterion of value for such seals is the fact that they do or do not exist elsewhere.

17. There are countless small signet seals scattered through the volumes of the *State Papers* at the Public Record Office.

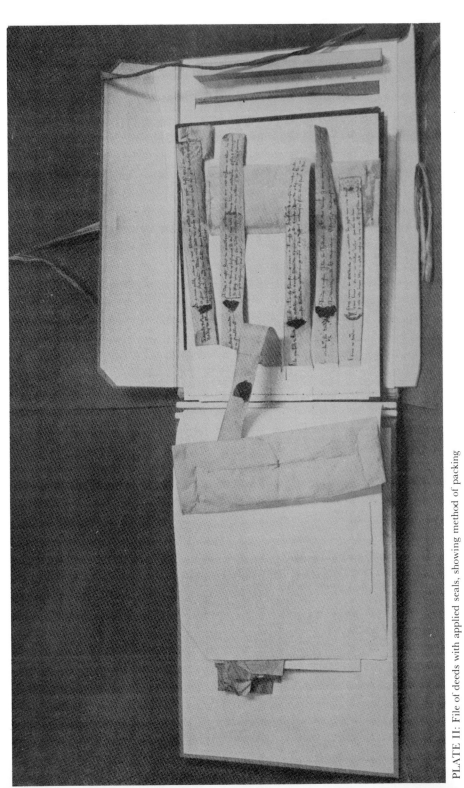

PLATE II: File of deeds with applied seals, showing method of packing

Cleaning and Restoring

The authorities at Stockholm and, I believe, at Dresden have devoted considerable time to the question of restoring their quality to seals which have 'perished'. The mixture which they recommend, and which we have used with some modification[18] at the Public Record Office, undoubtedly improves the consistency of brittle and flaky seals — it is particularly good for the natural wax seals which, to judge from the state in which they have come down to us, must frequently[19] have suffered from mould or had that admixture of chalk, or some similar substance, which has already been mentioned: it is also a very efficient cleaner if rubbed on plentifully with a very soft brush. Ordinary soap and water may also be used for cleaning, but if this is done great care must be taken in drying, especially at the point where the tab or cord enters the seal. It is also necessary to use only the softest brushes for these operations, for fear of scratches; the finest watchmaker's cleaning brush is the best.

Repairing

It is generally recognized that the best mending material is wax of about the same consistency as the original.[20] We have adopted the principle that it is the archivist's business not only not to fake a broken design, but also not to hide the modern work he puts into repairing in any way.[21] We therefore use deliberately a colour different from that of the seal, generally a natural brown; and do not adopt the plan of running into a crack wax from the back of the seal itself. The wax is applied warm and worked in with a hot knife or bodkin. In making up a seal of which only a fragment survives we add at the edges only enough to round off jagged pieces which might catch and cause further breakage. For preliminary holding together of small pieces spirit varnish (e.g. gum sandarac or a very thick solution of shellac) will be found useful. For extra strength heated metal pins, if the seal is thick enough to take them, may be thrust through from the edge so as to hold two pieces together. Should there be a number of small and fragile pieces it may be necessary to float them in a pad of new wax; but as little of this as may be should be used and finger and thumb marks, or any other marks on the back of the original, should be preserved. In view of the frequency of breakage it is wise to note somewhere (e.g. on its box) the state of the seal at the time of repair.

Leaden Bullae

The chief danger to these is that of corrosion as a result of contact with various impurities; in particular, seals placed in oaken receptacles will

---

18. We use a solution of bees-wax, turpentine, and benzine: see Baron de Fleetwood, *op. cit.*
19. See the suggestion made above as to the reason for this.
20. We use a mixture of wax and resin in the proportion of about two to one.
21. From this point of view the more skilfully the 'fake' is carried out the worse the crime.

become corroded as surely as though they were being deliberately converted into white lead by the ordinary Dutch process. If this corrosion has gone far it may be impossible to clean the seal without destroying all the design. One such was treated recently, upon the advice of the Government Laboratory, merely by saturating the surface with methyl cellulose; which, being a chemically stable substance, will, it is hoped, prevent any further damage. Others were coated with the same after a thorough brushing, first with spirit and ether, then with dilute hydrochloric acid (8 per cent.), then with dilute ammonia (8 per cent.), and then (very carefully) with distilled water, and a final drying by means of spirit. It is perhaps worth noting for the benefit of those who, like the writer, are not chemists, that the coating is not a celluloid; all celluloids being regarded as chemically unstable and therefore unsuitable.

Bullae which have to be exposed in oak show-cases at the Public Record Office are now protected from the volatile acids given off by the oak by being enclosed in air-tight glass boxes.[22]

MOULDING

From the point of view of the archivist the making of a permanent mould is perhaps the most important of all the processes connected with seals. The only satisfactory medium for this is plaster of Paris; the finest obtainable quality being used (that known as 'Dental') and even this being sifted through fine gauze (the reside may be used for backing). It is not impossible to use warm gelatine even on wax seals and gelatine moulding is an easy process: but as such moulds are not in any sense permanent, their only use for our purposes would be in the case where there is a great deal of overhang in a seal (due to collapse of the wax from age) and this condition can almost always be dealt with in other ways. Supposing gelatine to be used, a plaster cast would have to be made immediately and another mould made, in plaster, from that; which introduces a great deal of extra possibility of error.

Ordinary Plaster Moulds

When a pendent seal is to be moulded the document and its tab, tongue or cord are carefully wrapped in waxed tissue paper. The seal is then cleaned and carefully examined to see if at any point there is overhang. This most commonly occurs over the rim of the seal, where a matrix has been very deeply pressed into soft wax, and in extreme cases it may be necessary to cut away some of this superfluous wax; though as a general rule it is possible to

22. Pieces of glass jointed with cloth, which is waxed. The question of corrosion of lead objects is treated in *Bulletin No. 5* of the Department of Scientific and Industrial Research (*The Cleaning and Restoration of Museum Exhibits*, London, 1921, p.9); but the method of cleaning there described has not been followed.

soften the whole seal by immersion in warm (*not* hot) water and bend away the overhanging part. As a general rule, however, the overhang is very slight and small and a minute quantity of plasticine, or children's play wax, introduced temporarily beneath it will meet the requirements of moulding. Of course this method must always be used when the overhang occurs in the actual design of the seal. The seal, with its under side also protected by waxed paper, is now embedded in a pad of plasticine, or some similar soft moulding material, less than 1 mm. of its edge being left exposed — just enough to show the nature of the original or fractured edge. The plasticine outside this is bevelled away so that in the resulting mould the seal matrix may lie in a slight depression, which will enable the finished mould to stand face downwards (excluding dust) without the raised portion of the design coming in contact with the shelf. Having been made up in the pad the seal is very carefully oiled — we use olive-oil with a slight admixture of lard — by means of a fine sable brush, which it will be found best (especially for seals with a great deal of small and deep detail) to cut short and square at the end. It is essential that every scrap of the surface should be oiled and that the oil should not be allowed to soak in before the plaster is applied; but on the other hand the slightest amount of superfluous oil will cause bubbles and flattening in the mould.

A strip of thick lead foil of some standard[23] width is now bent round and pressed into the pad, forming a wall at a distance of 5 mm. or more from the edge of the seal; which is then ready for the plaster. For the quantities to be used in mixing this there is no fixed rule, different plasters varying; but roughly it may be said that the plaster should be gently shaken into the water (a teacup with an inch or so of water is a convenient mixing bowl) until the heap of plaster rises to the level of the water. It must then be stirred (very gently, so as to avoid bubbles; the finger is the best instrument) until it is of the consistency of cream and applied with a clean, fine brush in the same manner as the oil. Air bubbles, it will be found, are even more difficult to avoid than oil bubbles, and only practice is of use in this matter; but a good general rule is to follow with the point of the brush the lines of the design — not to go across them: as in small seals there are really no lines, only a number of deep, irregular depressions, it follows that the action of the brush on these will be a stubbing one, with a short and square-ended brush. There is a slight danger, if the 'painting' is continued when the plaster has begun to set (which it does very quickly), that the brush may pierce through it, with the result of a rough surface to the mould.

It is wise only to put a thin coating of plaster in first and then to fill up with one or more further lots, particularly in the case of large seals, where the mass of plaster generates considerable heat. The mould should be finished

23.   So that the moulds may all be of one height; we use a width of 3.5 cm.

with a flat surface level with the top of the foil. As soon as the plaster is sufficiently set the foil may be taken off to help the process of cooling, but some time — at least an hour — should elapse before any attempt is made to remove the seal; and if it does not come away easily it should be left for a further period.

The mould thus made must be allowed to dry very thoroughly in a warm room; the time required will vary with the size of the mould and with the weather, but it is not safe to try and hasten the process by putting the mould close to a fire. An easy test is to see whether the mould leaves any mark when laid for a few moments on a slate. The next process is that of hardening. For this the French use a *huile siccative* made by suspending a bag of litharge in a pan of boiling linseed oil; the boiling is continued for a considerable time — at least half a day; the pan being placed in an oven because of the fumes of the oil. In the mixture thus made the moulds are immersed, face downwards, to about two-thirds of their depth, and are left to soak for forty-eight hours. When they are taken out their surfaces are carefully freed from surplus oil. The treatment is then complete, save for the surface-drying of the oil, which will take some days more.

The process, though efficient, is a lengthy one. In Brussels a very quick and clean method is used, though not, perhaps, a very strong one — that of painting the surface of the dry mould with a few coats of a solution of shellac. We have endeavoured to compromise between the two plans. Our moulds are steeped on the French plan, but in the shellac solution,[24] in which they stand for five hours, by which time the mixture has penetrated right through them; they are then taken out and the surfaces very carefully freed from surplus shellac by means of clean spirit and a rag and brush. After this they will require to stand for a few days while the spirit evaporates, but this does not take so long as the drying of the oil. They are then stored, ready for use, face downwards on shelves.

The important point is the dryness of the moulds before the hardening treatment is applied.

Moulds from Applied Seals

No difference of method is to be observed here save that the seal cannot be made up in plasticine in the same way. Waxed tissue should be laid over the document and carefully pricked all round the edge of the seal; the paper exactly covering the seal can then be removed and a ring of plasticine formed on the paper round the hole thus made. If the paper is now held down very carefully on the document, a plaster mould may be made in the ordinary way without any danger of the damp reaching the parchment or paper of the

24. We use a solution of white shellac in methylated spirit, about three ounces to a pint. The method was suggested to me by Professor A.P. Laurie, to whom I am also indebted for advice on the subject of pigments.

document. It is to be noted once again that these applied seals are often bent and it may be necessary to give them support, by means of a curved pad of wax or other material placed underneath, during the moulding. Also they are generally very thin and frail, and extra care must be used in oiling and in the removal of the mould.

'Squeezes'

The method of taking a mould by means of soft wax pressed on to the seal may give a very accurate result, if carefully employed: on the other hand, the mould obtained has not the same strength, and the method cannot be used without some danger to the seal; and it should therefore be employed only for papered seals, where it is unavoidable. The seal should not be placed on a table but held in both hands in such a way that support is given to the whole surface from below by the fingers, the thumbs being used to press in the wax which is to form the mould. This pressure must be strictly vertical, or there will be distortion and side-cutting. The wax should be one which will go hard when cold.[25] It is to be softened in warm water or worked up in the hand till it is of the consistency of stiff putty; it is then rolled out into a cake with a slightly convex suface and over this a little French chalk is rubbed (no oil is used). The seal is laid face downwards on this and pressed lightly into it and then the whole is turned over and the wax pressed into the seal in the manner described. The wax should be allowed to go cold before being removed so as to prevent bending and distortion of the mould; indeed, it is better to remove the seal from the mould rather than the mould from the seal.

For the sake of permanency it is perhaps best to make a plaster cast from the squeeze and another mould in plaster from that; though this, as has been pointed out, introduces fresh possibility of error.

CASTING

There are many ways of making casts of seals, but the four materials most generally used are metal (by means of electrotyping), sulphur (with which powder colours may be mixed if desired), plaster and wax. Of these we have eliminated the first two; electrotyping because it involves extra machinery and produces a result which does not, after all, adequately represent a waxen original; and sulphur, because it is inflammable, is not very satisfactory as a representation of wax, and (since it has to be poured into the mould) gives a slightly blurred rendering of the finer lines. There remain, therefore, plaster and wax.

---

25.   The variety of children's modelling wax known as Play Wax is a good one. Or bees-wax and resin mixed in the way described below under *Casting* may be used.

Plaster Casts

These, while cheaper in material, are very much more expensive than wax ones in time and labour. Since their making involves a second oiling and a second possibility of bubbles, they also mean an increased proportion of error. The method of making them is exactly the same as that of making moulds, except that the foil is simply wrapped around the plaster mould, no setting in plasticine being necessary.

Wax Impressions

The ordinary way of using wax for casts is to pour it molten into the mould, which lays it open to the objection already urged against sulphur — that the fine lines are blurred. It is perfectly possible, however, with a properly hardened mould, using a softened (not melted) cake of wax rubbed with chalk (in the manner described under '*Squeezes*' above), to obtain an impression inferior to the original only in so far as there are any imperfections in the mould; and that in a few minutes, whereas a cast in plaster takes, by the time it is dried, many hours. The cake of wax is laid on the table and the mould pressed into it in a strictly vertical direction; or if the mould is a large one the pressure may be got by putting both in an ordinary copying press, taking care to put a piece of cardboard between the back of the mould and the iron platen and not to press so long that the face of the mould cuts through the wax and comes in contact with the bed of the machine. The cake of wax will need to be from a quarter to half an inch thick, according to the depth of relief in the mould.

Casts for Photography

The choice of materials in casting really depends upon the purpose for which the cast is required. A very frequent one is that of photography. The use of casts for this has the great advantage that it saves handling, and therefore risk to the originals; but from the photographer's point of view it is also very generally beneficial because the casts are easier to adjust, can, if necessary, be taken to the photographer's own studio, and can be made in any colour. We have therefore made some experiments in colouring plaster casts as well as in mixing coloured waxes; the problem being to make the detail of the design salient while retaining the characteristic surface of the original wax.

Considerable difficulty was experienced in colouring the plaster. Ordinary oil painting clogs and dulls the lines of the design; water colour or dry colour introduced into the plaster failed to give anything approaching the requisite depth of tone; and so forth. But we finally found that certain oil colours[26] (probably because they were particularly finely divided in grinding) could be

26. Orange vermilion, cadmium yellow, graphite black and oxide of chromium green were the best; the last could be darkened with Prussian blue.

mixed with bees-wax and turpentine and stubbed on to the surface of the cast with a fine brush and afterwards polished, giving quite a good effect. We also got a good result by painting with a solution of orange shellac. Experiments were then made by photographing groups of the same casts in seven different colours, with the result that a biscuit colour (produced by the orange shellac) was generally agreed to be the best.

Plaster casts for the slides for Mr. Fowler's paper were accordingly coloured in this medium; but the appearance of them on the screen was disappointing, the enlargement showing clearly that though the detail was good the surface did not suggest the wax of the original. We accordingly experimented further; first by steeping the shellac-coloured plaster casts in wax, then by preparing impressions in a special brown bees-wax; and then by reverting to the plan of mixing yellow ochre or brown pigment with the plaster and waxing the resultant cast. The last method has been fully approved, and the casts which will illustrate the paper in *Archaeologia* have all been prepared in this way. To secure the same depth of colour a large quantity of water is mixed with ochre beforehand. The casts when dry are plunged in melted paraffin wax[27] and left in it till air bubbles cease to rise and are subsequently brush-polished. The wax penetrates the plaster completely; and not only gets rid of a certain surface roughness due to the introduction of the pigment but strengthens the cast, which is liable also to be rather brittle for the same reason.

The above remarks apply to what may be termed average photographic work: the light brown or yellow undoubtedly give the best results as a whole. At the same time it must be added that a good photographer, taking the trouble to make the necessary adjustments and working with casts under suitable conditions, should be able to get good results from any colour or substance. In the illustration (plate III) three impressions in wax (scarlet, dark green and light brown), one cast in plaster shellac-coloured, and two casts in coloured plaster (brown and ochre) waxed — all from the same mould — have been photographed *separately*: and it will be seen that there is little to choose between the resulting reproductions, though there are distinct differences in the rendering. In the plate the casts follow the order given above.

It may be worth mentioning that we tried also to obtain colour by soaking the plaster casts with spirit stain;[28] subsequently soaking in paraffin wax in the manner described. The trouble with all dyes and stains appears to be that those made up from more than one colour show, when applied to the plaster, different rates of absorption, the results being parti-coloured and unreliable.

27. Melting point 160° F.: the wax should not boil.
28. Messrs. Gedge, of St. John Street, were good enough to make me up some special stains for this purpose; and I used also some of the ordinary spirit stains and dyes soluble in spirit. I was indebted to Mr. H.W. Fincham, F.S.A., for some suggestions on this point.

PLATE III: SEGILLIVN DE CONCILLIO DE BILVAO (1481) Impressions and casts in
wax and plaster of different colours

Even when this did not happen during staining it generally did during the waxing process; and though this might be got over by using only surface waxing the process was unsatisfactory.

Undoubtedly the most satisfactory method[29] of staining, as distinct from painting, was the use of aniline dyes dissolved in the paraffin wax, colour and wax being thus applied together. But here again the difficulty is to get the exact colour required, only certain anilines being wax-soluble and mixed colours proving once more a failure. We are still experimenting with this method.

Conclusion

There seems little doubt that, though the waxed plaster gives the best result for the camera, if casts are merely required for exhibition the method to be preferred is that of making direct impressions from the moulds in wax prepared from the same materials[30] as those used in the seals themselves. With the minimum of labour and of error in reproduction, and at no exorbitant cost, this gives us the nearest approach to a facsimile of the original.

29. Suggested to me by Dr. J.J. Fox, of the Government Laboratory, to whom I have been particularly indebted throughout.
30. See the analysis by Dobbie and Fox, *op. cit.* We use a proportion of roughly two of wax to one of resin. The best levigated powder colour should be used, vermilion and verdigris being the two normal ones. Only small quantities of these will be needed. The materials should not be heated more than is absolutely necessary in mixing; and the wax should never be melted afterwards, but only softened.

Medieval Tallies, Public and Private

INTRODUCTORY

It is now almost exactly twelve years since I first introduced this subject to the notice of the Society[1] in connexion with a then recent deposit of medieval Exchequer Tallies at the Public Record Office; and though I subsequently communicated two further notes[2] upon it, I may plead that even since those were made ten years have elapsed. During that time there has been a great change in our knowledge of Exchequer procedure. Two or three notable books have appeared and a considerable amount of work has been done,[3] though not all of it has yet been printed, upon the neglected Exchequer Records. Already we begin to look with quite different eyes at medieval financial problems, even though our knowledge of the great mass of the Memoranda Rolls, Receipt and Issue Rolls, Wardrobe Accounts and subsidiary documents still owes practically nothing to any publication of texts from those Records. I have accordingly thought it worth while to submit to the Society a further stage in our knowledge of the financial system, public, semi-public and private, of which Tallies formed so important a part. I have fortunately little to retract from what I said in my previous papers, but there are a few new points to note, some remarks to be extended, and a selection to be offered from a considerable accumulation of further illus-

1. *Archaeologia*, lxii, 367.
2. *Proceedings*, xxv, 29, and xxvi, 36.
3. R.L. Poole, *The Exchequer in the Twelfth Century*; T.F. Tout, *Chapters in English Administrative History and Materials for the History of the Reign of Edward II*; Conway Davies, *The Baronial Opposition to Edward II*; J.F. Willard, *Introduction* to the Surrey Record Society's volume of *Taxation Returns;* C. Johnson, *System of Account in the Wardrobe of Edward I*, in the Royal Historical Society's *Transactions*, 4th ser., vol. vi; Miss M. H. Mills, two articles on the *Adventus Vicecomitum* in the *English Historical Review* and a volume dealing with *Pipe Rolls* for the Surrey Record Society; H. Jenkinson, *The Financial Records of the Reign of King John* in the *Magna Carta Commemoration* volume of the Royal Historical Society and *Records of Receipts from the English Jewry* in *Transactions* of the Jewish Historical Society, vols. viii and ix.

trations.[4] In addition, there has very recently become available, from hitherto unsorted Miscellanea at the Public Record Office, a much larger collection of private tallies than had been known to exist anywhere before — a collection so large as to make possible deductions of some importance regarding a very widespread custom. These are dealt with in the second part of the present paper and analysed in detail in an Appendix.

It is to be feared that even now we shall not come to the end of Exchequer Tallies. The fact is that the more we examine financial conditions in medieval England and the *minutiae* of Financial History, as they are beginning to discover themselves through patient study of the Records, the more do we find that all development of this kind — development of the system of Public Accounts, of Exchequer Bills and their discounting, of Public Loans and Public Credit — is conditioned at every turn, to a greater or less degree, by that system of tally-cutting which was already well established in the twelfth century and which continued in action with very little alteration down to the nineteenth. Such investigations as I have suggested are in the province, it is true, of the Economist rather than the Antiquary: but it is not out of place to think of them here, because all must be based on an accurate understanding of the technique which governed the cutting of the original little slips of hazel; their importance and extent is therefore a measure of the value which a comparatively simple piece of antiquary's work may possess for students in other fields. I hope, however (though perhaps I am optimistic), that with the present note we may come near the end of the Antiquary's part in this matter of tally-cutting; and that the derivative questions (probably a large number) which will remain still to be treated may be more properly dealt with elsewhere.

It may perhaps be proper to recall here that my original paper was mainly devoted to examining the medieval Exchequer Tallies, then newly dis-covered, in the capacity of illustrations to a well-known but difficult passage in the *Dialogus de Scaccario*. It was possible to explain by their aid almost every point in this and to show that the system of cutting Exchequer tallies practically did not vary at all between the twelfth century and the date of our examples, and again between that and the nineteenth century; and for convenience the plates in the present paper have been chosen so as to repeat that illustration,[5] very nearly in life size. It was possible also to show that the

---

4. I am indebted to various friends for their contributions, but particularly and very greatly to my former student, Miss M.H. Mills, to whom I owe my information as to the Dividenda Tally (which she first investigated in the course of her own work) and the Dating of Tallies, as well as numerous other notes.

5. Thus we have illustrations of the marks for £1,000 (pl. III, no.9); £100 (pl. II, no.8); £20 (*ibid.*, no. II, and pl. III, nos. 3 and 7); £1 and half a pound (*ibid.*, nos. 4 and 6, and pl. II, nos. 1, 6, and 9, and I, no. 4); shillings and pence (*ibid.*, no, 6; pl. II, nos 3 and 4; pl. III, upper side of no. 7, etc.): the angle of the half-way cut and the right-hand end are well shown in pl. II, no. 11.

rules governing the inscription on the Exchequer tallies were equally rigid and almost equally unchanging; and to a certain extent to relate such small alterations as did occur to changes in Exchequer administrative procedure and to the Receipt Rolls upon which the tally inscriptions were copied. The paper dealt also with the enormous influence exercised by the tally form on every kind of financial development in this country; and finally attempted to examine, on the basis of a rather exiguous supply of illustrations, the technique of private tally-cutting.[6] Small additions to most aspects of the Exchequer tally previously treated, but especially to that of the development of assignment by tally and that of tally-procedure at a later date (the seventeenth century), were made in a subsequent note.[7]

SOME SMALL POINTS

It will be well to dispose first of a few questions arising out of these previous papers. Such are the matter of Nomenclature; the question why the tallies which have come to us survived in the Chapel of the Pyx; the reason for their survival elsewhere; further points about the Record Office collections; and some new points in the technique of writing and cutting.

Nomenclature

Mention of this may be justified by the fact that a new volume of the *Oxford Dictionary* has appeared since I first wrote. The word *tally*, in spite of its various Latin spellings, is well established: and so is the word *contratalea* or *contre-taille*[8] as an alternative for *folium*, the foil; where *contra* has that sense of a checking which we find in *counter-roll* and *controller*. *Contratalea*, by the way, must be distinguished very carefully from the *tally contra*, with which we have to deal below. One or two other forms, such as *dica*, have also been dealt with, but it is worth noting here that the confusion due to the fact that tally nomenclature includes the words *eschasse*, *scaccia*, scatch, scotch, scratch, score, and stock is one which even our best authority has not been able materially to improve. *Scotch*, we are told, is of obscure origin but probably not to be identified with *scorch*; though, without desiring to enter the field of Shakespearian criticism, I would venture to put forward the claims for consideration, in connexion with the second of these two words, of the Latin *cortex* and its derivative the French *escorcher* (*écorcher*). *Scorch*, according to authority, in the sense of incising is an alteration of *score*, perhaps after *scratch*; *scratch* is synonymous with *scrat*; and *scrat* is an Early English word of difficult

---

6. Private tallies were also dealt with in my later note in *Proceedings*, xxvi, 36.
7. *Ibid.*, xxv, 29.
8. The parts remaining with the Chamberlains of the Receipt are described as *countretailles* and also as *escaches des tailles* in the ordinances of 19 Edward II (*Red Book*, p. 964).

etymology. As to the use, in connexion with money, of the word *stock*, the *Dictionary* gives us a derivation from two senses of the word — that of *trunk* (which is undoubtedly the sense intended by the tally-maker, who used the word as a translation of *stipes*) and that of *base*. I still cling to the belief that *stocks*, in the sense of the Funds, may be derived from the tally; and some of the *Dictionary's* quotations, notably one of 1793, support this suggestion.

The Chapel of the Pyx

As a location this presents no difficulty, since the Chamberlains of the Receipt were the proper custodians of tallies and the Treasury of the Receipt the proper place for them to be kept in. The reason for the survival of this particular collection (with two exceptions[9] all stocks) is more obscure. We might infer from Agarde's Compendium[10] that they represent a known collection, set aside long ago for some purpose of which no record now remains. On the other hand, the highly miscellaneous character of the fragments of documents[11] which came to us with them seems to suggest a purely fortuitous sweeping together of accidental remainders. The truth perhaps lies midway between these two suppositions.

Exchequer Tallies in Private Custody

The Birmingham Free Library possesses no less than thirty, of which nine show Jewish script;[12] there is a good specimen at Manchester,[13] a tally of the younger John d'Abernon; another is in the Medieval department of the British Museum; one was brought to me only recently from a private collection in Wales;[14] and I know of two (purchased, I believe, at a London dealer's) in the possession of a Fellow of this Society. There can be little doubt that before the tallies were transferred to the Record Office, and before the Chapel was thrown open to the public, both were not infrequently exposed to visitors and that a certain amount of straying occurred; and we may be thankful that the collection remained as complete as it did. At any rate, no medieval Exchequer Tallies have come to light in private hands which were not of one of the dates represented in the Record Office series. On the other hand, we know that on occasion the medieval Exchequer was put out by accountants who had paid their debts and received their tallies, but

9.   See below.
10. Published in Palgrave's *Antient Kalendars*, vol. ii: see particularly pages 311 *et seq.* The work was compiled in 1610.
11. Two sets of these have furnished respectively material for an article on the *First Parliament of Edward I (Eng. Hist. Rev.*, xxv, p. 231) and illustrations for a book on *Palaeography and the Study of Court Hand* (Cambridge, 1915); and there are many others.
12. Among the Stone MSS., I am indebted to a former student, Mr. Leonard Chubb, of the Birmingham Library, for calling my attention to these tallies.
13. See Professor Willard's note in the *Bulletin of John Rylands Library*, vol. vii, no. 2, to be mentioned again below. I showed a tally of the elder John d'Abernon in my first paper.
14. This has since been exhibited to the Society.

who would not be troubled to come up and get their accounts acquitted[15] (which meant, incidentally, that the stocks were not returned to be tied up with the foils at Westminster); and it is therefore not absolutely impossible that a tally might have remained, generation after generation, in the private muniments of a family, to reappear as an antiquity in our own day. One other private collection — that of the Bank of England — is dealt with below; and another was referred to in my first paper.[16]

The Record Office Collection

This has been re-examined in some detail for the purposes of the present paper. It is now divided so as to preserve separately Tallies of the three periods; Tallies having added notes; Jewish Tallies (subdivided according to their several subjects); and Jewish Tallies with Hebrew script upon them. In each of these six classes there has been set aside also a tray of good specimens, and there are further special divisions containing tallies relating to a single county (Surrey), tallies *contra*, and curiosities of various kinds: these special divisions and specimen trays containing all the tallies illustrated here and practically all those reproduced in previous articles.[17] The arrangement, with the numbers in each division, is shown in Appendix I: the total, including the larger fragments, is 1300.[18] Appendix I contains also details of the arrangement of a number of late Exchequer Tally stocks derived from other sources, to which we shall refer again below.

An Exchequer Tally Foil

The chief result of the re-examination has been to produce one complete foil (pl. II, no. 1), the first of medieval date I have seen.[19] This is valuable as confirming my reconstruction, based on a badly split stock (pl. III, no. 2), of the way in which the writing was done; and because it shows (an important matter, as will be seen when we come to the Private Tally) that at the Exchequer the foil had the same inscription as the stock, in the reverse position as regards the notches: this is clear, though we have not, unfortunately, been able to find the corresponding stock. The conclusions drawn from it are also confirmed by the fragments of fourteenth-century and Jacobean foils,[19] discovered elsewhere in the Record Office since this paper was read, which will be described later.

15. We know that about 25 Henry III (e.g.) the Exchequer was finding it necessary to distrain accountants to come up for audit: cp. notes on L.TR. Memoranda Rolls 13 (mm. 14,15, and 16) and 14 (m. 14*d*).
16. The early 18th-century tallies at Martin's Bank.
17. *Archaeologia*, lxii; *Proceedings*, xxv; Jewish Hist. Soc., *Transactions*, ix; and *Surrey Archaeological Collections*, xxiii: one plate from the last-named is also reproduced in the Surrey Record Society's *Pipe Roll* volume.
18. I am indebted for some assistance in sortation to a small class of students, especially Miss D.M. Broome, Miss H.M. Chew, Miss M.H. Mills, and Miss C.A. Musgrave.
19. Now in E. 402/3 A, first tray.

Date of our Collection of Exchequer Tallies

Another result of re-examination has been to reveal some further [20] tallies which, to judge by their writing, are of an earlier date than the bulk of the collection: five are illustrated here (pl. I, nos. 1-5), two of them showing slight variation from the normal form of wording (nos. 4 and 5). It may be convenient to add here that the collection as a whole dates from the reigns of Henry III and Edward I; the two later of the three main classes dating apparently from a period of Exchequer reform (about 1280 to 1295).

The Technique of Tally-Cutting at the Exchequer

Our knowledge has been further increased during the re-examination by discovery of tallies bearing the mark for a halfpenny. We knew before that this — a punched hole — existed in the nineteenth century, but it is not mentioned in the *Dialogus* and no medieval evidence for it had been discovered. Curiously enough, one of the tallies shown[21] in my first article had this mark, but it escaped notice at the time and the printer successfully banished it from the picture; the hole in this case is round, but in a number of others the tool has not been held quite straight or was of a different shape, and the mark has come out as a semi-circle (pl. I, nos. 6-9). No attempt was made to split through it (the split in no. 9 is clearly accidental) and presumably it was repeated on the foil. That it must have been not infrequently in use is shown by the fact that the Receipt was prepared even, in case of need, to issue a tally for a halfpenny and no more;[22] and we may note in one of our examples (pl. I, no. 8) the precision which places the greater amount (pennies) on the lower edge of the stock and the halfpenny by itself on the upper.

A further point to be noticed is that the pound notch came gradually to be made with two cuts of unequal length, presumably to distinguish it from the shilling (contrast, in pl. II, nos. 1 and 6 with no. 9). The tendency may be seen in practically all the medieval Exchequer Tallies except some of our earlier examples; but it was not till later that the longer of the two strokes became exaggerated.[23] There is no sign in the medieval tallies of the enlargement of the shilling notch which is another late feature.

The Memoranda Tally

With another point in tally-making which was left doubtful before I have not been so successful: I am still unable to explain the passage in the *Dialogus*

---

20. One was reproduced in *Proceedings,* xxv, where it was conjecturally assigned to the reign of Richard I or John.
21. No. 23 in the article in *Archaeologia.* The accuracy of the reading of the amount has been established by tracking it on to the *Receipt Roll* in each case.
22. Cp. the case of Walter Hereman on Receipt Roll 123.
23. See below the notes on a Jacobean and later Exchequer tallies: see also below, p. 71.

regarding the Memoranda Tally. This was a device employed in connexion with the assaying of certain of the sums due on account of farms at the annual audit: as a tally was struck when the cash was paid in, and as the sum's value changed after 'blanching', some arrangement had to be made if the accountant's tally was to agree with the amount actually credited to him in the end: but the statement of the *Dialogus* does not make clear what this arrangement was. We have one possible suggestion to make in this connexion later, when dealing with added notes on Tallies. The matter is not very important, as actual 'blanching' died out at the end of the thirteenth century,[24] a conventional shilling in the pound for blanching-money replacing the assay in practice.

The Gold Mark

Another small curiosity in the *Dialogus* description is a statement according to which[25] the gold mark is indicated by an ordinary one pound notch placed by itself in the middle of the upper edge of the tally — not, one would think, a very distinctive arrangement, as ordinary pound notches are often in very much the same position; while the gold penny (presumably the besant) is to have the ordinary penny notch,[26] but cut straight, not obliquely (but the interpretation of this passage is doubtful). As the ordinary penny notch is cut straight across the edge of the tally, this can only mean that the cut was normally inclined inwards; whereas my experience is that it is not inclined at all (cp. the penny cuts on no. 7 in pl. III), or only so slightly that differentiation between the normal and abnormal would be impossible. We have here illustrated what might[27] be a mark of gold (pl. III, no. 3) — the only one I have been able to find, in spite of a special search. The matter is not, perhaps, of great importance; for, although debts were frequently collected in gold, or gold purchased, in the reign of Henry III,[28] we hear little of it afterwards; and when it did occur it would probably, we may conjecture, be represented by its current price (which varied[29]) in ordinary pounds shillings and pence.

24. We have not been able yet to fix any exact date: indeed the process seems to have been gradual.
25. *Marcam autem auri in medio talee sicut libram vnam incidas. Dialogus*, Oxford edition, p. 74.
26. *Aureum vero vnum non prorsus vt argenteum set ducto directe incidentis cultello per medium talee non obliquando sicut fit in argenteo. Ibid.*
27. The possibility is slightly increased by the fact that the tally records a receipt from a Jew and that it was not uncommon for gold coins to be procured through the Jews; but the point cannot be verified as the Receipt Roll for the Jewish talliage in question is missing.
28. See the printed *Close Rolls, s.v.* Edward of Westminster and others, who are frequently found handling marks' worth of obols of musc and besants (cp. pp. 232, 277, etc., under date 1244/5).
29. Thus in 15 Henry III (Pipe Roll 75, Oxford membrane) the *Telarii* of Oxford pay 6*l* for a gold mark and the *Cornesarii* 16*s*. for an ounce of gold. In 42 Henry III the *Pipe Roll* (Sussex, *Nova Oblata*) shows Geoffrey de Cruce owing 5 marks for a fine of half a mark of

Notes added to Tallies in addition to the Ordinary Inscription

I did not refer to these in my first paper, but have since identified them on about eighty examples — six or seven per cent. of the collection. They may occur, as will be noticed (pl. II, nos. 3 to 11), on any part of the tally, but the most usual place is the lower edge of the stock, where, in the later stage of tally development, the date is placed (pl. II, no. 3: also nos. 7 and 9). The most common is the statement *alloc[andum] vic[ecomiti]* etc. (pl. II, nos. 3 and 4), indicating that the payment made by some one else is one for which the sheriff or some other official had been charged and which must be allowed to him on the Pipe Roll: we have a number of cases of Essex tallies with the note *alloc' H. vic'* — one of the small indications that make me think the survival of these particular tallies was not due completely to chance, but that some of them had been set aside quite early for some special purpose or purposes.

Of the other notes illustrated here, one, *lib' blc'* (pl. II, no. 8), may possibly be important: a similar entry *(li.ars.)* is used on the early Receipt Rolls (see App. II); and while it undoubtedly means that the sum in question is in blanched money it is possible that it also represents the later stage of that Memoranda Tally of the *Dialogus* which puzzled us earlier. The note *de Itinere G. de Preston'* (pl. II, no. 6) is again one of a number; it serves to refer the transaction to its particular place on the Pipe Roll.

The remaining notes illustrated were probably all put on at the Receipt, being small memoranda touching the actual payment; one (pl. II, no. 11) indicates, perhaps, the identity of the hands which actually paid,[30] two (nos. 9 and 10) are anticipations of the later conventions which put county and date on the tally as a matter of rule.

Abnormals

Finally, we have to show a few examples of what can only be called abnormals. One (pl. II, no. 2)[31] has lost all trace of writing and we have therefore no means of saying that the hopelessly irregular cutting is certainly what it appears to be — that of a private tally. Another (pl. III, no. 1) is a definite Exchequer tally and the only example I have seen among 1,300 of desertion of the rules for placing the notches: probably the clerk who cut in a moment of carelessness went counter to the clerk who wrote; but, even so, he made a poor business of it.

We may add, in concluding this section, that re-examination of the tallies has shown no indication of any varying of the rules of cutting between the

---

gold; while in 26 Henry III Edward of Westminster is paying at the rate of a shilling of silver for a penny of gold, silver itself having its face value (Issue Roll 1205).

30. We have other examples with the addition *per manus* before the name.
31. Note the wrong angle of the central cut and the irregular and wrongly-placed notch.

three different periods; with the possible exception of the rule which, if there were no pennies, left the penny space bare. This rule certainly fell into abeyance later.[32] The foregoing remarks may suitably lead to one or two regarding the

MEANING AND USE OF EXCHEQUER TALLIES

My excuse for inserting them must be that private tallies are still mistaken for Exchequer ones, in spite of the fact that genuine specimens of the latter are distinguished by six unmistakable marks which are never found all together, so far as our present knowledge goes, in any private tally;[33] that Exchequer tallies are still misread; and that they are still spoken of as though they might conceivably be something other than what they originally were and always remained — receipts for payments. It is the failure to recognize this last very simple fact which has led distinguished authorities to misinterpret them. It is true, of course, that a receipt may become (as the tally became) hardly distinguishable from a cheque payable to bearer: but that does not alter its essential character nor the fact that the enrolment of the tally on the Receipt Roll means that the person concerned is credited with a payment at the Exchequer; and that is the key to the understanding of any transaction, however complicated,[34] in which the tally figures. I may add, by anticipation, that a similar key, firmly held, should be applied to the private tally.

THE RECEIPT ROLL

Since we have mentioned this we may go on to dispose of one or two small points in connexion with it. Without, at present, going in detail into the history[35] of this form of Record we may recall that there are four chief stages

32. See below, p. 63.
33. The marks of the genuine Exchequer tally are the angles of cutting at the centre and right-hand end, form and position of wording, and shape and position of notches: for which see my first paper.
34. For examples of complication the student has only to look under the Wardrobe headings in the double-columned Issue Rolls of Edward II or at the *pro* column in the later Receipt Rolls. Cp., e.g., the Issue and Receipt Rolls published in facsimile in Johnson and Jenkinson, *Court Hand Illustrated*, pls. xxii A, xxxv, and xxxix.
35. See my paper in Jewish Historical Society *Transactions*, vol. viii, with the facsimile in vol. ix; and cp. Appendix V to my *Manual of Archive Administration*, to be cited again below, p. 64.
    Since the above was written a number of very early fragments of Receipt Rolls have come to light among previously unsorted Miscellanea at the Public Record Office. As any new document of the reign of Henry II is of importance I have thought it worth while to summarize briefly in the present paper (see Appendix II) the state of our knowledge of the

in its development: first we have a primitive single-column roll arranged under counties; then multiple column rolls, also arranged under counties, first without, afterwards with, added 'sums' — we shall have to return to these later; then there comes the final form of a single-column roll arranged under dates, which persists from 21 Henry III till the end of the eighteenth century; the only important modification being the introduction of a series of notes on the right margin to show whether the transaction was or was not in reality an assignment — these at times assume the dimensions of an extra column. Throughout the character is or ought to be the same — that of a register of receipts, i.e. of tallies struck: one line on the roll should mean one tally.[36] Moreover, the stages of development in the Receipt Roll should undoubtedly reflect or be reflected by those similar stages in the growth of the tally form which we have already observed: the change which adds the name of the county to the inscription on the tally should indicate some change in the machinery of the Receipt Roll; and when we have settled the exact date (some time in the reign of Edward III) at which *pro* begins to appear on the right-hand margin of the Receipt Roll we should be near to solving the question when *pro* and *sol* tallies were introduced. One or two minor points concerning the Receipt Roll, such as the elaborate checking, indicated by a large spot or comma in the left margin,[37] which is given at certain dates to the Treasurer's copy, are also connected undoubtedly with Tallies;[38] but the habit of adding in the roll the name of the Teller concerned does not seem to affect them.[39]

DATING

Apropos of the Receipt Rolls a small question of some difficulty arises owing to the confusion between the calendar year, the ordinary regnal year, and the artificial Exchequer year of Edward I: the first Exchequer year of Edward I began technically at the last Michaelmas of Henry III, because Edward

early Receipt Rolls as it now stands. I shall hope to deal with the new documents in more detail elsewhere: they do not upset my previous theories as to the development of this type of Record.

36. Occasionally this is not so, and the fact is duly noted: see the *per duas tallias* notes in (e.g.) Receipt Roll 12 of 21 Henry III.

37. E. 401/376, a roll of 18 Edward III, is notable; fictitious loans (see below under 'Assignments') and an advance which had been returned are not marked with this marginal — a clear indication of the stage of procedure at which the checking took place. Compare the remarks above as to the correspondence of a single line in the Roll with a single tally levied, and see the note on later (17th cent.) procedure in *Proceedings*, xxvi.

38. Cp. Receipt Roll 147 of 27/28 Edward I, where we are told that a certain entry *punctuabitur* although *ignoratur si tallia fit vel non* — clearly an exceptional step. The forms of 'punctuation' on Rolls 139 and 140 are interesting.

39. See below, p. 62.

came to the throne in the middle of a Michaelmas term. Professor Willard[40] has connected the Manchester d'Abernon tally, which is dated Michaelmas 22 Edward I, with the Receipt Roll of 21/22 Edward I and the year 1293. This may be so, as the sum in question was paid in by d'Abernon both in that and the following Exchequer year; but other cases are in less doubt, and a number of them[41] makes it clear that tallies dated Michaelmas 22 Edward I refer to transactions of the year 22/23 Edward I and may be paid in as late as March 1295; and the same of course applies to other Michaelmas tallies of this reign. On the other hand, at least one example[42] has been noted of payment in advance.

It may be well here to insert a warning (since there has been some confusion) that the 'Exchequer year' is merely a modern phrase of convenience invented to cover the facts as to the beginning and end of the yearly activities of the Exchequer; that body would itself describe the Michaelmas Term (for example) of 1273, 1274 as *de anno primo finiente, secundo incipiente*,[43] when heading its rolls.

THE DIVIDENDA TALLY[44]

We come now to a quite distinct variety of tally, our knowledge of which is derived from the Receipt Roll only; whose history we must accordingly investigate in further detail. This *dividenda* must be distinguished from a document also known by that name which was no more than an indenture beginning with the words *Hec est dividenda inter*.[45] . . . The *dividenda* tally seems to appear as early as 15 John:[46] certainly we have it in the Pipe Roll of 22 Henry III, where we are told that a long list of debts was paid in *per duas tallias:*[47] I first had my attention called to it as a mysterious entry *dd* in the

40. *Bulletin of John Rylands Library*, vii, 2, p.270.
41. Robert de Glamorgan's tally, for example, for 27*l* 8*s* figured in *Surrey Archaeological Collections*, xxiii, is dated Michaelmas 22 Edward I, but was, as a matter of fact, paid in on the feast of St. Hilary 1295 (E.401/132): cp. in the same plate another Glamorgan tally for 22*l.*, paid in on 19 March 1295 (same Receipt Roll). Similarly a Glamorgan tally for 11*s* 8*d.*, dated Michaelmas 21 Edward I, is for an amount paid in Jan. 1294 (E.401/127).
42. See Receipt Roll 151 of 30/31 Edward I, where Ralph de Hengham pays four sums amounting to 666*l.* 13*s.* 4*d.*, one of which (336*l.* 6*s.* 8*d.*) is stated to be *de termino Sancti Michaelis proximo futuro*. One would like to see the tally for this.
43. Mr. H.G. Richardson has, I understand, a paper on this subject in preparation for the *Transactions* of the Royal Historical Society.
44. See note on p. 46 above.
45. Examples will be found in E. 101/282/23.
46. Receipt Roll 1564, m. 4*d*, *et omnes talee iste facte fuerunt de veteri dividenda*. The practice actually appears in the Pipe Rolls of 1206 and 1207, but without the word *dividenda*.
47. Pipe Roll 82, Devon, *Nova Oblata*.

right-hand margin of Receipt Rolls: the extension is given us by the Statute of Rhuddlan.[48]

The *dd* tally is indirectly one of the results of the legal reforms of Henry II. The Pipe Roll up to then had been a list of the debts and payments of people of some importance: but once the issue of Chancery writs to call cases into the King's Court became common, the Pipe Roll was threatened with submersion by a flood of small debts from small debtors for amercements, fines, and so forth; and while the officials of the upper Exchequer were finding the difficulty of adjusting their primitive machinery to changed conditions, those of the Receipt were being overwhelmed no less by the task of making out an ever-increasing quantity of tallies.[49]

The first attempt to meet this difficulty from the point of view of the audit was to devolve upon the Sheriff the task of collection. Locally the result was to set up ultimately an elaborate sheriff's office with full machinery of private Receipt Rolls[50] and private tallies:[51] centrally, we get, from the first beginning of a regular class of Receipt Rolls, the many-columned Receipt[52] Roll containing a certain number of groups of small receipts; for each of which groups the sheriff would receive one collective tally, which he had (morally) to split up among the debtors in the county, presumably by giving them private tallies of his own. The next development is the appearance of a single-column Receipt Roll[53] arranged under dates, in addition to the many-columned one: in these rolls appears the entry *per dd*,[54] which continues till the year 12 Edward I.[55] Now if we turn from these to the many-columned rolls[56] we find that these are changing their character and generally contain now only particulars of small debts. In other words, we have reached a system under which the single-column roll gives us all the receipts, the older

48. Item volumus et prouidemus quod Camerarii non faciant de cetero vicecomitibus seu aliis quibuscumque balliuis tallias diuidendas nisi receptis prius ab eis particulis summas et occasiones debitorum et nomina ea soluencium continentibus (Close Roll 101, m. 7*d*): cp. L.T.R. Memoranda Roll 51, m.9.

49. For Yorkshire alone, and in respect of amercements from a single Eyre, the Sheriff received in 2 John, 972 tallies; and about 120 more were required for individual payments: see Pipe Roll 46.

50. For examples (which have survived to us as vouchers to accounts) see L.T.R. Misc. Rolls 5/68 to 70 and E. 101 (K.R. Accounts) 505/6.

51. See the statute of Rhuddlan, quoted above.

52. Cp. Receipt Roll 4, of 5 Henry III. In Receipt Roll 5 we have a marginal *De itinere H. de Burgo totales*, which shows how close was the connexion of these rolls with the needs of the Pipe Roll: on the other hand the double character of the Receipt Roll (showing receipts issued to small debtors through the Sheriff) is well illustrated by the form of (e.g.) E. 401/11B, which may be contrasted with that of 3B.

53. e.g. Receipt Rolls 12, 13, 15, and 17 of the years 21 to 30 Henry III.

54. Or *per diuid'*, *per diuidend'*, *per particulas*.

55. Receipt Roll 103.

56. Receipt Rolls 22, 53, 54, all *circa* 38 Henry III.

form contributing the details of such of these as were *dividende*.[57] This older form is now known as *Particule (diuersorum) comitatuum* or *Rotulus de particulis*, while the single-column roll is simply *Recepta* or *Rotulus Recepte*.[58]

We have said that the Sheriff must have kept an elaborate system of records in his local office. In the next stage we find these, or fair copies of them, being utilized apparently to save the Exchequer the task of compilation. This came as a result of the Statute of Rhuddlan in 12 Edward I;[59] rather curiously, for though the desired result was attained — the submitting to the Exchequer by the sheriffs of proper lists of the debts they had collected — an additional and unforeseen effect was the disappearance of the *dividende;*[60] and with this went also the abolition of the many-columned Receipt Roll.[61]

The new records, compiled in the Sheriff's offices, which now make a brief appearance, are called *Particule totales et parciales* (i.e. particulars of wholly and partially paid debts) and seventeen of them have survived in the class of K.R. Sheriffs' Accounts.[62] In these the *tallie dividende* are replaced by tallies *de debitis plurium*, of which we have here (pl. III, nos. 4-7) some illustrations, showing slight varieties of phrase: *debitis plurium* (in the abbreviation *deb' plur'*, as a rule) was the final form, and many of our tallies bear that inscription. In one roll[63] which has survived we see the substitution of these for the out-of-date *dividende*.

The period covered by the rolls is very short — probably 1284 to 1287,[64]

---

57. Thus on Receipt Roll 76 we get, under Wiltshire, a list of small debts amounting to 46*l*. and 1 mark paid by Hildebrand de London: in Receipt Roll 75 we have simply *de Hyldebrando de London' vicecomite .xlvj.li. j. marc'. per d'd'*. Cp. the case of Thomas de Normanville's payments of 600*l*. and 200*l*. in Receipt Roll 88 and the long list of debts to his name in Receipt Roll 87. Note that the Receipt Rolls were kept normally in triplicate and that only the Treasurer's roll can be relied on for the *dd* note. The *dividenda* habit spread also to the Jewish Receipt Rolls (e.g. no. 1579). Very good examples will be found in Receipt Rolls 96 and 97.
58. See Appendix II.
59. See passage quoted above.
60. I have found no more of them on the Receipt Roll after 16 Edward I.
61. The last is one of 15 Edward I — E. 401/105, which is called *Rotulus parcialis diuersorum comitatuum de debitis plur';* it has marginals, *totales* as well as *parciales* — an important point, since it foreshadows the later Sheriffs' accounts.
62. Nos. 8/1 to 3 and 5; 19/2; 22/3 to 5; 29/7 and 8; 39/2 and 3; 41/2 and 3; 42/2; 46/1; and 47/8. In no. 8/2 we have one tally *de debitis plurium* for the *totales* (76 items) and one for the *parciales* (58).
63. *Ibid.*, 47/8: also Receipt Roll 97, where *dd* entries are struck through and *de debitis diuersorum* and *habet talliam* added later; but see more particularly Exch. of Receipt Miscellanea 5/23, a roll of 19-21 Edward I, called *Rotulus diuidendarum*, in which we see numerous officials, sheriffs, or bailiffs, all of whom appear to have held office before the statute (1284), receive new tallies for old. Cp. the *Tallie Innouate* Roll (Receipt Roll 1756).
64. At the outside 1280 to 1287.

during which time we find on the Receipt Rolls[65] marginal notes of *sine tallia* (generally struck through at a later stage) which seem to indicate the process of transition. What happened after 1287? Within a few years the Sheriff was keeping for himself a definite roll *de debitis plurium*, a type of which fragmentary remains have recently come to light: and this may probably be regarded as a final form. At the centre, the principle of the Sheriff's responsibility for small debts had been recognized in theory at the Exchequer of Audit[66] as well as that of Receipt. Gradually the result was felt in practice: in time the rule became universal of omitting the long lists of names from the Pipe Roll as they were omitted from the Receipt Roll and a regular system of Estreats — lists of debtors of the Crown extracted from the Records of the various Courts — took their place. But with this we are not concerned: we need only note that the Receipt Roll and the Tally now reached their final form — saving always the later *pro* and *sol* additions.

TWO SMALL NEW POINTS

Two small new points remain to be considered — the entries *de eodem* and *de crementis talliarum* on the Receipt Rolls. The first appears in the earliest of the Receipt Rolls[67] and simply marks an attempt to save time by adding a subsequent payment to an entry already complete.[68] There is a fair presumption that the original tally would be taken back and altered. The seond[69] is more complicated. It occurs quite frequently in the Receipt Rolls of Henry III and Edward I, being substituted, opposite the name of a county, for the normal entry of the name and payment of an accountant. We have generally *talliarum*, but sometimes *tallie*, the amount varying from a halfpenny[70] upwards. Occasionally the number of tallies altered is mentioned. The natural explanation would be that in some way this is connected with the payment of blanching money,[71] but the largeness of some of the amounts[72] makes this difficult, and besides the usage occurs in connexion

65. 104, 105, 107, 109, 110: cp. Exch. Acc. 238/9. But note that this inscription appears also on Receipt Rolls of an earlier date (nos. 14 and 15 of 26 and 27 Henry III).
66. Cp. the Ordinances *de statu Scaccarii* on Patent Roll 54 Henry III, m.22.
67. Nos. 1 and 2; and in the Northampton *Donum* (E. 101/249/2).
68. Thus in Receipt Roll 1 we have after an entry in ordinary form the addition *De eadem .iiij.s. In eadem tallia.*
69. It has been noted in the forms *crementis, cremento, incrementis,* and *incremento.* A parallel, but more exact , method, where we are told the exact sum which has been added to a specific entry, will be found under Notts. and Derby in Receipt Roll 117 of 19 Edward I, at the end of period here treated.
70. Under Dorset in Receipt Roll 44 of 45 Henry III.
71. Above, p. 52.
72. e.g. 74*s*. 2*d*. under Suffolk, Receipt Roll 19.

with amounts which would not be subject to blanching.[73] It occurs sometimes so frequently[74] that we can hardly put it down to a correction by the Exchequer of its previous arithmetic. Perhaps the explanation given above of the phrase *de eodem* is correct for this also and we have here merely a slipshod method, due to pressure of business, which disappeared after the reforms following on the Statute of Rhuddlan. Thenceforward we can safely rely on a normal equation between the number of tallies struck and entries made on the Receipt Roll[75]

ASSIGNMENTS

We cannot here go deeply into the matter of assignments; indeed it is, as has been said, an Economist's subject. But as the matter was first put forward, at any rate with emphasis, in my previous papers, it may be permissible here to outline some of the problems; one or two of them, also, are largely matters of tally technique.

Development of the Practice

Assignment, or anticipation of the Crown Revenue, was practised as early as the reign of Henry II, as I have pointed out in an article on a Flemish money-lender, William Cade, of that period. The King borrowed from Cade (and by the way a private tally may well have figured at this stage[76]) and repaid him by authorizing him to draw on Royal debtors in the Counties; the authority being probably always a writ to the debtor. Professor Willard, who furnished me with much illustration of this point on a previous occasion,[77] has lately worked out[78] the more fully developed system of the early fourteenth century in connexion with payments made by the Collectors of Taxation,[79] showing three stages. In the first of these a writ, whether under the Great or Privy Seal or out of the Exchequer, ordered the payment, directing the Collectors

73. *De Judeis de Stamford'*: Receipt Roll 12 of 21 Henry III.
74. Fifteen times in Receipt Roll 12 of 21 Henry III.
75. See above, p. 54. The entry has practically disappeared from the Receipt Roll by 13 Edward I.
76. E.H.R. *xxviii*, p. 209. Some of the original bonds of Cade's other debtors have survived, which I hope later to publish; but it appears from the roll that, instead of such parchment documents, he sometimes used tallies.
77. *Proceedings*, xxv, p. 29.
78. Surrey Record Society, xviii, *Surrey Taxation Returns*, Introduction, p. xv, and documents quoted.
79. Another good example for working is furnished by K.R. Subsidies 161/6, an account of the collection of the 15th in Oxfordshire in 30 Edward I, which should be worked in conjunction with the Receipt Rolls.

to take letters patent of receipt; in the second stage they were ordered to take letters patent on surrender of which the Exchequer would levy a tally for them; and in the third they were ordered to pay, taking in exchange a tally which had already been levied at the Exchequer and entered on the Receipt Roll under the same date as that of the writ sent to the Collectors and had also under that date been entered on the Issue Roll.

Note that in all these processes the writ or letter as well as the tally played a part.[80] The final stage would be reached when the writ dropped out. It is not perhaps inappropriate to recall here that we are working up a state of affairs when practically all payments will be made by assignment and the number of tallies so issued will be so large as to compel the conclusion that private firms must have undertaken the discounting of them; which (since we must suppose they exacted a consideration) gives us of course a starting-point for very wide deductions as to the state of the Public Credit.

Assignment and the Wardrobe

I venture on another illustration. Professor Tout has suggested that the practice of the Wardrobe was responsible for the origin of assignments by tally; and since one of the earliest beginnings of what is afterwards the *pro* entry in the Receipt Roll is the appearance of the word *Gard'* (*for Garderoba*) in that position he has attributed to the Wardrobe's activities the inauguration of the system. Examination of the documents,[81] however, during (e.g.) the last years of Edward I, will show that this *Gard'* must not be taken as marking an assignment of revenue to the Wardrobe: rather the Exchequer was here recognizing the *fait accompli*.

What happened was this. The Wardrobe armed with the power of buying necessaries one of its officials, who obtained what he required from X, say in January, giving a chit or private tally in exchange for the value — say twenty marks: X, if this was not a Wardrobe *billa* in the strict sense, presently exchanged it for one, and, armed with this *billa*, approached (say in March of the same year; but probably it was often much later) the Exchequer of Receipt.

As the Wardrobe had a general writ upon the Receipt for perhaps 10,000*l.*, that body would debit twenty marks to it upon the Issue Roll, describing this as paid *per manus X*. It might choose to pay cash, in which case there would be no entry on the Receipt Roll: if, however, the method of assignment was to be used, as, of course, it might quite well be, twenty marks would be credited to some Accountant on the Receipt Roll, a note *Gard'* written in the margin of that Record, and the tally for the amount handed to X. Note that under this

---

80. In 13 Edward II the amounts paid out by Collectors on a writ are respited because they have not yet received their tallies, the Treasurer being away (L.T.R. Memoranda Roll 90, m. 146).
81. Cp., e.g. Receipt Roll 1660 and Issue Roll 112.

arrangement the date of the Receipt and Issue Roll entries would be after that of the Wardrobe *billa*; and long after that of the Wardrobe's general writ for 10,000*l*. This fact, of course, strengthens the case for the independence of the Wardrobe, which clearly had no hesitation in incurring the liability first and authorizing payment out of the money due to it at the Exchequer afterwards; but the peculiarities of the procedure have nothing directly to do with the starting or encouraging of the assignment method of paying; which was being used in plenty of cases[82] which had not the *Gard'* or any similar note against them in the Receipt Roll.

It is to be observed, by the way, that the political significance of the comparative positions of Wardrobe and Exchequer may very easily be exaggerated. In any time of war the department which deals with Munitions will inevitably escape from control by the department of pure Finance; and with equal inevitability, so soon as a suspension or end of hostilities comes about, the Financial Department will be found taking control again and trying retrospectively to straighten things out. We need not necessarily assume a violent antagonism between the two; but only that Supplies could not wait upon Arithmetic, nor even upon the expert's evidence as to available resources. In point of fact the origins of Assignment go deeper than Wardrobe procedure: apart from the primary reason (the need to anticipate revenue), difficulties of coinage, of transport, and of the machinery of local Administration have probably far more to do with it.

Further Questions concerning Assignments

To other matters concerning Assignment we must not devote more than a passing mention. The method, viewed the naturally simple and straight-forward character of the Receipt Roll, led to endless confusion; to cancellation of entries when assignments had gone wrong, replacement of them by other entries, additions of notes of subsequent payment to rolls of an earlier date, and so forth: even when the clerks were careful it was a clumsy affair; and when they were not[83] the complications almost defy elucidation. The method of 'squaring' a muddle by means of a fictitious loan has been alluded to in an earlier paper: but to this has to be added the possibiity of loans that were genuine[84] being mixed in with the fictitious; not to mention a puzzling series, recently noted, where loans were apparently made in the morning and

---

82. See Issue Rolls 54, 57, and 59, and Receipt Rolls 94, 110, and 112 (16-18 Edward I) for some examples.

83. Cp. Receipt Roll 606 (20 Richard II) with the Issue Roll for the following year: cp. also Receipt Roll 639 of 8 Henry IV, where cancelled assignments are not struck through, with Issue Roll 596.

84. Examples in Receipt Roll 606 of 20 Richard II under date 22 August: cp. the case of Henry Beaufort's loan in the Receipt and Issue Rolls of 9 Henry V, an example for which I have to thank Mr. W.T. Waugh.

paid off in the evening or on the next day;[85] loans, too, by small officials and other unexpected people. The solemn use of a clumsy machinery for purely book-keeping purposes is perhaps seen at its best when we get the assignment of a tally for the benefit of the person supposed to be making the payment:[86] there is humour also in the case where on the same date two different authorities[87] assign the same debt to different people.

LATER EXCHEQUER TALLIES

A few facts have recently come to hand concerning late tallies which shed light on the continuation of the medieval practice into modern times. In the first place two fragments of Exchequer tallies have been discovered among the unsorted Miscellanea of the Exchequer. One of them is too small for any certain inference to be possible; but is probably part of an Exchequer tally (apparently a foil) of the fourteenth century. The other is much more interesting, being part of a foil of the Easter term of 8 James I.[88] The Receipt Roll[89] gives us the complete description.

Wiltes'	De Richardo Goddard armigero nuper vicecomite ibidem ——— $Cliiij^{li}$ ij^s $viij^d$ videlicet de exitibus juratorum $lvij^{li}$ $viij^s$ ij^d et de Remanentia compoti sui $iiij^{xx}$ xvj^{li} $xiiij^s$ vj^d	sol	Watson[90]

Enough of the tally remains to show (1) that there is no alteration in cutting conventions except that the £1 notch has already attained the wide modern shape: it had always tended to be made with one short and one long cut, though nothing is said of this in the *Dialogus*; (2) that the day of the month is given as well as the term; (3) that, though the small amounts are written in,

85. Cp. Receipt Roll 725 (9 Henry VI) under date 12 October with Issue Roll 696 under date 13 October. I am in hopes that the problem may presently be worked out by Miss D.M. Broome, who first noted its occurrence in the reign of Edward III.
86. Examples have been noted in (e.g.) Receipt Rolls 150 and 153 (*temp.* Edward II) and 747 (Henry VI): see also Receipt Roll 672 and Issue Roll 624, of 4 Henry V, under date May 11.
87. In 4 Edward III, one by a letter of privy seal and one by tally: see *Calendar of Close Rolls*, p. 91, and cp. p. 366.
88. This does something to fill a considerable gap. It has now been possible to examine in these papers Exchequer tallies of the early and late 13th century, the early 17th century, the early, middle, and late 18th, and the early 19th century.
89. E.401/1367, under date 8 July.
90. The Teller's name; I do not think this ever appears on the tally; it is a modern device, the Tellers having become persons of importance, to put it in the roll.

the total received is still expressed in notches only; (4) that the word *sol* is apparently not written on the tally; (5) that in all ordinary respects it conforms to our known rules and our inference that the foil reproduced the wording of the stock.

The second point to be noticed is the interesting discovery at the Bank of England[91] of a number of late eighteenth-century tally stocks. Belonging to the period before 50,000*l.* was fixed as the maximum to be notched on any one tally, they attain to an enormous size, one being 8 ft. 6 in. long. They apparently remained at the Bank (i.e. were never returned to the Exchequer) because they record an uncompleted transaction, being receipts for part of the original Government Debt,[92] which, of course, has never been repaid!

A collection of rather dirty and illegible stocks of a very late date (some are actually of the year 1826) exists at the Public Record Office and was alluded to in my former papers. A re-examination of these[93] has not yielded much of importance. There are a number of fragments and over 160 complete stocks. The latter include twelve preserved with draft accounts touching Gibraltar, to which they relate, for the years 1749-1760; twenty-eight with accounts of tax collecting in Berkshire, being almost[94] the only ones marked with the name of a county and not *Magna Britannia*[95] (the modern equivalent of the medieval *Anglia* on tallies of a non-local character): a few relating to Civil List accounts of the earlier part of George III's reign and still dated by the regnal year (an old fashion which seems to have been superseded by the use of the month and year date about 1802);[96] two having an established connexion with proceedings[97] in the Land Revenue Department; and a quantity of early nineteenth-century tallies relating mostly to a few matters only, such as Excise, the sale of Exchequer Bills, the Civil List, Naval Works at Leith, and Conscience Money[98] paid on various accounts. In addition to the points noted, they serve to establish the fact that *sol'* and the date were written in after the notching but before the splitting; that the shilling notch had now grown to the size of the original pound and more, the pound (as we saw in the case of the Jacobean foil above) being distinguished only by the uneven

91. I am indebted to Mr. H.G. de Fraine for an opportunity to inspect these. He has published an account of them in *The Old Lady of Threadneedle Street*, vol. ii, no. 13.
92. The familiar 11,015, 100*l.* of the Weekly Bank Return.
93. See list in Appendix 1 to this paper.
94. One for Rutland is practically complete, and there are a few other fragments.
95. One or two of the collection show a variant of this — *Brit*[*annia*] *sept*[*entrionalis*].
96. At which date a similar change may be noted in the Receipt Books.
97. Revenue of Leases on Crown property.
98. Two of these, dated 3 April 1806, are remarkable for having an inscription which begins *De J. Alcock* and then drops into English, the details of conscience money paid to the late William Pitt (in one case from America!) being too much for the clerk's Latinity: cp. the Receipt Book (E. 401/2216), where they are marked with the word *Anglic'*. Another (of 1809) relating to surplus fees in the Land Revenue Office is also in English; but the use is rare. Another occasional abnormality is the use of an inscription beginning *De pecunia* . . .

length of its cuts; that a farthing might appear in accounts and not on the tallies;[99] that the word *sol'* was sometimes omitted on the late tally; that the space for pence was not left blank when no pennies were to be cut; and that in other respects the rules of cutting were singularly close to the original medieval.[100] A late tally for one penny is curious because of its size. This and other typical specimens may be seen in the Public Record Office Museum.[101] A tally with the amounts written in beside the notches is probably a freak.

The provenance of these late Exchequer Tallies is doubtful: in the case of a few there are, as has been seen, some indications; but it is possible that the collection as it stands has been made up from several smaller ones. Clearly they represent, like the earlier examples, exceptional cases: otherwise we should have had foils, or foils and stocks, not stocks only.

Note — Since the above was written my attention has been called to yet another Exchequer Treatise, written by William Lowndes in 1691 and now among the Lowndes papers at the Public Record Office.[102] It resembles others of the seventeenth and eighteenth centuries, but throws some fresh light on the practice of his time with regard to Assignment Tallies.

LATER HISTORY OF THE RECEIPT ROLLS AND BOOKS

It is impossible here to investigate this matter in any detail, but for completeness it may be worth while to mention that since my earlier papers were written it has been possible to work out to some extent[103] the highly complicated adventures of the Receipt Rolls (which we have had occasion to quote so freely) and Issue Rolls. The splitting up of their series, their reunion, the division of a triplicate series into an unintelligible duplicate one in modern times, and so forth, with some account of alterations in administration made in the time of the Tudors, are matters of real importance because they often affect interpretation.

The last Receipt Roll is for Michaelmas Term 22 George III; the Receipt Book, which had grown up beside it, went on to the end of the old Exchequer system in 1834. Tally-making, it will be recalled, ceased in 1826.[104]

99. Two of the amounts in the Gibraltar Accounts contain a farthing but are reckoned to the next halfpenny on the tallies.
100. See my first paper, where Chisholm's Appendix to the *Report on Public Income and Expenditure (1869)* is quoted. Chisholm, by the way, appears to have had a foil before him when he wrote.
101. The Museum contains also a few specimens of medieval private tallies, to which it is hoped later to add some of the medieval Exchequer ones.
102. T.48/6. I have to thank Mr. R.D. Richards for the reference.
103. See Appendix V to my *Manual of Archive Administration* (Clarendon Press, 1922).
104. Recently I have discovered some examples of the 'indented cheque receipt' which was substituted for the tally in 1826: they will be found in E. 181/90.

MISCELLANEA

Before leaving the Exchequer Tally, we must mention what may be called the Miscellanea of the subject — notes which have accrued from time to time from various sources and will presumably go on accruing: information as to the writing of tallies;[105] new examples of attempts at forging[106] them, and what befell the offenders; fresh illustration of what occurred when a tally was lost or mislaid,[107] or having been mislaid was found again; cases of the emendation of tallies;[108] curious points of procedure[109] (including the treatment of the apposite clerks) when an accountant in the fifteenth century was getting his tallies through; and the like. All these are interesting, occasionally illuminating; and perhaps I may venture to say that I am always glad to hear of them, for their appearance is sporadic and cannot be predicted. In concluding this part of the subject we may comment on the lack of evidence of any parallel development of the tally outside this country. That is very curious, and, considering the importance of the tally in England, even confirmation of its unimportance elsewhere would be of value.

---

105. Notes like the following (from Receipt Roll 119, of Edward I) are probably not uncommon. *Hic incepit Radulphus de Manton' clericus domini Johannis de Theford' scribere tallias . . . quia dictus dominus fuit infirmus.* The *scriptor talliarum*, becoming a regular official, subsequently blossoms into the Auditor of the Receipt, an important person under the Tudors and later.
106. e.g. L.T.R. Mem. Roll 109 (II Edward III), m. 15: in 5/6 Edward I we have a description of how the tallies necessary for a sheriff's accounting could not be found in spite of much searching; how they were innovated, so as not to delay the account, and then *casualiter* found again in their proper place; and how the Barons of the Exchequer *huiusmodi mutacionem et translacionem talliarum suspectas habentes et sinistrum inde suspicantes* arrested William de Bradecote, one of the Chamberlains of the Receipt (Anc. Corr. 17/14 and K. R. Mem. Roll 5/6 Edward I, m. 3*d*). I am indebted for one of these references, and for some others, to Mr. R.J. Whitwell.
107. Cp., e.g., *Calendar of Close Rolls*, 14 Edward I, p. 384; Ryley, *Placita*, 450; *Rot. Parl.* i, p. 317b; Receipt Roll 905 (ii Edward IV), under date 28 October; *ibid.* 913, under date 2 March, containing a note of the elaborate precautions in case certain *pro* tallies, lost and innovated, should subsequently be found; and so forth. A writ ordering the arrangements for 'innovations' will be found on Receipt Roll 1756, m. 1*d*; cp. *Cal. of Close Rolls*, 1286, p. 385. The *Red Book*, p. 973, quoting Memoranda Rolls, says the Chamberlains might make no charge for searching for lost tallies; cp. *Cal. Close Rolls*, 1278, p. 487: but see note 3 below.
108. See *Tallie Innovate* Roll (Receipt Roll 1761), *temp.* Edward II.
109. *In expensis ad portam Westm' pro clericis Camerarii Scaccarii scrutantibus in les foyles . . .* MSS. Lord DeLisle and Dudley, i, 211 (*c.* 1460) — a reference for which I have to thank Mr. C.L. Kingsford. Such 'expenses' are the subject of an Exchequer poem printed not long since by Professor Haskins and Mrs. George (*E.H.R.* xxvi, p. 58). I hazard the suggestion that at Westminster Gate there was a place of entertainment, which would give point to a line in the poem (*ibid.* 65). Compare also Chancery Miscellanea 34/1/10.

PRIVATE TALLIES

Introductory

In my former paper I utilized very few private tallies and rather came to the conclusion that the subject was not one on which very many definite deductions could be attempted. At the time, the largest file of such tallies with which I was acquainted was one of fourteen, some of them fragmentary. After my subsequent supplementary notes and in time only for a brief postscript I heard of a file of twenty-seven; and had since then wondered from time to time, rather regretfully, whether some attempt at an analysis of them was not desirable — some effort to establish for ourselves what in the case of the Exchequer Tallies is given us by the *Dialogus*. The matter was clinched by the quite recent discovery, during the examination of hitherto unsorted Miscellanea at the Public Record Office, of three bags of the fourteenth century containing between them nearly 140 private tallies and fragments. As the matter stands at present I have been able thus to examine and classify nearly 250 separate tallies and fragments,[110] dating from the reigns of Henry III, Edward I, Edward II, and Edward III, with three of Richard II's reign, one of Henry V's, and one or two of later date. Most are from the reign of Edward III, round about 1350, but a reasonable proportion (about eighty) are of the earlier dates and clearly some more definite views should be possible.

Source of our Collections

Thirty-three different tallies or sets of tallies are described in Appendix II to this paper. Of these some are disconnected ones. In the case of those from the Record Office[111] it is possible to make some guess at their provenance and the official connexions which may have brought them there; but those from the British Museum[112] are more genuinely isolated.

More satisfactory specimens are the tallies which are preserved in some contemporary bags of leather (pl. IV) or sacking[113] (pls. V and VI), having writing upon them, and are themselves as a rule on their original twisted parchment filing strings,[114] perhaps with a descriptive parchment label in addition (pls. V and VII). These labels and

110. See list in Appendix III. Since this paper was read the number has been swelled by the discovery of another file of sixteen private tally foils. As they do not introduce any modification of what I had already deduced from the others, I have added them under sub-numbers in the Appendix to save alteration of the numbers cited at numerous points in the text and foot-notes.

111. Nos. 1 and 2, 3-6, 229 and 232.

112. Nos. 170, 217, 226, 231.

113. Nos. 29-31; 73-143 and probably 144-169; 171-201 and probably 202-216; 218-224. These are in two sacks with contemporary parchment labels attached and three leather bags, of which two are particularly fine specimens in white leather.

114. Most of those enumerated in note 112 above; also nos. 32-45.

writing on the sacks are nearly all, unfortunately, rather difficult to read; but they give us clues as to the nature of the tallies, the reason for their preservation, and their approximate dates. Thus the largest sack[115] (pl. V) has a label which conveys to us that it has to do with the accounts of . . de Manton', Keeper of the King's Wardrobe. This cannot be Richard de Manton', cofferer of the Wardrobe in the reign of Edward I, for so far as we know he never attained to the higher office; and we must accordingly relate it to William de Manton' who was keeper about 35 Edward III; a date which the tallies found in the bag, and presumably belonging to it, at least do nothing to contradict, while one of them actually supports it.[116] One of the parchment labels[117] (pl. VIII) tells us the number, date, subject, and amounts of the tallies:

In isto filacio sunt decem et quatuor tallie de vino capto ad expensas domini Edwardi Principis Wallie Annis regni regis Edwardi filii Regis Henrici xxjo xxijdo xxiijo xxiiijto et xxvto — Continentes viginti duas libras et duodecim denarios Item in isto filacio sunt nouem tallie continentes septem libras et sexdecim denarios debitos pro . . . de annis predictis.

Other labels[118] are similar though not so full of detail.

Thirdly, we have the tallies which are actually preserved with the accounts to which they belong,[119] giving us invaluable information. Among these[120] I have been so fortunate as to find some foils and stocks preserved together; which, as will be seen below, has made it possible to clear up several difficulties. The first collection is in Exchequer Accounts 261/21,[121] where we have Rolls and Counter-Rolls of Accounts, two sets of Tallies (stocks and foils) corresponding with the writings of the two accountants, and the original canvas sack (pl. VI).

Lastly, it is to be observed that our Tallies come from widely separated districts. Even among the Tallies found in the Manton sack a number of different counties are represented as well as a number of different hands.

Use and Importance of the Private Tally

In the first place we have to note the extreme popularity of the private tally. A curious example of the everyday nature of tally-cutting as a practice is

115. Containing eight original files and a number of loose tallies and fragments: this is E. 101/678/2. Two large leather bags are related respectively to the accounts of Thomas de Chubham sheriff of [E]ssex in xxxij. and xxxiij. [Edward III] and to those of Nicholas Raunche, reeve of Estwod'.
116. No. 92.
117. Attached to nos. 32-45.
118. Attached to nos. 73-83; 171-187; 188-201; 218-224: the last-named is inscribed *Tallie reseruande super compotum Nicholai prepositi de Estwod' anno xxxiiij.*
119. Nos 7-12; 19-24; 25 and 26; 27 and 28; 46-72; 225; 230.
120. Nos. 7-12 and 46-72: see also nos. 218-224.
121. Nos 46-72. Note that the fashion of cutting the tallies also differs, one set being abnormal, Exchequer fashion.

furnished by an inquisition[122] of the thirteenth century which tells us, without thinking it necessary to give any elaborate explanation, that two men, Henry and Walter, were lifting a table in the hall of William de Furnivall at Wytstan and Hugh de Chertevill, William's servant, was making tallies, holding his knife upright in his hand. Walter stumbled and fell on the knife — hence the inquisition; for us, the story is interesting for the suggestion it makes that an ordinary piece of stock work about the house would be the making, from time to time, of a bundle of tallies, perhaps even the splitting of them, ready for the use of the reeve or other official of the estate when he made his rounds. In this connexion we may note the number of tallies in our present collection (10 per cent.) which have the inscription roughly scratched on them,[123] with very often an ink inscription written in afterwards.[124] Another small indication is the spelling of the word tally in Latin[125] — clearly it is treated as if it were a vernacular word Latinized; and yet another is the fact (proved by the large square holes they were able to punch in them) that medieval folk must have used the wood green.

Nor are copious references to the use of tallies lacking. Money-lenders, we know, habitually used them from the earliest times[126] — the Jewish Plea Roll is full of references to them; and other passages[127] make it clear that the tally was a most ordinary accompaniment of all kinds of business. We note too that it was a general custom[128] at one time for the Crown, in making an order for the delivery of timber out of a Royal forest, to specify that a tally should be made between the forester and the recipient. The general use of tallies was, as we have seen, definitely recognized by the Central Administration, and on occasion regularized, in connexion with the collection of the King's revenue by subordinate officials; both by statute[129] and by special arrangement made from time to time.[130]

The use of private tallies was, in fact, fairly universal in the thirteenth and fourteenth centuries. When this popularity began and when it waned it is more difficult to say. We know that it has not entirely disappeared even in

122. See *Calendar of Miscellaneous Inquisitions*, i, no. 2169.
123. Examples of scratching without ink are nos. 73-81; 83: see pl. XVII.
124. The ink in some cases has run into the scratches.
125. *Talea, tallea, talia, tallia, taill'*, all appear: even the Exchequer's spelling is uncertain.
126. Cp. the case of William Cade, *temp.* Henry II, already quoted; and see the Jewish Plea Rolls, *passim*. A Jewish money-lender's tally is shown in the lower right-hand corner of pl. VII
127. e.g. Curia Regis Roll 26, m. 4, in an action over the sale of some salmon, *et inde producit sectam et talliam ostendit*.
128. Numerous examples will be found in the Record Office volumes of *Close Rolls*, Henry III (e.g. 22 Henry III, p. 28, which mentions tally and counter-tally) and some later.
129. Stat. of Westm. 3 Edw. I, c. 19, *q' les Viscontes facent tailles a tuz ceaux q' li paeront la dette le Rey*: we have dealt above with the statute of Rhuddlan (12 Edw. I).
130. For documents touching inquiry as to Sheriff's Tallies which were out in the country see, e.g., K R. Miscellanea, 24/17/3 and K.R. Sheriff's Accounts, 3/2 and 3/3.

our own time; but on the other hand we may safely conjecture that it began to give way before the more finished form of a parchment or paper receipt such as we find mixed with wooden tallies serving the same object on some of our files.[131] (pl.VIII), at a date a good deal earlier than was the case at the Exchequer; where, whatever the officials might say[132] as to its necessity for the safety of the King's revenue, a good deal of the tally's popularity was based on the vested interests of the people who made it. We must not press unduly any inference from the lack of examples of the private tally after the fourteenth century, and the examples given above of its mixture with parchment receipts is perhaps a little early; but we may conjecture a zenith of popularity in the late thirteenth and early fourteenth centuries and imagine that about the year 1350 old-fashioned officials would be grumbling that in their day the scratch of a knife on a slip of hazel was good enough for any man, but nowadays every knave who sold a few oats for the king's service must have parchment and ink and wax to content him. It is at least noteworthy that only two tallies[133] with an English inscription have so far come to light.

The matter is really worth study, for we have here, if we can establish the existence of a widespread system, a piece of the scattered and obscure, but valuable, evidence[134] for the activities, capabilities and fashions of a very important person, the *laicus litteratus*, the man of education who was not a cleric. The existence of a large body of such men, equipped as we know they must have been with what we should now call a commercial education of quite considerable range and finish, has a significance for the student of popular education and all it implies, which gives a value to any fresh addition to our knowledge on the subject.

Stock and Foil, Debtor and Creditor

With that preface we may turn to practical points concerning the private tally; which are many. The first which comes to mind is that of the connexion, if any, between the relation of stock and foil on the one hand and that of debtor and creditor in the transaction on the other. From this point of view it is to be noted that a large number of our private tallies are for goods (grain, forage, etc.) supplied for the King's needs; and since the persons who caused their preservation were Royal Officials, accounting at the Exchequer,

131. Nos. 25 and 26: cp. nos. 188-201.
132. Cf. the 17th cent. treatise quoted in *Proceedings*, xxv, p. 31.
133. Nos. 231, 232. One would not, of course, expect English on early tallies.
134. Other sections of the evidence are furnished by examination of the methods of the men who compiled the enormous mass of private Court Rolls, Accounts and Deeds of which a relatively small part has been preserved to us; together with Public Records of such a demonstrably local provenance as Sheriffs' Accounts, Inquisitions, and Assessments for Taxation. The wide distribution of knowledge of the elaborate rules for compiling such documents has not been sufficiently appreciated.

we may take it that tallies represented commodities collected by those
officials from the other persons named; whose claims for payment, for which
these tallies were vouchers, the Exchequer, through the Officials, had met or
was presently to meet. Now, in all but a few special cases it is the foil that is
thus preserved[135] and we are therefore entitled to argue that frequently, at
any rate in the thirteenth and fourteenth centuries, private tallying followed
the Exchequer rule by which the payer took the stock and the receiver the
foil. The suggestion is supported by cases (e.g. no. 25) where we have both
parties mentioned in the wording; and there is nothing anywhere to
contradict it. It is to be remembered that in the case of the Exchequer Tallies
the preservation of our collection of stocks is due to pure accident; but for the
fire of 1834 we should have had a collection of matched foils and stocks (since
the Exchequer exacted a return of the latter at Audit), *plus* some extra foils,
these being the part which remained in the Exchequer's possession
throughout.

Shape of the Private Tally

The distinguishing marks of the Tally's shape are four. First is the fact that
the complete tally is formed of two parts of uneven size by having a cut made
half through its thickness (generally at a distance of a quarter or a third of its
whole length from one end) and being split longitudinally from the other end
down to this point: this characteristic is universal with English medieval
Tallies both Exchequer and Private. Next we have the fashion of making the
half-cut just described. Third is the fashion of trimming the end which is
common to both stock and foil (the trimming of the butt end of the stock has
not been considered; as a matter of fact it seems to know no rule). Finally
there is the question of the position of the writing — the question which of the
two edges through which the split goes will be the upper and which the lower
if we hold the tally in a position for reading its inscription; or, to put it in
another way, whether the writing will run towards or away from the half-cut.
In the case of Exchequer Tallies all these are matters of immutable rule.
What of the Private Tally?

WRITING THIS WAY UP
ON FACE OF FOIL

In Appendix III the shape of the Tally has been marked as N. (Normal),
A. (Abnormal), S.A. (slightly Abnormal), and A.E. (Abnormal: following

---

135. The reason for the additional preservation of the stocks in a few cases (Appendix III, nos.
     7-12, 46-72) may be sought in the Accounts to which they belong: it naturally implies that
     they have been audited. Here we have only to take advantage of what it (it will be seen) a
     very lucky accident. We have altogether 34 stocks out of 248 examples.

Exchequer fashions), and it will be seen at once that there is a very great preponderance of Normals — 190 out of 248, not to mention 16 fragments. This 'Normal' shape of the foil (as has been remarked, most of our spcimens are foils) is here illustrated. The writing is on the face (the unsplit side): the half-cut across the tally forms the left end of the foil and is distinguished not by its angle to the edges of the face but by its angle to the horizontal plane, being sloped inwards from right to left: and the right-hand end is trimmed by a single cut making an acute angle with the upper edge of the foil. Further, it is to be observed that of the Abnormals twenty-one are only slight variations, due probably to carelessness or accident;[136] twenty-eight show evidence of Exchequer influence in one point or another[137] and only nine[138] are thoroughly abnormal. These figures are striking.

Shape and Position of the Notches

In the matter of *the shape of the notches* we have once more a marked normality: they are of the shapes and sizes (whatever they may have been meant to indicate) which were in use at the Exchequer. Thus we have the halfpenny mark,[139] the penny mark, and shilling and pound notches (see pls. IV to VIII); and a smaller, but still decisive, quantity of 20*l*. notches[140] (pl. VI). We have also the usual halves, but in addition a habit of halving the shilling mark, which is not done at the Exchequer but which is so common[141] in private tallies as to become a normality: in one case[142] it is used definitely for 6*d*. in money. There is distinct trace of the larger 1*l*.notch,[143] an exaggeration of the original one long and one short cut (examples on pl. VI); but that is at most an anticipation of later Exchequer practice.[144] Against these we have to set only six[145] cases where something like half a penny cut is used; and one absolute abnormal,[146] being a penny cut made obliquely across the tally edge.

In the matter of the *position of the notches* we have no such attention to rule. In certain cases where only one denomination (money) is involved and where there is an approximation to Exchequer form we get some trace of the

136. Cp. no. 102 in the Appendix, a case where careless cutting has made what should have been the stock into the foil.
137. There are some whose resemblance to Exchequer Tallies is only belied by their wording.
138. The first total shown in the list was 232; to which must be added the sixteen extra tallies mentioned above (note 110).
139. Appendix III, nos. 27, 229, and 230.
140. Nos. 46-57; 227.
141. Nos. 28, 74, 76, 78, 81, 111, 112, 115, 118, 122, 123, 125, 132, 133, 137, 140, 141, 142, 143, 175, 189, 211, 212, 215, 216, 217.
142. No. 229.
143. Nos. 19-24; 46-72; 218-224.
144. We have seen that it occurs in the Jacobean tally.
145. Nos. 44, 112, 115, 125, 217, 229.
146. No. 129.

Exchequer system of position, but for the most part the use of upper or lower edge and the position of the notches on it seems to have been at the will of the clerks: largely, this would result from the habit of putting more than one transaction on to a single tally[147] (note the uppermost file in pl. VII). We must also note a tendency to reverse Exchequer practice by putting the smaller notches on the left of larger ones on the same edge.

As to the meaning of the notches we shall have more to say later: but may remark here that when money is indicated the usual Exchequer senses are given to the different notches; and that there is even clear evidence of their being used in the nearest possible sense when commodities are to be indicated, a shilling being twelve times the penny cut and so forth.[148] Needless to say, the possibility of notches being used for varying purposes at once introduces an element of extreme uncertainty.

Writing

Here a glance at the Appendix will show that we have anything but a steady Normal: nor, indeed, would it be reasonable to expect it. The use of the face of the tally is regular enough, cases[149] where this is left blank and all writing put upon the edges being probably due to accident or carelessness. Nor is the commoner practice of continuing the inscription from the face on to the lower edge[150] very unreasonable: it is contrary to Exchequer practice, but then the Exchequer had always much the same thing to say and made the size of its tally accord. The use of the edge for a date or a place-name[151] or some special note[152] is quite natural: and granted the use of notches for more than one denomination, and sometimes for more than one on the same tally, it is logical to write on the edge for the purpose of distinguishing groups of notches,[153] for that of giving the price or the commodity[154] (whichever is not expressed in notches), or even for that of making it quite clear what the notches do mean[155] (see pl. VI and the tally across the lower part of pl. VIII: edge inscriptions may also be seen in pl. V). The last-mentioned mentioned information may equally well be given on the face,[156] indeed it is

147. A remarkable example is no. 230, where two distinct sums of money are put on the same tally; but to put on two or more commodities is common.
148. Appendix III, nos. 62-66. There is also clear evidence of the penny cut being habitually used for bushels and the shilling notch for quarters (nos. 121, 125, 217). Note however no. 228, where the pound notch is clearly used for twenty units but a score notch is used not for twenty times this but for 100 units.
149. Nos. 113, 123.
150. Nos. 1, 13, 14, 15, 23, 25, 27, 28, 96, 127, 226.
151. No. 137.
152. No. 2.
153. Nos. 8; 11; 35-37; 44, 45; 92-94; 106, 107; 109-113; 118; 123; 141, 142; 228.
154. Nos. 87, 88-94, 97, 119.
155. Nos. 46-57 (money); 58-71 (minerals); 217 (grain).
156. Nos. 135-139, etc.

continuation of that part of the writing. Similarly the edge writing may actually repeat the information given on the face.[157]

Wording

In all this there is, it is true, a considerable falling off from the staid following of what appear to be well-known rules; but that is, in a way, the logical result of multiplying the meanings which may be expressed by the notches: the Exchequer is only better off because it had practically abolished payment in kind before the date when its tally forms grew fixed. But it is when we come to consider the actual wording that we get the widest differences. Our Table shows us seventeen distinct forms, without going into the variations produced by the presence or absence of edge writing: forms which vary from the barest statement of a place-name to an elaborate explanation of the circumstances and which may equally well be introduced by *pro, contra* or *de*. The situation is complicated by the fact that in a large number of cases[158] we have an initial scratched[159] wording which is generally different, sometimes[160] very much so, from the inked inscription subsequently added (see the uppermost tally in pl. IV); that marked differences exist between tallies on the same file[161] and even between some which appear to be in the same hand; and that later additions[162] to an original inked inscription are also not infrequent.

On the other hand we find that, of 17 forms, 14 are distributed between only 51 tallies, whereas out of a total of 183 tallies three forms appear in, respectively, 83, 31 and 18 cases. The first of these is the form *Contra* (so and so) *de* (such a thing); the second is the same, substituting *pro* for *de*; and the third is the simplest form — that which begins (and sometimes ends) with a name. Clearly we have a wide choice of wordings but a great preponderance in the popularity of *Contra*; and this is well distributed over the whole collection and the whole period covered: several examples may be seen in the plates.

With regard to *contra* I have to confess to an error in my first paper, where I assumed that it must mean *against* and consequently refer to the position of debtor and creditor. The discovery of three sets[163] of tallies which include both stock and foil has proved not only that, contrary to the Exchequer custom, inscriptions on the two parts of the tally are not, or need not be, the same, but also that it is possible for *contra* to be used with the names of both

157. Nos. 98, 100, 103, 104.
158. Appendix III, nos. 140; 175, 176; 178; 180; 183; 190, 191; 198; 202; and eight fragments.
159. Probably with the point of a knife.
160. e.g. nos. 183, 198, 202.
161. e.g. nos. 114-131.
162. Nos. 171-174; 179; 185-187; 195; 229.
163. Nos. 7-12; 46-72; 218-224.

parties to the transaction,[164] implying a check on both rather than a debit on one. This gives us the further inference that in the large number of cases where we have a foil lettered *contra* (so and so) *de* (such a commodity) this is the receiver's counterfoil to an acknowledgement of goods received from the person 'against' whom it purports to be: which takes us a long way forward in the understanding of private tallies.

Dating

It is remarkable how generally we have been able to date our tallies and how seldom this has been on information supplied directly by the tally itself. A large proprotion give, it is true, some information, but comparatively few[165] of these go so far as to mention the King's name; and only seven[166] give the exact date: the rest of them are content with such phrases as *anno ix*. It is true that in practically all the remainder we can get a probable date either from the fact that dated and undated are filed together[167] or that a file or sack has a label on it. But there is hardly any sign of a date, even in the most abbreviated form, making a regular part of the inscription; much less is any regular position on the tally assigned to it, as was done at the Exchequer; and, as we have seen, in a single file some tallies may have it while others do not. Clearly the tally-writer relied generally upon his memory, or upon the order or position in which he kept his tallies, to give them a date: clearly also he had little conception of a date as essential to authenticity.

This may lead us on to the question of

Interpretation

It is clear from what we have said that the idea ôf the Private Tally as a thing to be read off by any one (in the way in which the Exchequer one can be read off) was by no means absolute, or even general. Private tallies, as we have them here, were very much things to be read in the light of a person's own knowledge or of accounts to which they might be attached or of a label attached to them.[168] The consequence is that though amounts, as we have seen, bear a pretty regular relation to the size of notches, *once we know what denomination is being used*, there are no cases where we can be sure of this from the notches alone: nobody troubled to devise a system which would give us a

164. Nos 46-72 afford particularly good instânces: the difficulty of interpreting *contra* when we had only one part of the tally was increased by the fact that the phrase *de . . . ab eo recept'*, which frequently follows it, might mean receipts *by* him or receipts *from* him.
165. Appendix III, nos. 1; 19; 20; 22; 23; 25 28; 89; 92; 96; 119; 131; 213; 217; 223; 226; 229, 230; 232. The habit of mentioning the King by his initial only, without any distinction, is of course not infrequent in other locally made documents.
166. Nos. 1; 92; 213; 226; 229, 230; 232.
167. Original files are nos. 32-45; 73-83; 84-88; 89-93; 94-101; 102-113; 114-131; 132-139; 171-187; 188-201, 218-224.
168. Such as that which tells that nos. 73-83 should amount to so much; giving us the inference that the notches represent shillings and pence.

difference between loads of hay and quarters of corn — probably nobody could. There is a fair number of cases (much larger than is ususlly assumed) where the meaning of the notches is made clear by what is written on the tally; either because the actual amount is given,[169] or because the wording makes it clear in other ways[170] (e.g. by using a phrase like *de denariis*); or because we act on inference, as for example when, price and commodity being both named, we find that the notches make an impossible large number of bushels or an impossible small number of pence. But there is also a considerable remainder where, in the absense of external evidence from accounts or a label, it is really impossible to settle the denomination of the notches with certainty — good examples are those which come from the sack of the sheriff of Essex.[171] In fact while it is true, as we have seen, that the tally-maker who puts more than one commodity on a tally will generally feel it wise to distinguish, by writing on the edge, the little pigs from the corn; while, also, there is a reasonable probability that by a shilling notch and a penny cut he will usually mean to indicate 13, it is only on rare occasions that a meticulous official will think it necessary to make it clear to the outside world that he means thirteen pence and not thirteen piglets.[172]

Conclusion

It would be unreasonable to expect private tallies to be governed by rules as fixed as the Exchequer ones; because the Exchequer (1) was dealing always with the same type of transaction in the same denomination (money) and (2) was a body of formalists: the *antiqua consuetudo* was, we may guess, a fetish already at Westminster in the thirteenth century. Still we can get from Exchequer practice a standard of comparison.

Let us summarize. The medieval Exchequer has absolute rules governing (1) the size of the tally; (2) the use of stock and foil and their relative size; (3) the way in which the tally was cut half through and (4) at the right end; (5) the size and (6) the position of the notches; (7) the way it was written on the face and (8) on the edge; (9) the form of wording employed, both on face and edge; and (10) the way in which it was split. The Private Tally-maker (allowing for abnormals)

(a) Agrees with the Exchequer in having rules for (1), (2) and (10) and, what is more, follows the same rules.

(b) Agrees with the Exchequer in having rules for (3), (4), (5) and to some extent (7), but has other, though similar, rules.

169. Appendix III, nos 1; 30; 38; 46-57; 218-227 (money): 25; 26; 117; 121; 125; 135-138; 141; 217 (grain): 60-71 (minerals): 228 (sheep).
170. Nos. 3-6; 16-24; 27, 28.
171. Nos. 188-216, two files relating to hay and litter: cp. the preceding file (nos. 171-187) relating to oats.
172. No. 101.

(c) Differs widely from the Exchequer in the matter of (6), (8) and (9) though he shows some tendency towards certain specially popular conventions.

A few inferences seem possible. First, it would appear that some considerable time before the Dialogus was written tally-making was a widespread custom in England and had reached a stage of considerable regularity in the matter of the size of the tally, the habit of making two parts of unequal length, and possibly the size of the notches. Secondly, we may infer that later (but again some time before the *Dialogus*; which speaks of an annual tally-season having existed before the *Scaccarium* system was invented) there had arisen a custom of deliberately differentiating the King's tallies, by certain peculiarities of cutting, from those made by the rest of the world: it was probably about this time that, contributions in kind becoming more and more commuted for money payments, it became possible for the Royal Officials to standardize the notches, and in particular the position of them, upon their tallies; giving a special significance to the upper and lower edges.

Finally, we may conjecture that the writing[173] on the tally (and its standardizaion at the Exchequer) was developed quite independently; and indeed it seems quite clear that in this matter the Exchequer, which had settled some of its forms early in the thirteenth century and practically all before the fourteenth, was far ahead of the private-tally maker, who is still using very primitive forms in many even of the fourteenth-century tallies in our collection. We can understand that the Exchequer official might adopt the opening preposition *De* to distinguish his tallies, just as he had adopted special angles of cutting at the ends: the curious thing is, not that other tally-makers did not use this form, but that they used so many others.

At the same time it is also an interesting comment, either upon the exclusiveness of the Exchequer or upon the strength of local tradition and training, that persons so closely connected with the Exchequer as most of those who have left us our private tallies, should have been so little influenced by its chosen forms.

THE TALLIES *CONTRA EDWARDUM DE WESTMONASTERIO*

I have left to the end consideration of the thirteen[174] tallies belonging to this section, two of which are shown in pl. III (nos. 8 and 9), because as a problem they seem to be between the Exchequer Tallies and the private ones.

173. The *Dialogus* tells us that there was writing on the Exchequer Tally and (inferentially) that it was placed in the way familiar to us later; but says nothing of any standard form of wording.
174. Four are fragments.

What is to be said of the tallies which are Exchequer in form, were found among the Exchequer specimens, and yet begin with the word *contra*? Seven of these tallies are for large amounts (they run into thousands): one of them (pl. III, no. 9) gives us a clue as to date, being annotated *post Pasch' anno xxxvjto*: and they are all stocks, i.e. (if the usual rule was observed[175]) belong to the person who had paid.

In the first place we may dismiss the idea that these are ordinary Exchequer Tallies. The Exchequer rule that a tally begins with the word *De* is by now too firmly established for us to discredit; but by way of extra precaution the Receipt Rolls covering the probable dates have been searched and revealed practically no payments made by Edward of Westminster, certainly none of these sums.

We turn to the word *contra* for light. A good deal has been already said about this in its purely private capacity. A certain number of references have been collected where it is used in connexion with Exchequer business, but here we only find either that the use is complicated by memories of local custom[176] or that a tally which we know to have been *De* so and so for money which he had paid in is spoken of quite literally as being *contra* the Exchequer. Can this be the clue? Can it be that Edward was being paid money, that we should look for these sums not on the Receipt but the Issue Rolls?

Here again the result of a good deal of search is disappointing: we have not found our sums on the Issue or Liberate Rolls. On the other hand we have found an extremely large number of other issues to Edward.[177] For years he is unfailing in his appearance on Issue Rolls and elsewhere[178] as a recipient of Royal moneys from the Treasury. The line of inquiry shifts accordingly to his biography.[179]

No attempt can be made here to give a regular sketch of this owing to the fullness of the material. He was by profession a melter and the son of a goldsmith, Odo, and appears acting in his professional capacity at the Exchequer in 1240[180]; and a first conjecture (discredited because the sums seemed too big) was that our tallies might refer to coin handed to him for melting. But he (and Odo too) had many other connexions with the Crown service. The two appear first together in 24 Henry III when we find them in

175. See above, p. 69.
176. e.g. in the curious document K.R. Subsidies, 161/6, where Exchequer Tallies which were perfectly normal (they have been duly followed on to the Receipt Roll) are spoken of as being *contra* the sheriff who had paid the money in.
177. In one roll, that of 24 Henry III (E. 403/1204) we find well over twenty, ranging from sums of shillings up to scores of pounds.
178. See the printed volumes of Close, Liberate, and Patent Rolls from the year 1240.
179. He does not appear in the *Dictionary of National Biography*.
180. Printed *Close Rolls*, p. 169: he may have succeeded John le Fundur, who was dead in 1235 (*ibid.*, 114).

charge of the King's wine and King's houses. But Edward is soon on his own feet. From a multitude of small jobs[181] — the provision of robes and vestments and gold cups and wood and candles and houses and obols of musc — we find him progressing to work more important and nearer to the King's heart; he buys land *ad opus Conversorum* in 1243[182]; he feeds 4,000 poor on an anniversary[183]: the forward step to borrowing the necessary money to feed 10,000 poor[184] is easy. Soon after[185] he has the difficult task of settling the King's debts *ne in aduentu nostro London' super hoc possimus inquietari*. He is appointed with others to tallage the City of London in 1252[186] and has many other financial offices entrusted to him such as that of talking[187] to the foreign money-lenders and persuading them to a gift, or at any rate a loan, in 1245. He is continually in association, official or unofficial, with the treasurer and continually figuring in Henry III's numerous shifts to get money and gorgeous plans for disbursing it.

But one employment in particular may engage our attention; both in general as antiquaries and for the purposes of the present paper. Edward was intimately associated with the King's work at Westminster Abbey, as apparently his father had been before him.[188] Large grants were made to him in this connexion about the year 1246[189] and he was appointed, with the Archdeacon, treasurer of the New Exchequer which the King had established for this purpose at Westminster.[190]

These references are merely, it must be repeated, a fraction of what might be brought forward concerning the mixture of craftsman, financial agent, and clerk of the works that was Edward son of Odo; but perhaps they are enough. I read them in connexion with the passage in the *Dialogus*[191] which tells us how, at an earlier period, the officials of the Exchequer dealt with cases where money had to be paid out without a writ. The Chamberlains (the officials who were responsible for the ordinary tallies) made tallies for these issues; and I suggest that our thirteen *contra* tallies are parallel to these —

181. See e.g. *Close Rolls* for 1240 and 1241, pp. 179, 253, 254, 255, 258, 266, 306, 308, 309, 310, 312.
182. *Ibid.*, 22.
183. *Ibid.*, 140.
184. *Ibid.*, 1243, p. 145.
185. *Ibid.*, 1245, p. 309.
186. *Patent Rolls*, p. 142.
187. *alloquamini et modis quibus poteritis inducatis diligenter . . .* but the letter is headed *De pecunia . . . extorquenda* in the roll (*Close Rolls*, 1245, p. 314). The charm of language of Henry III's letters has not yet been properly appreciated.
188. Issue Rolls, 1201-1203.
189. Patent Rolls, 475, 478.
190. *Ibid.*: cp. Brayley and Britton, *History of the Ancient Palace . . . , p. 53.*
191. Oxford edition, p. 88. *Item sunt ad Scaccarium liberationes constitute que statutis terminis sine breui regis soluuntur. Qualis est liberatio naucleri . . . De qua et consimilibus talee fiunt a camerariis quia de hiis breuia non habent.* Cp. the Introduction to *Calendar of Liberate Rolls*, p. viii.

evidences of sums issued to Edward of Westminster for which he may have been responsible to the King, but for which he certainly rendered no account at the Exchequer, and for which he probably had no writ.

Edward was living in 1264 and had apparently died before 13th March, 1265.[192] Some day I hope it may be possible to work out fully the career of this remarkable man: it should illustrate admirably the very curious qualities of his still more remarkable master; and perhaps throw light on artistic development in England in the thirteenth century.

192. *Patent Rolls*, pp. 245, 413. I have been indebted to Miss I.M. Cooper, Miss C.A. Musgrave, and Miss D.L. Powell for some notes on Edward of Westminster.

APPENDIX I

SUMMARY LIST OF EXCHEQUER TALLIES PRESERVED AT THE PUBLIC RECORD OFFICE

Reference.		Description.	Number of Tallies.
		EARLY TALLIES.[1]	
E. 402/1.	Tray 1	Tally stocks: no County or Date given. *Specimens.*	16
		Tally stocks: County, but no Date given. *Specimens.*	16
	2	Tally stocks: no County or Date given.	180
	3	" "	165
	4	Tally stocks: County, but no Date given.	108
E. 402/2.	Tray 1	Tally stocks: both County and Date given. *Specimens.*	20
	2	Tally stocks: both County and Date given.	85
	3	Tally stocks and fragments: with added notes. *Specimens.*	20
	4	Tally stocks: with added notes (*Alloc'*).	35
		Tally stocks: with added notes (various).	25
E. 402/3 A.	Tray 1	Tally stocks and fragments and two foils:[2] being curiosities of shape, cutting, state of preservation, and date.	22
	2	Tally stocks and fragments: relating to one County (Surrey).	32
	3	Tally stocks and fragments: *contra Edwardum de Westmonasterio.*	13
	4	Tally stocks and fragments: Jewish. *Specimens* (various).	13
		Tally stocks and fragments: Jewish. *Specimens* (with Hebrew script).	15
	5	Tally stocks: Jewish (tax of third part of movables).[3]	12
		Tally stocks: Jewish (tallage of 8,000 marks).	2
		Tally stocks: Jewish (tallage of 6,000 marks).	1
		Tally stocks: Jewish (Judaism).[4]	5
		Tally stocks: Jewish (tallage of 20,000 marks).[5]	58
		Tally stocks and fragments: Jewish (with Hebrew script).	27
E. 402/3 B.	Tray 1	Fragments: Jewish.	125
	Trays 2 and 3	Fragments: various (and a quantity of small pieces).	305
		MODERN TALLIES	
E. 402/3 C.		Account of George Burgess, Receiver General and Cashier at Gibraltar (1749–1754); with stocks of Exchequer Tallies complete.	9
		Abstract of Account of Edward Treadcroft in the same office (1758–176c); with stocks of Exchequer Tallies.	3
		Draft Accounts of J. Deane, Receiver General in Berkshire, in respect of Land and Assessed Taxation (1780–1788); with stocks of Exchequer Tallies and fragments.	29

---

[1] Of the reigns of Henry III and Edward I; with a few earlier and one later (in E. 402/3 A. Tray 1).
[2] One fragment of the reign of James I and one medieval foil.
[3] Twenty-five of the fragments also belong to this class.   [4] Five of the fragments also belong to this class.
[5] Fifty-eight of the fragments also belong to this class.

MEDIEVAL TALLIES, PUBLIC AND PRIVATE

Reference.	Description.	Number of Tallies.
	MODERN TALLIES (continued).	
	Specimens of Late Exchequer Tally stocks (now exhibited, with one of the preceding set, in the Public Record Office Museum) : including examples of all kinds of cutting, a Tally with the inscription in English, and Tallies relating to conscience money from America, the payment of the Prince Regent's debts, and other curiosities.	25
E. 402/3 D.	Tally stocks, 1784–1790 ; mostly relating to funds from suppressed offices devoted to the Civil List.	12
	Tally stocks relating to renewal of Leases on Crown Property (1809).	2
	Tally stocks (1802–1826), various.	36
E. 402/3 E.	Tally stocks (1802–1826), various.	60
E. 402/3 F. and G.	Fragments of Tally stocks (George III–1826), various.	110

APPENDIX II

LIST OF RECEIPT ROLLS OF THE EXCHEQUER, HENRY II TO HENRY III

to show alterations in the form of this Record and recent additions of new materials to the Class.

The Sheriff's Receipt Rolls (mentioned above, p. 301) have not been included here, not being documents of Exchequer origin.

Note particularly the changes, both in form and title, about 21 Henry III. The many-columned rolls apparently drop their Pipe Roll fashion of indexing about this time, and the entries marked *li ars.* disappear from them. These and *dividenda* entries appear practically throughout the single-column rolls.

Note that in the many-columned rolls each membrane usually consists of two smaller ones sewn together, Pipe Roll fashion, the large membranes thus made being sewn together at the head. In the single-column rolls the membranes are sewn head to tail, Chancery fashion.

MEDIEVAL TALLIES, PUBLIC AND PRIVATE

Reference.		Date.	Title or Description.	Membranes, etc.
Single Col.	Many Col.			
E. 401/1		7 Hen. II	Apparently a Receipt Roll though its form is nearer to that of the Pipe Roll than any other.	1 membr. fragm. New.
L.T.R. Misc. Rolls 1/1 and 1/2		31 Hen. II	Receipts arranged under Counties.	2 rolls.[1]
E. 401/2		32 Hen. II	do.	1 membr. fragm. New.
		c. 34 Hen. II	do.	1 membr. fragm. New.
		7 Ric. I	do.	small roll.
		c. 8-10 Ric. I	do.	1 membr. fragm. New.
E. 101/249/2		5 Ric. I	Jewish Receipt Roll (the Northampton Donum) arranged under Counties.	1 small roll.[2]
E. 401/3 A.		c. 6-9 John	Receipts arranged under Counties.	1 membr. fragm. New.
		8/9 John, East.	do.: with writs of *Liberate* on dorse.	1 membr. fragm. New.
		c. 8-10 John	do.: on dorse *liberaciones seruientum de Scaccario*.	1 small fragm. New.
		14 John, Hil.	Receipts of Ralph de Nevill' from the Bailiffs of Hugh de Nevill'.[3]	1 membr.
	E. 401/1564		*Rotulus Judeorum*. Receipts arranged under Counties.[4]	1 membr.[5]
	E. 401/3 B.	4 Hen. III, East.	*Rotulus Anni Quarti* and *Rotulus Judeorum*. Under Counties.[4] Contains also *Liberate*.	4 membr.[6]
	E. 401/4	5 Hen. III, East.	*Rotulus Anni Quinti*, etc. Under Counties.[4] Contains also Jewish Receipts and *Liberate*.	5 membr.[6]
	E. 401/5	6 Hen. III, East.	Titles as before. Under Counties.[4] Contains also Jewish Receipts and *Liberate*.	5 membr.[6]
	E. 401/6	7 Hen. III, East.	[No titles.] Under Counties.[4] Contains also Jewish Receipts and *Liberate*.	6 membr.[6]
	E. 401/7	9 Hen. III, Mich.	*Rotulus de Termino Sancti Michaelis*. Under Counties.[4] Contains also Jewish Receipts and *Liberate*.	7 membr.[6]
	E. 401/8	10 Hen. III, East	Titles, etc., as before. Under Counties.[4] Contains also Jewish Receipts and *Liberate*.	9 membr.[6]

[1] Published in facsimile by the London School of Economics.
[2] Printed in full in Jewish Hist. Soc. *Miscellanies*, part I.
[3] This is not strictly a Receipt Roll but has always been included in the series.
[4] Counties indexed at foot of membranes.   [5] A three-column roll.   [6] A two-column roll.

MEDIEVAL TALLIES, PUBLIC AND PRIVATE

Reference.		Date.	Title or Description.	Membranes, etc.
Single Col.	Many Col.			
	E. 401/9	10 Hen. III, East.	Partly duplicating above.	8 membr.[3]
	E. 401/10 A.	17 Hen. III, Hill.	*De termino* . . . Under Counties.[1]	1 membr.[2]
	E. 401/10 B.	17 Hen. III, East.	No titles. Under Counties.[1] Contains also *Liberate.*	5 membr.[2]
	E. 401/1565	17 Hen. III	*Rotulus Judeorum.* Under Counties.[1]	1 membr.[2]
	E. 401/11 A.	18 Hen. III, Mich.	*Rotulus de Termino* . . . Under Counties.[1]	1 membr.[3] New.
	E. 401/11 B.	19 or 20 Hen. III	No title. Under Counties.	1 membr. fragm.[3] New.
E. 401/12		21 Hen. III, Mich.	*Recepta de Termino* . . . Chronological arrangement : beginning 30 September.	Roll.
E. 401/13		25 Hen. III, Mich.	*Recepta* . . . Chronological : beginning 10 October.	Roll.
E. 401/14		26 Hen. III, Mich.	*Recepta* . . . Chronological : beginning 30 September.	Roll.
E. 401/15		27 Hen. III, East.	*Recepta* . . . Chronological.	Roll.
	E. 401/16	do.	No title. Under Counties.	1 membr.[2]
	E. 401/17	28 Hen. III, Mich.	*Rotuli de Termino* . . . Under Counties.[1]	4 membr.[2]
E. 401/18		do.	*Recepta* . . . Chronological : beginning 30 September.	Roll.
E. 401/19		30 Hen. III, Mich.	*Recepta* . . . Chronological : beginning 30 September.	Roll.
	E. 401/20	37 Hen. III, Mich.	*Particule Comitatuum.*	4 membr.[2]
E. 401/21		do.	*Recepta* . . . Chronological : beginning 30 September.	Roll.

[1] Counties indexed at foot of membranes.
[2] A three-column roll.
[3] A two-column roll.

From this point onwards the rolls run in regular series : Nos. 23–26, 28, 30, 31, 33, 34, 36–42, 44, and 46 being single-column rolls all entitled *Recepta* or *Rotulus Recepte*, while Nos. 22, 27, 29, 32, 35, 43, and 45 are many-columned and all entitled with some variant of the words *particule comitatuum.* None of these is indexed at foot. Nos. 1566 and 1567 are Jewish Rolls, also many-columned. Nos. 46 to 63 mostly single membranes and all of uncertain dates, but all belonging to the reign of Henry III. All are many-columned except No. 52. Nos. 47, 50, 55, 61, and 63 have two columns, the rest three. Nos. 61 and 62 have titles (*Particule . . .*).

MEDIEVAL TALLIES, PUBLIC AND PRIVATE

APPENDIX III

TRANSCRIPT AND ANALYSIS OF PRIVATE TALLIES
PRESERVED IN THE PUBLIC RECORD OFFICE AND ELSEWHERE.

NOTES.

In the second column the dates in square brackets are inferential.

In the fifth column N. = Normal (see above, p. 315): A. = Abnormal.

S.A. = Slightly abnormal: A.E. = Abnormal with Exchequer tendencies.

In the sixth column I = a single cut like the Exchequer penny.

v = the notch which at the Exchequer indicates a shilling.

V =   „   „   „   „   pound.

V =   „   „   „   „   score.

$\mathsf{v}\mathsf{v}\,\mathsf{V}$ = the halves of the above.

All these marks when reversed indicate notches on the lower edge.

In the transcript doubtful readings are given in [square brackets], words supplied by the editor being in addition put in [*italic*]. Writing on the edges is transcribed within ⟨angular brackets⟩.

MEDIEVAL TALLIES, PUBLIC AND PRIVATE

No. in this List.	Reference.	Date.	Stock or Foil.	Cutting.	
				Shape of Tally.	Shape, &c., of Notches.
1	Public Record Office Museum	1229	F.	A.E.	√V
2	do.	[c. 1229]	F.	A.E.	V
3	Exch. K. R. Misc. 1/43	1271, 1272	F.	A.	VVVVVVVVV
4	do.	1271, 1272	F.	S.A.	VVVVVVVVVVV II I ΛΛΛΛΛΛΛΛ
5	do.	1271, 1272	F.	A.E.	II VVVVVVV
6	do.	1271, 1272	F.	A.E.	VVVVVVVVVVVV IIII ΛΛΛΛ
7	Private collection [1]	1278, 1279	S.	N.	IIII VVVVVVVVVV
8	do.	1278, 1279	F.	N.	IIII ΛΛΛΛΛΛΛΛΛΛΛ
9	do.	1278, 1279	S.	N.	—
10	do.	1278, 1279	F.	N.	—
11	do.	1278, 1279	S.	N.	—
12	do.	1278, 1279	F.	N.	—
13	E. 101/5/7	[1294, 1295]	S.	N.	VVVVVVVV.

13. Fragment.

[1] Belonging (1902) to Sir Charles Lawes Wittewronge, of Rothamstead, and annexed to a bailiff's roll of the manor

MEDIEVAL TALLIES, PUBLIC AND PRIVATE

Denominations in Notches.			Writing.	No. in this List.
One or more.	Money.	Commodities.		
one	1*l.* 10*s.*		Thomas Godesire debet Joscy de Kant' Judeo .xxx. s. scilicet Medietatem ad festum Sancti Michaelis. anno gracie. M.CC vicesimo Nono et Medietatem ad festum Sancti Martini proximo sequens per cursum [*illegible*] plegii Andreas de [Mikelgot'?] ⟨*on lower edge* et Ing'ram Tallur⟩	1
one	1*l.*		Johannes ... Josceo de Kent' [*writing largely illegible but apparently similar to above*] ⟨*on upper edge Jewish script: on lower, part of word* Chirograph (?)⟩	2
one	9*s.*		contra prepositum de ledecumb de denariis ab eo receptis de arreragiis vnius firmarii anno .l. sexto	3
one	11*l.* 8*s.* 8*d.*		Contra prepositum de ledecumb de denariis ab eo receptis die sanctorum apostolorum petri et pauli anno .l. sexto. scilicet de firma et de redditu sancti Johannis	4
one	6*s.* 8*d.*		contra prepositum de ledecumb de denariis receptis de H [*illegible*] anno .lvj.	5
one	12*l.* 4*s.* 4*d.*		contra prepositum de ledecumb de denariis receptis [*MS.* d. d. r] de prima. annunciacionis. et redditu Hoked' anno. lvj°. per manum Johannis armigeri et Radulfi Hare	6
one	1*l.* 9*s.* 4*d.*		Whathamsted.—Tallia Roberti Bernereve ibidem de frumento tam dominici quam decimarum de exitu liberato Simoni Boleheved servienti ibidem post festum Michaelis anno vij°.	7
one	1*l.* 9*s.* 4*d.*		Whathamsted.—Tallia Simonis Boleved contra. Robertum Bernereve grangiarium ibidem de frumento de exitu tam dominici quam decimarum ab eo recepto post festum Michaelis anno vij°. ⟨*on upper edge* Frumentum dominicum : *on lower* Frumentum decimarum de Pyccotes⟩.	8
one	—	—	Whathamsted.—Tallia Roberti Bernereve ibidem de pisa de exitu decimarum ibidem liberata Simoni Boleheved servienti ibidem post festum Michaelis anno vij°.	9
one	—	—	Whathamsted. — Tallia Simonis Boleheved servientis ibidem contra. Robertum Bernereve ibidem de pisa de exitu decimarum ab eo recepta post festum Michaelis anno. vij°.	10
two	—	—	Whathamsted.—Tallia Roberti Bernereve ibidem de draga et avena de exitu dominici liberatis Simoni Boleheved servienti ibidem post festum Michaelis anno vij°. ⟨*on one edge* drag' : *on the other* aven'⟩	11
two	—	—	Whathamsted. — Tallia Simonis Boleheved servientis ibidem contra. Robertum Bernereve de draga et avena de exitu grangie dominice ab eo receptis post festum Michaelis anno vij°.	12
one	9*s.* 0*d.*	•	3 Contra Philippum Harneys et Thomam Aylred de denariis sibi liberatis de sexta domino Regi in villa ... ⟨*on lower edge* ad construccionem galie eiusdem domini Regis ibidem⟩.	13

of Wheathampstead : see a note by Philip Norman, F.S.A. in the *Archaeological Journal*, lix, pp. 288 seqq. ; from which I have taken the greater part of the above transcriptions.

MEDIEVAL TALLIES, PUBLIC AND PRIVATE

No. in this List.	Reference.	Date.	Stock or Foil.	Cutting. Shape of Tally.	Cutting. Shape, &c., of Notches.
14	E. 101/5/7	[1294, 1295]	S.	A.	ΛΛΛΛΛΛΛ
15	do.	[1294, 1295]	S.	A.E.	vvvvvvvv ΛΛΛΛΛΛΛΛΛΛΛΛΛΛΛ
16	Cha. Misc. 12/55 [1]	[1297, 1298]	F.	N.	vvvvvvVVV
17	do.	[1297, 1298]	F.	N.	—
18	do.	[1297, 1298]	F.	N.	
19	E. 101/505/34 [3]	1298, 1299	S.	A.E.	IIII
20	do.	1298, 1299	S.	A.E.	ΛΛΛΛΛΛΛ Λ ΛΛΛΛΛΛΛ
21	do.	[c. 1298]	S.	A.E.	—
22	do.	[do.]	S.	A.E.	—
23	do.	1296, 1297	S.	A.E.	ΛΛΛ
24	do.	1296, 1297	F.	A.E.	√VVV
25	E. 101/362/7 [4]	1301, 1302	S.	A.E.	VVVVVV
26	do.	do.	S.	A.F.	VVV
27	E. 101/482/22 [5]	1302	F.	A.E.	VVVVVVVV ΛΛΛ I●
28	do.	1303	F.	A.E.	VV ΛΛΛΛ IIIII
29	E. 101/77/16 A [6]	1303, 1304	F.	N.	VVV
30	do.	1305, 1306	F.	N.	VVVVVVVVVVV
31	do.	1306, 1307	F.	? N.	—

15. Fragment.   21. Fragment.   22. Fragment.   31. Fragment.
[1] Original file of three tallies and two indented parchment receipts, which give the date.   [2] Fragment.
[3] Tallies preserved with a quantity of vouchers to accounts of estate management.

MEDIEVAL TALLIES, PUBLIC AND PRIVATE

One or more.	Money.	Commodities.	Writing.	No. in this List.
one	7*l.*		₃Contra Philippum Harneys et Thomam Aylred de denariis sibi liberatis per manum Viuiani Seluestre et Laurencii Harold ⟨*on edge* Balliuorum Gypp' de frumento Johannis le Manner Mercatoris Alienigeni apud Gypp' vendito ad construccionem galie domini Regis ibidem⟩	14
one	15*l.* 8*s.*		₃Contra Philippum Harneys et Thomam Aylred de denariis sibi liberatis per manum Viuiani Seluestre balliui Gypp' videlicet de Warda . . . ⟨*on edge* le Countyf Mercatoris Alienigeni vendita ad construccionem galie domini Regis ibidem⟩	15
one		? grain	auena recepta de Magistro Ricardo de Abyndon' apud Kardoyl'.	16
? one		? grain	auena recepta de Mag . . . . . Abyndon' apud Holmcoltr . . . .²	17
? one		? grain	auena recepta apud Dunolm' .· . . . .²	18
one	17*s.* 4*d.*		¶ Contra Ricardum de Theford' de denariis sibi liberatis per manus J. de Tarent'· Anno. regni regis E. xxvij.	19
one	6*l.* 10*s.*		¶ Contra Ricardum de Haueringg' de denariis sibi liberatis [de] exitu ecclesie de Wfford per manus .J. de Tarentef Anno regni . regis . E . xxvij	20
one	—		¶ Contra Thomam Cachekute de denariis	21
one	—		[Contra *erased*] contra Petronillam de Manton' de xx s sibi lib . . . . de Manton' fratris sui . anno . r . r. E . xx	22
one	3*l.*		¶ Contra Willelmum de Colebrok' de denariis sibi liberatis .vj. die Augusti de exitu ecclesie de Vfford per manus Johannis de ⟨*on lower edge* Tarent' balliui ibidem anno regni regis E. xxv.⟩	23
one	3*l.* 10*s.*		· Contra balliuum de Plumstede [*and in another hand*] Anno Regni Regis .xxv.	24
one		grain	Tallia Rogeri de Munketon' seruientis Rectoris Ecclesie de Algerkirke. contra Reginaldum filium Sibille de Sancto Botulpho attornatum ⟨*on lower edge* vicecomitis Lincoln' de vjˣˣ quarteriis faborum cum auantagio. Eidem liberatis ad opus Domini Regis apud Algerkirke Anno Regni Regis E. xxx°.⟩	25
one		malt	. [*Same: but for 60 quarters* brasii hastiui cum cumulo].	26
one	8*l.* 3*s.* 1½*d.*		Contra Adam de Thorpp' Constabularium Castri Karlioli de expensis suis circa ⟨*on lower edge* operam Castri a festo Pentecostis anno Regis Edwardi .xxx. vsque festum Sancti Michaelis proximo sequens⟩	27
one	2*l.* 3*s.* 11*d.*		De denariis receptis de Ada de Thorpp' ad operam Castri a festo ⟨*on lower edge* Natiuitatis sancti Johannis Baptiste anno regis Edwardi xxxj° vsque festum Sancti Michaelis proximo sequens⟩	28
one		? wine	Vinum de Rofsestr' captum anno .xxxij.	29
one	11*s.*		Contra Ricardum Somner de .xj. s. debitis pro . . . . . . et sycero ab ipso captis apud . . . . anno .xxxiiij.	30
—	—	—	. . . . .vj. sextariis .iij. picheriis vini . . . . . . [ca]pti apud Hidingham a° .xxxv.	31

⁴ Tallies preserved with a number of parchment indentures of receipt of grain for purposes of King's Wardrobe.
⁵ Tallies preserved with the account to which they relate.
⁶ Found in contemporary leather bag.

MEDIEVAL TALLIES, PUBLIC AND PRIVATE

No. in this List.	Reference.	Date.	Stock or Foil.	Shape of Tally.	Cutting. Shape, &c., of Notches.
32	E. 101/678/1 (1) [1]	[*c.* 1305]	F.	N.	vvvv √
33	do.	[do.]	F.	Ṅ.	—
34	do.	1304, 1305	F.	N.	ı vvv
35	do.	[*c.* 1305]	F.	N.	v v v v
36	do.	[do.]	F.	N.	ııı vvv ∧∧
37	do.	[do.]	F.	A.	vv ∧ ∧
38	do.	1305, 1306	F.	A.	vv vV
39	do.	1305, 1306	F.	A.	vv √ vvvvvvv ııı
40	do.	1305, 1306	F.	N.	vvvvv vvv
41	do.	[*c.* 1305]	F.	N.	—
42	do.	1306, 1307	F.	A.	ıııvvvvvvvvvv
43	do.	[*c.* 1305]	F.	N.	—
44	do.	[do.]	F.	N.	v v ...[2]
45	do.	[do.]	F.	N.	v v v ∧ ∧
46	E. 101/261/21 (3) [3]	1316	S.[4]	A.E.	v ∧∧∧∧∧∧∧∧
47	do.	1316	F.[4]	A.E.	vvvvvvvvV ∧
48	do.	1316	S.[4]	A.E.	vvvvv√ ∧∧∧∧∧∧∧∧∧
49	do.	1316	F.[4]	A.E.	vvvvvvvvvv √ ∧∧∧∧∧ ∧
50	do.	1316	S.[4]	A.E.	∧ ∧∧∧
51	do.	1316	F.[4]	A.E.	V √VV
52	do.	1316	S.[4]	A.E.	∧∧∧∧∧∧∧
53	do.	1316	F.[4]	A.E.	vvvvvvvV
54	do.	1317	S.[4]	A.E.	vvvvv ∧∧∧∧∧∧∧∧ ∧∧
55	do.	1317	F.[4]	A.E.	vvvvvvvvv √V ∧∧∧∧∧

33. Fragment.   41. Fragment.   43. Fragment.   44. Fragment.

[1] These tallies preserved on original filing string with descriptive parchment slip.
[2] Three small straight marks, in length about half the width of the tally.

MEDIEVAL TALLIES, PUBLIC AND PRIVATE

Denominations in Notches.			Writing.	No. in this List.
One or more.	Money.	Commodities.		
one	? 14s.	or ? wine	Contra Johannem de Leycestria de Ebor' pro xiiij sextariis vini	32
—	—	—	pro ciphis vitreis	33
one	? 3s. 1d.	or ? cups	pro ciphis anno xxxiij	34
? one		? wine	Walton' ⟨also writing on edge : illegible⟩	35
more		? wine	Conyton' ⟨on upper edge iij parue iij sextarii vini : 'lower edge illegible⟩	36
more		? wine	Rameseye ⟨on upper edge ij parue : lower edge uncertain⟩	37
one	32s.		Contra Hamonem Le Tailuer de Notinggeham de .xxxij. s. sibi debitis pro .xxiiij. sextariis vini ab ipso captis .xvij die Junii anno xxxiiij.	38
one	? 7l. 12s. 3d.		¶ Contra Walterum Gome de Ebor' de .iij. doliis .xij. sextariis vini captis ab eodem anno xxxiiij.	39
one	? 2l. 15s. od.		Contra Gaceflour de Ebor' de .j. dolio vini .v. sextariis captis ab eodem anno xxxiiij	40
—	—	—	Abbotesrupt' ⟨on upper edge ? j quart' . . . . . .⟩	41
one	? 9s. 4d.		Tallia de .x. sextariis vini de tabernis [?] Rouscestr' anno .xxxv.	42
—	—	—	. . . aystowe Co . . . . vill' de	43
three		? grain	Wardeboys ⟨on upper edge ¶ pis' (?) frumentum bras'⟩	44
four		? grain	¶ Stiddingweth' ⟨on upper edge pis' bras frumentum : on lower ¶ ij quarter⟩	45
one	47l. 1s.		Contra Ricardum de Wigornia. Custodem Minere Regis. Deuon' de argento albo sibi liberato .xv. die Septembris. Anno .x°. per Ricardum . Lond affuratorem ibidem ⟨on lower edge xlvij li. xij d.⟩	46
one	47l. 1s.		Contra Ricardum Lond de argento albo in plat' ab eo recepto . xv die Septembris . anno .x°. ⟨on upper edge xlvij li. xij d.⟩	47
one	19l. 15s.		Contra . Ricardum de Wigornia [etc., as before] .iiij° die Octobris [etc., as before] ⟨on lower edge xix li. xv s.⟩	48
one	19l. 15s.		Contra Ricardum Lond [etc., as before] ⟨on upper edge xix li. xv s.⟩	49
one	51l.		Contra Ricardum de Wigornia [etc., as before] xvj°. die . Nouembris . anno Regni Regis Edwardi .x°. [etc., as before] ⟨on lower edge .Lj. li.⟩	50
one	51l.		Contra Ricardum Lond [etc., as before] ⟨on upper edge Lj. li.⟩	51
one	27l.		Contra Ricardum de Wigornia [etc., as before] .xxv. die Decembris [etc., as before] ⟨on lower edge .xxvij li.⟩	52
one	27l.		Contra Ricardum Lond [etc., as before] ⟨on upper edge xxvij li.⟩	53
one	39l. 5s.		Contra Ricardum de . Wigornia . [etc., as before] .xxviij° die Februarii et xxx°. die Marcii [etc., as before] ⟨on lower edge . xxxix li. v s.⟩	54
one	39l. 5s.		Contra . Ricardum Lond . [etc., as before] ⟨N.B. no writing on upper edge⟩	55

³ All these tallies preserved with rolls and counter-rolls of accounts to which they relate in original bag.
⁴ These tallies apparently in the hand which wrote the rolls. Note that the foil in each case follows in this list the stock to which it belongs.

MEDIEVAL TALLIES, PUBLIC AND PRIVATE

No. in this List.	Reference.	Date.	Stock or Foil.	Cutting.	
				Shape of Tally.	Shape, &c., of Notches.
56	E. 101/261/21 (3)	1317	S.[1]	A.E.	Λ
57	do.	1317	F.[1]	A.E	V
58	do.	1316	S.[2]	N.	v V / ΛΛ
59	do.	1316	F.[2]	N.	VV / ʌ Λ
60	do.	1317	S.[2]	S.A.	vvvvv / ΛΛΛΛΛ ʌΛ
61	do.	1317	F.[2]	S.A.	vvvvv √V / ΛΛΛΛΛ
62	do.	1316	S.[2]	N.	IIVvvvvvv / Λ
63	do.	1316	F.[2]	N.	V / IIΛΛΛΛΛΛΛ
64	do.	1316	S.[2]	N.	vvvvvvvvv / Λ
65	do.	1316	F.[2]	N.	V / ΛΛΛΛΛΛΛΛΛ
66	do.	1317	S.[2]	N.	vvvvvv / ΛΛΛΛΛΛ ʌ
67	do.	1317	F.[2]	N.	vvvvvv √ / ΛΛΛΛΛΛ
68	do.	1317	S.[2]	N.	—
69	do.	1317	F.[2]	N.	IV √ / IΛΛ ʌ
70	do.	1317	S.[2]	N.	IIIIVV / IIIIΛΛΛΛΛΛ ʌ
71	do.	1317	F.[2]	N.	IIIIVVVVVV ʌ / IIIIΛΛ
72	do.	1316	F.[2]	N.	√V / ʌ Λ

68. Fragment.　　　　　　　　　70. Tip broken.

[1] These tallies apparently in the hand which wrote the rolls. Note that the foil in each case follows in this list the stock to which it belongs.

MEDIEVAL TALLIES, PUBLIC AND PRIVATE

Denominations in Notches.			Writing.	No. in this List.
One or more.	Money.	Com-modities.		
one	20l.		Contra Ricardum de . Wigornia [*etc., as before*] .ij. die Junii [*etc., as before*] ⟨*on lower edge* xx li⟩	56
one	20l.		Contra Ricardum Lond [*etc., as before*] ⟨*on upper edge* xx li⟩	57
two		minerals	Contra Ricardum de Wygornia [*etc., as before*] de tot lad' ei liberatis .xxviij. die Augusti anno .x°. ⟨*on lower edge* Nigre Mine *and near the notches* lad' : *on upper edge* Albe Mine⟩	58
two		minerals	. . Contra Thomam de Blakwell' et socios suos Minerarios de Mina de eisdem recepta .xxviij. die Augusti et .xx. die Septembris anno decimo ⟨*on upper edge* .xl. lad' Nigre Mine : *on lower edge* . albe . Mine.⟩	59
two		minerals	Contra Ricardum de Wygornia [*etc., as before*] xij. die Februarii anño .x°. ⟨*on lower edge* xxxv lad' Nigre Mine : *on upper edge* Albe Mine.⟩	60
two		minerals	Contra Hugonem de Litton' de Mina ei[3] liberata[3] xij die Februarii anno decimo ⟨*on upper edge* xxxv lad' Nigre Mine : *nothing on lower*⟩	61
two		minerals	Contra Ricardum [*etc., as before*] .vj. die Octobris anno decimo ⟨*on lower edge* Nigre Mine : *on upper edge* vij. lad' .ij. disc'. albe Mine⟩	62
two		minerals	Contra Thomam de Blakwell' et Willelmum de Ashford' de Mina ab eis recepta .vj. die Octobris anno decimo ⟨*on lower edge* albe Mine⟩	63
two		minerals	Contra Ricardum [*etc., as before*] .xx. die Nouembris ⟨*on lower edge* xx. lad' Nigre Mine : *on upper edge* ix. lad' albe Mine⟩	64
two		minerals	Contra Henricum le Bagger de Mina ab eo recepta .xx. die Nouembris Anno decimo ⟨*nothing on edges*⟩	65
two		minerals	Contra Ricardum [*etc., as before*] .v. die Februarii anno decimo ⟨*on lower edge* xvj. lad' nigre Mine : *on upper edge* vj. lad' albe Mine⟩	66
two		minerals	Contra Ricardum de Bouteshale et sociis suis [*sic*] de Mina ab eis recepta .v. die Februarii anno x. ⟨*nothing on edges*⟩	67
two		minerals	Contra Ricardum de Wygornia [*etc., as before*] .xxiiij. die . . . . . . ⟨*on lower edge* Nigre Mine .xj. lad' .j. discus : *on upper edge* . albe Mine .xij. lad' .j. discus⟩	68
two		minerals	Contra Hugonem le Taillour et Simonem Trout' de Mina ab eis recepta .xxiiij. die Maii . anno decimo ⟨*nothing on edges*⟩	69
two		minerals	Contra Ricardum [*etc., as before*] ix. die Marcii anno decimo ⟨*on lower edge* .xvj. lad' .iiij. disci Nigre Mine : *on upper edge* ¶ albe Mine⟩	70
two		minerals	Contra Hugonem de Litton' et socios suos de Mina ab eis recepta ix. die Marcii . anno decimo ⟨*nothing on edges*⟩	71
two		minerals	Contra Hugonem le Taillour de Mina ab eo recepta .xx. die Octobris [?] Anno decimo ⟨*on lower edge* .x. lad' [? j] disc' albe⟩[4]	72

[2] These tallies in the hand which wrote the counter-rolls.
[3] These words marked [3] apparently repeated by mistake from the stock.
[4] No stock of this tally preserved.

MEDIEVAL TALLIES, PUBLIC AND PRIVATE

No. in this List.	Reference.	Date.	Stock or Foil.	Shape of Tally.	Shape, &c., of Notches.
73	E. 101/678/2 (1)[1]	[1335, 1336]	F.	N.	||||||
74	do.	[do.]	F.	N.	||√
75	do.	[do.]	F.	N.	||||
76	do.	[do.]	F.	N.	√√ ||||
77	do.	[do.]	F..	N.	√
78	do.	[do.]	F.	N.	√√
79	do.	[do.]	F.	N.	√
80	do.	[do.]	F.	N.	√
81	do.	[do.]	F.	N.	√√
82	do.	[do.]	F.	N.	√ |
83	do.	[do.]	F.	N.	||
84	*Ibid.* 2 (2)[4]	[? c. 1335]	F.	N.	||||√√√√√√√ ∧∧∧∧
85	do.	[? do.]	F.	? N.	[missing]
86	do.	[? do.]	F.	? N.	|||√√
87	do.	[? do.]	F.	N.	|||√√
88	do.	[? do.]	F.	N.	√
X. 1	*Ibid.* 1 (4)[5]	[1346, 1347]	F.	N.	| / / √ √
X. 2	do	[do.]	F.	N.	|||∧∧
X. 3	do.	[do.]	F.	N.	√√√√√
X. 4	do.	[do.]	F.	N.	√√√√√√
X. 5	do.	[do.]	F.	N.	√√√√√√√√√√√√√√
X. 6	do.	[do.]	F.	N.	√√√√√√√ ||
X. 7	do.	[do.]	F.	N.	√√√√√
X. 8	do.	[do.]	F.	S.A.	|| /√√√√√√ √
X. 9	do.	[do.]	F.	S.A.	|| /√√√√√√
X. 10	do.	[do.]	F.	N.	√√√√√√√ [broken]
X. 11	do.	[do.]	F.	S.A.	√√√ | [broken]
X. 12	do.	[do.]	F.	S.A.	|||| | √√
X. 13	do.	[do.]	F.	S.A.	√√√√ √

85. Fragment.   86. Fragment.

[1] A parchment tab attached to this foil shows that there should be twelve tallies (only eleven remain) for litter belonging to the year ix and amounting to 12s. 2d. They are on the original leather filing strip.

[4] Inscription scratched, not in ink.

[5] Inscription in ink, as usual.

MEDIEVAL TALLIES, PUBLIC AND PRIVATE

Denominations in Notches.			Writing.	No. in this List.
One or more.	Money.	Commodities.		
one	? 6d.		Contra Willelmum de . . . . pro lit'.[2]	73
one	? 8d.		Contra Alissiam Relictam Johannis in selone [?] pro stramine[3]	74
one	? 4d.		Contra Hugonem [?] . . . . . . pro . lit'[2]	75
one	? 1s. 10d.		Charleton . pro . lit'.[2]	76
one	? 1s.		Contra Katerinam de Wyteuill'. pro . lit'[2]	77
one	? 1s. 6d.		Contra Rectorem de . . . . pro lit'[2]	78
one	? 1s.		Charleton pro lit'.[2]	79
one	? 1s.		Charleton pro lit'.[2]	80
one	? 1s. 6d.		Contra Robertum de Stedeleie . pro . lit'.[2]	81
one	? 1s. 1d.		Contra Haric' de la [?] stil' pro lit'[3]	82
one	? 2d.		[? Contra] [illegible] [? Monachorum][2] ⟨some words on upper edge : ? lit'⟩	83
?	?	? grain	[? contra] Ricard[um] Gregory pro ffag'	84
—	—	—	¶ Johannem . . . . . et	85
one	—	? grain	¶ Const' de Wes . . . . precium quarterii vj s.	86
one	?	? grain	Const' de bledelowe . . . . . pro frumento precium quarterii vj s ⟨on upper edge xiiijs. 3d.: on lower edge something illegible, ? buck'⟩	87
one	?	? grain	Const' de bradenston [?] pro frumento . . . . vj s ⟨on upper edge vj s: on lower buck'⟩	88
one	—	—	ℙ Avena De Abbate Glouc'	X. 1
two	—	—	Tallia Abbatis Westmonasterii Puls' ⟨on upper edge auena, solutum est and pro auena in 3 writings : lower edge illegible⟩	X. 2
one	—	—	Tallia Abbatis Westmonasterii de Puls'	X. 3
one	—	—	Puls' De Abbate Glouc'	X. 4
one	—	—	ℙ Tallia Abbatis Glouc' [De Puls' added later]	X. 5
one	—	—	ffolium contra balliuum de Horton' et Hembury de frumento ab eo recepto ad opus domini Regis precium quarterij .iij. s. iiij. d. quia debilis anno .xx^{mo}.	X. 6
\? one	—	—	Contra Willelmum Balliuum de Iddebur' de frumento recepto, etc.	X. 7
one	—	—	ℙ Bybur'[6] tallia ffratris[6] de Bybur' pro v. quarteriis frumenti	X. 8
one	—	—	¶ Tallia Ade de Wylkewone[6] de Hudicote[6] [illegible] . pro .ij. quarteriis frumenti.	X. 9
two	—	—	ℙ Contra Rectorem de Swyndon' pro iij. quarteriis frumenti et iij. quarteriis puls'	X. 10
two	—	—	ℙ Tallia Abbatis de Alicestr' pro . iij. quarteriis frumenti et vj. quarteriis puls'.	X. 11
one	—	—	¶ Tallia Rectoris de Marchton' Sicca pro . v quarteriis et ij. busselis . frumenti ad opus Regis . pro [word illegible]	X. 12
one	—	—	ℙ ffrumentum de Episcopo Herefordensi	X. 13

[4] On original filing slip: apparently not all in same hand.
[5] File of 16 foils on original parchment slip.
[6] Reading uncertain.

MEDIEVAL TALLIES, PUBLIC AND PRIVATE

No. in this List.	Reference.	Date.	Stock or Foil.	Cutting.	
				Shape of Tally	Shape, &c., of Notches.
X. 14	E. 101/678/1 (4)	[1346, 1347]	F.	N.	vvvvvvvv √ III
X. 15	do.	[do.]	F.	S.A.	V ΛΛΛΛΛ
X. 16	do.	[do.]	F.	N.	I VV . IIII
89	*Ibid.* 2 (3) [1]	1348, 1349	F.	? N.	[missing]
90	do.	[do.]	F	? N.	[missing]
91	do.	[do.]	F.	N.	v
92	do.	[do]	F.	? N.	[missing]
93	do.	[do.]	F.	? N.	[missing]
94	*Ibid.* 2 (4) [2]	1348, 1349	F.	? N.	vvvvvv [broken]
95	do.	[do.]	F.	? N.	[missing]
96	do.	1348, 1349	F.	N.	vvv IIIvv
97	do.	1348, 1349	F.	? N.	IIIIvvvvvvv [missing]
98	do.	1348, 1349	F.	N.	IIIIvvvvvvvvv
99	do.	[do.]	F.	? N.	[missing]
100	do.	1348, 1349	F.	N.	Ivvvvvv
101	do.	[do.]	F.	N.	IV
102	*Ibid.* 2 (5) [8]	1348, 1349	F.	A.	III
103	do.	[do.]	F.	N.	III
104	do.	1348, 1349	F.	N.	IIII
105	do.	[do.]	F.	? N.	[missing]
106	do.	[do.]	F.	N.	vv IIII

89. Fragment.   90. Fragment.   91. Fragment.   92. Fragment.   94. Fragment.   95. Fragment.   97. Fragment.
 99. Fragment.   105. Fragment.

[1] These five tallies, on an original leather, appear all to be in the same writing.
[2] Eight tallies on original parchment strip : apparently not all in same hand.   [3] [*Sic*] MS.

MEDIEVAL TALLIES, PUBLIC AND PRIVATE

Denominations in Notches.			Writing.	No. in this List.
One or more.	Money.	Commodities.		
one	—	—	℞ ffrumentum De Abbate Westmonasterii	X. 14
two	—	—	Contra Archiepiscopum Eboracensem de frumento et fabis captis ⟨on upper edge frumentum ; on lower fabe⟩	X. 15
one	—	—	ffrumentum de Abbate Glouč	X. 16
—	—	—	Tallia contra Willelmum atebrokende de stepelmorden ...... eo empt' anno Domini Regni Regis Edwardi xxij videlicet j quarterium	89
? one	—	? malt	Contra Ricardum ..... de [?] bras' pro	90
one	—	? malt	.. Johann' de ..... ton' de bras' ab eo [? perqui]s' ..... precium .vj. s.	91
—	—	? grain	Contra Willelmum clericum de Badborouha const ..... ab eodem recept' / anno Domini Regis Edwardi tercii post conquestum .... ⟨on upper edge bras' ordei Chilford'⟩	92
? more	—	pigs, etc.	Contra Willelmum Michel et Robertum [illegible] Wat..ich de bras' pro [illegible] ⟨on upper edge writing, perhaps placename : on lower edge ix d. ... iij bacones d ...⟩	93
more	—	? pigs, oxen, etc.	Contra Robertum Jakes de Sutton' de victualibus .... victual' ville de Caleys anno .xxij° .... ⟨on upper edge Bacon' precium baconis .ij. s. Pis' precium quarterii ... s. : on lower edge carcos boum precium ....⟩.	94
—	—	—	Contra Rogerum ...... de prisa p ..... ⟨some writing on lower edge illegible⟩.	95
two	? 3s. and 2s. 3d.	? grain and pigs.	Contra Robertum Hewe de [? 'gruele] constabularium de Pisa pro[3] ad opus domini Regis [illegible] de eadem villa Anno regni ⟨on lower side Regis Edwardi post conquestum xxij : on upper edge Item iij paruas bacones precii iij s⟩	96
one	? 7s. 4d.	or ? grain	.leueryngton' ℞ Anno .xxij° precium quarterii .iiij s. ⟨on upper edge . ffab'.⟩	97
one	? 9s. 4d.	or ? grain	Tyd . ℞ . Anno .xxij°. de ffabis . precium quarterii iiij s. ⟨on upper edge ffab'.⟩	98
one	—	—	Well' ℞ de ffabis ad opus Regis ..... [and some writing illegible]	99
one	? 6s. 1d.	or ? grain	[?] EI .. ℞ de ffabis . contra . Regem Anno xxij°. precium quarterii .iiij s. ⟨on upper edge ffab'.⟩	100
one	1s. 1d.		Contra Willelmum peperstok' constabularium de he' [illegible][4] de j paruo bacone precii xiij d	101
? one		? grain	Caldecote Anno xxij°.	102
? one		? grain	Contra Saram Mott' de ... de pisa ab ea recepta ⟨on upper edge pise⟩	103
? one		? malt	Contra dominum W. capellanum de K [illegible] de brasio ab eo recepto anno xxij°. ⟨on upper edge bras'⟩	104
—	—	—	Catteworth' magna	105
two		? grain, etc.	Contra constabularium de bokeden' de pisa et baconibus ab eisdem captis ⟨on lower edge paruo ba : on upper edge pisa⟩	106

[4] This tally has had the upper edge pared off after the writing was done, perhaps for the notches to be altered.
[5] File of twelve tallies on original parchment strip : probably not all in same hand.

MEDIEVAL TALLIES, PUBLIC AND PRIVATE

No. in this List	Reference.	Date.	Stock or Foil.	Cutting. Shape of Tally.	Cutting. Shape, &c., of Notches.
107	E. 101/678/2 (5)	1348, 1349	F.	S.A.	IIIIIII Λ
108	do.	[do.]	F.	? N	[missing]
109	do.	[do.]	F.	? N	[missing]
110	do.	[do.]	F.	S.A.	ΛΛ ⟨missing⟩ I VV V V
111	do.	[do.]	F.	S.A.	II IIIVV IIIVV VV
112	do.	[do.]¹	F.	S.A.	Λ ...III IIIΛ
113	do.	[do.]	F.	A.	II ʃ
114	*Ibid.* 2 (6)²	[do.]	F.	? N.	[missing]
115	do.	1348, 1349³	F.	N.	VV ·III
116	do.	[do.]	F.	N.	VVVVVV
117	do.	1348, 1349	F.	N.	IIII Λ
118	do.	1348, 1349	F.	N.	VV IIIII IIIIIΛΛ
119	do.	1348, 1349	F.	N.	V V Λ
120	do.	1348, 1349	F.	N.	VV
121	do.	[do.]	F.	N.	I:IIIII
122	do.	1348, 1349	F.	N.	VV IIII
123	do.	[do.]	F.	N.	III VV IIʃIII
124	do.	1348, 1349	F.	N.	VV
125	do.	1348, 1349⁴	F.	N.	ʃ · · ·III

108. Fragment.   109. Fragment.

¹ The notches on this file, here represented by dots, are single cuts made with the point of the knife and not drawn right across the edge of the tally.

MEDIEVAL TALLIES, PUBLIC AND PRIVATE

Denominations in Notches.			Writing.	No. in this List.
One or more.	Money.	Com-modities.		
two		? grain, etc.	. . dnesbury. De brasio et pisa ab eis receptis anno xxij° ⟨on lower edge pis' and bras'⟩	107
—	—	—	[Apparently place-name.]	108
three		? grain, etc.	Aylynton' ⟨on lower edge ij parui bacones: on upper pis' and bras'⟩	1c9
[more]		? grain, etc.	Alwalton' ⟨on upper edge j. paruus and bras' and fr'm⟩	110
four		? grain, etc.	Contra Hugonem ffarset ⟨on upper edge [? parui] and pis' and bras' and fr'm⟩	111
three		? grain, etc.	Ouerton' ⟨on lower edge bras' and pis' and fr'm⟩	112
two		? grain, etc.	⟨Caldecot' on lower edge: face blank: on upper edge fr' and bras'⟩	113
—	—	—	t contra Regenaldum constabularium [illegible]ton' de frumento ab eodem ad opus [illegible]	114
one		? grain	tallia contra Nicalaum [?] Gernon constabularium de stepelmorden de frumento empto de cecilia Hor . . anno domini Regis xxij	115
one		? grain	tallia contra Johannem de caldecote et Johannem valentin constabularios de villa de orwell' de frumento ab eis recepto.	116
two		? grain	Contra constabularium de Abington' parua de frumento eius ad opus domini Regis anno regni Regis xxij precium iij s ⟨on lower edge bras' .j. quarterium⟩	117
three	? money		Contra Thomam Kydeman de schenegeye de pisa prouisa ad opus domini Regis anno xxij ⟨on lower edge Pis' Arningforde Hn'd: on upper edge j paruus baco and ta[llia] de frumento⟩	118
three		peas, grain, etc.	Contra Her' de stoke[vpton?] de frumento. pisa vj s ab eo emptis ad opus Regis Anno regni Regis ⟨on lower edge e xxij precium quarterii vj s bras': on upper edge precium quarterii iij s and pis' viij d and precium vj s and frumento⟩	119
one		? grain	tallia contra Ricardum ate Crouch constabularium de villa de Weston coluill' de receptione frumenti anno xxij	120
one		grain (bushels)	tallia de frumento empto ad opus domini Regis de Matillíde Ace de Walsham ⟨on upper edge frumento and [? bocell']⟩	121
? one		? grain	Contra Johannem de [?] Gontell' de frumento ab eo empto ad opus domini Regis Anno xxij	122
two		? grain	⟨Face bare: on upper edge [? Syntone] . de frumento Recepto ad opus domini Regis: on lower edge tallia de Brasio ab eisdem empto ad opus domini Regis⟩	123
one		? grain	tallia contra Robertum [? Hewe] de [? grafele] de frumento empto ad opus domini regis anno regni domini Regis xxii	124
one		grain	tallia contra Johannem [? Bray] constabularium de swafham priour de dimidio quarterio . frumenti iij bussellis iij p . . . . anno regni Regis xxij	125

² File of eighteen tallies on original parchment strip: possibly all same writing.
³ The dot . among the notches for this tally represents in the original a single cut extending half across the edge of the tally: the tally looks as if it were not hazel.
⁴ The three dots among the notches for this tally represent in the original single cuts extending half across the edge of the tally.

MEDIEVAL TALLIES, PUBLIC AND PRIVATE

No. in this List.	Reference.	Date.	Stock or Foil.	Cutting.	
				Shape of Tally.	Shape, &c., of Notches.
126	E. 101/678/2 (6)	1348, 1349	F.	N.	IIIIV
127	do.	1348, 1349	F.	N.	V
128	do.	[do.]	F.	N.	VV
129	do.	1348, 1349 [1]	F.	S.A.	III
130	do.	[do]	F.	? N.	[missing]
131	do.	1348, 1349	F.	N.	V
132	*Ibid.* 2 (7) [2]	[? c. 1348]	F.	N.	IIVVV
133	do.	[? do.]	F.	N.	IIV [missing]
134	do.	[? do.]	F.	? N.	[missing]
135	do.	[? do.]	F.	N.	? VVVV
136	do.	[? do]	F.	N.	V
137	do.	[? do.]	F.	N.	IVVV
138	do.	[? do.]	F.	N.	VV
139	do.	[? do.]	F.	? N.	III [missing]
140	*Ibid.* 2 (8) [3]	[? do.]	F.	N.	IIV
141	do.	[? do.]	F.	S.A.	II V VV [missing]
142	do.	1348, 1349	F.	N.	VV III^ IIII
143	do.	[? do.]	F.	? N.	I
144–169	*Ibid.* 2 (9) [5]	[? do.]	one S rest ? all F.	? all N.	—
170	British Museum Tally	1356, 1357	F.	? N.	IIII VVV AAA
171	E. 101/678/2 (10) [6]	[1357–1359]	F.	N.	VVVVVVV AA
172	do.	[do.]	F.	N.	IIIIIIIVVVVVV AA

130. Fragment.   133. Fragment.   134. Fragment.   139. Fragment.   144–169 Fragment.   170. Fragment.

[1] The dot among the notches for this tally represents a single cut; but sloped, not at right angles to the edge.
[2] File of eight on original parchment slip.   [3] Four tallies found loose but belonging apparently to this sack.
[4] Has incised as well as ink writing.
[5] Twenty-six fragments, of which one is that of a stock, apparently belonging to this sack. Four have incised as well as ink writing. There are in addition sixteen smaller fragments (two showing the incised writing) and a quantity of minute pieces.

MEDIEVAL TALLIES, PUBLIC AND PRIVATE

One or more.	Money.	Commodities.	Writing.	No. in this List.
one		? grain	tallia contra Johannem de colne constabularium de Caxstone de frumento emto [*sic*] ad opus domini Regis	126
one		? grain	Contra Johannem le taylour constabularium de villa de [?] napwell' de frumento empto ad opus domini Regis ⟨*on lower edge* anno regni xxij⟩	127
one		? grain	Contra Johannem smart de papwortheford' de frumento liberato per eundem constabularium	128
? one		? grain	tallia de Roberto le [? Wistler'] de [? hyldrsham] de frumento empto anno xxij	129
—	—	—	tallia contra Thomam [? tergaunt] constabularium . . . de frumento prouiso ad opus domini anno . . .	130
one		? grain	Contra constabularium de villa de Papworth' [*illegible*] ys Anno regni Regis Edwardi xxij ⟨*on upper edge* frumento⟩	131
? one		? grain	Contra Constabularium de Rous . . e et [*illegible*] prec' ij s de ij quarteriis et vj [? bussellis] [*illegible*]	132
		? grain	Contra Constabularium de [?] Sout [*illegible*] quarterii ij s [*illegible*] ⟨*on lower edge: illegible*⟩	133
—	—	—	Contra constabularium . . . . . . quart' iiij . bus' au	134
one		grain	. . . Constabularium de ffifede pro auena prec' quarterii ij s viij d [*remainder illegible*]	135
one		grain	Contra Constabularium de Bampton' pro j quarterio auene precium quarterii ij s viij d.	136
one		grain	Contra Constabularium de Charyndon' pro ij quarteriis v bucellis quarterium ad ij s vj s j d ob' ⟨*on lower edge* . . . . yndon'⟩	137
		grain	[? Contra] Constabularium de Abbesse Rochyng' pro auena precium quarterii ij s viij d Summa . vj s iiij d	138
? one		? grain	. . Constabularium de parua . . . . . pro auena precium	139
? one		? grain	¶ Const' de Wynchyndone pro frumento . . . . vj . . . ⟨*on upper edge writing illegible*⟩ [4]	140
? 4		grain, pigs, etc.	Sautre ⟨*on upper edge* ij parue j quarterium [? frumenti] bras'⟩	141
? 2		? grain	Contra constabularium de geldemordon' de frumento et pisa [ca]ptis anno regni Regis xxij ⟨*on lower edge* fr' : *on upper* [? fr']⟩	142
one	?	?	*No sign of writing on face* ⟨*on upper edge much writing, illegible*⟩.	143
—	—	—	[*All apparently in one or other of forms already noted.*]	144–169
? one	?	?	. . . . rueys pro litera liberata pro equis domini . . . . Regis anno xxx^{mo}	170
? one	?	?	₱ contra constabularium de Holm de ffeno Greyne [7]	171
? one	?	?	₱ stoke abb' de [8] eadem villa de auena [8]	172

No abnormality of shape or notching has been noticed; and the writing, so far as can be judged, always resembles one or other of the forms already noted.

[6] Original file of seventeen tally foils with parchment label; giving date 31 and 32 [Edward III]. It is possible that this file should properly be preserved with the leather bag (E. 101/678/3, listed below).
[7] Words in paler ink: ? added later.   [8] to [8] Words in darker ink: ? added later.

MEDIEVAL TALLIES, PUBLIC AND PRIVATE

No. in this List.	Reference.	Date.	Stock or Foil.	Shape of Tally.	Shape, &c., of Notches.
173	E. 101/678/2 (10)	[1357, 1359]	F.	N.	VVVVVV ΛΛΛ
174	do.	[do.]	F.	N.	IIIIVVVVVVVV ΛΛΛ
175	do.	[do.]	F.	N.	IIII V VVVV ΛΛ
176	do.	[do.]	F.	N.	IIIIVV Λ
177	do.	[do.]	F.	N.	VVVVVV ΛΛΛ
178	do.	[do.]	F.	N.	II V IIII
179	do.	[do.]	F.	N.	VV Λ
180	do.	[do.]	F.	N.	VVV IIIIΛ
181	do.	[do.]	F.	N.	IIIVVV IIIIIΛ
182	do.	[do.]	F.	N.	IIIIIV IIIII
183	do.	[do.]	F.	N.	VVVVVV ΛΛΛ
184	do.	[do.]	F.	N.	IIIIIIIIVVVVVV ΛΛ
185	do.	[do.]	F.	N.	IIIIVVV Λ
186	do.	[do.]	F.	N.	VVVVVVV ΛΛ
187	do.	[do.]	F.	N.	VVV Λ
188	*Ibid.* 3 (1)[10]	[1358, 1359]	F.	N.	VVVV √
189	do.	[do.]	F.	N.	VV √VVVV IIIΛ
190	do.	[do.]	F.	? N.	[missing]
191	do.	[do.]	F.	? N.	[missing]
192	do.	[do.]	F.	? N.	VVVVVVVVV [missing]
193	do.	[do.]	F.	N.	IV
194	do.	[do.]	F.	N.	[missing]
195	do.	1358, 1359	F.	N.	VV
196	do.	[1358, 1359]	F.	N.	VV
197	do.	[do.]	F.	N.	V
198	do.	1357, 1358	F.	? N.	Λ [missing]

190. Fragment.   192. Fragment.   194. Fragment.   198. Fragment.

[1] Words in paler ink : ? added later.   [2] to [3] Words in darker ink : ? added later.
[3] Ink written over incised inscription *Cram ffelde.*
[4] Written over incised inscription *Contra balliuum manerii de Cram . . . felde.*
[5] Ink over incised inscription *tusterne.*   [6] Ink over incised inscription *sto ne.*
[7] Ink over incised inscription *Abbddus astone.*
[8] Ink over incised inscription *Herte welle.   auena* in paler ink ? added later.

MEDIEVAL TALLIES, PUBLIC AND PRIVATE

Denominations in Notches.			Writing.	No. in this List.
One or more.	Money.	Commodities.		
? one	?	?	Contra constabularium de Wasdon' de Auena capta Greyne [1]	173
? one	?	?	ℙ Const' de Langefelde auen' de [2] comitatu de Bedeforde [2]	174
? one	?	?	Contra villatam de carnefelde de auena [3]	175
? one	?	?	Contra Balliuum Manerii de Cranfelde de auena . de comitatu Bedeford' [4]	176
? one	?	?	¶ Contra constabularium de Wodell'. de auena	177
? one	?	?	¶ De villata de Tusterne de auena [5]	178
? one	?	?	contra villatam de Barton de auena	179
? one	?	?	Contra villatam de Ston' de auena [6]	180
? one	?	?	¶ Contra villatam de Abbodes Aston' de auena [7]	181
? one	?	?	¶ Contra villatam de Hertwelle . auena [8]	182
? one	?	?	¶ contra villatam de Wynghe de auena [9]	183
? one	?	?	¶ contra prepositum de Adewell' de auena	184
? one	?	?	Contra Mydelstoke de [2] eadem villata pro auena [2]	185
? one	?	?	Villa chalgraue de [2] auena [2]	186
? one	?	?	¶ swenescombe de [2] eadem villa pro auena [2]	187
one	?	?	Contra constabularium de Estwyk' pro litera capta equis domini Regis per manus Ricardi atte feld'	188
one	?	?	contra Constabularium de Estone vij . s viij d. pro litera xx d. capta per Henricum Brayb'f	189
one	?	?	De constabulario de Bun . . . . [11] ⟨on upper edge xiij⟩	190
one	?	?	De constabulario de Lydesden' pro litera [12]	191
one	?	?	Contra Henricum Bray de litera capta de Johanne Reynald' de Heebregg'	192
one	?	?	Const' de Stanewey pro litero	193
one	?	?	Const' de [? Tol . . . .] litero	194
one	?	?	contra constabularium Stanewey pro [13] litera anno xxxij [13]	195
one	?	?	Const' de [? Alphinston'] pro litera	196
one	?	?	Const' de ffordham pro litero	197
one	?	?	Contra Abbatem de [? Stratford'] pro 1 . . . . atteffelde anno xxxj [14]	198

[9] Ink over incised inscription *Tallia de Wenke de auena recepta.*
[10] Original file of fourteen tally foils and one parchment receipt; with parchment label.
[11] Ink over incised inscription, mostly illegible.
[12] Ink over incised inscription, mostly illegible but beginning *contra.*
[13] to [13] Added later in smaller hand.
[14] Ink over incised inscription *pro litera de Abbate Str . . . .*

MEDIEVAL TALLIES, PUBLIC AND PRIVATE

No. in this List.	Reference.	Date.	Stock or Foil.	Cutting.	
				Shape of Tally.	Shape, &c., of Notches.
199	E. 101/678/3 (1)	[1358, 1359]	F.	N.	vvvvvvv
200	do.	[do.]	F.	N.	vvv [missing]
201	do.	[do.]	F.	S.A.	IIIIᴧᴧ
202	*Ibid.* 3 (2)¹	[? do.]	F.	S.A.	Iᴧᴧ
203	do.	1358, 1359	F.	N.	vvvv
204	do.	1358, 1359	F.	N.	vvvvvv
205	do.	[? do.]	F.	N.	vvvvvvvv
206	*Ibid.* 3 (3)⁴	[? 1357–1359]	F.	N.	vvvvvv√
207	do.	[do.]	F.	N.	VVVVVV
208	do.	1357, 1358	F.	N.	vvvvvvV
209	do.	1358, 1359	F.	N.	IIIIvvv√
210	do.	[? 1357–1359]	F.	N.	vvvv
211	do.	[do.]	F.	N.	√vvvvvv
212	do.	[do.]	F.	N.	√VVV
213	do.	1358, 1359	F.	N.	√v√V
214	do.	[? 1357–1359]	F.	N.	vv
215	do.	1358, 1359	F.	N.	IIIIvv
216	do.	[? 1357–1359]	F.	N.	Iv√
217	British Museum Tally⁶	1358, 1359	F.	S.A.	·III ᴧ
218	E. 1C1/678/4⁷	1361, 1362	F.	N.	HIIvvv√VVV
219	do.	1361, 1362	S.	N.	IIIIᴧᴧᴧᴧᴧᴧᴧ
220	do.	1360, 1361	F.	N.	IIIIVVVV
221	do.	1361, 1362	F.	S.A.	ᴧᴧ
222	do.	1361, 1362	S.	S.A.	VV

200. Fragment.   206. Fragment.

¹ Four broken tally foils found loose : probably belonging to previous file.
² Ink over incised inscription *Const' Pateswik' pro litera.*
³ Ink has run and writing is blurred.

MEDIEVAL TALLIES, PUBLIC AND PRIVATE

Denominations in Notches.			Writing.	No. in this List.
One or more.	Money.	Commodities.		
one	?	?	Contra abbatem de stratforde pro litero ad opus domini Regis captum [sic] per manum Ricardi atte ff[elde]	199
one	?	?	Contra constabularium de Kelveden' pro litera	200
one	?	?	Contra constabularium de Coggeshal' pro litera	201
one	?	?	Contra constabularium de Pateswik' pro litera [2]	202
one	?	?	Contra .... de R .... de litera capta etc. per R' atteffelde anno xxxij [3]	203
one	?	?	De litera capta per Radulfum [sic] atteffelde in Abbatia de Stratford' anno xxxij.	204
? one	?	?	Contra Constabularium de Claydon' pro [? ij quarteriis] [illegible] xxj. s.	205
one	?	?	...·... Dagenham pro feno capto per Ricardum atte	206
one	?	?	Contra dominum Reginaldum Mannyng' pro feno capto per [illegible] atte ffelde	207
one	?	?	Contra constabularium de Langham de feno Anno xxxjmo	208
one	?	?	Contra Henricum Bray pro feno capto de Johanne Reynold de Hebregg'. Anno xxxijo.	209
one	?	?	Constable de [? stistede] pro feno	210
one	?	?	Tallia contra constabularium de [? reydone] de ffenis captis per R' atteffeld'	211
one	?	?	Contra vicarium de brokesbourne pro feno capto per Ricardum atte ffeld'	212
one	?	?	Contra Constabularium de Coggeshal' [pro] [? herbagio] recepto Anno regni regis Edwardi tercij a conquestu xxxijo.	213
one	?	?	Contra constabularium de B [illegible] de feno [5]	214
one	?	?	¶ Contra constabularium de West [? xxijd] straminis anno xxxij	215
?	?	?	[Writing very faint and illegible].	216
one		grain	Tallia de Willelmo West de Fousmere Anno Regis Edwardi post conquestum [? x]xxij [de] brasio ⟨on lower edge dimidia quarteria iij bussella dimidium⟩	217
one	3l. 13s. 4d.		anno xxx vltimo preterito — contra Willelmum de Hynton' balliuum de honore de Reylegh' Liij s iiij d per istam talliam et non mensionem h[abet] plus quia xx s sunt in vsu.	218
one	3l. 13s. 4d.		[Stock of above] Tallia Willelmi Hynton' . . . contra Nicholaum [etc.]	219
one	4l. 4d.		Contra Nicholaum Colman balliuum de Reylegh' de denariis ab eodem receptis anno xxxivto.	220
one	2l.		Estwode Tallia Nicholai Raunche prepositi ibidem contra Nicholaum Colman balliuum de Reilegh' de denariis ab eo receptis xxij die Marcij Anno xxxvto.	221
one	2l.		[Stock of above] Tallia Nicholai Colman contra [etc.].	222

[4] Eleven tally foils found loose but apparently belonging together. Not all in same hand.
[5] Ink very faint.
[6] The dot among the notches represents a line extending half across the edge of the tally.
[7] Original file of seven tallies (four foils and three corresponding stocks) and five parchment deeds with seals and descriptive parchment tag : preserved in contemporary leather bag (see above, p. 312).

MEDIEVAL TALLIES, PUBLIC AND PRIVATE

No. in this List.	Reference.	Date.	Stock or Foil.	Cutting.	
				Shape of Tally.	Shape, &c., of Notches.
223	E. 101/678/4	1361, 1362	F.	N.	VVV
224	do.	1361, 1362	S.	N.	ΛΛΛ
225	Private collection [1]	1367, 1368	F.	N.	VV
226	British Museum Tally [2]	1368	S.	A.E.	vvvvvvvvvv
227	M.A. 856/10	1388	S.	N.	ΛΛΛΛ
228	do.	1388	S.[3]	N.	ΛΛΛΛΛΛΛ
229	E. 101/678/1 (2) [4]	? 1390, 1391	S.	S.A.	IIII
230	M.A. 1122/15	1417, 1418	F.	N.	VVVVVVVVVVVVVVV
231	British Museum Tally [7]	[15th cent.]	F.	N.	IIΛΛΛΛΛΛ ●IIIIIΛΛΛΛ vvvvvvv V ΛΛΛΛΛΛΛΛΛΛΛΛΛ
232	E. 101/678/1 (3) [8]	Henry VII or Henry VIII	F.	A.	VVVV

[1] Belonging (1895) to Mr. J. G. Moore, of Appleby: see note by W. Paley Baildon in *Proceedings*, xv. 309. This tally is attached to the roll of accounts to which it refers: a second receipt for money paid to the lord is on parchment.
[2] An exceptionally long stock, more than three times the length of the foil.
[3] Very long stock.

MEDIEVAL TALLIES, PUBLIC AND PRIVATE

Denominations in Notches.			Writing.	No. in this list.
One or more.	Money.	Commodities.		
one	3*l.*		ℙ Estwod' contra Nicholaum Colman balliuum de Reylegh' de denariis ab eodem receptis de reddital ad terminum Pasche anno regni regis Edwardi etc xxxv^to	223
one	3*l.*		[*Stock of above*] ℙ Tallia Nicholai Colman contra [*etc.*].	224
	2*l.*		Tallia Johannis prepositi de Appelby de — xl s liberatis domino Ricardo de Vernon' per manus Johannis atte Halleyate ante Pasch' anno xlij°	225
one	? 10*l.*		Contra Radulphum Spigurnell Constabularium Castri Douerr' et custodis quinque portuum De Warda de Grauesende ⟨*on lower edge* intr' vij° die Octobris Anno regni regis Edwardi tercij a conquestu quadragesimo secundo⟩.	226
one	13*l.*		Horton Tallia Thome Symond' prepositi ibidem de xiiij li liberatis Stephano Velewet de diuersis proficuis Manerii ibidem Mense Septembris Anno regni Regis Ricardi secundi post conquestum duodecimo	227
one		sheep	Horton' Tallia Thome Symondes prepositi ibidem de cccc^mlx ouis [*sic*] de stauro Manerij liberatis Johanni Farwell' post [festum Michaelis *struck through*] [Mensem Septembris *interlineated*] Anno regni regis Ricardi Duodecimo videlicet de Multonibus C^m.iiij^xx.vj. De ouibus Matricibus Hegg' ferc' et Hurtard' Ciiij^xxxviij. Et de Agnis — lxxvj	228
one			De [? Ricardo Bautre] misso apud [*illegible*] Anno regni regis [?] Ricardi .xiiij°. pro^5 [? tf] contra Hugonem Armigerum dominj.^5	229
one	14*l.* 13*s.* 5½*d.* 6*s.* 8*d.*		Tallia de denariis solutis domino per manus Johannis Kent' balliui de Wattecombe anno quinto . Henrici . quinti	230
two		? wood	p^d to M . . . . . } for xx lodes } The } p^d to billettes and } ·tayle } John Bryght xvj lodes tallwood } lackyng } ⟨*on lower edge* Tallwood : *on upper* Billettes⟩	231
? one	?	?	[*Illegible*] regni regis Henrici [?] vij^mi fowr dussan [*illegible*]	232

⁴ Another exceptionally long stock : the dot among the notches represents a stroke half across the edge of the tally.
⁵ to ⁵ Added in another hand. In the first hand the ink has run and it is very illegible.
⁶ Two sums are entered on the lower edge, 13*s.* 5½*d.* and 6*s.* 8*d.* This tally is preserved with the document to which it belongs.
⁷ A parchment tag attached, mostly illegible, is in Chancery hand and signed *Southwell.*
⁸ Large and clumsy : position of writing and notches quite abnormal.

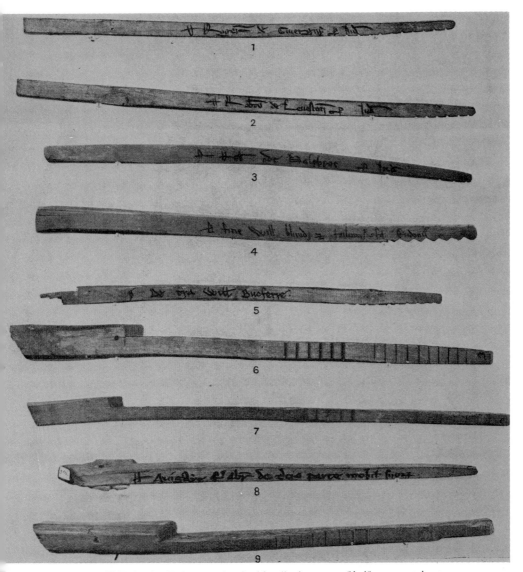

PLATE I: Exchequer Tally Stocks. Early examples, Jewish tally, instances of half-penny notch, etc.

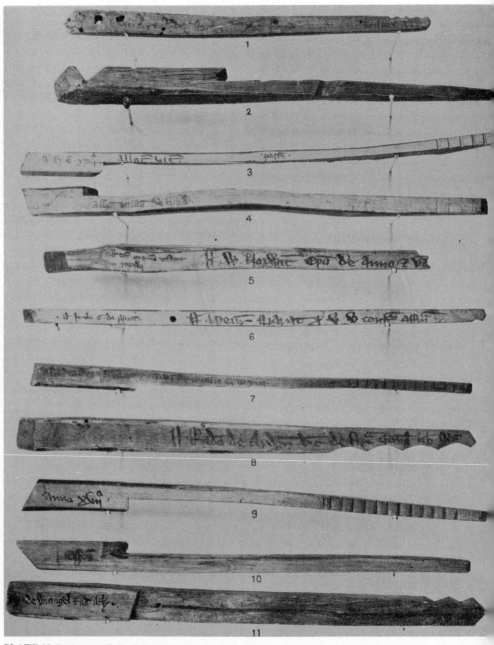

PLATE II: Exchequer Tally-Foil and Stocks, showing added notes etc.

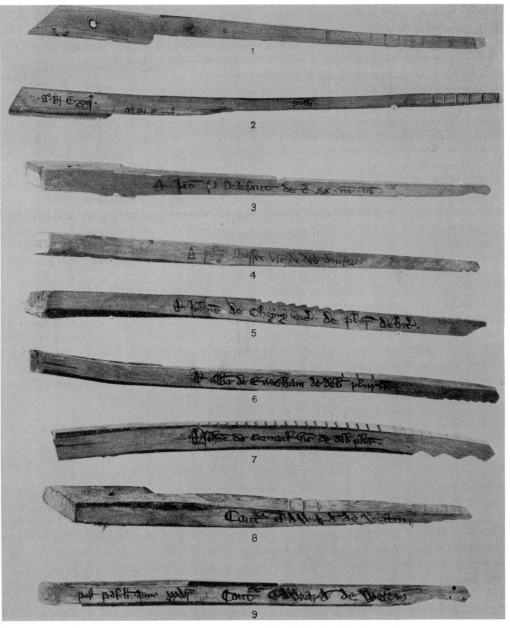

PLATE III: Exchequer Tally Stocks, showing tallies 'de debitis plurium', tallies 'contra', etc.

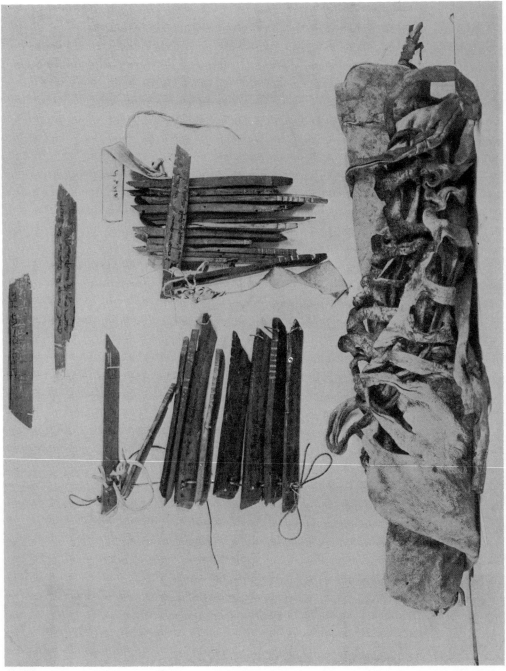

PLATE IV: Private tally, fule and leather bag

PLATE V: Private tally foils and sack with labels: 14th cent.

PLATE VI: Private tallies, stocks and foils, with canvas bag, descriptive label and rolls of accounts

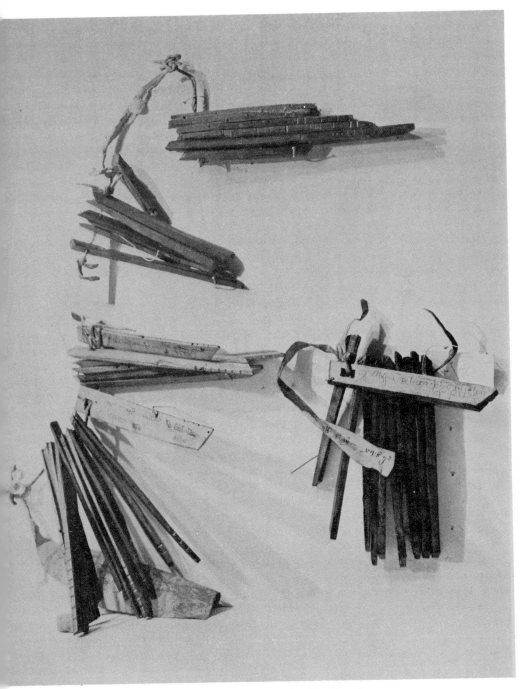

PLATE VII: Private tally foils, showing incised inscription and variety of notches

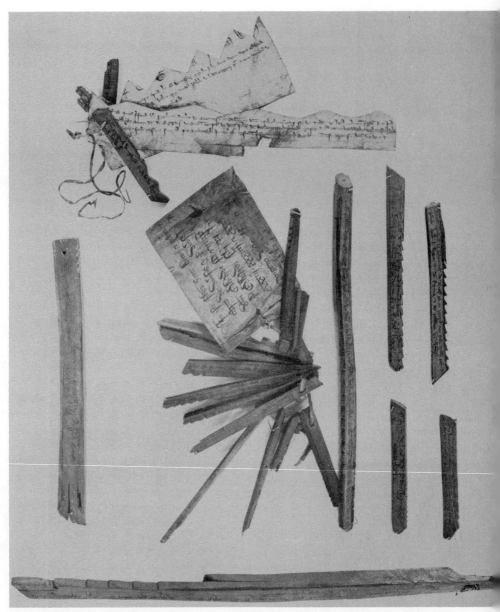

PLATE VIII: Private tally stocks and foils, showing tallies filed with parchment indentures, file of tallies with label, Jewish money-lender's tally etc.

The Librarian as Archivist

The subject of archive science has almost ceased to be a stranger in the librarian's syllabus of studies. For quite a number of years, for example, it has figured in that of the Library Association, and it has been a regular feature in the summer school organised by Dr. Ballinger at Aberystwyth. Most important, perhaps, because most formal, was the recognition given to it when it was included in the syllabus of the new School of Librarianship started nine years ago at University College, London. It has continued to be a necessary part of the training in that school, and every year from twenty to forty students, destined, many of them, to take positions in the public libraries of the country, have dedicated thirty or forty hours of lecture, and much more of private work, to the study of this subject in combination with palaeography. Moreover, the School of Librarianship has been responsible for the appearance of what was, good or bad, the first attempt made anywhere at a complete *Manual of Archive Administration*,[1] a book written largely to meet the needs of the class there. I hope, since I happen to have been the teacher charged with the duty of organizing this study at University College, I may be forgiven if I regard this approach of a new type of student to a new subject as a matter of some interest; and if I take the opportunity (finding myself in a gathering of distinguished librarians) to set out for information, and perhaps criticism, my own view of the reason why archive science is a subject proper for the attention of English librarians, and of the lines along which it should be studied.

Archives — if I may begin with a definition — are the pieces of writing, on whatever material made and in whatever form (whether originals received or drafts prepared for despatch or memoranda of transactions), which business men and business offices, public or private, have tended everywhere to

1. Clarendon Press, 1922.

accumulate and preserve by way of reminder and summary of various aspects of the work of which they formed a part; and during the last century or two it has become recognised that the masses of archives which have survived to us after their original purpose had long ceased to be of any importance form a mine of information as to the doings of the past not only quite independent of the narrative accounts, more or less contemporary and more or less prejudiced, which had hitherto formed the basis of our histories, but actually superior to them very often in wealth of detail and always in authenticity and impartiality. So much have archives gained in estimation and there is almost a danger lest the use of those derived from the past, and the preservation of those which are being piled up in the present by an age of card-indexes and duplicators, should alike be overdone. That, however, is a point we need not labour here: what interests us is the fact that there is in our time no subject of serious research which may not — which does not, frequently — turn to them for its illustration. Just as there is no human activity or interest which does not, sooner or later, become involved in the machinery of the world's business, so there is none which may not be found figuring in archives of one kind or another, often in the most unexpected places: the best specimens of early English wallpapers and of eighteenth-century patterns of dress materials (to take two recently-noted examples) are among the public records. And since the librarian is the servant of research the subject of archives, at least from a bibliographical point of view, of their whereabouts and availability, of the means of approach to them and of the books in which they are made public, has become an essential part of his stock-in-trade.

But it is not because other people studying archives may require his intelligent assistance that I have ventured to suggest for the librarian the role of archivist. That word, as I see it, is properly applied not to the research-worker who takes from archives what interests him or helps his work, but to the man who, armed with the necessary special knowledge, undertakes the task of preserving them and of producing them when required — of doing for them, in fact, what the librarian does for his books. It was with the object of training young librarians for this task that the archives course at University College was planned; and the questions I wish to try and answer in this paper are, first, why should the English librarian be asked to undertake this extra labour? and, second, why and how is the training necessary for the keeping of MSS. which are archives different from that required for the keeping of other MSS. or of books?

To answer the first of these questions involves a brief survey of the official position of archives in England. In most countries the State recognises and controls, at least in theory, the archives produced by all grades of public administration, from the central Ministry down to the least important hamlet: generally the central and controlling authority is that which has the actual care of the most important central collections.[2] In England we have no such system. The Public Record Office Acts of 1838 to 1898 and the Order in Council of 1852 give to the Master of the Rolls control over all legal records within the direct jurisdiction of the High Court and, with some modification, over the accruing archives of existing public departments; but with only one exception (to be mentioned presently), although various Acts[3] have from time to time recognised an obligation upon this or that local authority to make and preserve records, no attempt has been made to face, by way of statute, the problem of enabling and enforcing their preservation under proper conditions. This being so, it need hardly be said that there has been no statutory attempt to deal with the question of the preservation of the archives of semi-public bodies or of private persons or institutions, though the Historical MSS. Commission, in the 150 odd volumes it has published since 1870, has done valuable work by calling attention to their existence and importance.

It is in respect chiefly of the classes of private archives, though to some extent also of those of a semi-public nature,[4] that some of us who are interested in the possibilities of documents have endeavoured to invoke the aid of the librarian. It is hardly necessary to emphasise here the value of the documents or the magnitude of the peril — they have been made the subject of denunciation or appeal for many years at numerous conferences of the learned, and only last year the Congress of Archaeological Societies devoted the larger part of its annual meeting to the subject — but I permit myself one example of what may occur: Since the passing of Lord Cairns' Act, some fifty years ago, made the preservation of the older title deeds to land no longer a practical necessity it is literally true that hundreds of thousands of such deeds, many of priceless value for local history, have been destroyed or scattered. One could give countless detailed illustration of the effect of uncontrolled ignorance, combined with a little cupidity and a good deal of apathy, upon what should have been a recognised national inheritance.

It may be asked — why pick out the librarian for the part of *deus ex machina?* Frankly, the answer is that one takes the best one can get. Local interest in local history, which so often does (as it always should) find a natural ally in the local librarian, is the strongest motive force for the safeguarding of documents: but the fundamental question, as experience has shown again and again, is that of repository space. 'You want me,' says the owner, 'to refrain from selling my family papers; but have you any place in which, if I

2. Thus in France it is the *Archives Nationales*, the institution which looks after the archives of most of the great departments of State, past and present, which is the head of the whole Archive Administration of the country.
3. A notable example is the Local Government Act of 1894.
4. For instance, those of schools and charities and of commercial firms or public committees, such as those formed during the Great War, whch have ceased to function.

offered to deposit them for public use, they could be securely and permanently bestowed?' And inevitably, though we know the difficulty it too has to face in this connection, we turn to the local library.

One more word about the position of the local library as an archive repository. I spoke earlier of an exception to the rule that this country knows no central control over local archives. Lord Birkenhead's Act of 1922 seemed to many scholars as fatal potentially to the Court Rolls — the records of that wonderful system of local jurisdiction which was such a remarkable feature of medieval England and so strong an influence in moulding the growth of later local institutions — as fatal to them as was Lord Cairns' Act to the Deeds; and on this occasion timely agitation produced an amending measure by which the Master of the Rolls, the head of the Public Records, is given power to prevent the destruction and dissipation of Court Rolls and under certain circumstances to order their deposit in local repositories to be approved by him. The administration of these powers is a delicate and difficult task, and the Master of the Rolls, with a committee which he has appointed, has been engaged so far principally in encouraging the discovery and listing of these records — for at present everyone is in the dark as to the number and extent of existing accumulations — and in finding and approving local repositories both suitable for and willing to take local deposits when these may offer. Of about fifty repositories so approved up to date two-thirds are libraries — a sufficient evidence of the way in which this newest of archive problems is touching the librarian: and as some indication of its extent I will venture to quote in conclusion the case of my own county, Surrey. Here we have just had issued by the County Council, in collaboration with the Record Society,[5] as complete a list as we could make of Surrey Court Rolls; and though this county, owing to its semi-suburban position, will probably prove to be one of the poorest in such survivals we have been able to list rolls from over 200 manors, twelve collections dating from the thirteenth century and twenty-four more from the fourteenth. Of three Surrey repositories so far approved two are libraries — the Minet Library at Camberwell and Croydon.

So far we have suggested that the local library is, by force of circumstances, not only the natural centre for information about local archives, but often also their custodian. Numerous examples might be given — from large libraries, such as those of Birmingham, Cardiff, and Croydon, downwards — where such work has already been taken in hand, but space forbids. I turn to the question — what should be the special training given to a young librarian in view of these facts?

The principal classes of topics which may be the subject of his instruction are, I think, three. First there is the *physical care* of documents, embracing the question of the conditions under which paper, parchment, ink, and other

5. Surrey Record Society, No. XXVIII.

writing materials may best be conserved, questions of binding and receptacles, the problem of suitable buildings and fittings, problems of protection from fire, vermin, and other enemies. Next we have the *moral defence* of archives, including all problems attendant on the archivist's task of making his archives available for students and the problem (if he feels called upon to face it; I do not myself think he should) of selecting what is worth preserving. Finally, there are the studies required by the archivist in so far as he finds it necessary to read his archives for the purpose of *arranging, listing,* and perhaps *publishing.*

In regard to the first and second of these groups, but particularly the first, the librarian should not have much to learn, for he should have studied, or be studying, in connection with his more ordinary duties the questions of library architecture, the atmospherics of the library, the qualities of binding and parcelling materials, and the natures of paper, parchment, ink, and so forth; and similarly he should be acquainted with all the received views as to 'production' from repository, the supervision of students, and the like questions. It might be thought that in addition to his ordinary training the librarian would require little here save a few demonstrations of the special requirements of some unfamiliar forms of material or make-up, such as parchment rolls or seals. That is, with one exception, true: apart from a few trifling specialities there is only one thing, one piece of knowledge which the librarian lacks or should lack. But that one is a principle which governs so strictly (if I am right) and so universally the whole of archive work — make-up, repair, labelling, listing, supervision and production, publication — that it is necessary to emphasize and enforce it by illustration or demonstration of its application in every department.

The piece of knowledge about which I have made so much ado is nothing more than the fact that whereas the ordinary collection of books (or of any other objects — the MSS., for instance, in the British Museum) is the result of selection by persons interested in the object which that collection serves today, the individual pieces having no other necessary relation than the fact that they were all chosen for the same reason, a group of archives is a single organism which has not been made but has grown for reasons and under circumstances quite independent of the interests which now make use of it. This is responsible for every particularity which one has to prescribe in the treatment of archives: it is responsible (for example) for the extreme importance attaching to the question of custody, an unblemished reputation in this respect being, it cannot too often be repeated, the *differentia* between an archive and a plain document: it is responsible for a like preciseness as to the place or connection in which an archive was first found: two copies of the *London Gazette*, for example, which to the librarian are two copies of the *London Gazette*, taking on for the archivist totally different values and characters because one is (shall we say) an enclosure to Foreign Office correspondence, while the other is merely part of the office miscellanea of the Admiralty. One might multiply examples of the way in which this archive character, which consists in the relation of every piece to the administrative machinery which produced it, governs or should govern every action of the archivist's official life; but space once more forbids. May I merely say in conclusion, deliberately, that there is in my opinion no item in all the dismal catalogue of errors and crimes in the past treatment of archives in this and other countries by their appointed custodians which was not the result of ignorance or neglect of this fundamental fact?

There remains the question of the necessary acquirements for an archivist-librarian in the matters of palaeography and other preliminaries to reading; they may be stated briefly. He will need in the first place a trifle more of the outlines of English History than generally remains after an average education; a trifle of the History of Law, especially that of real property, if (as they almost certainly will in a collection of any size) his documents are to include deeds; some Latin if (once more) the collection is of any size or age, and if it is a medieval one some French as well; not to mention some idea of the medieval modifications of those languages, though this is not so severe a task as it sounds; a specially good bibliographical knowledge of the authorities upon Family History and Topography; and a more detailed acquaintance with those relating to his own neighbourhood; a familiarity with the actual Scripts employed in the period and variety of documents with which he is concerned; and some knowledge of Administrative History.

The last two — Palaeography and Administrative History — raise a point of some difficulty. The necessity of Palaeography of a kind is obvious; and elsewhere[6] I have endeavoured to show that the necessity for Administrative History, if less obvious, is really greater; though indeed it should not require much proof that to understand documents which formed part of a business process one must understand the process which produced them. The trouble is that, while one is anxious to restrict the studies of the aspiring archivist to the period and variety of document with which he will have to deal, one cannot in practice make him a reliable reader without giving him a knowledge of the earlier forms out of which those belonging to his period were evolved; nor can he practice upon earlier documents without knowing something of the administration which lies behind them also. In a modified form the same difficulty attaches also to the other preliminary studies we have named; he may not, for example, find Latin in his own documents, but may need it for the reading of earlier ones, the study of which seems essential for understanding the scripts of his own period. The case is one where it is very difficult to prescribe. Perhaps the best we can do is to lay it down, as a rough guide, that if the documents to be dealt with are not earlier than the

6.   Palaeography and the Study of Court Hand: Cambridge, 1915.

eighteenth century they may, at a pinch, be tackled without preliminary palaeographical work; that the reading of sixteenth — and seventeenth — century hands ought to be based on a knowledge of those of the fifteenth; and that for earlier hands than this last one really requires to begin *ab ovo* — say from Domesday. With this we may couple a hope that the student will make his studies as thorough as possible and an assurance that he cannot have too much practice and that he will not find the subject dull.

It may be useful if I end this paper with some description of the effect upon the student, so far as I have been able to observe it, of such training as we were able to give under the circumstances, and on the lines, I have mentioned. Our students were of the London University Matriculation standard, and they were expected to pass, at the end of a year's course, an examination which fell into two parts, one of Archive Science and one of the reading, explaining, and annotating of documents, including transcription from 'unseen' facsimiles of medieval manuscripts. Most of them succeeded in reaching a forty per cent. pass in both. To attain this I found that they needed no more than five or six lectures and demonstrations, with the corresponding amount of private work, on Archive Science; all the rest of the time (more than two terms' work out of three) being given to reading practice, elementary Palaeography, and what I have called Administrative History. The students at the end of this training were not, of course, experienced archivists; but they had a good idea of their own ignorance and of the means of correcting it. They gave quite a definite impression that they found the subject, or subjects, interesting, and I was certainly very sorry when I had to give up the pleasant task of teaching them.

General Report of a Committee on the Classification of English Archives

INTRODUCTORY
1. TERMS OF REFERENCE

In May 1933 two letters were received almost simultaneously by the Council: one was from the Northamptonshire Record Society asking that the Council should take steps to formulate a scheme for the Classification of Parish Records, both Civil and Ecclesiastical: the other was from the Sub-Committee charged by the Committee of the Anglo-American Historical Conference with the duty of reporting on the Accessibility of Historical Documents and on the Migrations of MSS., enquiring as to the possibility of classifying Documents in connexion with Local History. The Council then decided itself to appoint a Committee to report on the questions raised by these two applications.

Subsequently a Motion from the Conference of November 1934, asking the Council to investigate the possibility of a Uniform Scheme for the Cataloguing of Deeds, was also remitted to this Committee: and in connexion with another Motion from the same Conference the Committee was asked to deal with the question of Records in the custody of Clerks of the Peace.

2. MEMBERSHIP AND MEETINGS

The Members appointed to the Committee were the Right Honourable Sir Matthew Nathan, G.C.M.G. (Chairman); Dr. G.H. Fowler, C.B.E. (Chairman of the Anglo-American Sub-Committee mentioned above); Mr. S.C. Ratcliff, I.S.O. (Secretary of the Historical MSS. Commission); Miss Joan Wake; Dr. Gordon Ward; and the Honorary Secretaries of the Association (Miss Irene J. Churchill, D. Phil., and Mr. Hilary Jenkinson, F.S.A.). Sir Matthew Nathan found it necessary to retire during the latter stages of the Committee's work but has continued to receive drafts throughout; though he does not join as a Member of the Committee in the presentation of the Report.

Great difficulty has been experienced, at times, in arranging dates for Meetings; and this, with the complex nature of the enquiry submitted to the Committee, must account for some slowness of progress; but every matter here treated has been the subject of lengthy deliberation; and while it was inevitable that individual Members might feel they would have expressed certain points differently, the Report may be taken to represent as a whole the collective opinion of the Committee.

An *Interim Report* was submitted to the Council in 1934.

3. THE COMMITTEE'S TASK

The Committee, after due deliberation, has concluded that it would best fulfil the objects for which it was constituted, if it proceeded in the first place to submit for consideration a General Scheme covering the whole body of English Archives. Relations between different categories of Archives are so continual and so complicated, that every writer or archivist who has been called upon to deal with any considerable body of Archives (whether from the point of view of their arrangement or from that of their use for any kind of historical purpose) has invariably found it necessary to construct some such scheme for his own purposes; and it would obviously be for the advantage of all, if a single one could win general agreement. Following this the Committee proposes to submit first a description of the various *Archive Groups* to be found within each of the Primary Divisions or Categories of English Archives described in the General Scheme; the word 'Group' being used in the technical sense of the *Body of Archives resulting from the activities of any independent unit of Public or Private Administration or Business*, such for instance, as a Borough, a Parish or a private Business Firm. Finally the Committee has prepared detailed schemes for the Classification of *Parish Records* (in accordance with the request mentioned in section 1. above) and of *Private Muniments*, and a revised *List of Archives to be found in the Custody of Clerks of the Peace.*

The Report therefore as submitted to the Council of the Association, consisted of four parts:

    i. the present *Introductory Remarks* (sections 1-3);
    ii. the *Primary Divisions of Archives* (sections 4, 5);
    iii. existing *Groups of English Archives* (sections 6-12); and
    iv. schemes for the *Internal Classification of certain Groups:*

to which was added an

    Appendix on the various possible methods of *Cataloguing Deeds*: based on the replies to a Questionnaire sent to Institutional Members following a resolution of the Conference of 1934.

It will be observed, however, that whereas Parts i. to iii. form a single complete whole, Part iv. may be expanded in the future, if that is desired, by the preparation of Schemes for Internal Classification covering other varieties of Archive Groups: the Committee has, for example, a certain amount of material already in hand for the preparation of a schedule of Classes of Archives to be found in Ecclesiastical Muniment Rooms other than those of Parishes. It has been decided therefore to print these separately in successive Numbers of a new series of *Reports of Committees: the first of which* (the present publication) contains only Parts i. to iii. above. The *Appendix* has been issued by itself and formed the basis for a discussion at the Conference of November, 1935.

PRIMARY DIVISIONS OF ARCHIVES
4. MAIN HEADINGS

In pursuance of the above conception the Committee proceeded first to fix a series of primary divisions into which all surviving English Archives might be considered to fall. Taking the accepted meaning of Archives as the documentary remains of Business, Judicial, or Administrative Transactions of any kind, it would propose to describe English Archives under six Main Headings.[1]

I. *Documents resulting from the work of Central Public Administration.*

These are the Groups of Archives preserved either at the Public Record Office or in other repositories belonging to the Royal Courts of Justice and to the various Government Departments.

II. *Documents resulting from Local Public Administration.*

These are the collections to be found (taking present day illustrations) in the possession of such Administrative Units as County Councils or Boroughs.

III. *Documents resulting from Semi-Public Activities.*

This description is intended to cover the large and increasing quantities of Archives resulting from business which, in origin founded and conducted, like those under the following heading, for private advantage or satisfaction, have (owing to the nature of their work) a certain public quality; receive accordingly from the State special recognition and privileges; and are charged with functions of at least a semi-official character. Examples are Public Utility Companies, such as Turnpike Trusts or Railways, and many Educational and Charitable Institutions.

1. During the progress of the Committee's work a *Guide International* to European Archives was published at Paris by the *Institut International de Coopération Intellectuelle*. In the Section there devoted to the United Kingdom, English Archives are described under the 'Main Headings' here adopted. The section also describes the Archives of Ireland, Scotland, Wales (so far as these exist separately) and the Channel Islands: and the important Archives of Scotland are also treated under these headings.

It may be added that this semi-public character has a marked effect upon the form of Archives.

IV. *Documents resulting from the conduct of Private Affairs for Private Purposes.*

This description covers the documentary results of every kind of Undertaking or Jurisdiction conducted for private advantage or satisfaction, whether by an Individual or by a Corporation or Institution. Family affairs, the conduct of an Estate, the organization of a Social or Educational Movement, the activities of a Business House, Manufactory or Commercial Concern — all alike give rise to Archives which may be included under this heading.

V. *Documents resulting from the work of Ecclesiastical Administrations.*

The activities of the Church have, of course, largely developed on lines separate from the State. It has been, however, in the past much concerned (for instance, as a land-owner) with temporal as well as spiritual activities; it has also had judicial and other functions some of which (such as the control of Testamentary Dispositions) have subsequently been transferred to the State. These facts will naturally give rise to a number of difficulties in the classification of its Archives: and necessitate a considerable amount of cross-reference between this and other divisions.

It should be noted also, that in respect of the post-Reformation period, there will be included under this heading the Archives produced by the activities of Religious Bodies other than the Church of England.

VI. *Documents of Historical Interest artificially collected.*

Normally and properly preserved Archives fall into 'Groups' corresponding to the Business Interests which give rise to them; every document in any given Group having thus a definite relation to others in the same Group; and each Group being preserved in custody either of the individual or institution who created it (or their successors) or of some properly constituted Archive Authority. There are, however, large quantities of documents which have lost connexion with their natural Group and can be regarded only as isolated specimens.

Such documents form the *Collections* which the present heading is designed to cover.

SUMMARY

The first four main divisions of English Archives under the Committee's scheme may thus be described shortly as

I. *Public, Central;*
II. *Public, Local;*
III. *Semi-Public; and*
IV. *Private:*

all these being the result of Civil activities. The next division is that of

V. *Ecclesiastical:*

and to this, owing to the vicissitudes through which many Archive Accumulations have passed, has to be added

VI. *Artificial Collections.*

ENGLISH ARCHIVE GROUPS
6. DIFFICULTIES OF DETAILED CLASSIFICATION

Border-line Cases and the Need for Cross-reference

Before proceeding further to distinguish in more detail under the above headings varieties of Administration or Business, and their resultant Archive Groups, and to define in certain cases the *Classes* of Archives to be found within particular *Groups*, the Committee would lay stress on the fact that while classification is necessarily rigid, the institutions concerned are fluid; so that there must always be a certain number of border-line cases, varieties of Administration (and Archives), which according to different points of view might figure almost equally well in either of two possible places. For example, Probate Jurisdiction, as has been already remarked, was for centuries in the hands of the Church and in close relation with other Ecclesiastical Jurisdiction: and for that period its Archives would seem undoubtedly to be classed best under our fifth heading: but in the middle of the 19th century both the Administration and the Archives of Probate were transferred to the control of what is now the Supreme Court. Are we therefore to make a violent division and classify them down to the mid-nineteenth century under Heading V, and after that under Heading I? Again, the Ecclesiastical Parish was from the time of the Tudors down to the Parish Councils Act of 1892 increasingly used by the State as a unit of the Local Administration organized largely by and through the Justices of the Peace: and the Archives of this Civil work are accordingly to be found often (but not always) in the Parish Chest. Are we for that reason to take Parish Administration with its Archives out of division V and describe it under division II? Similar difficulties are to be found very frequently in regard to the distribution of Archives as between Headings II and III. In dealing with such cases, the Committee will be guided wherever possible by the present location of control over the whole or the larger part of the Archives concerned: and will attempt to prevent any misconception by a free use of cross-reference from possible alternative places of classification.

Classification Distinguished from Arrangement

The Committee would take occasion also to emphasize the vital distinction between *classification on paper* for the convenience of study and the *physical arrangement* of documents. While these two should, and do very often, coincide, it also frequently happens that circumstances have brought about abnormal administrative arrangements and a corresponding abnormality in the arrangement of the Archives. In one or two cases to be mentioned later (such as that of the Lord of a Manor who owns also a Hundred Court and keeps the Records of his two jurisdictions in a single documentary series) it would obviously be dangerous, if not impossible, to attempt an actual physical division of the documents in accordance with what would be a perfectly legitimate method of *classifying* items on paper: but in other less obvious cases a like caution has to be observed. It is to be noted that merely theoretical *Classification* on paper, if it is wrong, will produce no permanent harm; whereas if a mistaken *Classification* is translated into terms of physical *Re-arrangement* of the documents it may produce, as it has done in the past many times in specific cases and among important Archive Classes, irreparable damage. The *Special Collections* among the Public Records, created by a mistaken zeal and a false scheme of classification in the past, and the havoc wrought by successive 'Methodizers' among the *State Papers*, are well-known examples. It should be remembered that if documents are conveniently classified on paper, the fact that their actual numerical arrangement does not correspond with this is, in general, at most a trifling inconvenience; and in the great majority of cases they should be left, physically speaking, as they were found; not only because past students may have used them (and taken references to them) in that order, but also for fear lest after all the classifier should be making a mistake.

Miscellanea

This is a useful term but dangerous if used carelessly. The Committee would remark that in almost any large assembly of Archives, and particularly in important Private Collections, there will be found some documents which have no obvious connexion with the activities of the particular Administration or Organization which gave rise to the main body of documents. Such documents fall into two broad divisions. First some of them will be found, on closer examination, to have survived in their present location owing to some topographical or family connexion: a good example is provided by the *Muster* papers cited in illustration below[2] which may be found in a Private Collection either because they are private memoranda kept for his own use by some former member of the Family who was a Lord Lieutenant, or occupied some similar official post, or because, though they are really Official Papers, the person in question omitted to transfer them to

2. See Note 27.

an official Repository. The classification of such papers will depend upon a decision as between these two possibilities: but either as 'subsidiary' to the ordinary activities of the family, or as 'strays' from another collection to which cross-reference will be made, they can find a place. But when all such allowances have been made there remains the second division — that of Papers whose survival in their present position is apparently due to some unexplained accident and which have no traceable connexion with any other collections. To these documents, which are neither 'Subsidiaries' nor 'Strays' — and so far as possible to them only — the title of *Miscellanea* may be applied.

7. ARCHIVE GROUPS RESULTING FROM PUBLIC CENTRAL ADMINISTRATION

The first of the primary headings given above (*Public, Central*) need not be further sub-divided here. The boundaries of the various Groups of Archives within it, derived both from living and defunct Administrations, are already fixed and their character well-known from official publications.[3] It may be well, however, to remind readers that most large Government Departments maintain to a greater or less extent branches which function (and accumulate documents) locally; such as the Commands of the Army, the local Registries of the Supreme Court and the numerous local establishments of the Ministry of Health. These branches are strictly subordinated to the central offices, and their Archives (if they are ultimately preserved) become classes of the main *(Central)* group formed by the Department from which they depend. They are not to be confused with the independent and truly *Local* Administrations and Archives, which will be dealt with in the next section: any more than the Archives of British Consulates and Embassies (which are local branches of the Foreign Office) are to be confused with those of the Foreign Countries in which they are situated.

It may be convenient to add here a very brief note as to Departments of Central Administration whose Records are not deposited in the Public Record Office. These include

(a) something like thirty Departments of varying importance which, though they have accepted the 'Rules' of the Master of the Rolls, have

---

3.   See the official *Guide to the Public Records* by M.S. Giuseppi: also the *First Report* (pub. 1912) of the Royal Commission (1910) on Public Records; with the earlier authorities cited in both of these works. Mr. Giuseppi has further compiled for the Surrey Record Society (No. XXIV) a *Guide* which gives a good idea of the contents of the Public Record Office from the point of view of a Local Historian. See also *A Handbook to Kent Records* compiled by *Miss* Churchill for the Records Branch of the Kent Archaeological Society in the series of *Kent Records*, Vol, II., 1914.

not yet felt obliged by the age of their Records or the pressure on their space to make any transfer[4]: and

(b) a few Departments which, owing to peculiarities in their constitution, do not and possibly never will transfer custody of their Records. The most important of these are the India Office, the Land Registry, the Houses of Parliament, the Principal Probate Registry (controlling the Records of all ancient Courts of Probate) and the College of Arms.[5]

8. ARCHIVE GROUPS RESULTING FROM PUBLIC LOCAL ADMINISTRATION

(i) Counties and sub-divisions of the County.[6]

The most important persons or bodies controlling Local Administration in England have always been those whose activities covered a *County* Area; or, in the case of larger Counties, a part of such an Area equivalent in size to a smaller County. At the period when our earliest records begin the chief Local Official was the *Sheriff*, who had at his disposal in addition to his office staff

4. The most convenient Guide to existing Public Departments is the *Imperial Calendar*, published annually. As to the Records of those which do not deposit in the Public Record Office, see the *Second Report* (pub. 1914) of the Royal Commission (1910) on Public Records; and the numerous other authorities there cited. One or two Departments issue leaflets regarding their own Records; *e.g.*, the Ministry of Agriculture *(1934: Form 701/L.G., etc.)* and the Registrar General *(Regulations concerning Registrars . . . in the custody of the Registrar General)*.

    Certain Departments which have not yet deposited Records in the Public Record Office have accepted the Rules of the Master of the Rolls regarding the disposal of their Archives and have 'Schedules' for the destruction of those which are not deemed worthy of permanent preservation. These Schedules are printed in order to be laid before Parliament and those of a date before 1914 have been reprinted and issued as a volume (*Statutes, Rules and Schedules governing the Disposal of the Public Records: 1914*).

5. As to the India Office, see the publications of that Office, and particularly Sir W. Foster's *Guide to the India Office Records, 1600-1858:* as to Parliament, see the series of volumes of *Manuscripts of the House of Lords* begun by the Hist. MSS. Commission: as to Probate Records, see the official *Return of all Courts empowered to Grant Probate* (1845) and *Reports on Probate Registries* (1927); also G.W. Marshall's *Handbook to the Ancient Courts of Probate* (1895).

    The peculiar position of the India Office, Land Registry and Principal Probate Registry is due to the Statutes under which they were created. For the position of the College of Arms, see note 16 below.

6. The following works should be consulted for further details: the *Third Report* of the Royal Commission (1910) on Public Records and its appendices (1919): Surrey Record Society Publications, Vol. XXXII (*Guide to Records of Justices of the Peace*), and the works of Professor B.H. Putnam and other authorities there cited: Sidney and Beatrice Webb, *English Local Government* (1906-8), volumes which are specially valuable for their bibliographies; Hubert Hall, *Repertory of British Archives* (1920); G.H. Fowler, *Care of County Muniments* (1928); Helen M. Cam, *The Hundred and the Hundred Rolls* (1930); *Gladys Scott*

the machinery of the *County Court* and, below this, that of the *Hundreds* and *Tithings* and certain other less normal divisions which need not be particularized here. No official accumulation of the organized Archives which resulted from these activities is known to have survived, except in the case of certain of the lower divisions (Hundreds, etc) which were by privilege in private hands: but in recent years a number of accidental survivals of County Court Rolls and other Records which undoubtedly originated in a Sheriff's Office have been identified by Scholars among the accumulations of the Central Authorities, in Private Muniments and elsewhere: and it is necessary therefore to leave in any scheme of classification a place for these most important discoveries and for any others which may accrue.

Parallel to the activities of the Sheriff and also of great antiquity were those of the *Coroner*: of whose Archives the same is to be said as of those of the Sheriff.[7] The activities of the *Escheator* might perhaps have been placed here, but it seems proper to treat that office, so far as Archives are concerned, as a branch of the Central Administration rather than as an office of Local Government.[8]

During the later medieval period, and with increasing rapidity in and after the reigns of the Tudors, the control of Local Public Administration passed from the Sheriffs to the *Justices of the Peace*: who functioned mainly through *Quarter* and other Sessions, through the office machinery gradually created by the *Clerk of the Peace*, and below these partly through the old *County* machinery (described in the first paragraph of this section), but largely also through that of the Parish; which up to the Tudor period had been a purely Ecclesiastical unit. Two categories, therefore, of organized Archives which resulted from the activities of Local Public Administration are found surviving in increasing quantities from the sixteenth century onwards; the first in the offices of the Clerks of the Peace, and the second among the Archives of purely Ecclesiastical business in Parishes. Both these categories will be covered in more detail by later Numbers in this Series.

Thomson, *Lord Lieutenants in the Sixteenth Century* (1923); and Northamptonshire Record Society Publications, Vol. VII *The Montagu Musters Book.*

The Surrey Volume cited above gives (p. 34) a list of Counties from who *Sessions Records* Publications have been made; to this should now be added recent volumes for Oxfordshire, Staffordshire and Warwickshire.

Over 60 volumes from 18 Counties were shown, in the Exhibition of Publications issued by Local Authorities, at the Association's Conference in November, 1935.

7. The Coroners, though their Courts are 'of Record,' seem always to have taken the view that their Record-making was their personal concern: see Royal Commission (1910) on Public Records, *Second Report* (1914), Part II, p. 143, and the earlier Departmental Report there quoted.

8. The same applies to a number of other officials directly controlled by the Central Government, such as Collectors of Customs and other Taxes.

To the local activities mentioned in the preceding paragraph must be added in chronological sequence those of the Lord *Lieutenant,* an office first created in the sixteenth century but later united in one person with the older one of *Custos Rotulorum;* who was a senior member of the Commission of the Peace charged from an early date with the duty of ensuring the preservation of Sessions Records.

The Lieutenants were originally appointed to discharge certain functions which were previously undertaken by the Sheriffs and by various Commissioners of Array and Musters in connexion with the organization of the armed forces of the County. The not unimportant documentary remains of the earlier activities of Lords Lieutenant and their Deputies which have come to light in recent years have been accidental survivals, mostly among Family Muniments. The Clerks to the Lieutenancy have still charge of the ordinary administrative Archives of that Office[9]: but in more modern periods the Clerks of the Peace for the Counties have generally acted as Clerks to the Lieutenancy, and have consequently preserved the documents compiled by the latter among their own Archives. Under the Territorial and Reserve Forces Act[10] the Lords Lieutenant were made *ex officio* Presidents of the County (T.F.) Associations: but the purely military Records of these activities belong to the War Office.

The last stage in the history of *Public Administrations covering the whole County Area* was the transfer of most administrative (as opposed to judicial) activities from the Justices of the Peace to the *County Councils* created by the Act of 1888: in practice the offices of Clerk of the Peace and Clerk of the County Council are almost invariably combined in the same hands and the Archives are therefore in the same custody. Almost at the same time (by an Act of 1894[11]) subordinate administrative activities throughout the Counties passed also to new authorities in the shape of the (Civil) *Parish Councils or Meetings* and the *Urban* and *Rural District Councils.*

(ii.) Other Areas

It remains to mention three categories of Local Administration, which neither covered the whole County Area nor occurred with regularity throughout it; but whose activities have created, or may have created, Groups of Archives.

(a) The first of these is the category of Authorities having by privilege the independent exercise of functions elsewhere discharged through the

---

9. The duties of clerks of General Meetings of the Lieutenancy, in regard to the appointment of Deputy Lieutenants, are laid down in the Militia Act of 1882.
10. 7 Edward VII, c.9.
11. 56, 57 Victoria, c.73.

County machinery: chief among them being the *Boroughs*[12], specially privileged towns, which from the earliest times, discharged through their own Officials the duties performed elsewhere by the Officials and Courts of the County, and have accumulated Archives accordingly.

(b) The second category is that of the bodies grouped by Mr. and Mrs. Webb in their History of Local Administration[13] as *Statutory Authorities;* which functioned for the performance of Social Services over special areas devised for the purpose. Such for instance, were the *Sewers Commissions* whose modern activities begin in 1532, the voluntary *Unions of Parishes* for Poor Law Administration which were first sanctioned in 1782, and the *Commissions for the Improvement of Towns* established by special Acts of Parliament in the late 18th and the 19th centuries[14]

(c) Finally, as part of that general movement for national reform in many directions which produced the Reform Act of 1832, there were created by legislation certain administrative bodies of which some were partially and some wholly elective; whose area of work might cover a parish or some other specified district not necessarily lying within a single County. Such were the *Boards of Guardians* created by the Poor Law Act of 1834, the *Highway Boards* and *Districts* which came into being under the Acts of 1835 and 1862, and the *School Boards* set up in 1870. Some of these produced large quantities of Archives before their functions were transferred by statute to County Councils in 1888, 1902 and 1925, or to District Councils in 1894.

9. ARCHIVE GROUPS RESULTING FROM SEMI-PUBLIC ADMINISTRATION[15]

It is not always easy to distinguish the Administrations and Archives figuring under this heading from those described at the end of the previous Section

12. For further details and information, see Adolphus Ballard and James Tait, *British Borough Charters* (1913, 1923); Charles Gross, *Bibliography of British Municipal History* (1897); Hubert Hall, *Repertory of British Archives* (1920). The last-named compiles (p. 257) from seven Reports of Royal Commissions and Committees (including the two Commissions on Municipal Corporations) a list of nearly 400 'Municipal and Reputed Boroughs.'
    Nearly 120 volumes from the Records of 40 Cities and Boroughs were shewn, in the Exhibition of Publications by Local Authorities, at the Association's Conference in November, 1935.
13. Cited above, note 6.
14. Hall (*op. cit.*) gives (p. 103) a 'Select List' of 'Statutory Authorities and Trusts' of this kind. The problem of the location and preservation of their Archives has given rise to serious anxiety (see the pamphlet on Poor Law Records published by the British Record Society) and was the subject of discussion at the Conference of the Association in November, 1935.
15. There is no general Authority for the Archives described under this heading but valuable indications will be found in H. Hall, *Repertory of British Archives* (already cited) and in the *Third Report* of the Royal Commission (1910) on Public Records. The Archives of a certain

under the title of *Statutory Authorities*: there is even occasionally a possibility of confusion as between *Semi-Public* Institutions and some of the more independent units of *Local or Central Public Administration*[16]

The point of differentiation (as has already been suggested) is that in the case of the bodies now to be described the private satisfaction, advantage or profit of individuals is the prime consideration which brings them into existence: the public duties which they undertake (and the privileges consequently accorded to them) are incidental to this, their original and main purpose.

There is a similar possibility of difficulty in distinguishing between these *Semi-Public* bodies (which might equally well be called *Semi-Private*) and the *purely Private* concerns to be described in the next Section: it is not always easy to say that a commercial Company, or other private organization, has absolutely no public functions; and in fact the tendency of modern legislation is to give to certain types of originally private concerns (Banks, for instance, Insurance Companies and Friendly Societies) something of the character of Public Servants.

This Committee being charged with the duty of preparing a Scheme of Classification (necessarily a matter of definite divisions) can only call attention to the fact that at either end of the category now under discussion are to be found border-line cases — Institutions, and corresponding Archive Groups, which might figure almost equally well under either of two Headings. The Committee would also make it clear that it has attempted only a description, not an enumeration, of the Bodies now to be treated: those specifically mentioned below are named solely for the purpose of illustration.

Semi-Public Institutions then, and their Archives, may be described within four divisions.

(i.) Statutory and Chartered Bodies

These may again be sub-divided according as they are

(a) *National* in the scope of their work; or
(b) *Local*.

(a) will include obviously such Institutions as the *Bank of England, Lloyd's*

number of the older Institutions have been described separately in *Reports* of the Historical MSS. Commission (see the List of Owners upon whose Collections Reports have been issued in that Commission's *Nineteenth Report*). Other works dealing in detail with the Archives of particular Institutions are in general too detailed to be cited here; but one or two covering collectively a number of such bodies will be noted below; with a few outstanding examples of publications of a more individual kind.

16.   An extreme example of this is furnished by the College of Arms, which is always reckoned a Department of Public Central Administration and has been so described in section 7 above: the College does undoubtedly occupy this position but it is also a chartered body dating from the fourteenth century and still enjoying certain rights as a private institution.

Corporation Exchange and Registry; and *Trinity House*. Under (b) will come all Authorities administering *Docks and Ports*, and *Public Utility Companies or Trusts*, dealing with Roads, Transport, the Supply of Light or Water and similar Public Services over dates which range form the 16th or 17th Century to the present day. It is unnecessary to describe the numbers of Companies of this kind which have come into existence in modern times. The older onew, with their Archives, have sometimes been absorbed by later concerns or even by Public Authorities.[17]

(ii.) Endowed Institutions.[18]

These include *Colleges and Universities*; *Schools; Hospitals;* and *Charities* of all kinds. As nearly all have at some time held, and may still hold, landed property they very frequently have at least collections of Deeds and other documents relating to the administration of their Estates: and these do not, of course, differ in character from the similar collections in private hands to be described below. Apart from such documents the smaller Endowments will sometimes be found to possess little beyond their Foundation Charter: but in a surprisingly large number of cases Minutes, Registers and other working Records survive in addition. It may be remarked also that there will be found to be a very large number of Endowments (especially the Educational ones and Hospitals) which are either themselves of medieval foundation or have incorporated older institutions; and that their Muniments are sometimes correspondingly ancient.

(iii.) Learned and Professional Societies and Corporations

Outstanding examples in this division are, of course, the four *Inns of Court*, the *Law Society*, and the *General Medical Council:* all being bodies which undertake the organization and control of the Professions with which they

17. For example the *Metropolitan Water Board* is the modern representative of, *inter alia*, the *New River Company* founded in 1608: and the Archives of defunct *Turnpike Trusts* of the eighteenth and nineteenth centuries have sometimes passed, with the Roads, to modern Local Authorities.

18. The best means of information as to existing institutions of this kind is to be found in the *Reports* published by the Charity Commissioners from 1819 to 1840. A *Guide to the Records of . . . Endowed Institutions*, published by the Surrey Record Society (No. XXXI.) may be useful as an indication of the survivals to be expected: they are remarkably numerous (some 60 collections, large and small) for what is probably a poor County in this respect. The important Muniments of Cambridge and Oxford Colleges have been the subject of a number of Reports by the Historical MSS. Commission, as well as more individual publications, and the volumes of *Alumni* published at Cambridge give remarkable evidence of what may come out of University and College Registers. Among Schools Winchester College, with a fourteenth Century Muniment Room, is not perhaps to be quoted as typical; but there must be a number with collections almost or quite as extensive as those (for example) at *Alleyn's College of God's Gift at Dulwich* catalogued by G.F. Warner (1881) and F.R. Bickley (1903), though there is nothing in the nature of a general Guide to them.

are concerned. Beside these may be set a number of other Bodies having a similar qualification, in that membership of them is or has been recognised as conferring a professional status.[19]

(iv.) The City Companies of London and similar Bodies[20]

These partake to a varying extent of some or all of the characteristics mentioned in connexion with the three previous divisions: they sometimes discharge public functions; they not infrequently regulate the organisation of their Trade or Profession; and they often have large endowments which they use for Charitable or Educational purposes: but it has seemed better to give them here a separate division. The London Companies are well known but the existence and importance of similar institutions elsewhere is not, unfortunately, a matter upon which much information is at present available.

10. ARCHIVE GROUPS RESULTING FROM THE CONDUCT OF PRIVATE AFFAIRS

It is not possible at present even to guess at the number of existing sets of Archives which come under this Heading. The Private Institution which was most productive of Records in the medieval period was the Manor, and the Master of the Rolls' Register of Manors now numbers 18,000: how many more will be added to this total and from how many of them Archives will ultimately be found to have survived it is impossible to predict; but certainly the number of Archive series will be extremely large.[21] When we come to later times and the general survival of Family Papers of a more obvious kind it is even more difficult to estimate quantities: and supposing that the

19. The very important early Records of the Inns of Court, dating from the fifteenth and sixteenth centuries, are well known: a number of volumes having been published by all four Inns. Among the most valuable Records of Bodies of this kind are naturally the Registers of their Members: but at present little information is available as to the existence and extent of these apart from those of the Inns and a few others.

20. An enumeration of the 12 'Great' and 66 other Companies in London may be found in Whitaker's Almanac and similar books of reference. The *Report* (1884) of the Royal Commission on the Livery Companies is the best general account of their History, and gives some idea of their Archives. Individual publications based on, or describing, particular Collections, are too numerous to be cited here, but volumes published by the Carpenters', Cutlers', Drapers', Grocers', Skinners' and Weavers' Companies during the last fifty years, and those produced by the Bibliographical Society from the Records of the Stationers' Company, and by Sir Ambrose Heal from those of the Goldsmiths, may perhaps be mentioned as particularly notable.

21. In one County in which a known Series of Court Rolls have been listed the number reached 200 (see Surrey Record Society, No XXVIII): and Surrey is probably one of the poorer Counties in this respect.

Historical MSS. Commission looks forward to covering eventually all Private Collections of importance in this Country, it is probably true to say that no one can yet make more than the most distant guess at the proportion of its whole task which is represented by the 180 odd volumes it has so far published.[22]

It is also practically impossible to divide up this mass of Private Records (as has been done in the present Report for other Categories of Archives) on the basis of a Classification of the authorities which produced them: because individuals, and even Institutions, often act in a dual capacity, both public and private. Thus a Manor (to take again that example) may be owned and administered by a private person or a Corporation, by a Cathedral Church, a House of Religious or (as sometimes happens) an Official or Department of the Central Government: the only effect of this variety of ownership upon the documents is that what are essentially Private Archives may be found in the Official Collections of all the Institutions so far described in this Report; and that sometimes, since more than one kind of business may be done by a single Official or a single piece of Office machinery, they may survive to us in combination with others of a totally different kind in a single series. For instance, the Lord who owns a Hundred Court may conduct it by means of the same Official who conducts his purely private Court Baron; and the Records of the two may be either kept singly or inextricably mixed: or, to take a more modern example, a Public Official may mingle his public with his private correspondence in a single letter book.

For the purpose of Classification, however (as distinct from Arrangement), all activities and Archives which are essentially private in origin may properly be treated together under the present Heading. The Committee proposes to distinguish six broad divisions.

(i.)   Archives resulting from *Manorial Administration and the Ownership of Land:*

(ii.)   Archives resulting from *Household Administration:*

(iii.)   *Personal Correspondence* and Papers connected with *Family and Social Relations:*

(iv.)   Documents resulting from the *Tenure of Office in a public or semi-public capacity:*

(v.)   Archives resulting from *Commerce and the Conduct of Business:* and

(vi.)   Documents resulting from the organization of *Artistic, Literary, Scientific or Social pursuits* and of Philanthropic and other *Public Work* by Private Bodies: including the Proceedings etc. of Learned Societies.

In a later Section the Committee will attempt a more detailed internal classification of some of these. Without anticipating this it offers here the following brief comments.

(i.)   will obviously be subdivided immediately (if only to conform with the accepted

---

22.   The Commission, first appointed in 1869, has dealt with about 300 Collections up to date, some 80 being treated in detail: for the Collections examined see its *Nineteenth Report.*

definition[23] of 'Manorial') between *Manorial Records* proper and *Muniments of Title*. The former may date from so early as the first half of the thirteenth century: the latter not infrequently go back a century further.[24]

(ii.) *Household Records* regularly made (apart, that is, from stray Memoranda) are exceedingly scarce for the Medieval period: in fact very few Collections are known though there is one large survival from the fourteenth century.[25] It is the more desirable to locate even fragmentary remains.

(iii.) *Family Papers* which again (save for accidental and occasional survivals) can hardly be said to begin till the late fifteenth century[26] also lend themselves readily (so soon as they become plentiful) to a first subdivision: classes of *Correspondence* and *Documents connected with Legal Business* separating themselves almost automatically from more miscellaneous survivals.

(iv.) *Official Documents* will need to be distinguished carefully into two categories: for on the one hand we have from quite an early date the possibility of documents which are purely official, and ought to have been officially preserved, surviving in the family of a person who had held the office in question[27]; and on the other hand we find increasingly in family papers from the sixteenth century onwards documents which were genuinely the private property of the person who placed them there, but which resulted from his official work rather than his private business.[28]

(v.) Here again regular survivals hardly begin till after the fifteenth century. Collections of *Commercial Records*[29] become considerable only in comparatively modern times though there are outstanding examples dating from the seventeenth century.[30]

(vi.) Learned and other Societies, now very numerous (works of reference show some hundreds), are mostly of comparatively modern date; though probably in provincial

23. Under the Amendment (1924) to Lord Birkenhead's Act of 1922.
24. On the subject of the earliest known Manorial Records see F.W. Maitland's Introduction to the Selden's Society's volume of *Select Pleas in Manorial and other Seignorial Courts* (1888).
25. The *Clare Household* Accounts now preserved in the Public Record Office.
26. The *Paston*, *Cely* and *Stonor Papers* are the best known examples: the last two contain also fragmentary remains (not all yet published) of Household and Commercial Accounts.
27. For example two of the few known Records of Medieval County Courts have survived in the family collections of the persons who occupied the offices of Sheriff and Coroner in the Counties in question; see English Historical Review XLIII, p. 21; *Cambridge Historical Journal* I, p. 103; and the *Rolls from the Office of the Sheriff* . . . published by the Bedfordshire Historical Records Society.
28. Good examples are supplied by a number of the Tudor Muster Papers which have survived in the families of Lords Lieutenant of the period. See the volumes of such Records published by the Northamptonshire and Surrey Record Societies.
29. They are the special concern of a body affiliated to the British Records Association, the Council for the Preservation of Business Archives; which has already made considerable progress in the locating and listing of such Archives and may be able presently, as a result, to produce a more elaborate classification than can here be attempted.
30. Such are certain London Banks (e.g. that of Messrs. Hoare), a few Commercial Houses (for example Messrs. Twining) and one or two of the great Trading Companies such as the Hudson's Bay Company: with others now defunct or incorporated in later bodies, though their Archives have survived, as (for example) have those of the African, Levant and other Companies among the Public Records.

towns there may be considerable survivals from the eighteenth century. A few in London — the Royal Society, for example — date from the previous century.[31]

Finally the Committee would repeat the warning already given as to border-line cases lying between the *Semi-Public* and *Private* divisions (this relates particularly to divisions (v) and (vi) above); and would emphasize the necessity for cross-reference in such circumstances. Similarly it will be clear from the observations made in regard to division (iv) above that cross reference will also be necessary from time to time from *Private* to series of *Public Local Archives*. On the other hand it is to be remembered that every category of Administration previously mentioned, *Central, Local* and *Semi-Public*, and the *Ecclesiastical* Administrations which will be described below, may on occasion act in a *Private* capacity (for instance in that of Lord of a Manor) and accumulate Archives which will be essentially *Private* in character and should be classified as such.[32]

11. ARCHIVE GROUPS RESULTING FROM ECCLESIASTICAL ADMINISTRATION

It will be apparent from the outset that this title must include Archives of Authorities differing very widely in every respect of functions, powers and antiquity. A first division may therefore not improperly be made between those whose roots and Archives in this country go back behind the Reformation of the sixteenth century and those which are of post-Reformation and recent establishment. Under the first division will be placed the Church, *Ecclesia Anglicana*,[33] round and under which can be grouped all those Ecclesiastical and Religious Bodies which functioned in the pre-Reformation period. Under the second will come all Ecclesiastical Authorities other than the Church of England.

To these two divisions should be added two others, *Statutory Bodies* and *Religious Societies*; though the first will be dealt with to a certain extent by way of cross-reference to other headings. Under the second will be included the Society for the Propagation of the Gospel in Foreign Parts, the Society for the Promotion of Christian Knowledge, and other Bodies of a similar nature. We thus have as *Secondary Divisions* under the Main Heading which stands as title to this Section.

31. A Society of Antiquaries was founded so early as 1572 by Archbishop Parker, but was discontinued in 1604.
32. An obvious example is supplied by the enormous mass of Manorial Records now in the Public Record Office: which should be incorporated with those in Private hands in any complete list of Manorial Records.
33. For justification of the use of this title see discussion by Z.N. Brooke in *The English Church and the Papacy* (Cambridge: 1931).

(i.)   *Ecclesia Anglicana;*
(ii.)   *Ecclesiastical Authorities other than the Church of England;*
(iii.)   *Statutory Bodies concerned with Ecclesiastical Matters* and
(iv.)   *Religious Societies.*

Taking these Secondary Divisions the Report may now proceed to a further analysis or subdivision; setting out under each the varieties of Administration belonging to it, with the Archive Groups, or series of Archive Groups, which they produce.

(i.) Ecclesia Anglicana

The Church has in the past presented the dual aspect of a Temporal Magnate, with secular estates and affairs to manage, and a Spiritual Authority with a corresponding jurisdiction over some sides of the life of the Country. Both these activities produced Records: but while those on the Spiritual side were of a judicial and administrative character, and by their nature quite distinct from those of all the Administrations with which this Report has so far dealt, those resulting from Temporal activities did not differ to any important extent from the series already described in the Section above devoted to Private Administration and Archives. Moreover temporal activities of this kind, and the resultant Archives, have for the most part passed away from the Church: the Muniments of Religious Communities which have been dissolved have perished or been scattered or passed to the new owners of Church property: and following the re-arrangement of Diocesan Areas and Episcopal Incomes, and the re-organization of Cathedral and Collegiate Churches, consequent on the recommendations made by the Church Inquiry Commission of 1835-6, the remaining temporal possessions of the Church, with the Archives belonging to them have in most cases[34] been transferred to a Statutory body — the Ecclesiastical Commission set up in 1836 — and come under an earlier heading in this Report.[35]

Although therefore, it is true that the two functions of the Church were sometimes exercised through a single organization, with the result that the Records may be inextricably mingled in a single series, the present Section must be taken to deal almost exclusively with the Archives of spiritual activities; and these may be considered under the natural divisions of purely Ecclesiastical Administration.[36] We shall thus have as our first three subdivisions.

34.   There are some exceptions among capitular Authorities.
35.   See a note under the heading *(iii.) Statutory Bodies* below.
36.   For a general description of the making of Ecclesiastical Records see the work under that title by Dr. Claude Jenkins, in S.P.C.K. *Helps for Students of History* No 18; see also an analysis and classification of these Records in Hubert Hall's *Repertory of British Archives* (1920) pp. 134-144. The Reports of the various Commissions appointed in the nineteenth and twentieth centuries (1800, 1833, 1837, 1883, and 1912-1919) give the series of

(a) *Provincial Archives*[37]

(b) *Diocesan Archives*[38]

(c) *Archidiaconal Archives*[39]

These are normally in charge of their respective Registrars; but quite numerous exceptions can be found where, for example, the Diocesan collection is preserved partly in the Palace and partly by the Diocesan Registrar: and the Archidiaconal for purposes of convenience may be housed with the Episcopal Records or even deposited in the Muniment room of some Local Authority or Public Library. Also under the Church Measure of 1929 (sect. 12) some Diocesan Record Offices, independant of the Registrar, have now been set up.

(d) Of a similar nature to Archidiaconal Archives are those which relate to Deaneries of *Peculiar* or (as they were more often termed in the medieval period) *Immediate Jurisdiction:* for the authority wielded by the Deans over these districts included juridical, testamentary and visitational powers. Peculiar Jurisdictions arose when the Church or Rural Deanery concerned was exempt from the authority of the Ordinary or Bishop in whose Diocese it lay; being either a Royal Peculiar (as in the case of a Chapel exempt from any jurisdiction save that of the Sovereign) or one subject to the jurisdiction of

documents in different custodies so far as they were listed and included in returns then made. That of 1883 on the Ecclesiastical Courts contains an *Historical Appendix* by Bishop Stubbs; which will be found of considerable value, though the researches of later writers on certain points may necessitate a modification of some of his statements.

37.   i.e. those of Canterbury and York; and since June, 1920, the Province of Wales, formed from the four Welsh dioceses previously in the Province of Canterbury: see G.K.A. Bell, *Randall Davidson, Archbishop of Canterbury (1935)*, chapter lx.

38.   Before the Reformation there were in all 22 Dioceses in the two Provinces, nineteen (including Canterbury) in the Province of Canterbury, and three with York in the Province of York. Three more were created in the sixteenth century for the Southern and one for the Northern Province. Many more have been added in the course of the nineteenth and twentieth centuries: see the current edition of Crockford.
On the subject of *Bishops' Registers* see R.C. Fowler in No. 1 of the S.P.C.K. series already cited and the publications of the Canterbury and York Society. A scheme constructed to cover Oxford Diocesan Records in the Bodleian Library was printed in the *Bulletin* of the Institute of Historical Research in June 1930 (Vol. VIII, p. 14). An Inventory of the Books and Papers preserved in the Diocesan Registry at Durham has been published in the *Proceedings* of the Society of Antiquaries of Newcastle-on-Tyne, 3rd Series, Vol. V, p. 167.

39.   The number of Archdeacons in a Diocese varies considerably, but two or three are usual numbers. A single Registrar may often be found acting for more than one Archdeaconry. Lists of the Documents relating to the Archdeaconry of Leicester (*Chronicle of Convocation*, New Series, Vol. XXIII, 1906. No. 403: Appendix to Report on the Collection and Custody of Local Ecclesiastical Records), and to the Archdeaconry of Huntingdon (in Vol. IV. of *Proceedings* of the Cambridgeshire and Huntingdonshire Archaeological Society (1930) pp. 165-208) are valuable, though the arrangement is under subjects and not according to Administrative structure.

the Bishop of another Diocese or to that of the Archbishop of the Province, or (as happened more particularly in the case of Churches and Parishes) to that of a Dean, Chapter or Prebendary. Peculiars were practically abolished by various legislative Acts of the nineteenth century[40] and the districts covered by them came again under the jurisdiction of the Dioceses within which they lay. The Archives in so far as they have survived should be classed separately (though presumably they now come under Diocesan control) and make here a fourth sub-division. Like those of Archdeacons they may be found in Repositories of various kinds and even in private custody.

It will be convenient to interpolate at this point a note that certain elements of Spiritual jurisdiction, as well as the control over Temporalities, have passed from the Church in post-Reformation times. The most notable example is furnished by *Testamentary Jurisdiction* which (with all the Archives of the Ancient Courts of Probate) has passed[41] into the control of a division of the High Court of Judicature: which has taken over also control in Matrimonial cases. As has been remarked already[42] the Archives involved are best treated under the Administrative division to which they now belong and may be mentioned here only by way of cross-reference from the four divisions of *Ecclesia Anglicana* set out above; all of which at one time exercised jurisdiction in these matters.

(e) In any scheme of classification a place must be left for the possibility of Archives belonging to the office of *Rural Dean*.[43] It was, however, a position of varying importance at different dates; and does not seem to have produced Archives as a general rule; although from time to time in the medieval period glimpses of the activities of Rural Deans are obtained. It may quite well be that if Archives existed and have survived at all they will be found among Archdeaconry Records. The functions of the Rural Deans appear to have suffered a decline for some centuries, but the office was re-invigorated in the nineteenth century: even now, however, it does not appear to produce regular Records.[44]

---

40. In particular 10 and 11 Vic. c. 98. For other relevant Acts see R. Phillimore, *Ecclesiastical Law of the Church of England* (ed. 1895) p. 215.
41. It should be noted that the transfer of Archives was not always very carefully supervised: so that Records of Ecclesiastical Jurisdictions have nothing to do with Probate or Admimistration sometimes passed, in error, along with the 'Probate' Records.
42. Above p.9.
43. W. Dansey, *Horae Decanicae Rurales* (2nd ed., Rivington, 1844) remains the quarry from which all subsequent writers on this subject have in the main derived their material.
44. Notes from a valuable modern Ruridecanal Register covering a considerable period (1829 to 1905) were published in 1912 in *Surrey Archaeological Collections*, XXV, p.116; it was then in the custody of the Rural Dean for the time being. It would be interesting to know how far similar Records exist elsewhere.

(f) We come next to *Parochial Archives*[45]: and following these account must be taken of the Archives of

(g) *Capitular Bodies* (Deans and Chapters of Cathedral foundations);[46] some having collections of Monastic origin; and

(h) the Archives, when they can be reconstituted, of *Monastic Houses*[47] of pre-Reformation date which no longer exist in original custody.

Sub-divisions of *Ecclesia Anglicana* will therefore tabulate as follows.

(a) *Provincial;*

(b) *Diocesan;*

(c) *Archidiaconal;*

(d) *Peculiars* or *Immediate Jurisdictions;*

(e) *Ruridecanal;*

(f) *Parochial;*

(g) *Capitular;* and

(h) *Monastic:*

(d) and (h) figuring generally by way of cross-reference to other Archive Groups, not necessarily Ecclesiastical.

(ii.) Ecclesiastical Authorities other than the
Church of England
General Note

The Committee has been largely indebted to Archivists, Librarians and others, connected with the various Communities mentioned under the present heading, who have been good enough to answer letters addressed to them in this connexion: their names will be given in footnotes at the appropriate places.

The information thus collected, even when reduced to the most abbreviated dimensions, fills so considerable a space in comparison with earlier

---

45.   At the time of the Census of 1831 there were about 11,000 Parishes: the number has been considerably augmented since that date.

    On Parish Records see A. Hamilton Thompson (S.P.C.K. *Helps* No. 15). A.M. Burke, *Key to the Ancient Parish Registers in England and Wales* (1908) is also useful: publications of such Registers are too numerous to be cited; at the Association's Conference in 1934 fifty recent volumes of this kind were shewn.

46.   The only general guide to the Archives of individual *Deans and Chapters* is to be found in various Reports of the Historical MSS. Commission. In the case of certain Chapters more detailed work has been published; but Lists and Summaries are badly needed.

47.   The best available List of Monastic Houses in England is that published in Gasquet's *English Monastic Life*, though it needs revision; an elaborate work on surviving cartularies of Religious Houses was planned by the 'Migration of MSS.' Committee of the Institute of Historical Research, but has been (it must be hoped only temporarily) abandoned.

sections of this Report (where Readers who desire more detail can be referred in a brief footnote to published works) that the Committee has thought it best to reserve it for issue in a separate Report which will appear simultaneously with the present publication.

The Bodies in regard to which the Committee has been able to obtain information will be treated in the following order.

(a) *English Roman Catholics* (i.e., for the period subsequent to the withdrawal of the English Church from Papal Jurisdiction);

(b) to (i) *English and Welsh Nonconformist Bodies*, mostly incorporating communities which seceded from the Church of England in the seventeenth and eighteenth centuries and including *the Baptist Union, the Calvinistic Methodist or Presbyterian Church of Wales, the Methodist Church, the Congregational Union, the General Assembly of Unitarian and Free Christian Churches, the Society of Friends* and *the Countess of Huntingdon's Connexion;*

(j) *The Moravian Church in England*, with Records dating from the mid-eighteenth century.

(k) and (l) *Foreign Protestant Refugee Churches (Dutch and French)* dating from the sixteenth century;

(m) *Communities of the Orthodox Greek Church in England*;

(n) *Anglo-Jewry*, since the Resettlement in the seventeenth century.

There is, however, one category of Records which is common to nearly all the Archive Groups just mentioned: and this may best be dealt with in a single collective statement before any detailed description of individual Groups is attempted.

Registers of Births or Baptisms, Deaths or Burials, and Marriages

In 1838 a Commission, originally appointed by William IV. and renewed by Queen Victoria, published its Report on the 'State, Custody and Authenticity' of the Records described above in England and Wales, other than the Parochial Registers. It had had transmitted to it 'about 7000 Registers from 3630 religious congregations' (the Roman Catholics and the Jews declined) and it recommended that these should be kept together under the care of the Registrar General. In 145 pages of Appendices it set out the detailed results of its inquiries in regard to French and other Foreign Protestants, the Three Denominations (Baptists, Presbyterians and Independents), Wesleyan Methodists, Methodists (New Connexion), Primitive

Methodists, Bible Christians,[48] Inghamites,[49] Moravians, Lady Huntingdon's Connexion, Calvinistic Methodists, Swedenborgians, and the Society of Friends. A further Report under practically the same Title[50] published in 1858 by another Commission records the transmission of 292 more Registers from the same bodies, the Roman Catholics and Jews being still unable to agree to deposit.

A leaflet issued by the Registrar General's Office under the title 'Registers and Records of which the Originals or Certified Copies are deposited in the Custody of the Registrar General' summarises in one of its sections the result of the above Reports. It also indicates that there may have been some deposits since these Reports were made. This Leaflet is reprinted in the *Second Report* (1914) of the Royal Commission (1910) on Public Records.[51]

Other Churches and Religious Denominations not of English origin, whether Catholic, Orthodox, Protestant or non-Christian may be found established from time to time; and it would probably be correct to say that in most cases such Archives as they may have accumulated in England would be in this country in the custody of the acting head of the particular body, to whom enquiries on the subject should be addressed. This would be the procedure for example in the case of the old Catholic Church (now centred at Utrecht) which had no following in England before the early years of the twentieth century, and for the British Conference of Seventh Day Adventists, whose main organisation is in the United States.

(iii). Statutory Bodies concerned with Ecclesiastical Matters

These correspond with the bodies similarly named which in the previous (Civil) portion of this Report have been treated under the *Public Local* heading. Of the five Authorities to be mentioned three — the *Ecclesiastical Commission* (dating from 1836), the *Welsh Church Commission* (dating from 1914) and the *Governors and Treasurer of Queen Anne's Bounty* which took over in 1837 the work of the *First Fruits* Department of the Exchequer — rank as Public Departments. The remaining two are the *Representative Body of the Church in Wales*, which came into existence as a result of the Welsh Church Disestablishment Acts of 1914 and 1919, and the *National Assembly of the Church of England* constituted in 1919.

48.   The Bible Christians, according to the Commission's Report, had some thirty communities in Cornwall, Devonshire, and the Southern Counties in the early nineteenth century.
49.   The Inghamites at this time had apparently seven communities dating from the eighteenth and early nineteenth centuries in Lancashire, Yorkshire and Nottinghamshire.
50.   The Commissioners are described as reporting on 'Certain Non-Parochial Registers of Records . . .'.
51.   Part ii, p. 297.

Concerning all these a fuller account is given in the Separate Report mentioned in the previous section, to be issued simultaneously with the present publication.

(iv.) *Religious Societies*

Continuing the parallel previously instituted between *Ecclesiastical* and *Civil* Administration and Archives the Committee would remark that to treat separately the Archives the Committee would remark that to treat separately the Archives of Private Individuals which have a specially Ecclesiastical or Religious significance is quite impossible. Private Societies and organisations having as their object the prosecution of some Ecclesiastical or Religious aim are more readily separated: but even here the subject can only be treated very broadly and only the most obviously outstanding bodies can be selected for mention.

In the separate Report already mentioned the Committee has accumulated some information concerning the Archives of six bodies which may be considered as specially important and typical — namely, *the Society for Promoting Christian Knowledge, the Society for the Propagation of the Gospel in Foreign Parts,*[52] *the Church Missionary Society, the British and Foreign Bible Society, the London Missionary Society* and *the Salvation Army.*

12. DOCUMENTS OF HISTORICAL INTEREST ARTIFICIALLY COLLECTED[53]

There is no need to describe here the Public and Private Libraries, Museums and Repositories in which such collections as these are found: nor are the documents which compose them in many cases susceptible of any scheme of classification in the sense in which that word has been used in the present Report. Though in origin Archives, the *Deeds* and other documents brought together in this way have lost that character through separation from the connexion in which they were originally preserved: their importance now lies

52. In S.P.G. *World Wide Series No 2* Mr John W. Lydekker has printed a brief but very interesting account — the first fruits of the Society's recently organised work upon its Archives — of the new Muniment Room; with an appreciation of the Records stored there, particularly the Colonial Sections.

53. No attempt can be made here to cite individual works in which such collections are described; though reference may perhaps be made, exceptionally, to the useful summaries, relating to collections in the Bodleian Library, the British Museum and the Cambridge University Library, published in S.P.C.K. *Helps for Students of History* (Numbers 31, 43 and 46) and to the *List of Unpublished Catalogues, Hand-Lists and Schedules of Manuscripts, Documents, etc.,* published by the National Library of Wales. Mention may also be made, by anticipation, of the Bibliography of *Printed Catalogues of Collections of Manuscripts in Great Britain* projected by Mr. Seymour de Ricci under the auspices of the Institute of Historical Research.

in their individual value; and systems for their arrangement are a matter purely of the convenience of Students. Fortunately, however, Libraries and Museums have become increasingly aware in recent years of the collective value of sets of documents taken over from their original owners as a whole. In such cases, and even in cases where some considerable proportion of an original whole has been transferred as it stood to a public Collection, the Archive Group may, and should, be reconstituted: the Curator or Librarian becomes in effect the Custodian: and the documents take their place as Private, Semi-Public and even Public or Ecclesiastical Archives within the divisions already described in the earlier Sections of this Report.

The Committee would use this opportunity of urging that the policy of taking over integral sets of Documents and preserving them in their original grouping (even though some may be intrinsically uninteresting to the Collector) should be adopted in every possible instance. It welcomes the fact that most of the Depositories recognised by the Master of the Rolls for the custody of Manorial Documents have not confined their attention to Manorial Records within the meaning of the Act but are prepared also to give a safe home to the connected Muniments of Title which are often in even greater danger. But the principle enunciated here does not relate solely to documents having to do with the tenure of land: it applies to all categories of Archives. *In a collection of Letters, for example, those of the unimportant persons (individually negligible) form not infrequently, if preserved in their original setting as part of a single unit, a background which enormously enhances the value and aids in the interpretation of the more obviously important and interesting pieces.*

The Study of English Seals: Illustrated Chiefly From Examples in the Public Record Office

INTRODUCTORY

A very large amount of work has now been done upon English Seals: one has only to look through the *Proceedings* of any Archaeological Society — the *Journal*, for example, of the British Archaeological Association — to see that English Sigillography has had, if not as large a share as the enthusiast would like, at least some considerable proportion of the attentions of English Antiquaries during the last fifty years and more. There are outstanding names — for example, those of Henry Laing,[1] W. de Gray Birch,[2] the brothers Wyon,[3] Sir William St. John Hope[4] and (happily still labouring in this field) Mr Hunter Blair[5] — to which very substantial contributions must be credited: and the number of writers who have published notes or articles upon this or that small point runs into hundreds.[6] At the same time one has to record the facts that no single large work[7] has yet been published in

1. *Descriptive Catalogue of Impressions from Ancient Scottish Seals* . . . Edinburgh 1850, 1866.
2. Editor of the *Catalogue of Seals in the Department of Manuscripts* published by the British Museum (1887, etc.): he published also a *History of Scottish Seals* . . . (Sterling, 1907).
3. A.B. and Allan Wyon, *The Great Seals of England* . . . 1887: and a number of articles in the British Archaeological Association *Journal* and elsewhere.
4. Between 1885 and 1917 he wrote on the Seals of *Cambridge Colleges*, the Seals of *English Bishops*, the Seals of *Archdeacons* and the Seals of *Kings of Arms and Heralds;*on *Seals of the Statute Merchant*, on the *Municipal Seals of England and Wales* in general and on the individual Seals of various *Cities and Boroughs* in particular; on Great Seals of *Stephen* and *Henry* III; and on a number of other individual Seals of special interest: see the *Bibliography* of his works published with an Introductory Memoir by A. Hamilton Thompson in 1929.
5. See particularly his work on Durham Seals in *Archaeologia Aeliana*, 3rd Series, Vols. VII, VIII, IX, XI, XII and XIII and 4th Series I: and in *Archaeologia*, Vols. LXXII and LXXVII.
6. The Card Index in the Library of the Society of Antiquaries of books and articles on the subject of Seals numbers some 1,500 Cards; of which about 900 relate to English Seals or Matrices.
7. As a small sketch should be mentioned Mr. H.S. Kingsford's useful work in S.P.C.K. *Helps for Students of History*, No. 30.

English in which every aspect of the study receives due attention; that there is no adequate bibliography of the extremely scattered printed sources of a later date than 1866;[8] that detailed descriptions of some of the most obviously important series — such, for instance, as the numerous series of Royal Seals[9] — either need revision or (more often) do not exist; and that in most cases the preponderant interest of the herald, the genealogist, the artist and the local historian in the design and wording of Seals has been allowed rather to dwarf, if not to exclude, humbler but still important studies such as those of the materials of surviving seal impressions, the methods used for affixing them to documents, and in general their Administrative employment and significance.[10]

It is hardly necessary to say that the present article makes no attempt to fill these gaps, or any one of them: but it has been thought that Amateurs of a very interesting and very vast subject may welcome a brief and summary statement of its various aspects and a few illustrations of them. The latter have for convenience been taken almost entirely from examples in the Public Record Office. No Catalogue of the Seals in that Office has yet been printed but a Card Index begun by Sir William St. John Hope and continued by the late R.C. Fowler (who described it in an article published in 1925[11]) is still in slow progress and numbers at present something like 14,000 cards. The difficulty here is the very large number of classes of Records which may contain Seals and have therefore to be searched in detail. If it is ever found possible to bring the Catalogue to anything approaching completeness it will

---

8. The Victoria and Albert Museum published in that year a valuable *List of Books and Pamphlets . . . illustrating Seals*. For a recent attempt at a Bibliography of European proportions *see* Mariette Tourneur-Nicodème, *Bibliographie Générale de la Sigillographie*: Besançon, 1933. Official publications on Seals have been more numerous in France than in any other country: among them, as an introductory work on Sigillography in general, may be mentioned specially the elaborate *Éléments de Sigillographie* prefixed by Douet d'Arcq to his *Collections de Sceaux* published in the Series of *Archives de l' Empire* (Paris, 1863). See also, as examples of French sigillographic work, G. Demay's *Inventaires* for Artois and Picardy, Flanders and Normandy.

9. As to the present state of our knowledge of the Great Seal and related Departmental Seals see articles by the present writer in *Antiquaries' Journal*, XVI, p. 8 (1936) and *Archaeologia*, LXXXV. Sir H.C. Maxwell Lyte (*Historical Notes on the Use of the Great Seal of England*, 1926) has described (pp. 42-49) the Privy Seals from Edward I to Victoria. On the Signet there are valuable notes (but for limited periods only) in T.F. Tout *Chapters in the Administrative History of Medieval England*, Vol. V (Manchester, 1930), F.M.G. Evans, *The Principal Secretary of State*, 1518-1680 (Manchester, 1923) and M.A. Thomson, *The Secretaries of State*, 1681-1782 (Oxford, 1932). The numerous lesser but still important Royal Series whose existence may be inferred from the survival of stray examples noted in the British Museum Catalogue, are practically unworked fields awaiting investigation.

10. The works of Sir H.C. Maxwell Lyte and Tout (cited above) are outstanding exceptions.

11. In *Archaeologia*, LXXIV, p. 103: in the present article I have had the advantage of using some of Mr Fowler's notes as well as my own.

be by far the largest and most comprehensive in England and perhaps the largest from a singe Repository in Europe.[12]

The present survey is limited by its title to English examples and the word *Seal* will throughout be used to signify *impressions* which are or were attached to documents: for the instrument, generally called by the same name, by which they were formed, the word *matrix* will be employed. As a *terminus a quo* I have taken the period when the use of Seals first begins to be at all general — that of the Norman Kings.

SCOPE OF THIS ARTICLE

As a point of departure I have ventured to take a Seal, though it is already well known, which happens to have been one of the first in which I was personally interested. It has the advantages of being an exceptionally beautiful example of the Engraver's art and of having furnished the material for a note by Sir William St. John Hope; who discovered at the Public Record Office the unique example by which it is known and published an account of it in 1914.[13] A brief description[14] might run as follows.

An impression in dark green wax from a round, double matrix, a little over 4 inches in diameter, appended by plaited laces of red and lilac silk to letters patent[15] dated 1 April 20 Edward III, by which John de Warenne,[16] Earl of Surrey and Stratherne, granted to the King certain Castles, Towns and Manors in Surrey, Sussex and Wales. The Seal is of Royal size and character, doubtless because of the owner's Palatine position in regard to his Earldom of Stratherne.

The *Obverse* shows the Earl in robes, seated on a throne, panelled and carved, and holding a flower in his right hand: the background, in allusion to his family name, consists of a warren, with rabbits, a hart, etc.: Legend — [+*Sigillum: Iohannis: Comitis: W]arennie: et Strathernie: et : Comitis : Palacii* in "Lombardic" capitals.

The *Reverse* shows the Earl in armour, on horseback, galloping to the right; the horse's trapper and the Earl's shield and ailette showing the checkered device of Surrey: the background, similar to that of the obverse, shows a pool with swan and cygnets, and storks: Legend — [+] *Sigillum: Iohannis: Comitis: Warennie : et : Surr . . .*

A good impression, but about a quarter of the seal (on the right, as one looks at the obverse) has been broken away and the Earl's left arm (on the reverse, his right arm with sword) is missing: together with some of the legend in each case.

Both sides of this Seal are shown in our first Plate.

12. The very large collection of casts (between 50,000 and 60,000) at the Archives Nationales described by Auguste Coulon (*Le Service Sigillographique*: Paris, 1916) contains examples from the Departmental as well as the National Archives. Douet d'Arcq's *Collections de Sceaux* enumerates nearly 12,000 examples. The six volumes of the British Museum *Catalogue* of originals and casts in that collection contains over 23,000 numbers, but many of these are for duplicates.

13. In *Proceedings of the Society of Antiquaries*, Series II, XXVII, p. 4: also in *Surrey Archaeological Collections*, XXVII, p. 123, and *Sussex Archaeological Collections*, LVII, p. 180.

14. I have omitted description of the Earl's clothes and armour.

15. Public Record Office, *Ancient Deeds*, A.S. 244.

16. Born 1286; succeeded his grandfather as Earl of Surrey and Sussex in 1305; created Earl of Stratherne by Edward Balliol in 1333.

SUBJECTS OF STUDY

In enumerating the lines of inquiry suggested by the description given above we may begin by excluding what may be called purely personal considerations. Obviously such a seal as that illustrated here may have, for an individual student, associations with some person, institution, place or event in whch he has a particular concern; but the investigations which this will suggest to him are not necessarily of general interest nor have they primarily anything to do with the making and use of Seals. Apart from these, however, a dozen questions or more might occur to a person who had not previously studied the subject but whose interest was aroused by the sight of this seal.

THE USE OF SEALS. For what purpose or purposes was sealing originally designed and subsequently employed? What were the Administrative processes surrounding it?

THE USERS. What classes of persons may be assumed, at any given time, to have possessed seals?

THE MATRICES. In a sense, these might be regarded as forming a separate subject: but we can hardly avoid asking a question or two about their materials and form and the way in which they were made and distributed: also about the mechanical means by which they were employed. This may lead to questions about

SIZE AND SHAPE: and this in turn to

SEALS PROPER — THE IMPRESSIONS. Of what materials were they made at different periods?

What colours were employed? and had these any special significance?

What were the methods of attaching them to the documents?

THE DEVICES. What varieties and styles can be distinguished?

THE LEGENDS. What forms of wording do we find? and what styles of lettering? and how are they placed on the Seal?

Finally, three questions of a more modern and practical nature:

THEIR PRESERVATION. What safeguards can be employed?

SURVIVALS. Can we form any idea of the number that await our study?

THEIR RECORDING. Do any regulations or recommendations suggest themselves?

To touch on each of these, even summarily, will be a very sufficient task for a single paper.

THE USE OF SEALS

It is a point rather frequently overlooked that the chief if not the only purpose of Seals was originally to authenticate: they were the equivalent of the modern signature at a time when the principals in any business or administrative transaction could seldom read and still more seldom write.

This fact is important because it affected materially the way in which the seal was affixed: and still more so because of the influence which it gave to the persons who, in any administrative organisation, controlled the Sealing Department: to this day a Secretary of State is admitted to his high Office by receiving the Seals. The use of sealing to authenticate survives in the apologies for Seals which we affix to our modern conveyances and in the more genuine "Common Seal" which most corporate bodies still find indispensable: but obviously we must expect to find it on the decline so soon as the art of writing begins to be general in use, that is in the 16th and 17th centuries.

The use of the seal to close a document, and thus guarantee not only that it was genuine but also that it had not been interfered with *after it was made*, became general in practice later; but survived in certain classes of document when authentication by signature made the older use of the seal unnecessary, and is, of course, the ordinary use for a seal at the present time. "Sealing to close" has also naturally its effect on the method of affixing and the material used: but these are matters to be dealt with later.

THE USERS OF SEALS

Investigation of this matter has been restricted up to now by a natural preponderance of interest in the more eminent personages of the past and the more beautiful or interesting seals: and in fact outside the Ecclesiastical, Municipal, Official and (especially) Armorial Classes, only seals which had some exceptional peculiarity or beauty of design have, as a rule, been noticed by those responsible for making our Catalogues. This is to be regretted because the seals of smaller people are an important matter in Social and Commercial History and their neglect in the past means that Collections which have already been searched may have to be examined all over again. It is probable that by the 14th century the ownership of a seal was quite a common matter: certainly there was a presumption that anyone of any standing had one; for the Central Government, when asking for Local information, would often require that the Inquisition returned should be under the seals of the Officials who took it and of the sworn men by whom the inquiry was made. It is true, we may suspect, that not infrequently some of these seals were no more than lumps of wax or alternatively that more than one *juratus* used the same matrix;[17] but the extent to which such practices

17. The way in which the Seal maintained for centuries its position as an absolute essential for the authentication of any document of importance, while at the same time men might be quite careless about the particular Seal they used, is one of the curiosities of Administrative History. A singular illustration is furnished by the Warrant for the execution of Charles I, now preserved in the House of Lords; on which the Seal of one of the Regicides (Cromwell!) is used twice.

were carried at any given period is exactly the kind of thing which we need to know; and on the other hand there is ample evidence that already in the 13th century the burgess of a small town, or the small land-owner, frequently thought the written business that came his way (though we cannot imagine that its volume was very great) quite sufficient to warrant the possession of a seal. An agreement preserved at the Record Office between Ranulph, Earl of Chester and Lincoln, and the men of Frieston and Butterwick, has appended to it (see Plate II) the seals of the "Men" to the number of no less than fifty, all different; and one would like to know how far this state of affairs is typical: but such questions will be solved only when a sufficiently large number of Seals has been described for analysis to be made and reasonably accurate inferences drawn.

It seems probable that plenty of small Seals of this kind were available ready-made: the superior ones offering a choice of devices from which the purchaser might select something which he regarded as symbolical: and the best grade having a blank space in which his name could be engraved.[18] The question of the cost will be mentioned later.

At the other end of the scale of persons who used Seals in the medieval period are the classes indicated at the beginning of this section — the Corporate Bodies, large and small; Dignitaries and Officials, lay and ecclesiastical; Knights and Ladies; Lords and Prelates; and finally the Sovereign himself. These, according to their rank, would naturally have Seals of greater or less elaboration. The greater ones among them would even find a single Seal insufficient for their needs, as the business they had to transact in writing grew more and more extensive and complicated and the staff who conducted it for them more and more numerous: so that we have the King, for example, by the end of the 14th century, using three certainly, and perhaps four[19] — *a finger ring* for his most intimate affairs, a *Signet* for his Secretary and a *Privy Seal* which was a step between his Secretary and his Chancellor, head of the busy department which controlled his *Great Seal* and authenticated his most formal acts. The elaboration of these processes in Royal Administration is the subject of much of the work of the late Professor Tout and Sir H.C. Maxwell Lyte, cited above. Parallel developments in the establishments of Lords, Dignitaries and Officials are extremely interesting but have been as yet little investigated.

It may, perhaps, be added that peculiarities of phraseology, in documents of all kinds, bearing on the methods of sealing, *and on the witnessing*, are likewise very important, and that these again (save in the case of the Royal Great Seal) have had very little investigation.

---

18. Not many years ago a medieval seal matrix was found in which a space, clearly left blank for this purpose, had never been filled.
19. See Tout, *op. cit.*, Vol. V, for illustrations of the smaller seals of Richard II.

MATRICES: THEIR MAKE AND EMPLOYMENT

The large proportion of medieval Seal Matrices were undoubtedly made of the kind of bronze called Latten: but silver also was fairly common and we hear of a Great Seal of England which is said to be of gold.[20] Gems set in rings occur but were not, apparently, very common medievally: they have, of course, recurred in later times. The design was normally cut, but in the case of some of the cheaper smaller ones casting might be used, and it is even possible that large and important ones might have been made in this way and finished with the tool.[21]

When a double seal was required, the two matrices would be flat slabs each with from two to four projecting "lugs" pierced with holes: vertical pins stretching from the lugs on the lower matrix to those on the upper secured correct super-position of the one matrix over the other. Single matrices had very often a flat piece projecting at right angles from the middle of the back which, being generally pierced (indeed, on small seals it was practically a ring) served at once as a grip to pull the matrix off the wax impression and as a means of attachment to a chain. Sometimes, however, this projection was enlarged into an elaborate ornament as in the case of William of Wykeham's Seal Matrix at New College, Oxford, which we illustrate here (Plate III).[22]

When the matrix was double, the lower (*reverse*) one was placed on the table face upwards with a cake of wax on it, softened probably by immersion in warm water (anyhow it was not melted): on the top of this lay the laces, tag or tongue[23] by which the seal was to be attached to the document, on the top of them another cake of softened wax and on this again the upper matrix,

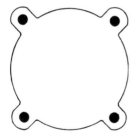

Fig. 1. One side of double matrix for round seal, showing projecting lugs.

20. A Great Seal of Henry IV, used also by his son and grandson: see Wyon, *op. cit.*, p. 43. The Seal matrix in a picture of the Chancery to be mentioned below is shown in gold and is perhaps meant for this one.
21. The suggestion has been made that the use of casting might help to explain an extraordinarily long series of changes in what is apparently a single matrix in use in the Court of Common Pleas, from the reign of Edward III to that of Henry VII. See an article by the present writer to be published in *Archaeologia*, LXXXV.
22. For leave to reproduce these photographs I have to thank the Warden and Fellows of New College, Oxford.
23. See later for description of these.

face downwards, to form the *obverse* of the impression. Pressure was applied (we may see the method in a 15th-century picture reproduced[24] in plate V) originally by means of a roller: later, perhaps, by a lever press and finally by the screw press[25] Medieval sealers may have used[26] a dusting of chalk on the wax to make the impression come off easily.

When the matrix was a single one of any size, the method was probably first to impress it lightly and then to press the wax into it with the fingers and thumbs.[27] The projection behind makes any kind of mechanical pressure on the matrix impossible unless a hollowed block is placed over it, and anyone who has tried to take an impression simply by downward pressure with the hand on (for example) Wykeham's seal will realise the difficulty of that method. When the wax was sufficiently pressed into the matrix, the sealer would shape up the back of it, and often ended by digging his finger into this (or his thumb and two fingers, if it was large enough) and so getting a grip on it when he wished to pull off the matrix.[28] Occasionally, having done this he would press into one or all of the depressions so formed a small finger ring. A good example in which three ring-seals figure on the back of a seal of Merton Priory, in the Public Record Office, is shown in Plate IV. Sometimes a secret or privy seal matrix was pressed into the back of the impression from a larger one: this is generally referred to as a *counter seal*: and as the Great and Privy Seals would be normally kept by different officers, its addition constituted a second authentication. A common trick, in the case of small seals was to press into the wax a ring made of twisted rush — no doubt picked up from the floor — by way of framing and holding together the impression: less common is the pressing of leaves into the back of the seal.[29] perhaps to prevent the wax sticking to the table or hand when the matrix is first pressed into it. Abnormalities, such as the inclusion of a small coin in the wax,[30] cannot be described in detail.

24. Now in the possession of the Inner Temple Library: it was reproduced and described in 1862 in *Archaeologia*, XXXIX; and is figured here by kind permission of its present owners.
25. An early screw press is illustrated by Hunter Blair in *Archaeologia*, LXXVII, p. 176.
26. It is used in making wax impressions from moulds at the Public Record Office.
27. This, of course, applies only to Seals appended to a document: for those applied to the face of the parchment or paper direct pressure on the matrix would be necessary: for the use of these two methods of affixing see later.
28. Particularly fine impressions of the thumb and first and second fingers of the sealer may be seen in the back of a seal on the foundation charter of Ripon Grammar School.
29. An example may be seen on *Victuallers' Recognisances* (E. 180), 151, in the Record Office, and two very good ones were recently noted on 16th-century documents in the possession of Corpus Christi College, Cambridge.
30. See for an example *Ancient Deeds, c.*4889 (*temp.* Henry VI) and for another (*temp.* Elizabeth) *State Papers Domestic, Supplementary,* 79, f. 186b.

The development of the metal-worker's craft in the making of matrices is really a separate subject and we must pass lightly. Mr Kingsford[31] has some interesting remarks on this, including mention of abnormal ingenuities by which (for example) a portion of the design was impressed separately: he also cites a number of cases in which matrices have survived. It is unfortunate that we so seldom know anything of the personality of the early engravers: but the progressive publication of contemporary Accounts may do something to remedy this, particularly in the case of Royal Seals.[32]

SIZE AND SHAPE

In the case of the more important Seals, shape is practically[33] confined to two forms — the round, and the pointed oval (*vesica*). Royal, Military and Official (Lay) Seals are generally round, and Secret or Privy Seals (where the owner has more than one) very usually take this shape. The oval for Great Seals is particularly favoured by Ladies and Ecclesiastics and is used a good deal, though not invariably, by religious foundations. Double Seals are normally round: but it is not impossible to find combinations of large round and small oval:[34] and the opposite (large oval and small round) is common.

Smaller seals of the medieval period follow much the same conventions: but we find abnormal shapes such as the triangle, square, oblong, diamond-shape, hexagon and octagon; the spade-shape and heart-shape; and, not infrequently, the shield.[35] When we get to the later seal rings showing shields of Arms, supporters and motto, there is a natural tendency towards a shape (rounded oblong or oval) whose breadth is greater than its height.

In general it may be said that the spread of the writing habit and the consequent substitution of signature for authentication by seal killed the Great Seal, save in the case of Royal and semi-Royal Departments, Ecclesiastical Offices of a like dignity, and Corporate Institutions of all kinds; except in such connexions we find very few new Great Seals from the time of the Tudors onward: and the same applies to the formalized Privy Seal of the Middle Ages. There survived only the small Signet or still smaller Signet

31. *Op. cit.*, p. 12 *et seq.*
32. cf. a note in *Antiquaries' Journal*, XVI, p. 9; and some examples in Lyte, *op. cit.*
     Mr Kingsford (*op. cit.*, pp. 20, 21) has a useful note on this subject and on the cost of matrices. For the cost of a number of small official seals of *auricalcum* (latten) in the reign of Richard II, see *Exchequer, King's Remembrancer, Accounts Various*, 550/40.
33. Not quite completely: see for example the early diamond-shaped Seal of the town of Dunwich.
34. The early round Seal of Nostell Priory shown in Plate IV has a small oval *Contrasigillum* (so described).
35. Examples of each of these shapes in the Public Record Office are on *Ancient Deeds*, A. 1803; B.S.300; BX.480(a); A.5134; A.6073; B.3684; B.9455; and A.S.154: some are illustrated in Plate VI.

Ring. As we shall presently note, the same period saw changes in the type of design and legend, in the material used and in the manner of affixing the Seal.

An average size for the Great Seal in *private* use in the 13th and 14th centuries was about 3 inches in diameter; or, in the case of an oval one, in height. The Great Seal of England increased in size from 3¼ inches (William the Conqueror) to 6 inches (Queen Victoria). Privy or Secret Seals in private use were generally from 1 inch to 1½ inches in diameter in the 14th century (the Royal Privy Seal grew gradually much larger). Other Seals were of various heights or diameters from about 1½ inches downwards. An economy sometimes effected in Royal Seals (I know of no example elsewhere) by the use of a "half" or "quarter" Seal must be mentioned only in passing.[36] Still more curious was the use of a tiny spot of wax which was pressed on to the part of the Great Seal matrix depicting the Sovereign's head for the purpose of certain documents[37] which issued up to modern times from the Irish Chancery.

MATERIALS

Medieval seals were made with one material only [38] — true sealing-wax, consisting of about two-thirds of beeswax to one-third of some kind of resin.[39] Used as described above it was ideal for pendent impressions from deeply-engraved matrices. It was not so suitable for Seals "applied" to the surface of documents (they tended to crack off); nor indeed are deeply-cut matrices suitable themselves for such work: and as paper became commoner in the 15th century the habit developed of laying a piece of this over the wax and impressing "through" it with a small seal engraved in low relief. The same method was adapted later for pendent seals; but meanwhile, as trade grew with the Indies in the 16th century, a new material — shellac — was introduced: and shellac has continued a favourite down to the present day: quite rightly so long as it is confined to small and applied seals.[40] The papered seal, however, was by no means ousted and, indeed, paper enjoyed

36. See some description of these seals in Lyte, *op. cit.*, p. 307.
37. Writs for return of Members of Parliament.
38. Lead, in use at the Roman Curia and elsewhere, was never employed in England so far as I know. So-called "golden bullae" (Henry VIII employed one for the seal on a Treaty with France) are generally Smith's work, not seals: though I have seen (in a Foreign Repository) an actual impression on thin gold.
39. Analysis of a number of fragments from the Public Record Office has shown that there was not much variation during the medieval period: see an article by Sir James Dobbie and Dr J.J. Fox in *Transactions of the Chemical Society*, CV, p. 797.
40. It is most unsuitable, owing to the rapidity with which it hardens, for large and for pendent seals.

considerable popularity about the 18th century in company with a new and abominable invention — the wafer of flour and gum. All these materials survive in at least occasional use in our own day; and the shellac is, of course, the ordinary "sealing-wax" normally bought and used by ordinary people.

The so-called wafer of (sometimes coloured) paper in use[41] in the 19th century need not detain us, but the modern embossing seal with the same design in relief in one matrix and in intaglio on a second, for use with paper only, is worth a word. Government Offices (and possibly others) have latterly tried various expedients ranging from a mixture of paraffin wax and tallow (recently noted in Exchequer Seals of the reign of Queen Victoria[42]) to a cellulose acetate thermo-plastic moulding compound at present in use in the Crown Office for the Great Seal. During the reigns of William IV and Queen Victoria (possibly earlier), a most curious invention was employed — that of leather stretched over a cake of some material and having the seal impressed on it[43] and guttaperch, which was used for casts in the 19th century, may also have been employed for actual seal impressions.

COLOUR

The normal medieval colourings were three: natural wax, red (got by the addition of pure vermilion colouring) and green (verdigris). A good deal of variation in shades occurs according to the amount of colour used (the expense of the pigment was no doubt a consideration) and natural vermilion itself varies to a very orange tone: variation also occurs if wax is re-melted (as no doubt it was for a second or third use) owing to burning of the resin. It is possible that some very dark seals which survive contain carbon. An economy practised in early days (it appears in Great Seals of the 12th century) was to colour natural wax impressions with a coating of reddish varnish or paint: and a curious revival of this was noted recently[44] in some Exchequer Seals of George III which were painted green. A singular yellow mixture, sometimes used for the Great Seal in Queen Victoria's reign, was probably intended to simulate natural wax. The shellac seals seem from the first to have been normally scarlet or black.

In Royal Seals, at least, of the medieval period the colours had signifi-cance: natural wax being used with the Great Seal for all routine business, green for grants of perpetuities[45] and scarlet (sometimes at least) for

---

41. Its use may even be statutory: see Lyte, *op. cit.*, p. 327.
42. e.g. in *Exchequer, Special Commissions* (E. 178), 132/6846.
43. There is an example of the reign of William IV in the County Muniment Room at Bedford: the Society of Antiquaries has a good specimen, *temp.* Queen Victoria.
44. For an example see at the Public Record Office *Loose Seals*, O.76.
45. cf. Lyte, *op. cit.*, p. 310, for a 17th-century ruling on this subject: but it appears to have been an accepted convention much earlier.

diplomatic purposes: at the Exchequer a particular use of green gave its name to a class of documents (*Summonses of the Green Wax*): for the Privy Seal — at any rate when "warranting" a letter out of the Chancery — scarlet was always employed.[46] It seems probable that investigation of the practices in sealing departments elsewhere would produce evidence of an accepted significance of colours in some of these also: a curious elaboration which occasionally appears, when a piece of different coloured wax is inserted at the back of a Great Seal for the impression of the Secret (Counter) Seal,[47] is possibly an evidence of this. On the other hand, a thin layer of the (more expensive) coloured wax was sometimes set in a thick saucer-shaped lump of the "natural": the seal of John Drewe, shown in Plate VI, is an example.

METHODS OF ATTACHING THE SEAL

These fall into two broad groups, seals being either *appended* by a strip of some material attached to the document or *applied* to the surface of it. The first method is the older and long continued in general use for documents, whether public, or private, which announced formally to all concerned a gift, grant, commission, or agreement; though in conveyancing, as the seal became a mere accompaniment of the signature, and as shellac sealing came in (*i.e.* from the late 15th and 16th centuries onwards), the applied seal tended to oust it.

In describing varieties of attachment within these two groups, we shall experience some trouble over nomenclature. One would like to use names based on contemporary practice but is met with the difficulty either that none is known or that there is more than one name for the same process: so that having found the word "label"[48] used for a strip of parchment, one accepts that only to discover that another contemporary calls the same thing a "pendicle." These questions are not without importance in view of the great desirability of securing homogeneity in the description of such matters by the editors of catalogues, and one has always to remember that apparently meaningless differences of method may have had, certainly did have in some cases, a significance for the people who used them. On the whole, therefore,

---

46. According to Lyte (p. 49), its use for the Privy Seal was universal: but the trouble about this Seal is that very few examples survive and those nearly all of a single category (*Warrants* to the Chancery).

47. An example of double colouring will be found on *Ancient Deeds*, B.S., 185, at the Record Office (Seal of Battle Abbey).

48. Sir Henry Maxwell Lyte (*op. cit., p. 300*) has discovered some authority for "label" and in a letter of Henry VII to the Major of Lyme Regis it is described as a *lambewe (French lambeau)*. *Pendiculum* appears in a late 14th-century document quoted in H.T. Riley's *Memorials of London and London Life* (1868), p. 528.

the best course is probably to take an agreed modern series of descriptions: and we may suggest in the first place that the time has come to cease using French names[49] for English practices. An Anglo-American Committee on Editing, in its *Report* published in 1923,[50] suggested a system which with one or two small modifications and the addition of some phrases to cover the mixed practices of later periods will be found to serve very well. I shall venture to describe them at a little length.

(1) APPENDED SEALS. The simplest method employed was (Figure 2) by means of a single cut running nearly across the foot[51] of the parchment to make a *tongue* on which either a double or single seal could be made *pendent* in the manner described above. Sometimes a much narrower *tie* would be cut in the same way either by itself or in addition to the *tongue*: both are shown in the Figure. The use of the tie will be described below. The spot at which *tongue* or *tie* remain attached to the parchment, we call the *root*.

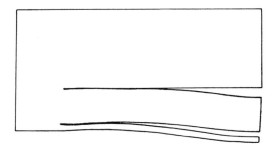

Fig. 2.

The more elaborate method of appending was to fold the parchment over at the foot and through this to make either (Figure 3) a series of cuts

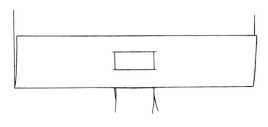

Fig. 3.

49. *En placard, simple queue* and so forth.
50. Institute of Historical Research, *Bulletin*, No. 1.
51. In the case of the top part of a duplicate indenture, it may be cut from the top edge: see, *e.g.* in the Public Record Office, *Ancient Deeds*, L.4.

(generally two cuts through both layers and one at the fold) or (Figure 4) a series of holes. Through the former (the cheaper and more usual method) would be passed a doubled *tag* of parchment, vellum or leather, and through the latter, *laces* consisting of cords or loose threads or strands of silk, or occasionally a woven[52] ribbon, braid or other material.

The free ends of the tag were not infrequently twisted together, or even slit[53] in the middle and passed through each other, so as to form a projection at the spot where the seal was put on and help to retain the wax. In the case of deeds to which there were a number of parties, we find either several *tags* or a single *tag* with several small Seals on it: sometimes these are placed tandem-wise, sometimes the end of a broad tag is slit up to make a separate tag for each seal. *Tongues* also may have more than one seal on them; placed in the same ways.

The silk laces were generally two double ones of different colours and the four free ends (shown in Figure 4) were usually plaited together before they

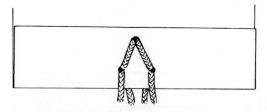

Fig. 4.

entered the seal. For very important Royal Grants in the 15th century and later, gold or silver thread was frequently mixed with the silk: and later, in the cords used for Treaties, it became preponderant. Whether the difference between silk and bullion meant anything more than a difference in the fees[54] paid is doubtful but certainly the comparative use of *tongue, tag* and *laces* had administrative significance in the Royal Chancery and very possibly in other places.

In this connexion we may mention the subject of the boxes of basket work, turned wood, ivory and bone, or metal which became common in the later part of the medieval period and are generally known as skippets.[55] Usually they were shaped to fit the seal with holes for the *tongue, tag or laces*: but

52.   Early Charters (*e.g.* some of Richard I) provide interesting examples of tablet weavings used for this purpose. Ordinary ribbons occur later: but plaited strands or threads of silk are by far the most common.
53.   Some examples of the 13th century have been described by Dr. G.H. Fowler in *Associated Archaeological Societies' Reports* (1933).
54.   For fees paid in the 17th century, see Lyte, *op. cit.*, p. 349.
55.   "Small basket" is perhaps nearest to the original meaning of the word.

sometimes (especially in foreign practice) a single-sided matrix was impressed on wax already embedded in the box. In the late 18th century it became normal to issue letters under the Great Seal with skippets of tin plate: and with the addition of a coat of japanning these are in use at the present day. It also became normal to have exceedingly elaborate ones of silver or silver gilt decorated with Arms, etc., for Treaties:[56] and other very important documents were at various times similarly distinguished.[57]

(2) SEALS APPLIED. Little more than has been said above is necessary here, but we may note the habit observed from the 14th century onwards of making a number of converging cuts in parchment documents, arranged in something like the pattern shown in Figure 5, at the spot where the seal was to be applied, in order that the cut points, turned back, should reinforce the wax.[58] The rush ring was also used occasionally on an applied seal for the same purpose.[59] A trick sometimes employed in the late 14th century with

Fig. 5.

Fig. 6.

the smaller Royal Seals (and perhaps elsewhere) was to *apply on a cross* made of two strokes drawn on the document in the soft wax. This method could be used when the seal was *applied to close* over the edge of a folded paper document,[60] as shown in Figure 6.

Applying to close in the case of *parchment documents* was rather more complicated and made use of the *tie*. The document was generally folded once longitudinally and this was then folded again, sometimes several times, into a small packet; the tie was wrapped round the packet: and the Seal (or as much of it as there was room for) was applied on the face of the packet over the tie. The precise process varied in different departments of Royal Administration, and no doubt elsewhere. Legal Writs, from the Chancery, for example, were

56. The Record Office has a large collection among *State Papers Foreign* and in the Records of the *Foreign Office*.
57. Earlier examples (*temp.* Henry VIII) of silver skippets, with fine enamelled decoration, may be seen in the Record Office Museum.
58. See an example in *Chancery Warrants*, II, 711 (*temp.* Henry VIII).
59. See *e.g. Treasury of the Receipt, Scottish Documents*, 96/26.
60. It was so used on the example shown in the Record Office Museum: see also one in *Chancery Warrants*, I, 1365 (*temp.* Henry V).

made up into particularly small packets,[61] some of which may be seen in our Chancery picture (Plate V) lying on the table; and were sealed in a fashion different to that used at the Exchequer. The method used for warrants under the Privy Seal addressed to the Chancery was so unusual as to deserve description: here the document was folded once longitudinally and twice across this; making six folds, through which a slit was cut: a tie (broader than usual, in fact more like the normal *tongue*) was turned over and thrust through this slit and the seal *applied* on the otherside partly over the projecting tongue.

What happened when both a *tie* and a *tongue* were cut I do not know: presumably a seal pendent on the tongue was left hanging out of the folded document; but what seal was then used on the tie? The arrangement appears not infrequently in private deeds[62] where folding and closing seem (in any case) superfluous: it is not improbable that it may have been used for correspondence, especially by persons who had more than one seal.

(3) LATER METHODS OF ATTACHMENT. We have space to note only two matters. First there is the trick of cutting the *paper* used with *applied seals* in the 17th century and later to an elaborate pattern such as that seen in Figure 7.[63] I have seen also, later, small squares of paper with gilt edges. On the other hand, for extreme simplicity one might make a small slit, or two slits, in the corner or at the side of a paper document, turn over the slit portion, as shown in Figure 8, and *apply* the seal *through* this.[64] Secondly, we

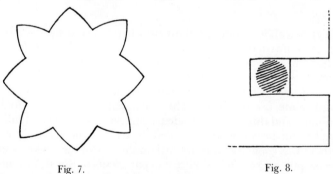

Fig. 7.   Fig. 8.

61. One is illustrated in the Plate prefixed to Sir Henry Maxwell Lyte's work: but I differ from him about the sealing of it. Certainly there was a small spot of wax on it and (on an analogy derived from the modern Irish Chancery) I think this may probably have been pressed on a small spot of the Great Seal matrix!

62. It is seen for example in a 12th-century deed — one of the earliest known bonds for debt: see an article in *Essays presented to R.L. Poole* (Oxford, 1927), p. 194.

63. A much more elaborate example (*temp.* Charles II) is illustrated by Miss F.M.G. Evans, *op. cit.*

64. See an example in *Exchequer, King's Remembrancer, Accounts Various*, 64/30 (*temp* Elizabeth).

must be prepared for innumerable mixed methods of sealing in late documents. A Treaty, for example, may be written in book form, the folded sheets of this sewn with a silk cord and the ends of the cord used for a *pendent* seal. On the other hand, the famous "Scrap of Paper" Treaty was sewn with ribbon which was turned over inside the book and had the seals of the Plenipotentiaries *applied* over it. The post-medieval use of *papering* for *pendent* seals has been already mentioned: it is particularly common in the 18th century, when it is used for Bishops' Seals (cp. the latest seal shown in Plate IX) and even for (Colonial) Great Seals: but examples could be found from the two preceding centuries.

Completely abnormal methods may of course be found at any date, though medievally they are rare: an amusingly simple and certainly abnormal plan is seen in the case of the 19th-century impression from a medieval matrix shown in Plate VIII. Two earlier examples recently noted are perhaps worth quoting. First we have two Irish documents of the reigns of Edward I and Edward II to each of which both the Great and the Exchequer Seals of Ireland are attached, two parallel tongues being cut for the purpose.[65] Secondly, there is the case of some Bordeaux documents of the 15th century:[66] here a large document had the usual fold made at its foot and through this two slits; but the slits were made *vertically* and through them was passed a tongue cut on a second smaller document; and the seal on this served to authenticate both.[67]

THE DEVICES ON SEALS

Reaching this subject we come to the region of Sigillography which has been most explored: and shall for that reason, as well as on account of its size, pass rapidly. But there are two main subjects on which we may perhaps usefully say a few words — those of *periods and styles* and of *types of design*.

Styles in seal-cutting provide an even better example than usual of the danger of attempting to date antiquities: the possibility of error is indeed, in this case, a double one. Apart from the fact that we know (as has been said) so little, as a rule, of the persons who executed the matrices, and the circumstances under which they worked — so that in any given case we may have before us the work of a man of nineteen or ninety, that of a provincial or a London craftsman, an importation from abroad or a native product — it is a well-established fact that the same matrix was often continuously in use

---

65. The documents are described in Royal Irish Academy *Proceedings*, XXXV, C., pp. 126-128: but the very unusual method of sealing is not mentioned.
66. *Exchequer, King's Remembrancer, Accounts Various*, 189/13.
67. A similar device was used for fastening a second (confirmatory) document to the *Bishop's Certificate*, from which our fourth (18th century) example is taken in Plate IX.

through successive generations. Even Kings have frequently used, with or without alteration, the seals of their predecessors;[68] similar usage was without doubt fairly common, probably more than that, in the case of private seals with lettering on them; while in the case of simpler matrices, with nothing personal about them, the possibilities of continued employment over a long period (viewed the lasting character of bronze) are almost unlimited. Religious and Charitable Foundations frequently used the same Seal for a very long tim; and there are plenty of Corporations who have in action to this day matrices of medieval date[69] or close copies of them: see for example the Seals of the Priories of Merton and Nostell and the 15th-century Seal of the Borough of Colchester shown in our Plates.[70] Occasionally a later copy has been marked by the insertion of some small variation, even of a date;[71] and indeed, we might venture to recommend to Institutions who follow the admirable practice of safeguarding their medieval matrix by using a modern reproduction[71] that they should in some way distinguish the latter: but in general, seal-users in the past have not been so provident for the comfort of scholars of a later age.

THE DEVICES ON SEALS: STYLES AND PERIODS

It seems clear from the foregoing remarks that we must beware alike of crediting the date which might be assigned to a matrix on the ground of the document to which an impression from it is affixed, and of discrediting it on the ground of style. There is, however, a sufficient number of Seals whose matrix is of known or approximately known date to enable us to fix certain styles which may be said at least to be characteristic of certain periods: for

---

68. Thus, Edward III's "Brétigny" Great Seal Matrix, of 1360, was altered for himself later, altered again for his grandson Richard II, and again for Henry IV, and used so late as the reign of Henry VI: similarly matrices of Edward I were altered by the addition of a castle for Edward II and by that of a fleur-de-lys for Edward III: the case of the Seal of the Court of Common Pleas has already been mentioned: and, to take a modern example, the King's Remembrancer was using throughout the reign of King George V the Exchequer Seal of King Edward VII without alteration.
69. cf. articles by Sir W.H. St J. Hope cited on opening page.
70. Plates IV and VIII: see also notes on these in the Appendix.
71. The insertion of a date in a matrix, whether for this or any other purpose, is not very common: but Mr Kingsford (*op. cit.*, p. 51) has noted a number of examples, and a late one may be seen on No. 4 of our Plate IX.
72. Perfection of the mechanical methods of reproduction (for instance at the Mint) has led, I believe, to action of this kind in a number of cases by Colleges and similar bodies in recent years. An impression from the "reproduction" Seal of New College is shown in Plate III, side by side with the original matrix; by courtesy of the Warden and Fellows of the College.

convenience we may add here a description of the styles of lettering (which might otherwise be given below) to which they are roughly parallel. Naturally, the student must assume a transition by gradations between each of the periods we shall name. *First*, then, we have the *Primitive Style*, associated with legends in almost pure.

ROMAN CAPITALS

Sufficient examples of both may be seen in the Great Seals from William the Conqueror to Stephen.[73] Compare the style of the Nostell Priory Seal shown in Plate IV, the matrix of which may be ascribed to the 12th century. The next stage in lettering is that of what are generally called

LOMBARDIC

Capitals: and these occur during the transition from the most primitive style of cutting through that of (say) the Great Seals of Richard I[74] (the late 12th century) to the *Second Style* — *the finished workmanship of the 13th century*: a very fully-developed example of this would be the Great Seal of Edward I:[75] and stages in its development may be observed in the two Great Seals of Henry III:[76] or the student may compare any of the Baronial Great Seals affixed to the letter to the Pope of 1301 in the Record Office Museum with that of the same Baron's predecessor say seventy years earlier: the Warenne family provides good examples, as may be seen in Plate VII. Early signs of a change from this to the *Third Style* — *the elaboration of the 14th century* — may be seen in the extraordinarily deeply-cut matrix used by Merton Priory (Plate IV) and the full development of 14th-century skill and beauty in the Warenne Seal with which this article began and some of the small seals in Plate VI: this third period is associated with a change from Lombardic to

black letter

the small letter forms being chiefly used: but the association must not be pressed too far. Finally, from this style we slide easily into the *over-elaboration of the late 14th and 15th centuries, a good example of which is seen in the almost-ridiculous architectural adornments of the Br*ē*tigny Seal*[77] (1360) of Edward III and still more in the "Golden" Seal used by Henry IV,[78] Henry V and Henry VI: a more restrained use of elaborate detail is seen in the New College Seal (Plate III). These later and final stages of the *Third Style* are definitely associated as a rule with black letter.

73. Wyon, *Great Seal*, Plates II to IV.
74. Wyon, Plates V and VI.
75. *Ibid.*, Plate VII, Nos. 47, 48.
76. *Ibid.*, Plates VI and VII, Nos 41-44.
77. *Ibid.*, Plate X, Nos. 63, 64.
78. *Ibid.*, Plate XII, Nos. 73, 74.

With this we end the medieval period. A *Fourth Style* and period is the *Renaissance* or *Classical*: with which is associated a lettering in pure

ROMAN CAPITALS

and a marked tendency to much lower relief in the cutting. But it took a considerable time for all the "Gothic" elements to disappear: in the case of the Great Seal, though Renaissance elements begin to be seen in the second and third of Henry VIII[79] and are to be noted in increasing quantities thereafter, it can hardly be said that we have a type with no "Gothic" elements in it at all till we get to Cromwell.[80] Meanwhile the sealing habit has largely disappeared: little is left save the small seals, displaying an initial or conventional pattern, in use by non-armigerous persons, and the armorial signets of more important folk, with mantling, crest and so forth, which may be seen rapidly developing into the forms we know in our own time. Seal-cutting in the grand manner was dead: and if we wish to make a *Fifth Style*, with (in some cases) **SANS-SERIF** lettering, out of modern developments from the *Renaissance*, we have only a restricted number of Royal and Official seals on which to base it. The student may compare the Renaissance and later styles with the medieval in the Episcopal Seals shown in Plate IX.

CLASSES OF SEAL DESIGNS

We can only deal broadly with this subject in regard to which the student will find much useful information in Mr Kingsford's work already cited. Here it must suffice to indicate a few main divisions of the subject, and perhaps give some idea of its vast and unexplored character.[81]

(1) ROYAL AND SEMI-ROYAL GREAT SEALS. These are throughout distinguished by a single convention, due perhaps to their Anglo-Norman origin: they show normally two portraits of the Sovereign, one enthroned and one riding. So strong is this convention that the holders of Palatinates imitate it, as we have seen in the case of John de Warenne: even a Bishop may do so.[82] It is to be noted, however, that many specialised Great Seals were developed, to discharge functions originally part of the work of the one Seal kept by the Chancellor, and that these followed the Baronial convention of a portrait on one side and a shield of Arms on the other.[83]

79. Wyon, Plates XVIII and XIX, Nos. 99-102.
80. *Ibid., op. cit.,* Plates XXXII-XXXIV.
81. This is not intended as an ideal classification. Mr. Kingsford has suggested (*op. cit.*, p. 31) a scheme for this under four headings (Royal, Ecclesiastical, Local and Personal or Private) with numerous sub-headings.
82. See examples in Hunter Blair, *op. cit.*
83   For a summary description of these Seals see my article in *Archaeologia* already cited. Note that the latest type of these seals — the Colonial ones — tend to a very fanciful setting of the Sovereign's portrait: or even eliminate it altogether in favour of a view.

(2) LESSER ROYAL SEALS. These, again following the Baronial convention, display a shield of Arms with (as time goes on) an increasingly elaborate architectural or other surround and background.[84]

(3) OTHER SEALS OF ROYAL ADMINISTRATION. The series of these — some apparently an official issue, some a personal supply — are too numerous and in most cases too little investigated to be more than mentioned here: reference to the British Museum *Catalogue*[85] will give some slight idea (but only an incomplete one) of their number and diversity. A large proportion have little in their design to distinguish them from private ones, though not infrequently emblematic: a Sheriff for instance seems to choose or be given the device of a castle; a Household official may display a key; and so forth.

(4) BARONIAL GREAT AND PRIVY SEALS have been described above by implication: the portrait of the lord is always equestrian. Note that a great lady also may have seals of a like importance if her business requires it: her Great Seal tends generally to the vesica shape and a standing portrait.[86]

(5) ECCLESIASTICAL SEALS may be divided into those of

(a) DIGNITARIES (Bishops, Abbots, etc.) who have generally a standing portrait[87] (see Plate IX); and

(b) RELIGIOUS INSTITUTIONS which may use, in vesica or round shape, and in sizes that vary according to their importance, the figure of a Saint, a picture of their building, or a Biblical or religious story: examples of the first of these from Nostell and Merton Priories are shown in Plate IV.[88]

To these must be added (to be again left undescribed) the host of seals of smaller Ecclesiastical Offices and their holders: we can only say that their devices, also, will often be to some extent emblematic; and that they too await the labour of scholars.[89]

---

84. See the illustrations of Privy Seals and Signets given by Tout, *op. cit.*, Vol. V.

85. See Vol. I, pp. 141-156: but many local officials must be sought in the topographical section of the Catalogue — under Counties, Hundreds, Towns, etc.

86. A good example of the 14th century is provided by the Seals of Mary de Sanco Paulo, foundress of Pembroke College, Cambridge: see *Archaeologia*, LXVI, Plate XXXI. See also, *ibid.*, the early seal of her College and the great and privy seals of the Earl of Pembroke, her husband.

87. Note that in later times, Bishops have taken to armorial devices. Episcopal Seals have been the subject of numerous scattered articles.

88. For a single work on this subject, see Gale Pedrick, *Monastic Seals of the Thirteenth Century*, 1902.

89. One or two categories which have been treated generally in published works (as indicated in a note at the beginning of this article) may serve as pointers to the work yet to be done in connexion with the seals of these smaller Ecclesiastical Offices; and with the corresponding lay ones also.

(6) COLLEGES, SCHOOLS AND SIMILAR FOUNDATIONS.[90]
These (or at least the first-named) have seals of such importance as to merit a
separate section. The figure of a founder with Saints is of frequent occurrence
in the case of the Colleges (see Plate III). The Schools are, as a rule, later
and less interesting: something symbolical or topical is generally their device.
The vesica shape for all these is probably the most usual.

(7) CIVIL CORPORATIONS.[91] The most important are Towns, Cities
or Boroughs; smaller institutions being either of a religious character (as in
the case of Guilds) or of a private nature and akin to the *non-armorial* seals
mentioned below. The Boroughs tend to a round seal of fair size depicting in
many cases a local feature — a bridge, tower or other building. The strength
of this convention is amusingly illustrated by the 18th-century seal of
Madras, depicting the fort and seaboard.[92] Boroughs also used, fairly often,
a Patron Saint or some kind of allusive picture such as a ship. The addition of
the Royal Arms is not infrequent. The seals are sometimes double ones: an
example (Colchester) of the 15th century is shown in Plate VIII. We can
only mention, in passing, the smaller official seals — those of the Mayor and
so forth — which might properly come under this heading and which are
represented by large numbers of surviving impressions.

(8) PRIVATE ARMORIAL. These are the seals of armigerous persons of
lesser degree. Their shape (apart from the abnormals already mentioned) is
generally round, though the pointed oval occurs. The history of their design
is that first of increasing decoration (often of an architectural character) in
the surround to the shield, and then of the addition of badges, supporters,
crested helm, mantling and finally motto; which brings us to the modern
armorial signet. Of the heraldic interest of these Seals we cannot speak here:
it has led to their receiving more attention than, perhaps, any other class:
but, unfortunately, not beyond the point (in the 16th century) when Records
of Heralds' Visitations begin to be regularly preserved. Examples may be
seen in Plate VI.

(9) PRIVATE NON-ARMORIAL. Three grades have been already
indicated — the completely ready-made; the partially ready-made; and the
specially-made, generally allusive to their owner's name. The last class may
use as a subject almost anything — a popular story, a patron saint, a
merchant's mark, initials; the first will display any small conventional
decoration — a cross, a fleur-de-lys, a bird and so forth. I would once more

---

90.   On College Seals of Cambridge, see the article by Sir W. St. J. Hope already cited. On the
      Seals of Schools, see articles in British Archaeological Association *Journal*, XII and XIV.
91.   The Seals of Cities and Boroughs have been treated in scattered articles too numerous for
      mention here: for single works, see Gale Pedrick, *Borough Seals of the Gothic Period* (1904),
      and Alexander Porteous, *Town Council Seals of Scotland* (Edinburgh, 1906). See also Sir
      W.H. St. J. Hope's work already cited.
92.   An example has been noted on a document dated 1781.

plead that these seals are sometimes amusing, always (in the present state of our ignorance) worth examination. The early examples, in Plate II, have already been mentioned: a few more will be found in Plate VI. An outstanding seal in this Plate is the early but very graceful figure of a woman on the seal of Eva de Broch: it is of the 12th century. The seal of Nicholas de Hugate shows the miracle of St. Nicholas of Myra: that of Adam de Howtone (showing Adam and Eve) has a legend which will be mentioned below. Both these last are on documents of the first part of the 14th century.

THE LEGENDS ON SEALS

Of the successive *styles of lettering* we need say little more: antiquaries not so many years ago were bold enough to use them as evidence for very exact dating, but for the reasons given above, that form of *expertise* is now discredited: the final blow to it was given in an article published by Mr Kingsford in 1929.[93] The ·order of succession, however, remains unquestioned.

Of the *placing*, again, there is little to say. Throughout the medieval period, the normal place is in a band going completely round the device, no matter what the shape of the Seal may be; though variants, such as a double band,[94] a legend beginning at the foot or across the top or down the side,[95] or running two ways,[96] are to be found from time to time in all parts of the medieval period, and there are even examples of legends on the rim of the impression.[97] We have also occasionally supplementary lettering on a scroll or other device worked into the general design: examples are the space allotted on some of the Royal Seals for the King's Bench and Common Pleas for an additional note explaining the precise nature of the Seal.

THE WORDING. Here again we have, with one big exception,[98] a norm which is followed in the vast majority of cases in the medieval period. The legend starts on the reader's right at the top, with (very often) a cross and after this *Sigillum*[99] (or S, or some other abbreviation) followed by the name and titles of the owner: the words being separated very often by a colon or some small conventional device. Sometimes (if he uses more than one seal)

93. "The Epigraphy of Medieval English Seals": *Archaeoligia*, LXXIX, p. 149.
94. An example (that of Boxley Abbey) is cited below.
95. Examples of these peculiarities will be found on the following *Ancient Deeds* at the Public Record Office: A. 13718 (foot); A. 6853 (top); A. 11652 (side). Note also the text beginning at the foot of the Colchester Seal on Plate VIII.
96. See *e.g. Ancient Deeds*, DS. 28.
97. *e.g.* on Seals of Norwich and Rochester Cathedrals.
98. The frequent use on Royal Seals of a plain name and title in the nominative as on coins.
99. An occasional variant is *Secretum*, implying that the owner has another and larger *Sigillum: contrasigillum* also appears, as in the case of Nostell Priory, already noted.

there may be at the end a statement of the use to which this particular one is dedicated: for instance, on the Scottish Seal of Edward I, the words *ad regimen regni Scocie deputatum* occur in this position.[100] Sometimes, as we have seen, this may be placed elsewhere, especially in later Seals. If the Seal is two-sided, the same legend may appear on both sides; or there may be a variation — a multiple title being divided between the two, as it is (for example) in one of the earliest Great Seals in our period,[101] or (as in the case of Philip and Mary, whose combined titles were much too long for any one legend) a single sentence may be continued from one side to the other;[102] or (as may be observed in most of the Exchequer Seals) the *reverse* may be used for statement of the functions of that particular seal.

The above remarks apply, *mutatis mutandis*, to the smaller armorial seals and to many of the non-armorial: but with the last-named we begin to get variations. This applies even in the case of large ones; a Religious Found-ation, for instance, which displays on its Seal a picture of the Virgin and the figure of its patron, Thomas Bek, Bishop of Lincoln, using for legend a verse

Salva prece pia Thomam Bek Virgo Maria.[103]

This kind of legend seems to have been very popular with Ecclesiastics; who doubtless enjoyed composing the verses even if they made false quantities. But the lure of religious and allusive legends is not confined to Ecclesiastics, as may be judged from the text seen on one side of the Borough Seal of Colchester shown in Plate VIII; and flights of fancy were not infrequent also in the owners of small fancy seals; ranging from verse again — for example (on a seal shown in Plate VI) —

Est Ade signum vir femina vipera lignum[104]

down to short more or less allusive mottoes either in Latin or in the vernacular.[105] Naturally, the smaller the matrix the greater the temptation to

---

100. See *Antiquaries' Journal*, XI, p. 229.
101. The legends of the "fourth" Seal of Henry I are *Henricus Rex Anglorum* and *Henricus Dux Normannorum*: see Wyon, Plate IV. Compare the two verse legends used by William the Conqueror, and for a later example see that of John de Warenne in our first plate.
102. See Wyon, Plate XXI. This is also the case in the Scottish Seal mentioned above.
103. The Seal of the Hospital of St. Thomas in Billingford co. Norfolk. This is a very simple example: at the other end of the scale is the elaboration of a 14th-century Seal of Boxley Abbey which has, on double bands, first an ordinary legend and then three verses, one punning on its name, one containing a prayer to St. Bernard, and one invoking St. Benedict. Examples of these and many others may be found in the British Museum *Catalogue*
104. A small seal of Adam de Howtone, about 1315, depicting the Garden of Eden: it might be rendered in verse not much worse than the original:
    "This is the mark I, Adam, make —
    A man, a woman, a tree and a snake."
105. Such as the merely descriptive *Sum Leo Fortis* in combination with the device of a lion; or the more elaborate *Loke wel forth* on the seal (depicting a fox emerging from a hole) of one

cut down the lettering to vanishing point; and without considering the cheaper ones (where the question of lettering would in any case not arise) we may suppose that anyone who had a great as well as small seal, and used the latter only for his more intimate affairs, might well be content with no more than his heraldic identification or even less than that.[106]

This brings us to the final stage in which the post-medieval heraldic seal has dropped altogether the explanatory legend, while the motto has become a family matter, a regular part of the armorial achievement: this convention survives to our own day and is too familiar to need illustration.

The *Language* of the more conventional seal legends continues to be predominantly Latin down to a late date: and that language is still employed in some cases on such seals. On the small non-armorial seals, as may be judged from the note above, English occurs quite early: and French is not unknown.

THE CARE OF SEALS

On the treatment, repair and packing of Seals, an article has been published elsewhere,[107] to which reference may be made. Here then we need only say summarily:

(1) that Seals should *never* be severed from their documents — the relation is vital;[108]

(2) that in Repair the main principles are
(a) to repair so far as possible with the same material, but
(b) to distinguish — generally by colour — the new from the old;

(3) that in Packing, numerous *ad hoc* devices may be invented, but that the principles are
(a) to avoid absorbent packing materials in the case of Seals made of true wax,
(b) to prevent pressure (this again relates specially to wax Seals) and bending, and
(c) to take the weight off tongue, tag or laces;

and finally

(4) that since, after all our care, Seals may still get broken, it is wise to take moulds, for Record purposes, of our more important specimens; and that this is an interesting craft to practise.[109]

John Foxholes, about 1426. Examples in English have been noted on Seals in the Record Office so early as the 13th century.

106. Curious examples are some of the earliest Royal Signets or finger rings: notably one of Richard II which bears simply the word *richard*.

107. By the present writer in *Antiquaries' Journal*, IV (1924), p. 388. I may perhaps take this opportunity of correcting a printer's error of some importance on page 396: 8% of dilute hydrochloric acid should be 0.36.

108. Numerous melancholy examples in Public Collections of "Loose Seals" which have lost half their significance — or more than that — point this moral.

109. Methods of moulding are described in the article cited.

SURVIVALS OF ENGLISH SEALS AND THE RECORDING OF THEM

The answer to the question propounded above should already be clear by implication: even if we exclude all but medieval Seals — say, all after 1550 — the number of possible survivals is incalculable. By far the commonest type of document on which Seals are preserved to us is the *Deed*, and until late in the 19th century, when "long title" was abolished, Landowners had every interest in the preservation of Deeds of any age relating to their property; and although the number of these documents which have been destroyed since then is terribly large, the survivals are still extremely numerous. It is not uncommon to find in any reasonably well-kept Muniment Room — that of a College for example — bundles of 100 to 200 deeds of medieval date, all complete with Seals, for each property held.

The apparent hopelessness of the task is sometimes made an excuse for not attempting to record for the purpose of study at any rate the less important Seals: moreover, the number of persons who, though interested in historical and archaeological matters and particularly in documents, are not yet aware of the importance of this subject, would seem to be still very large. From the answers to a questionnaire recently sent out by the British Records Association, it appeared that about twenty-five out of seventy Institutions who are interested, from the point of view of cataloguing or publication, in Deeds, make no allusion to Seals in the lists or descriptions of these documents which they prepare for their own use or for printing. I would venture to conclude this article by urging that it is time everyone adopted a policy of invariably recording Seals in such cases: and I would emphasize once more that until we know much more than we do at present, it will be impossible for us to say that any seal of medieval date, however trifling its design, however unimportant the position of its owner, can be regarded as entirely lacking in interest.

Naturally the amount to be said must vary with the nature of the Seal: where the subject demands anything of a description I would plead, in the interests of scholarship, for a general adoption of the standard phraseology suggested in the *Report on Editing* already cited. I might also perhaps venture to suggest that Cataloguers of Deeds should get together in order to arrive at a more or less fixed use of such terms of comparison as "part" or "portion," "fragment" and "incomplete"; and again, to agree on the sense in which they will use the words "good impression," "defaced," "mutilated" and "damaged"; it is not always realised that a "fragment" may be a "good impression." Moreover, even if circumstances prevent anything approaching full description, I would still suggest that a little thought will enable Cataloguers and Editors to give in a surprisingly small space at least some information about the Seals in their description of any Deed. Supposing, for instance, the Parties to a Deed are numbered in the Catalogue entry of it, the facts that on an elaborate Deed in which five parties were concerned, the Seals of A, B, D, and E survived and were appended each on its own tag, while that of C was represented by a tag only, that those of A and D displayed their Arms, that B's seal contained his name, and that E's was merely of a conventional pattern, could all be conveyed in the form:

Seals: (1)(4) Arm.; (2) Name; (5) Conv.: 5 *Tags*.

which is considerably less than a line of ordinary typescript or print: and even

Seals: 1,2,4,5: 3 *lost*

would convey some information.

At the present moment there is more interest in such matters than there has ever been before in this country: and at the last Conference of the British Records Association an inquiry into the possibility of securing an uniform system of Cataloguing Deeds was referred to a Committee for further consideration and Report. It is much to be hoped that in the near future co-operative work by many hands may lead to the gradual enlargement of our knowledge of a very interesting subject.

POSTSCRIPTS

Since this article was written, I have been asked to add to it some remarks about the *Forgery of Seals*. The subject is much too large and too difficult to be treated with any fullness here, but two remarks may be made.

The forging of a Seal was long regarded as a very serious offence: forging the King's Seal, for instance, was high treason:[110] and although forgery, given a suitable original to forge from, would not be difficult (plaster of Paris and the like were no doubt available), it is doubtful if the medieval counterfeiter would normally think of making a matrix. On the other hand, there is a number of recorded cases where documents were challenged because their seals were not right; and a further number of cases, discovered by modern scholars, where what appears to be a right seal is attached to a very wrong document.[111] The explanation is, I think, that in the one case the "forger" tried to pass muster with a more or less formless lump of wax, or

---

110. By Statute, 25 Edward III, st. 5, c. 2.
111. See for example the alleged charter of Henry II as Duke of Normandy, illustrated on Plate XXIX of C.L. Kingsford's article on the De L'Isle and Dudley documents in *Archaeologia*, LXV (1914). This is a 16th-century forgery: a good medieval example is an alleged charter of Henry I to St. Peter's, Gloucester (Public Record Office, *Ancient Deeds*, A.S., 308), which was probably produced in the 13th century.

some similar trick, while in the other he slipped, from its tag or tongue on a document he did not want, a genuine seal, and transferred it to a spurious writing which he proposed to get confirmed at the Royal Chancery or to use for some other practical purpose, such as a law suit.

My second point is that the proceedings just mentioned should not too hastily or indiscriminately be labelled "forgery" with the full modern connotation of that word: there is little doubt, for example, that a few at least of the known cases of monastic "forgeries" may prove an investigation to be nothing worse than the more or less intelligent reproduction of a genuine charter which had been lost: very improper, of course, but not necessarily immoral. The whole question requires minute investigation.

APPENDIX

LIST OF ILLUSTRATIONS[112]

Note. *The dates given (save in the case of Plates III and V) are those of the documents to which the Seals are attached: but the matrices from which they were made are in some cases of much earlier date.*
Line blocks in the text are not included in this List.

---

112. The Plates (except Nos. II, III, V and VIII) are from photographs of yellow plaster casts, waxed — and the material approved for this purpose at the Record Office.
113. See description and notes above, p. 95.
114. See B.A.A. *Journal,* XII, p. 147: an engraving of the seal is given *ibid.*, Pl. XVIII.
115. Date assigned in the British Museum *Catalogue.*
116. This matrix is said to have been made three centuries earlier (1241): see British Museum *Catalogue* No. 3637, with references to Dugdale and to Manning and Bray.

(2) Seal of Nostell Priory with figure of St. Oswald[117] 1280[118]
Public Record Office: Ancient Deeds, B.S., 378 and A.S.,484.
Plate V. The Court of Chancery[119] ... ... 15th century
Note, on the table, the Great Seal Matrix and the writs
folded ready for despatch.
MS. *in the Inner Temple Library.*
Plate VI. Small Seals ... ... 12th century to 16th century
From Ancient Deeds in the Public Office: as follows.[120]

(1)	*Dominus* John Drewe (A.S. 340)	1 Henry VI
(2)	Joan, wife of Henry, son of R[einer] (A. 1803), ...	[12th century]
(3)	John D'Engayne (L.S. 173)	30 Edward III
(4)	William Chaucede (B. 3007)	5 Edward III
(5)	John Bellewe (PP. 177)	1 and 2 Philip & Mary
(6)	Adam Howtone (D. 7941)	9 Edward II
(7)	Eva de Broc[h] (L.S. 55)	[later 12th cent]
(8)	Nicholas Hugate (W.S.60)	18 Edward III
(9)	Petronilla de Benstede (L.S. 165)	33 Edward III
(10)	William de Dodingesele (C. S. 91)	[late 13th cent.]
(11)	Thomas, son of Richard Viel (B.S. 97)	13 Edward I

Plate VII. Warenne Seals ... ... 13th and 14th centuries
(1) William de Warenne (Obverse only) ... ... [c. 1230]
Public Record Office: Ancient Deeds, L.S., 223.
(2) and (3) John de Warenne (Obverse & Reverse) 29 Edward I.
Public Record Office: Exchequer (T.R.), Barons' Letter.[121]
(4) John de Warenne (Privy Seal) ... ... 12 Edward II.
Public Record Office: Ancient Deeds, A.S., 101.
Plate VIII. 15th-century Seal of the Borough of Colchester,
attached to a modern document, with cast to show the
other side 1888
The seal shows (obverse the figure of St. Helen and (reverse) a walled town with the text *Intravit Jesus,* from Luke

117. A small oval seal used as Counterseal is not shown here. As to these seals, see William Salt Society *Collections,* ... N.S. VIII, p. 130, printing a description not quite correct) given of it in 1375.
118. The matrix is ascribed to the early 12th century.
119. See a note on this and three companion pictures of the Courts of Exchequer, King's Bench and Common Pleas, with coloured illustrations, in *Archaeologia,* XXXIX (1862).
120. The numbers give the position in the Plate reading from left to right by rows: the first row contains numbers 1, 2, 3; and the third numbers 6, 7, 8; the central (oval) seal being No. 7. The Deed references are given in brackets.
121 See M.S. Giuseppi, *Guide to the ... Public Record Office* (1923), I, p. 201: and authorities there cited.

x, 38. Note the very abnormal method of attachment, a
hole being bored in the impression and a ribbon passed
through it.

From Public Record Office: Chancery, Liquidation Proceedings, 129.

Plate IX. Seals of Bishops of Bath and Wells[122] 13th to 18th centuries
(Note persistence of the Cross of St. Andrew, even in the arms on
late Seal.)

From Ancient Deeds in the Public Record Office : as follows.

(1)   Robert [Burnel] (A.S. 296) . . . . [1275-1293]

(2)   Ralph [de Salopia] (B.S. 410) . . . . 37 Edward III

(3)   William [Knight] (BB. 128) . . . . 33 Henry VII

and from P.R.O.: Exchequer, First Fruits, Bishops'
Certificates, 4/23/470.

(4)   Edward Will[es] 1744

---

122.   On the subject of Episcopal Seals in this Diocese, see an article by Sir W.H. St. John
Hope in Somerset Archaeological and Natural History Society's *Proceedings,* XXXVI
(1889), p. 29.

PLATE I: Seal of John De Warenne, Earl of Surrey and Stratherne: 14th cent.

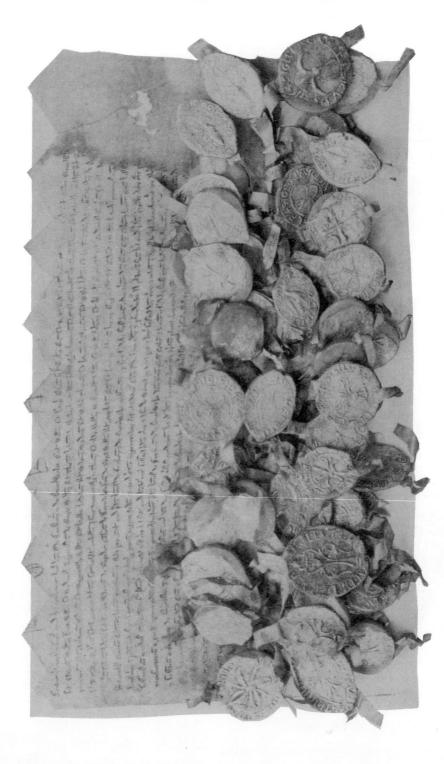

PLATE II: Seals of men of Frieston and Butterwick, Co. Lincoln; early 13th cent.

PLATE III: Wykeham's seal for New College: 1386

PLATE IV: Seals of Nostell and Merton Priories: 12th and 13th centuries

PLATE V: The Court of Chancery: 15th cent. Ms.

PLATE VI: Small seals: 12th to 16th century

PLATE VII: Warenne seals. Early and late 13th cent. and early 14th cent.

PLATE VIII: 15th cent. seal of Colchester on document of 1888

PLATE IX: Seals of bishops of Bath and Wells: 13th to 18th century

The Choice of Records for Preservation in Wartime: Some Practical Hints

Let it be said at once that the title to these notes is not to be taken either as condoning by implication the destruction of Records or as suggesting that any qualities of scholarship or experience will make it possible for anyone to "choose" with certainty out of a mass of Records those which future historians will find most useful. Records ought not to be destroyed: the necessary selection of *current office documents* for final preservation as *Records* should have taken place long before the "Record" stage is reached. But it frequently happens that Local and Private Records are the result of an accumulation of office documents over which there has been little or no control; and in such cases the Records, which have survived because no one troubled to destroy them, are particularly liable to perish in times of stress because no one is sufficiently interested to preserve them; and to perish indiscriminately, important and unimportant together.

It is such indiscriminate raiding of Local and Private Muniments in time of War that the British Records Association, as is made clear by the letter of the Master of the Rolls, which is reprinted on the opposite page, has set itself to prevent so far as possible: and in attempting this task the Association turns naturally for help to the Librarians; who were among the first to study seriously Archive questions in this country and to provide harbourage for Records the owners of which had ceased to be interested in their preservation. To commend to such an audience the importance of the work would be preaching to the converted: but it is thought that some of the librarians who, it is hoped, will be consulted, may not have had much direct experience in dealing hastily with large masses of documents. Hence the following suggestions.

(i) In the first place we would say to librarians consulted, "*Do not imagine that there will be time normally for examination of individual documents*": accumulations which are worth the attention of the paper merchant will be much too large for that. Little as you (or we) like it you will have to make sacrifices to urgency and the necessity for speed.

(ii) It is particularly necessary for the same reasons to *solicit the advice and help of the Owner:* his practical experience and knowledge of the documents, even though he does not think them worth preserving, may be invaluable: he may know of old Lists, or of an Official on the staff who has inherited knowledge of the contents of the Muniment Room.

(iii) Faced with a big accumulation your first task will be to get set aside for examination *likely classes of documents, boxes with suggestive titles and any distinguishable smaller collections* such as those of a commercial concern, a public institution, or charity, or a body of trustees. The greatest variety of documents will probably be found in Solicitors' offices: members of the firm may have acted as *Town Clerks* or as Clerks to *Enclosure Commissioners, Boards of Health* and *Guardians of the Poor, Turnpike Trusts* and all sorts of other trusts and charities; they may have been Secretaries to Committees dealing with *Railway* or *Canal construction* and many other kinds of public business; and in innumerable instances they have been *Stewards of Manors.* The documentary results of any of these activities, and even of the employment of solicitors as *Clerks of Assize, Clerks of the Peace* or *Ecclesiastical Registrars,* have been found in the past and may be found again in their Muniment Rooms. Here, then, are quantities of really important Record classes which may have to be singled out before we can afford to look into the more problematical value of boxes labelled "Executors of X.Y.Z., Esq."

(iv) If and when you proceed to more detailed examination of (for example) any of the collections suggested above it is vital to remember that the criterion by which the importance of Records must be judged *is not that of sentiment or aesthetic value.* Interesting autographs, "association" pieces, charming sketches — these are not what you are to look for: though they may reasonably be preserved if found without looking.

The very brief time you will probably have at your disposal is to be spent in finding out and preserving if possible (and this is where the knowledge of the owner or the official may be so valuable) the series of *documents which were in their time the essential ones for office work*; and which consequently preserve for us still, in the smallest space, a Record of what the business, or institution, or individual in question was engaged upon when they were made.

(v) It follows that normally, whatever else goes, an effort should be made to preserve *Surveys, Estate Maps and Plans* and *Particulars of Sales* (especially marked copies); *Court Rolls, Minute Books* and other *Records of Proceedings; Ledgers* or (failing these) *Journals* or *Cash Books; Rentals, Rate Books* and *Assessments* and any other official *Lists of Names; Abstracts of Title* and, at any rate down to the end of the seventeenth century, original *Conveyances of Real Property, Marriage Settlements* and Records of *Legal Transactions. Correspondence* of a date before 1700[1] should also be kept if possible: nor must it be forgotten that really important printed matter — unique copies of pamphlets, for instance, and early local newspapers — have been found and may be found again among Records.

If these and their like can be saved, the destruction of masses of old Correspondence, Petty Cash and Cash Books, Vouchers and Miscellanea need not be reckoned so great a loss.

1. Date is not a sound criterion to go by in general, because in one class a document of (say) 1600 would be a very early and important example while in another it would be late and comparatively valueless. It may be useful, however, to bear in mind, as a guide, that in the case of the Public Records the rule is that nothing of a date earlier than 1660 may be destroyed.

The Expert Care of Archives: Dangers of the War and Post-War Periods

INTRODUCTORY

My excuse for obtruding my views personally on this Conference is primarily that in a world rather full, just now, of chances I was better able to guarantee my own presence than that of many of our Members who would have liked to discuss this theme. But I may perhaps also say that for the last twenty years, I have been as much interested as anyone in promoting the consideration of Archive Science as an independent subject, to be treated and studied as such. I have indeed been accused sometimes of endeavouring to force the word *Archives* on a reluctant world and it is a fact that some English people are still a little shy of it: I use it because it is more comprehensive than *Records* and because its universal occurrence in other European languages emphasises the possibility of the study of Archive Science on international lines, improbable as that may seem at the present moment. It is, however, with a purely domestic problem that I am concerned to-day.

ARCHIVE WORK IN ENGLAND IN THE PAST[1]

Less than twenty years ago there were still many persons concerned with Record work for whom their subject began and ended with the Public Records; who would not allow much importance to any classes even of those, apart from the *Chancery Enrolments*, the *State Papers*, and a few others; and for whom the needs of the Student meant only the needs of Family History or Topography. If the suggestion had been made to them that for the Archivist all classes of documents in his custody must from certain points of view be said to have an equal value, they would certainly have considered that the

---

1. I have ventured here to use again words which I wrote in 1937 in reviewing development which had occurred since the first publication of my *Archive Administration*.

person who put it forward was trying to gain a cheap reputation by the use of paradox: and to talk of Archive Science in such company was to run the risk of being thought rather silly. Outside the Public Record Office, though a number of official Reports had drawn attention to the quantity, nature and importance of our Local Records, there were not more than two or three Local Authorities which had yet even considered the desirability of making special provision for the organization and maintenance of an Archive department: and after fifty years of demonstration, in the publications of the Historical MSS. Commission, of the quality and quantity of Private Collections in this Country local enthusiasts were still struggling with little success in most neighbourhoods to obtain that first requisite — a Local Repository where they could find housing and custody for documentary collections in danger of dispersal or destruction.

PROGRESS SINCE 1918

How great an advance from this state had been made in the period 1918-1938 one has only to look at the current number of our *Year's Work* to see. We may summarise it under eight heads.

I. *Publishing Societies.*
Not only had the Local Societies recovered from the last War but there was plenty of fresh development: old Record Societies had started on enterprising new series of publications and new Societies had been formed in connexion with Counties (such as Warwickshire and Wiltshire) and other bodies and Institutions (such as the City of Bristol and the Hudson's Bay Company) which did not possess them before. When in 1934 our Association brought together a display of volumes thus produced we were able to show over 350 as the result of only five years' publication by 60 Societies.

II. *General Interest in Care of Documents.*
We were slowly but steadily removing the reproach that England, probably the richest Country of the World in local and private survivals of Archives, though it might be prepared to spend money in publishing cared nothing for their physical welfare. I will take only, as an index to this development, the single matter of Repair. The special staff engaged in this work at the Public Record Office is allowed to undertake it privately in the limited time available outside Office hours and during the ten years preceding the present War a very remarkable number of public, semi-public and private institutions had taken advantage, some to a small, some to a very large extent, of these facilities. Glancing only at the more important, one finds them to include among Local Authorities ten Counties, some thirty ancient Boroughs, a sprinkling even of such modern bodies as District Councils, and more than a score of Public Libraries and Museums; among Educational

Institutions at least ten of the Cambridge and Oxford Colleges, five other University bodies, two of the Inns of Court, the Royal College of Surgeons and a small number of Schools; on the Ecclesiastical side half a dozen Dioceses and as many Chapters and at least sixty Parishes figure in the list, with several other important institutions such as the Society for Promoting Christian Knowledge, the Society for the Propagation of the Gospel and the Church Missionary Society; and among other public or semi-public bodies we have to note eight of the Livery Companies of London, three Hospitals and three Banks. That, for a comparatively new development, is a remarkable list: and of course the Record Office is not the only place where such work is done.

III. *Archive Science as a Subject*

The Local Libraries had always been good friends to the movement for the preservation of Documents in the interests of Local History: not infrequently (as for instance in the case of the Minet Library at Camberwell) they had provided during the lean years the only possible refuge for those un-wanted *Deeds* whose value for County History is now so widely recognised. And more recently both the Library Association (for its Diploma) and the School of Librarianship established in London University in 1920 by giving this subject a definite place in their curriculum had made possible the elaboration of a technique new in this country — that of the Specialising Archivist. Two great services for which the Librarians deserve much gratitude.

IV. *New Repositories and Archive Organization.*

The proposals of the Royal Commission of 1910 had never born fruit: but what formal recommendations for statutory action had failed to bring about was beginning to be accomplished by individual enthusiasm. Bedfordshire, under the inspiration of Dr. G.H. Fowler, had shewn that an Archives Department was a practical possibility as part of the ordinary machinery of County Administration: County after County (especially in the years immediately preceding the present War) had followed this lead and so had a number of Boroughs (Bristol, for example, and Coventry), of Religious Authorities or Institutions such as the Diocese of Lincoln,[2] the Dean and Chapter of Ely and the Society of Friends, and even the owners of some of the great accummulations of purely private Muniments such as those at Chatsworth, Hatfield and Woburn.

V. *The Professional Archivist*

The last named movement had done much to stimulate the development already mentioned under III. above: recognition of the utility or necessity of

---

2.   We must not forget in this connexion the effect of the Church Measure of 1929 which permits the setting up of Diocesan Record Offices; the effect of which was just beginning to be felt when War broke out.

a special Repository for Archives, even of a special department for their administration, implied the recognition of a need for Archivists; and the demand quickly created supply. Would-be Archivists had in fact for years been waiting only for some modest prospect of a career before turning to specialisation in this direction. More recently still, similar indications had begun to reach us from the Dominions and Colonies: this Association had even received from one (Southern Rhodesia) the request that we would ourselves institute a special Diploma purely for Archive work.

VI. *The Master of the Rolls and Local Repositories.*
The Amendment (1924) to Lord Birkenhead's Act, coming into force in 1926, accomplished two very important things which those who framed it had perhaps hardly contemplated. In the first place it gave to the head of the Central (and only official) Archives Establishment in England, for the first time, a definite official relation with, and control over, one section[3] of Local or Private Archives — the Manorial: a very significant and interesting innovation in this Country though in most Continental Archive Systems it had long been the rule. In the second place it led to the Master of the Rolls 'recognizing' at least one manorial Repository for every County, very often the existing Muniment Room of a County Council; and this has already had far-reaching results: quite soon, with the late Lord Hanworth's sedulous encouragement, Local Authorities and other Bodies began not merely to accept but to seek such recognition; and once opened the Muniment Rooms generally did not stop at housing merely Manorial Records.

VII. *Records Preservation.*
As a result when the British Record Society in 1929 took up the task of saving for Students Records which were un-wanted by their owners it found at least one part of the old problem — that of finding homes for them — in a fair way to be solved.

VIII. *The B.R.A.*
Finally when our own Association came into being in 1932 with the object of co-ordinating all the interests and enthusiasms which I have just described it met with a success which even its most enthusiastic promoters would have hesitated to predict. It is true that our position in 1939 was the result of a great deal of hard work by many people of good will: but with all the good will and all the work we could command I think none of us had hoped to achieve in seven years a Membership of 900, including 300 Institutions and representing, thoroughly, every kind of Archive-owning interest in England. In addition our Conferences and Exhibitions, speaking with all modesty, have been remarkably successful and have attracted a considerable amount of public attention: we have a very respectable body of publication to our

3. A clause in the recent Tithe Act makes this now two sections.

credit: people have begun to call on us for assistance and advice: and (a most gratifying feature) the more technical sides of our work have not been behind the others in arousing interest outside our own Membership.

WAR-TIME AND POST-WAR DANGERS

So much for the positions we have gained: I turn to the dangers from which, I suggest, it is our duty to defend them. It is hardly necessary to say that Economies, the cutting down of expenditure on most of the Activities I have been describing, are inevitable at the present time: equally inevitable are the depletion of Staff owing to the calls to military or other War service and the transfer of many of that army of voluntary workers upon whom in Peace time we rely for so much of our work — even of the most senior of them — to tasks of a more immediate urgency. We must be resigned to publish less, repair less, sort less, consult less; and view with as much equanimity as we can the temporary disappearance of the School of Librarianship or the closing of a Students' Room. There is no complaint; and indeed, as you may see from the *Year's Work* which will be issued with these *Proceedings*, Archivists, amateur and professional, are somehow contriving without (as we have reason to know) neglecting other duties to keep old interests alive to a surprising extent. But probably the worst pinch is yet to come and it is against this and its after effects that we should be forewarned and so far as possible fore-armed. There seem to me to be four principal dangers — risks to which the developments in which we are interested are particularly liable because they are for the most part young and tender growths.

THE DANGER TO WORK IN HAND

There is more than a chance, unless we are very careful, that many enterprises of *Research* and *Publication*, which have had to be 'temporarily' stopped may not be resumed; for any one of a number of reasons. It was only with difficulty, in many cases, that one found the editor, or the money, or the facilities, or the time for them: and after the War, *they will not be resumed automatically:* it will need a fresh effort, perhaps a greater one than before, because there will be many competing interests, to ensure that they do not follow the line of least resistance and fade out; but that effort ought to be foreseen and undertaken.

THE DANGER TO PROGRESS IN LARGER AFFAIRS

The risk of which I have just spoken is one which I think threatens all that amateur, private, and unpaid effort, much of it perhaps in comparatively small fields, which taken as a whole has produced such a great body of succesful work in recent years. When we turn to the larger schemes in which are involved not only the contributions in enthusiasm, time and money of Individuals but also the interest and co-operation of Institutions and Public Authorities we face a fresh danger: because it is to be remembered that a large proportion of the members of such bodies who have been moved in recent years to agree to the diversion of small (generally very small) amounts of the funds they adminster to Archive purposes — to the building of a new Repository, to the Repair of a considerable part of their ancient Records, to Publication, or to the payment of an Archivist — a large proportion of these do not share our enthusiasms; they are at best mildly interested, at worst apathetic; and on the other hand, they have very often enthusiasms of their own. We must anticipate in some cases after the War a *considerable effort*, supported by plausible arguments, *to cut out further expenditure* on the Repair and Publication which had been so happily begun, to *postpone* till the Greek Kalends the building of that new Repository, *to refrain* 'for the present' from filling the place of an Archivist who has been absorbed elsewhere.

It is not my object in the present connexion to suggest practical measures but I will venture at this point to stress the value (if no better may be) of merely keeping alive — of securing a 'token' amount of repairing and publication or other Archive work in default of complete and immediate restoration of the status quo: *the fatal thing would be to let the work which has been begun lapse altogether.*

THE DANGER TO THE PROFESSION

This is really implicit in what I have just said; for it there are no professional openings for them there will be no Archivists. I will venture to call the keeping alive of that particularly young and tender plant, the Archivist's profession in this country, the most important of the tasks I have been describing. Of all the Archive developments of recent years it has been the most difficult to secure: for volumes and buildings are at least concrete things — there is something to shew for the money expended; whereas many people can still see no need to spend money on such a luxury as trained Assistants; still cling to the view that the administration of Archives requires no special knowledge; still hug the even more ingenuous belief that if you provide a building it will somehow contrive to run itself without staff. On the other hand *if we can keep in existence a body, even a small one, of men and women trained to Archive work and zealous in their calling and other things we desire will be added:* the Archivists can be trusted to see that somehow work for the care and arrangement of their documents and their accessibility to Students does go forward; and, what is almost equally important, that technical research for the betterment of their own knowledge and method is not neglected.

THE DANGER TO OUR OWN ASSOCIATION

I need not labour this final point (though it is not the least important of those I have to suggest) for it has already been put in the Appeal addressed to Members by our President in the first year of the War. I will venture to quote again two passages in particular. The Association, he pointed out, had already made for itself a position which might truly be called national. 'That it has been able to do this is due to the large and representative Membership: both of Individuals and Institutions, which it has succeeded in securing: a remarkable feat which has only been accomplished by an exceptionally large amount of patient and unremitting labour. It is very doubtful if such an effort could be repeated.' . . . The financial support it demands is not large, but, on the other hand, the numerical strength of its supporters is one of its chief assets. Moreover, Membership of it is not directed merely to securing for the Member the advantage of receiving publications or attending meetings: rather it is an affirmation of belief in the national importance of Archive Work; and that is a belief which should not be allowed to perish even in time of War.'

I will not offer any concluding apology but merely say this in continuance of our President's last remark. Archivists may be as modest as they will about their own proficiency and performance: and they should certainly be as modest as they can in any demands they make for the continuance of their activities in times of national stress. But I venture to add that they should not be at all modest about the importance of the work entrusted to them nor backward in proclaiming that importance, even in times like the present, when fit occasion offers. Of all forms of written evidence on which the progress of human knowledge depends, Archives — I use the word in its widest sense to include ancient and modern, public and private, civil and religious, legal, political, economic and social — Archives, if conserved with fidelity and used with intelligence, give us the best chance of arriving at the facts, at undiluted Truth. And it is for the maintenance of Truth as the only sure basis of Conduct that we are now fighting.

The Classification and Survey of English Archives

The subject which I have been invited to cover here is so vast, and the space in which to do it comparatively so small, that I think, though naturally flattered by the invitation, I should have declined it if it were not for the recollection of two words to which I most strongly object and about which I have been wanting to say something ever since a *Congrès Mondial* on Documentation which I attended at Paris in 1937. I did, in point of fact, say something at the Conference at Oxford in the following year: but I do not feel that I (or other Archivists, for I claim no monopoly) have said nearly enough: hence this paper. The two words are "and Archives" or "and Records", and I need hardly say that I have no objection to them as words. What I dislike is the way in which they are dropped in, as a hardly necessary after-thought, at the end of long lists of other things to which Records or Archives bear no relation: no relation at any rate which justifies that casual "and". The Director of Salvage and his enthusiastic followers have taken to doing it lately: 'hand over for pulping,' they tell us 'your old Newspapers, Music, Pictures, Maps, Photographs, Prints, unwanted Books *and Records*'.

The exponents of scientific documentation (I am afraid we must admit), when propounding large schemes for the classification and utilization of the sources of human knowledge are prone to make the same mistake: not, of course, with effects so immediately devastating, but with the result of a darkening of council which is quite sufficiently confusing and might well be actually dangerous to Records, if their proposals were taken seriously by Archivists.

The subject being so large I hope I may be forgiven if I concentrate on setting out plainly its main headings and if my style becomes in consequence rather tabular.

I. **In the first place** *What are Archives?*

To give a quite un-technical definition[1] they are the Office Documents (with annexures) which accumulate in the course of business, are kept more or less deliberately for reference, and thereafter survive in the custody of their original owners, or subsequent representatives of those owners, for any one of a number of reasons; including mere inertia — the fact that no one can find time or energy to decide whether they still have practical value. The Business with which they are connected may be of any kind — Lay or Ecclesiastical, Central or Local, Public or Private, Ancient or Modern, large or small: most people, in fact, in an age when writing is in general use, make Archives, as Monsieur Jourdain made prose, *sans le savoir*. Whatever its size or kind all Organized Business accumulates Office Documents and all these documents may presently emerge from a kind of cocoon stage as Archives. In the past they have generally been manuscript but that is not a necessity.

II. **My next point is that of the** *Qualities of Archives* **which result from that definition: I shall specify five.**

(1) *Archives are Accumulations, not Collections*: that is to say, they came together by a natural process — like Topsy, they growed: they are parts of an organism: they were not singled out for preservation on account of their believed value for aesthetic, historical or literary purposes by the more or less fallible judgment of an expert. It would be a service to clarity if the word 'Collections' could be reserved for Museum specimens and banished for ever from the description of Archives.

(2) *Archives were not normally drawn up for the information of Posterity*: they are in fact used as a rule by Posterity for purposes quite different from those which caused their compilation. Even in the exceptional cases when (for example) a document is expressly stated to be addressed to all present and to come, *omnibus presentibus et futuris*, or to be drawn up *in perpetuam rei memoriam*, the result is the same: it is safe to say that most of the deductions which Historians and Lawyers have made from *Magna Carta* never entered the heads of King John who granted it, the Barons who extorted it, or the Chancery Clerks who copied it.

---

1. The more detailed definition of which this is a summary was worked out in my *Manual of Archive Administration* in 1922 (second edition 1937). Though circumstances in different countries induce naturally a varying point of view in Archivists it has not been, so far as I know, seriously attacked: and appears to agree very closely with an earlier definition independently worked out in America by Dr C.M. Andrews, of which I was not at the time aware. See *Third Annual Report of the Archivist of the United States* (Washington: 1938), pp. 4 and 5, quoting both definitions.

(3) *The fact and nature of Custody are all-important for Archives.* Two matters in particular are involved here.

(a) *The impartiality and authenticity of the Archive.* Obviously if the persons who preserved it (and their successors — an important point) did so for reasons quite independent of our interests, of which they were in fact ignorant, we start with the enormous advantage of knowing that there can be no intention on the part of the document to mislead us: we can only go wrong owing to our own incorrect interpretation of it. An example frequently used but so good that it will perhaps bear one more repetition is that of the entry in a Revels' Account, made and preserved to justify certain expenditure by a Court Official in 1605, but used by us to give a date to one of Shakespeare's plays: for which it would have furnished unimpeachably evidence if it had not been known to have spent some time out of the custody of the Audit Office and in the keeping of a Shakespeare enthusiast. A dozen or so of books[2] and articles have been written to prove (a) that Peter Cunningham did, or (b) that he did not, forge the all-important entry.

(b) *The Effect of Custody on Interpretation.* By this I mean the relation of the particular custody in which a Record is preserved to the nature of the evidence it offers. To take the simplest example, a letter, or copy of a letter, addressed by X. to Y., if preserved in the custody of X. is evidence of despatch: whereas if you find it in the custody of Y. it is evidence of receipt. In neither case, of course, does it prove the truth of the statements made by X.: and it will probably be used eventually to prove or disprove statements by a later writer upon some subject not specifically mentioned in it at all.

The above remarks may show why the good Archivist insists, sometimes to the annoyance of students who want 'facilities', on the importance of 'unbroken custody'. He has to guard a character in his Archives which gives them *a value possessed by no other form of written evidence.*

(4) *Archives were an actual part of Administration.* This means that to be sure of interpreting an Archive correctly you have to know something of the Office routine which lies behind it: because *in a document intended for their own or their colleagues' or correspondents' information* (not ours) people will naturally use a technique of abbreviations, omissions, verbal forms, and the like which they will not think it necessary to explain. Everyone does it. A frivolous modern example is that of the small boy who constantly marked items of expenditure in his cash account S.P.G.: had his Mother known as much as she should of his office technique she would not have been so pleased with his devotion to the Society for the Propagation of the Gospel. At the other end of the chronological scale is the well-known T.R.E. of Domesday. My own favourite example is one in which a mere dot in the margin plays an important part: it

2. The most recent is, I think, the late Mr A.E. Stamp's *Disputed Revels Accounts* (Oxford: 1930).

is that of the medieval Receipt Roll which in certain circumstances appears to record the payment, at Westminster on the date in question; with nothing, on the surface, to distinguish these entries from neighbouring ones which mean exactly what they say. *Knowledge of the History and Machinery*[3] *of Administration is essential for the intelligent use of Archives.*

(5) *Inter-relation of Archives.* In any business the actions of the several departments are bound to be related and the same remark applies with even more force to their Archives, the written remains of those actions: the significance of the *Ledgers* for instance, of an Accounting Section may be lost without reference to the *Correspondence* of the Executive. It follows of course that normally no document preserved as an Archive is to be considered separately, *per se*, as it would probably be if it were a Museum specimen: also that documents intrinsically dull or unimportant may be of the greatest value as an essential part of the whole organism: and in particular that *the first approach to any accumulation of Archives must be an investigation of them as a whole.*

But this inter-relation goes further. Nearly all business has at least two sides — the fact that A. writes a letter postulates the existence of a correspondent, B.; *and of B.'s Archives.* In fact it is not too much to say that in a period like our own, when writing is in general use for business purposes, there is no action of any private person or public body which has not its potential reaction in the business, and therefore in the Archives, of some other. This means, of course, that there is no conceivable subject of human interest which may not find illustration in Archives. More important for our present purpose — it means that, while we need not push our argument to its logical conclusion by going outside this country, within England *any Group of Archives, of any kind, public or private, must be regarded as potentially related to any other Group belonging to the same period.*

III. *The result of these Characteristics and Qualities in Archives is seen, or should be seen, in the treatment we give to them.*

This may best be demonstrated by contrasting at two or three points the view and practice of the Archivist with those of his first cousin, the Librarian. Take, for instance, the question of the duplicate: for the Librarian this is a thing of regular occurrence: something he can sell, exchange, destroy or keep in reserve. For the Archivist it practically does not exist, because even modern multiplied typescripts, if they are preserved for him in more than one filed example, have survived in different connexions and have a different significance. This does not mean that all are necessarily to be preserved

---

3.   This may extend to the smallest details: I have known an important point of interpretation turn on the sand used for drying the ink.

permanently: it does mean that each has to be considered in relation to its own environment. Again the Librarian, unless an old binding has some intrinsic beauty or interest, can order re-binding without considering anything more than the adequacy of his binder and the suitability of the binding chosen for the protection of the book: for the Archivist the binding is part of the Record and the smallest detail of it — the nature of the sewing holes,[4] for instance, or the fact that the old boards were of layers of brown paper, not mill-board — furnishes potential evidence for its interpretation which must not be destroyed or obscured: he cannot just send his volume to the Binders. Or contrast (for a third example) the precautions which the Librarian and the Archivist may think necessary in relation to their students: the Librarian concerned almost entirely with the possibility of material loss or damage; the Archivist preoccupied with a moral problem in the necessity for preserving unbroken custody. I could pile up examples drawn from all sides of Archive work: but there are two aspects which we are specially to consider here and I must turn to these; with an apology for the unconscionable time I have taken in reaching them.

IV. *Classification*

It is obvious from what has been said that to a very large extent this word must mean to the Archivist something quite different from what it means to the Librarian or Bibliographer. Archives are, or should be, treated both in physical arrangement and in description, almost exactly as a Botanist or Zoologist treats a specimen: that is to say as part of a living, or once living, organism; which is itself one of a larger family; which in turn is one unit in a yet larger natural division. In the case of Archives Species, Genera and Orders are represented by *Classes, Groups* and *Categories* of Records: which are, to an almost equal extent, natural, not artificial, divisions. The fact may be most easily appreciated by contrasting the volume in a Library with the volume in an Archive Repository. The former will normally be *labelled* with a *press-mark* showing its position (a matter of convenience) on the shelves: and will be *catalogued* in various orders quite independent of this according to its Author, its Subject and so forth. The Archive volume normally will be marked with a purely structural *reference* consisting of three parts: the first the Group to which it belongs, the second its Class within that Group and the third its number (or number and sub-number) within that Class. *This reference will normally govern alike its place on the shelves and its place in the List;* and be subject to *no change.*

4.   I have myself many times identified strayed fragments on no other evidence; but there is no indication which it is more easy to confuse: a single re-sewing through new holes will do it.

It is true that the *Category*, which tells us the kind of Administration that produced any Group of Archives in which we may be interested, is to this extent an artificial division that there is sometimes room for doubt to which Category a Group should be assigned. It is also a fact that the *Group*, which is the term used to describe the set of Archives resulting from a single independent administrative unit (such, for instance, as a Government Department, or a Parish, or a Business House), is to this extent a changeable thing that an Archive may start life as a member of one Group and end up in another: to take an obvious example a large Business or Professional Firm may swallow a small one, and its Archives. Finally it occurs sometimes that the assignment of documents to a *Class*, which should be a division of Archives, within the Group, corresponding to the division of office work which produced them, is complicated by the fact that a single person performed more than one function and recorded all his activities in a single series, register or roll. But these difficulties, though annoying to the tidy mind, are only illustrations of the fact that Nature is constantly changing and must be described at the stage in which we find her. I understand that even the Zoologist has to put up with some creatures which upset all systems of classification. These vagaries have to be met, of course, by the use of cross-reference.

The symbols used to express each element in the reference are purely matters of convenience: but the Record Office system may be taken as typical. There —

C.O. 5/1000

means the thousandth *Piece* (volume, container, file, etc) in the fifth *Class* (that known as 'America and West Indies') of the Colonial Office *Group* of Records.

V. *English Archives*

The application of the scheme just indicated to English Archives was first suggested in the Introduction to a *Guide* published by a Local Record Society in 1925[5] and used later in other publications; including a volume issued by the London University School of Librarianship in 1927.[6] Then in 1934 it formed the basis of the *Royaume Uni* contribution to a *Guide International des Archives* published by the League of Nations and in its final state it was adopted by the British Records Association.[7] It may therefore be regarded

5. Surrey Record Society, Number XXIII.
6. *The Uses of Libraries*, edited by Ernest A. Baker.
7. British Records Association, *Reports from Committees*, Number 1 (1936): See pp.

now as fairly generally accepted and I do not propose to repeat it here save in outline.

English Archives, then, fall into two great divisions — Lay and Ecclesiastical: the latter containing only those which result from the jurisdiction of the Church in spiritualities.

A. *Archives of Lay Administration*

(i) *Those resulting from Public Administration* (past or present) *at the Centre.*

This includes all *Public Departments and Royal Courts of Justice*: most of the more important have already made transfer to the Public Record Office and the Archives of practically all are by Statute 'in the custody' or 'under the charge and superintendence' of the Master of the Rolls. Those who have actually transferred to the Public Record Office, or whose Archives have been inherited by it, number nearly seventy; but wherever they are, the documents of each Department may be regarded as forming one Group of Archives belonging to this category of *Public, Central.*

It is to be remarked that these 'Public Records' offer particularly numerous examples of the phenomenon already described by which the Archives of one Group are swallowed by another: so that the seventy mentioned above really represent a much larger number. Most Public Departments have absorbed the functions and Archives of one or more predecessors (indeed in the rapidly moving conditions of war one can often see the process going on): some have even taken over from authorities belonging to another category; the India Office, e.g. taking over from a Private Body (the old East India Company), and the High Court of Justice having assigned to one of its Divisions the previously Ecclesiastical jurisdiction in Probate, with a wealth of Records drawn from a large number of Ecclesiastical Groups.

The Archives in the Public Record Office and many of the others are reasonably well provided with Guides, Lists and so forth showing the Classes within each Group (there are nearly 3,000 Classes in the Record Office alone) and the individual Documents contained in each Class.

NOTE

Before going further it will be convenient to set out a highly curious fact — at least it would appear so to any continental Archivist. Practically none of the Archive-owning bodies or individuals we are now to enumerate owe any allegiance to the Central Authority (the Public Record Office) or, with certain comparatively trifling exceptions,[8] are

---

8. The Ministry of Health sometimes issues directions to Local Authorities concerning particular classes of Local Records: Bishops or Archdeacons occasionally instruct

accountable for their treatment of their Archives to anyone save themselves.

(ii) Archives resulting from Local Public Administration.

I am, of course, alluding here to independent Local Authorities, not to mere local establishments of Central Departments such as the Port Authorities dependent on the London Customs and Excise Department. The chief unit of Local Administration has always been the County and three types of Authority have successively (but overlapping each other) held almost complete control over its activities. The first was the medieval *Sheriff*, acting for all purposes through the *County Court* and the *Hunred and other lesser Courts* below it: but of all the masses of documents which must have resulted only strays have survived. The Sheriff was presently superseded as principal authority by the *Justices of the Peace*, who between the sixteenth and nine-teenth centuries gradually added to their original judicial functions practically all administrative ones, acting through the old lower machinery but also, increasingly, through that of the (ecclesiastical) *Parish*: of their Archives large quantities survive still in the custody of the Clerk of the Peace.[9] Finally in 1889 most administrative activities were taken over by *County Councils*, whose seat, officials and Records, however, remain closely associated with those of the Justices: since 1894 they have had under them *District* and *Parish Councils* which have taken over civil duties, and sometimes Records, from the Parishes. I have mentioned these and other inferior authorities in order to show again how interwoven are all administrative functions and Archive Groups.

Of antiquity comparable with that of the Sheriffs we have the *Coroners*, likewise based on the County: yet here again centuries of activity are represented by little more than strays in the way of Archives. But inde-pendent of the County we find a host of authorities exercising for themselves, by privilege, most or all of its functions within their own borders: principally of course there are the *Boroughs*, where Archives have very generally been conserved with care: and since Boroughs of ancient foundation number between 300 and 400 it will be seen that we are making with these big

Parochial Clergy; and so forth. But in no cases is there a superior (Archive) Authority to provide buildings, appoint Archivists, inspect conditions, lay down rules of conservation or in fact do any of the things that need doing to ensure careful *and homogeneous* treatment of Archives. It was this fact which brought into existence in 1932 the British Records Association, which endeavours to secure the desired effect by voluntary effort.

9. Those Archives furnish an extreme example of the possibility of doubt as to correct distribution in Categories: for there has lately been a strong tendency to hold that they are in fact Records of Central Administration! It is unlikely, however, that existing arrangements for their custody by the Clerk of the Peace will be altered: and he is in practice Clerk also of the County Council — an unquestionably Local Authority.

additions to any list of English Archive Authorities. But we have still to add for the modern period a number of *Trusts* and *Statutory Authorities*, some of them partially elective, to whom, about the period of the Reform Bill (1832) were given, over districts whose boundaries often transcended those of the Counties, the task of dealing with a multitude of social works, from Paving and Lighting to Education, from Road-making to Poor Law Administration. The extent of the survival from these of what might well be exceedingly interesting Archives is not yet established: often they are preserved (if at all) by the later Authorities who have inherited their functions.

(iii) Archives resulting from Semi-Public Activities.

For *Semi-Public* might equally well be written *Semi-Private*. The description covers all those bodies and institutions which, functioning primarily for their own private advantage or satisfaction, yet do in effect work of a public character and in consequence hold a privileged position. Their character varies widely; ranging from that of the Charitable Endowment, founded *pro salute anime mee* yet doing the obviously public work of maintaining a School or Hospital, to the Bank of England or Lloyds; from a Public Utility Company to a Cambridge College; from the British Broadcasting Corporation to the British Medical Association: and the tendency of modern Legislation is to add to their number, using the big Insurance Companies, Banks and Friendly Societies (for instance) for all kinds of Public Work.

It is to be noted that the border line between this Category and the 'Local' one above it, or the 'Private' below is sometimes difficult to draw and it is here that a certain element of artificiality creeps in even to our system. On the other hand the objective view of these bodies as partaking of the characteristics of both the other categories is very necessary for the comprehension of their place in English Archives as a whole.[10]

(iv) Archives resulting from Private Activities

The Archives which have survived to us from the medieval period mostly result from the ownership and occupation of land: including the activities of all those Courts whose varied jurisdictions (many of them Royal ones exercised privately by privilege) are generally grouped together under the title 'Manorial'. It is these last-named Records (producing, by the way, well over 10,000 separate small Groups) which furnish one of the few examples in England of control by the Central Archive authority of Private Archives; for they are, by recent statute, under the charge and superintendence of the Master of the Rolls. From the sixteenth century onwards, as the use of

10. At the time of the compilation of the *Guide International* I found this category one which my foreign colleagues had some difficulty in understanding: but they ended by admitting its necessity.

writing for all purposes spreads gradually to all classes, more and more accumulations begin to survive to us in private hands; and they are related more and more to every kind of human activity — commercial, professional, scientific, social; till 'private' or 'family', or 'business papers' attain the character we know now.

Two points only need special mention. First, that 'Private' may of course describe corporate as well as individual activities. Second, that Private Administration and Archives furnish the largest number of those cases, to which we have already alluded, in which the dual capacity of a single administrator may result in some confusion in Archives: for example any Authority — Central, Local or Semi-Public — may be the *private* owner of a Manor and accumulate the appropriate Archives. Property-owning Ecclesiastical Authorities in the medieval period are particularly good examples: the elaborate *Pipe Roll*, for instance, and other Archives relating to the large estates formerly owned by the Bishops of Winchester, have nothing to do with their Ecclesiastical Office and should be classified as *Private*.

B. Archives of Ecclesiastical Administration

The principal Archives to be described under this heading are those of the English Church — *Ecclesia Anglicana*, deriving its authority at first from the See of Rome and later from the Sovereign in his capacity of *supremum caput*: highly important Archives are very numerous, but for reasons of space and other causes we must pass very lightly. Enough to say that, following the organization of the Church *in spiritualibus* they have left us five main Categories, each containing a number, large or small, of Groups, from the two *Provinces* down to the 11,000 and more *Parishes*; with Categories of *Diocesan* and *Archdeaconry* Archives, and those of *Peculiar* or *Immediate Jurisdictions*, in between. A sixth category which might have been included (*Rural Deaneries*) can hardly be said to have produced Archives; but we must make separate ones for the independent *Religious Houses* of the Middle Ages and the still surviving *Chapters and Colleges*; and the Church Assembly and other *Statutory Bodies* require another. The Church, moreover, like the State, has its *Semi-Public* category including Private Societies of all kinds which do Church work: but the *Private* category cannot be said to exist separately from the Lay one of the same name.

Finally, *Religious Denominations other than the Church of England*[11] are obviously classified most conveniently in this place: each having a separate category. Dating from the seventeenth or eighteenth century many have very valuable Archives.

---

11. Ecclesiastical Authorities other than the Church of England, and their Archives, have been described with some fulness in another (Number 3) of the British Records Association's *Reports from Committees*.

VI. *The Survey of English Archives*

So we come to our final topic. In a sense, and by implication, I have already attempted this superficially in the preceding section.[12] From this it will have been obvious that there is already available a certain amount of information as to the existence of Archives belonging to my various 'Categories' and 'Groups': and in fact for a long time now, and increasingly in recent years, Commissions, Committees, Local Societies and individual enthusiasts of various kinds, in addition to the one or two I have specifically mentioned, have been publishing Reports and Lists which, taken together, do give us the beginning of a Survey of the field as a whole. For example the Royal Commission (1910) on Public Records,[13] gathering up the results obtained by its predecessors and calling itself for fresh returns, has dealt to some extent with the larger Local Authorities: a few of these (Counties) have called for returns from the smaller Authorities below them and one or two have even published the result; and Local Societies have sometimes seconded these efforts[14]: the Institute of Historical Research has made wide inquiries (and published the result) from the point of view of facilities for Students in Archives other than those at the centre: the Historical Manuscripts Commission has for seventy years pursued its investigations into Private Archives and into some belonging to others of our categories; though it rather turned aside, early in its career, from the survey of such Archives in general, to the publication of particularly fine ones: Parliamentary and other Reports of a wide variety of dates from 1831 onwards[15] tell us something of special classes such as Probate Records of various ecclesiastical Categories and Parish Registers: and the London Chamber of Commerce not long ago gave us indirectly some indication of what we might expect to find in the way of Commercial Archives.[16] The trouble is that these publications, valuable as they are and grateful as we should be for them, all (taken as parts of a scientific survey) suffer from one or more grave defects — those of being partial, incomplete, lacking in detail, or out of date. The Local Societies' surveys of Parish Records are admirable but have only been worked out in two or three Counties: the Report on County and Borough Archives is

12. I hope I have also given sufficient indication of the enormous *bulk* of the accumulations we are considering. In case I have not it may be worth while to mention that those in the Public Record Office alone occupy about 35 miles of shelving.
13. *Third Report*, 1919.
14. Surrey County Council (e.g.) in conjunction with the Surrey Record Society has compiled and published *Guides* to the Archives of *Parishes, Manors, Endowed Foundations, Boroughs* and *Quarter Sessions* within the County (S.R.S., Numbers XXVI, XXVIII, XXIX, XXXI, XXXII): and very valuable work has recently been done upon Parish Records in Lincolnshire and Somerset.
15. The Census Returns of that year give information about Parish Registers.
16. 'Century-old Business Houses' in *London Chamber of Commerce Journal*, July, 1939.

complete as far as it goes, but jejune, not brought up to date and compiled from un-checked returns: the Historical Manuscripts Commission's Reports on Private accumulations are some of them sixty or seventy years old and do not represent the present state of affairs: and soforth.

What is wanting? The present is no time for the launching of ambitious schemes nor for thinking over-much of their possibiity. But we are fighting for a world in which Truth will be restored to its supreme position as the ideal and directing force in men's lives and the pursuit of sound learning be once more honoured: and even in our war work we have from time to time occasion and opportunity to think for a moment of what our own particular task in that new world might be. I recently had occasion to assist in compiling[17] for the benefit of the Regional Commissioners for Civil Defence, a first attempt at a single list, topographically arranged, of all the places in this country where valuable accumulations of Archives, in all the categories I have named, might be expected. It contained (with Manors and Parishes excluded and only the greatest adumbration of possible survivals in the offices of Solicitors and Business Firms) nearly 2,000 addresses: and though its incompleteness and the multitude of errors which (one was sure) had found their way into it, were displaying, it did give for the first time a view of the subject of English Archives as a whole and did seem to point the way to a piece of work which when happier times come, might be brought to fruition.

Archivists in this country, at the time the War broke out, and especially those responsible for the activities of the British Records Association, were beginning to feel their way towards the formulation of a national policy at various points of Archive work. There was talk, for instance, of the possibility of an Inspectorate of Archives on the lines of the Inspectorate of Ancient Monuments; of the necessity of making all Custodians of Archives in this country (including the private and the modern) conscious, as already some have become, of the importance and the technical requirements of their charges; of the need of a school and diploma for English Archivists; not to mention more specialized but hardly less important matters such as the conservation and utilization of Scientific and Business Archives. What is the one essential preliminary to the realization of these and other like schemes? I think there is only one answer — the construction of a General Plan, a Directory, a complete Survey of our National Archive wealth: and I am optimist enough to look forward to the time when we shall be at liberty to attempt it. When we do I hope that the Humanists will have the co-operation of the Scientists, the Student of the past that of the Administrator in the present time: for the Business Papers of to-day are the Archives of to-morrow and their use is not, or should not be, confined to Scholars working in any particular fields.

17.   The work was undertaken by the Public Record Office, the Historical Manuscripts Commission and the British Records Association in collaboration.

British Records After The War

Being a Summary of the
Reports and Memoranda
Prepared by a Special Committee for the
Council of the British Records Association

ENGLISH ARCHIVES: THEIR NATURE AND PRESENT DANGER

(1)   A very large proportion of the Historical Documents preserved in this Country are, or have been, Records or Archives: i.e., Documents *accumulated* in the course of organised business, social activity, or family affairs, by a natural process of growth — *not collected* because they were thought to be interesting.

> It is this nature which gives such Documents their evidential value: because they represent not what someone wishes us to believe, but the facts: and they have that value in the highest degree when they have survived in undisturbed series in the custody of their original compilers or those compilers' direct representatives.

(2)   Survivals of Accumulations of this kind in their original state are probably more numerous in England[1] than in any other country in the world.

> To name only a few categories — practically every County preserves still its ancient *Sessions Records*; *Ancient Boroughs*, all of which should have accumulations large or small, number between 300 and 400; *Ancient Parishes* (all preserving their Registers and many of them having much larger accumulations) are about 11,000, ancient *Manors* whose Records are known to have survived, 13,000 with more to come; ancient *Endowments* and *Private Corporations* still surviving (Colleges, Hospitals, City Companies and the like) must be reckoned certainly by thousands and often retain their Records in a comparatively undisturbed state from very early periods; and *Commercial Concerns* over 100 years of age, many of which are known to have preserved continuous series of their Archives, have been listed to the number of over 1,400 in London alone. The aggregate of Classes of Documents within these and other Groups of Archives must be put at a very high figure of thousands: the aggregate of Documents at a large number of millions.

(3)   The National Value of these Documents is now generally, if vaguely, recognised: it is very great and should be stated uncompromisingly.

> They are more than evidences for English History — they are actual parts of it: survivals from the past life of the Nation, as important in their way as Buildings or any other

---

1.   It has been considered best to frame this Report in terms applicable primarily to Archives in England; it is hoped, however, that with certain modifications the proposals made may be adapted to the special cases of Scotland, Wales and Northern Ireland. See para. 32 below.

Historical Monuments and in some respects even more important. And, like the Monuments, whatever the Ownership in which they have survived they must be regarded as having a public value, forming part of the Nation's heritage.

(4) The Archive Nature of such Documents, which gives them their value, is also the source of their greatest danger.

There are two reasons for this. First, being accumulated primarily for business purposes they are liable, when those purposes have been served, to be considered of no importance: and though they may survive in spite of that there comes a time when the space they occupy is grudged, or when their value as saleable Antiquities (or as Waste) is appreciated. Secondly, being not a mere collection of isolated pieces but a body of related documents they may be ruined almost as effectively by dispersal as by destruction.

(5) The Dangers of Destruction and Dispersal through ignorance (especially in the case of Private Archives) were already pressing before the War: with the Dispersal danger supplemented by increasing value in the Sale Room. After the War all these dangers will be accentuated.

The disuse of Large Mansions, the breaking-up of Properties, the closing down of old Business Houses or their agglomeration in larger concerns, the discontinuance of certain types of Social Activity, and all the other accompaniments of post-war reconstruction will affect Archive accumulations of every kind: but notably those in Private or Semi-Public custody.

Classification of English Archives: the Absence of Central Control.

(6) The Classification of English Archives now generally accepted divides them into Public (Central); Public (Local); Semi-Public; Private; and Ecclesiastical.

The last (Ecclesiastical) is really a division parallel to all the other four: the Administration and Archives of the Established Church and other Religious Bodies falling into sub-divisions (by Provinces, Dioceses, Archdeaconries, Parishes, Chapters, Unions, Societies, Congregations, and so forth) which correspond in matters spiritual to the Public (Central and Local), Semi-Public and Private divisions of Civil Administration.

(7) English Archives, if they are to be governed by the most intelligent and efficient policy possible, must be viewed as a whole.

The point is that Archives being the result of business or social activities, which depend upon relations between one individual, or one body, and another, are themselves potentially related, as between Group and Group[2]: the complement to the information contained in one set of Archives is to be sought in another of, perhaps, quite different character — the Records of a War Department, for example, being supplemented by those of a Parish. This fact should condition their treatment.

(8) The Control of Archives has never been centralised in England as it has in most of the greater European Countries.

The Public Record Office Act brought together, or arranged to bring together, under one Authority the Archives of nearly all divisions and departments of Central Government: but

2. The word *Group* is used to indicate a set of Archives resulting from the activities of a single independent Unit of Administration, Public or Private. Thus the activities of a Public Department, a Parish or a Family each result in an independent Group of Archives.

it established no relation between this Authority and the Local, Private and Ecclesiastical Custodians or Owners. Nor, speaking generally, has any Act or Measure established any inter-relations between these other Authorities and Individuals, or made them anything but autonomous in the matter of their Archives.

(9)   Though this is the general position the State has in fact intervened sporadically in regard to all the Categories of Archives named above: enough to create a precedent.

It has done so by means of a number of official Inquiries; and by a small number of Acts or Measures which affect particular Groups or Classes of Archives — for instance the Local Government Acts of 1894 and 1933, the Amendment (1924) to the Law of Property Act of 1922 and the Church Measure of 1929: and there have been a number of abortive proposals of a larger kind, notably those of the Royal Commission (1910) on Public Records.

(10)   State Intervention in other fields — notably that of Historical Monuments — has been of a wider and more definite kind: and has given to such work an official connexion with a Public Department.

The present *Royal Commission* on Historical Monuments was set up in 1908 and has been at work ever since: but in its first Report (1910) it called attention to the necessity for an Executive Authority and this was set up by legislation in 1913[3] in the shape of an *Inspectorate* forming part of the Office of Works.

Proposals for State Intervention: What is Needed.

(11)   The present contention is that the time is ripe for a step forward in the matter of Archives; and that new or increasing dangers, existing or immediately threatened, make it urgent that this step should be taken.

The work of the British Records Association since 1932 has done much both to reveal and to foster increased and practical interest in Archive work on the part of Individuals, Institutions and Local Authorities throughout the Country: and paradoxically the dangers which threatened from Salvage Drives, owing to the measures which the Association has felt obliged to take in that connexion, have in many ways added both to this public interest and to the Association's power of directing it. On the other hand though this remarkable improvement in general recognition of the importance of Archives encourages the opinion that any measures which might be proposed would have a public support sufficient to carry them through, it is not by itself strong enough to counteract the dangers of the time. Hence the Association's action in bringing together the Reports here summarised and the mass of information on which they are based: and in making concrete proposals.

(12)   Intervention by the State should be as limited as is consistent with effectiveness.

Apart from considerations of economy the very nature of Archives as defined above demands it: it is highly desirable that they should remain in their natural custody if that has so far subsisted unbroken and can be continued without danger of loss, deterioration or dispersal. But some intervention is urgently necessary.

(13)   What is needed in the case of Semi-Public and Private Archives is
(i)   *Prevention of Loss of Disperal;*
(ii)   *Prevention of Sale where this would mean Loss or Dispersal;*

3.   Superseding the ineffective Act of 1882.

(iii.) Proper Upkeep; and

(iv.) Reasonable Facilities for approved Students (reserving private rights, especially in the case of documents which are, in any sense, confidential).

(14)   What is needed in the case of Local and Ecclesiastical Archives is

(i.)   Prevention of Loss of Dispersal (in certain instances: the danger is not so universal her as in the preceding case);

(ii.) Recognition or Establishment (where they do not already exist) *of Local Repositories properly organised and staffed*[4];

(iii.) Organisation of facilities for Repair and othe Technical Services (on a co-operative basis as between Repositories); and

(iv.) An Organised Relation of Local Repositories
   to each other,
   to Central Authority (the Public Record Office), and
   to semi-Public and Private Archives.

A National Register of Archives.

(15)   To secure these ends, the First Requirement is a National Register of Archives.

The *basis* of this would be the List prepared by the British Records Association in co-operation with the Historical Manuscripts Commission for the information of Regional Commissioners for Civil Defence.

Since it is required for immediate and practical work *its form in its first edition must be simple and un-detailed and no other, more elaborate, work must be allowed to interfere with the completion of this stage.*

It must be accurate and for this and other reasons *will require the co-operation not only of local Archivists but of many bodies not primarily concerned with Archives:* for example, Professional Institutions and Chambers of Commerce.

(16)   The Register should serve three purposes: it should be a Directory for the information of Central Authority, a Basis for detailed Safe-guarding Measures, and an Instrument for the Guidance of Students.

This means that the original Register should be in a form which makes it possible for it to be consulted while still in process of compilation; should be preserved centrally but in a position where it can be made available to accredited Students; and should be kept indexed up to date.

It is not necessary to contemplate publication of the Register but it would be very desirable to arrange, by co-operation with local bodies, for duplications of the relative portions to be preserved, and kept up to date at regional centres. It would also be very desirable to arrange by means of local co-operation, for the parts relating to certain categories of Archives to be re-made later in an expanded form. The form of entries in the Register should be such as to allow of this.

'Scheduling': its Benefits and Restrictions

(17)   Scheduling — i.e., the marking of certain Documents or Accumulations of Documents entered in it as of outstanding National Importance — should proceed as far as possible *pari passu* with the compilation of the

---

4.   Development on natural lines will vary locally; cp. the schemes at present under discussion in Lincoln and York.

Register: provided that the preparation of the latter is not in any way delayed by it.

> The announcement to Public or Private Custodians or Owners that their Archives had been scheduled would immediately make such Archives subject to certain restrictions, while entitling them also to certain benefits. Following the precedent of procedure adopted in the case of National Monuments it would probably be found desirable to arrange for a system by which the announcement of a proposal to schedule would have the same restrictive effect for a limited time as actual Scheduling.
>
> On the other hand care must be taken not to overload the Schedule or include in it any doubtful cases.

(18)   In the case of Semi-Public and Private Archives the benefits to be derived from Scheduling should be stressed from the first.

> It should be emphasised that what is required is a partnership between the Owner and the State for the purpose of accomplishing a valuable national service.
>
> There should be a Competent Authority which should be in a position to offer the Owner[5]

(i.)   advice and in certain cases practical help in *arrangement*;

(ii.)   in the case of Modern (accruing) Documents advice as to *what should or should not be preserved;*

(iii.) advice and practical help in regard to *housing, make-up* and *repair;*

(iv.)   protection against unnecessary demands for *consultation;*

(v.)   *temporary deposit* in a suitable public institution, where any of the preceding services demanded it, with full reservation of the rights of the Owner; and

(vi.)   arrangement of special advantages in the case of documents *permanently deposited* in a National or recognised Local Repository.

> Scheduled Documents should be automatically entitled to *Exemption from Death Duties* under the scheme already in force in regard to Heirlooms of approved national value.

(19)   Restrictions attaching to Semi-Public or Private Documents scheduled must give power to the Competent Authority to provide for safety and accessibility.

(i.)   be kept informed of the *address* at which scheduled Documents are housed;

(ii.)   have power to *inspect;*

(iii.) have power to arrange *temporary or permanent deposit in a public institution* (as set out under (18) above) where safety or accessibility require it; and

(iv.)   have power to *forbid sale* where this would endanger the documents, interfere with their accessibility or lead to their dispersal.

(20)   The definition of Archives affected by these provisions should be framed so as to include Documents of any kind preserved with the ordinary Muniments of Individuals, Families or Corporate Bodies; and should be extended so as to cover, when necessary, Documents demonstrably of an Archive character even though they have not survived in the possession or keeping of their Natural Custodians.

> The words of *any kind* are to be understood literally. It is particularly important to remember this in connexion with Family Papers, among which Private Correspondence,

---

5. *Note.* — In practice these benefits might advantageously, when means allow, be extended to certain non-scheduled documents; but their provision should be a definite condition in the case of those scheduled.

Diaries, Memoranda and Compilations of all sorts may be included with perfect propriety. It is the circumstance of their accumulation by a natural process, rather than their form, which gives to Documents their title to be included amongst Archives. If, to take an extreme case, a British Ambassador to Rome accumulates, *in the course of transacting public or private business there*, Italian Documents, these will have a legitimate place in his public or private Archives; if an Englishman on the grand tour collects out of curiosity similar documents they will have, so far as this Country is concerned, only the value of Library or Museum pieces.

The Special Case of Local and Ecclesiastical Archives

(21)   In the case of Local and Ecclesiastical Archives a large number of the more important accumulations would be scheduled as a matter of course.

There can be no question that, taken as a whole, the Archives of certain bodies — e.g., a Borough, a County, a Diocese or a Chapter — should be declared of National value: though, as in the case of the Public Records, such accumulations should be subject to limitation, in the matter of modern accruals, which must of necessity be 'weeded.' Apart from this question of eliminating unnecessary documents the dangers of Loss or Dispersal are not, in the case of Local and Ecclesiastical Archives, the principal problem: which is rather than of Organisation, Maintenance and Accessibility.

(22)   These Accumulations are very large and numerous and it would hardly be practicable even if it were thought desirable, for the State to take over their care and custody from their Natural Custodians: a proposal which would not in fact command general acceptance.

(23)   On the other hand the number of cases in which they are at present cared for by an adequately equipped and staffed Archive Department is relatively small.

Even among the Authorities (County Councils) which have in recent years done most to effect improvements in this resect, efficient Archive Departments are still found in only a minority of cases: and elsewhere the number of efficient establishments, where housing, maintenance and accessibility are all of a satisfactory kind, is very small indeed.

The dangers due to lack of proper housing and maintenance are progressive if not arrested: and are therefore, in view of the importance of the Records concerned, urgent.

(24)   In many instances this neglect is due to apathy or ignorance: but in a large number, especially on the Ecclesiastical side, the trouble is lack of resources.

Few Ecclesiastical Authorities would question the desirability of making the Records in Diocesan Registries more accessible to Students, but the truth is that as a rule Diocesan Registrars have neither the space nor the staff necessary, nor the funds to provide them. Similarly, the state of Arrangement, Housing and Repair of Chapter Archives is, it is generally admitted, most undesirable in many cases: but for the most part no solution of the problem has been found.

It is not enough to make a single great effort and by raising a fund or securing a grant arrange to put a Building or a set of Archives into a state of repair: the problem is one of maintaining the interest of the authority concerned, with the corollary of an expenditure, for upkeep and staff, small perhaps but continuous and regular.

(25)   Where important Local and Ecclesiastical Authorities have failed

(for whatever cause) to provide adequately for their own Archives it need hardly be said that they have done even less to assist bodies or officials of the grades below them in this matter.

> The Local Government Act of 1894 assigned powers and duties to the County Councils in regard to the Archives of Parish Councils and Parish Meetings, but, except for some inquiries in a few Counties, practically nothing has been done. A Church Measure of 1929 gave power to Bishops to institute Diocesan Record Offices and through these arrange for the better care and custody, where necessary, of Parish Records: but (largely, no doubt, because the necessary funds were not available) little action has resulted.
>
> This is not to say that good work has not been done in many Parishes: but it has been dependent on the interest of individuals; has been, relatively, small in amount: and carries no guarantee of continuance. Actually, apart from other dangers, recent experience has shown that in the case of these Archives the risk of loss or dispersal is almost as great as in that of those in Semi-Public or Private custody.

The Possibilities of Co-operation.

(26)   In two or three notable instances local developments have gone far towards solving some at least of the problems indicated: nearly always by co-operation between different Authorities. Such solutions, if they could be brought about in sufficient numbers and sufficiently soon, are clearly better than a single scheme imposed from above because they make allowance for special conditions and local requirements.

> The most ambitious project (at present only in the stage of planning) would combine, if carried out, in one Repository the Archives of the three Councils of a single County, the Boroughs of the same, the corresponding Diocese (both Registry and Diocesan Record Office) and a Chapter — the obvious economic and other advantages: in two instances at least Bishops have solved the difficulty of securing a Diocesan Record Office by arranging to occupy space in the County Council's Repository: in a few cases also County Councils have taken over Archdeaconry Archives and the Tithe Records from Diocesan Registries: and numerous Local Authorities provide custody for Manorial Records and, by a natural extension, for other Private Muniments.

(27)   Enough has been done to shew the feasibility and value of co-operative effort[6] and the possibility of its application not only as between Local, or Local and Ecclesiastical, Authorities, but also as between such Authorities and Semi-Public or Private Owners.

> If an efficient National Archive Service is to be established, co-operation will be particularly necessary for the provision of certain technical services: few Local Repositories, for example, could afford to maintain solely for their own work, fully equipped and staffed Repairing or Photographic Departments. These technical services, together with accommodation (temporary or permanent) in order to make documents available for Students, are also the matters in which Semi-Public and Private Archives will most require assistance from Public Bodies, National or Local.

---

6.   The desirability of such effort has been stressed in previous Reports, e.g., that of the Departmental Committee of 1901 and the Royal Commission (1910) on Public Records.

Need of a Co-ordinating Authority

(28) It is generally agreed by those most qualified by interest and experience to speak of Archive work in Local and Ecclesiastical Repositories that what is now needed is a Co-ordinating Authority closely connected with the Public Record Office and charged with the duty of inspecting and advising those Authorities which have already taken up such work seriously upon technical questions and questions of policy: of encouraging and aiding others who have not done so to follow their example; and of organising, where this is required, co-operative work.

> *Technical questions* include not only the questions of housing, make-up, packing and repair of documents but also such problems as those of arrangement, listing and photography. *Questions of policy* are notably those concerned with the elimination of unnecessary accruals, the physical form and make-up of documents which are destined for permanent preservation, and relations with other Authorities and Custodians.

The Necessary Machinery

(29) For the production of a National Register (above paragraphs 15 and 16) arrangement could be made by means of a Royal Commission (i.e. without Legislation) What is required is a small permanent whole-time staff with a strong Advisory Committee meeting frequently and having power to invite the assistance of Local Societies and other interested bodies or persons.

(30) For the work connected with Scheduled Documents the 'Competent Authority' already mentioned (above paragraphs 17-20) would require Statutory Powers. The same remark applies to the Authority which (above paragraph 28) should act as an Inspectorate of Local Archives. The two functions overlap and would clearly be discharged most economically and efficiently by a single Authority.

> Following the model of the Inspectorate of Ancient Monuments this Authority would be based upon a Public Department — in this case, presumably, the Public Record Office. Whether it would be better to make its functions in relation to the inspection of Local Archives dependent in the first place on the acceptance of an invitation by individual Local Authorities is a question for discussion.
>
> In any case the assistance of the Local Authorities — many of whom have already expressed themselves in favour of the idea of an Inspectorate — should be sought for the drafting of any legislation. The last two paragraphs apply also to Ecclesiastical Authorities.

A Temporary Safe-guard

(31) As a temporary safe-guard to a particular danger to Semi-Public or Private Archives (that of sale out of the Country) should be met by extension of the present Order requiring a Board of Trade Licence for their export.

Northern Ireland, Scotland and Wales

(32) The extension of certain of the Provisions here desired to Northern Ireland, Scotland and Wales would be a matter for settlement by local opinion based on local conditions.

> In the case of Scotland there are fundamental differences of administration which would make some parts of the proposals submitted in this Report definitely inapplicable: but other parts might, it is considered, with advantage be adapted to meet Scottish requirements. Here, and in Northern Ireland, the governing idea of the Report — the necessity for co-ordination and co-operation — would be accepted by Archivists without question. The last remark may be made also in regard to Wales: but in the case of that Country it has been represented that there is a strong case for a different method. It is urged that a large measure of Centralisation of both Lay and Ecclesiastical Archives has already been achieved through the National Library of Wales with satisfactory results: and that all the facilities advocated in the present Report — a central Advisory Authority, adequate housing facilities, the necessary financial . resources, technical equipment, expert staff, availability for Students in conjunction with the necessary works of reference — could be best provided by a continuation and extension of the same policy.
>
> The Committee of the British Records Association records these views, communicated by specialist Members, without comment.

British Archives And The War[1]

I may perhaps be allowed to begin by saying how much I appreciate the compliment implied in the invitation kindly conveyed to me by Mr. Buck to take some part in an annual conference of American archivists, and how truly I wish it were possible for me to be present on that occasion. I shall venture to hope that pleasure may prove one day to have been merely postponed, and meanwhile send my most sincere wishes for a successful meeting. I have only to add to these preliminary remarks some apology for a contribution which will be found to be little more than a series of notes; and, what is worse, notes compiled from a personal angle. Archivists in this country — that is to say those few out of a small band whose activities have not been diverted by the needs of the time to other services — have been fully occupied up to now in efforts to preserve their charges from the immediate dangers which successively presented themselves; and if, in happier circumstances, we are now venturing occasionally to turn our minds towards the problems of post-war reconstruction the change of attitude (pleasant as it is) does not make us any less busy. In short it has not been possible as yet to bring together the materials for that comprehensive survey which my title might suggest and which I should have liked to offer.

THE CLASSIFICATION OF ENGLISH ARCHIVES

In order to make these notes intelligible I must begin by reminding you very briefly, what English archives are. You will notice that I say English. That is not because English archivists are out of touch with their Scottish, Irish, and Welsh colleagues. On the contrary, the closest possible co-operation is

1. A paper read by Solon J. Buck, archivist of the United States, in the absence of the writer, at the dinner meeting of seventh annual meeting of the Society of American Archivists, Princeton, New Jersey, November 15, 1943.

maintained. On a small committee of the British Records Association, for example, which has been considering lately important plans for post-war development, three members represent the three sister countries. But in Scotland and Northern Ireland both public administration in general and archives administration in particular differ in important respects from those of England, and the same may be said, with some modifications, of Wales. It is our usual custom therefore, in studying any large question of archival economy, to examine it first as it bears upon, or is illustrated by, archives in England — which are of course larger than those of the other three countries — and then to inquire how far and with what reservations the conclusions reached apply to the remaining parts of the United Kingdom. A similar observation may be made in regard to the archives of the dominions and colonies, which should certainly be included when one speaks of British archives; though here the distinctions are, of course, more marked and the extent to which co-operation between archivists has been developed at present much less.[2]

English archives then, from which my illustrations will be chiefly drawn, fall, according to a classification now generally recognized,[3] into five categories: public (central), public (local), semi-public, private, and ecclesiastical. The first comprehends the surviving archives of all those bodies which we now call public departments or ministries — divisions of the central government which have in the past administered, or do now administer, under King and Parliament, the affairs of the nation as a whole; from the Exchequer, Curia Regis, and Chancery of the twelfth century down to the Treasury, Supreme Court and Home Office, Foreign Office, etc., of the twentieth.

The second (public, local) includes the archives of all those bodies which carry on, and always have carried on, those parts of the country's business which can be decentralized because they affect districts rather than the nation. The machinery through which this is done has altered a good deal through the centuries, but the regional divisions have remained much the same — the counties, the great boroughs which maintain a jurisdiction independent of the counties, and below these a multitude of smaller administrative units. The machinery which concerns us here, because it is represented by existing archives, was from, roughly, the sixteenth century down to the end of the nineteenth in the counties that of the justices of the

---

2. One of the works in progress which the war has stopped is the proposed second volume of the *Guide International des Archives*, which would have covered the archives of all British dominions and colonies, including Cyprus and Malta. Much of the necessary information has actually been collected and will, I fear, be obsolete if, or when, the project can be renewed.

3. It is that used in the *Guide* mentioned in the preceding note and adopted by the British Records Association in Number 1 of *its Reports from Committees*.

peace whose jurisdiction, in origin purely legal, gradually came to cover every department of public administration; in the smaller districts it was that of the parishes, to whose primarily ecclesiastical functions activities of a purely lay character were similarly added. Modern legislation, some fifty years ago, transferred most of these acquired administrative functions from the justices to county councils, from the ecclesiastical parishes to separate civil parishes or to rural and urban district councils. The ancient archives were left for the most part with their original compilers.

In my third division (semi-public) are included all those institutions and corporations so characteristic of this country which, though their original object was and remains private profit, advantage, or satisfaction, have come to discharge public functions — educational, charitable, or social — which are recognized and which give them a certain official status. City companies; universities, colleges, and schools; hospitals and charitable foundations of every kind; the great institutions which govern the legal, medical and other professions; public utility undertakings; commercial bodies such as the great banking and insurance corporations, from the Bank of England and Lloyds downwards — all these come under this heading. All, needless to say, are by their nature compilers of archives; many have been in existence for a very considerable time; and some are of great antiquity, dating back three, four, five centuries or even more, and preserving from those early times a substantial quantity of records.

On the field covered by my fourth category (private archives) I need not expatiate, but there are three points to be noted. First, that it includes of course the archives both of institutions and of individuals; second, that among these are to be found the great accumulations of family papers which sometimes — when members of the family have played an important part in public life — have an official character and may even approximate, as in the case of the Cecil family, the importance and character of state papers; and third, that from dates much earlier than the sixteenth and seventeenth centuries, when "family papers" begin, there have survived in these same accumulations very large masses of documents connected with the tenure of landed property and in particular the records of manorial jurisdiction. Let us add for completeness that it includes also, of course, at the other end of the scale, most of the enormous and increasing mass of commercial and professional archives.

My fifth category (ecclesiastical) is really a series of categories. For the division of archives which result from the activities in matters spiritual of the provinces, dioceses, archdeaconries, parishes, and other divisions of the Church of England, and those of the unions, congregations, and so forth of other churches, are really parallel to the civil divisions — national, local, semi-public and private — which we have been distinguishing. In the case of the Church of England, too, the archives almost equal those of civil administration in antiquity, and a number of the others date back for two or three centuries.

The total quantity of archives surviving from all these activities may be gauged by the reflection that the English have always been a conservative, though not a careful, people in such matters, and have had very few revolutions. Actually there are well over ten thousand ancient parishes, practically all preserving at least some archives of a reasonable antiquity, and an even larger number of manors whose records have been listed up to date. The total of charitable foundations of some importance for our purpose must reach well into the thousands. Ancient boroughs number between three hundred and four hundred. But I must not delay you any longer with statistics and estimates of bulk; indeed I owe renewed apologies for the length of this exordium.

THE NEED FOR CO-ORDINATION

The point to which have been leading may now be briefly stated. England differs from all the other great archives-owning countries of Europe in that there is no central control of all this mass of archives. The public records, my first category, have indeed been for a century with only a very few special exceptions under the general superintendence of a single official, the Master of the Rolls, acting through the Public Record Office. But with, again, only a very few exceptions, neither the Master of the Rolls nor the Public Records Office has any authority over the remaining custodians of archives, individual or corporate, nor is there any other authority charged with the duty of supervising any section of them. The Archbishop of Canterbury for example, although naturally he might exert great influence in the matter if he saw fit, is not regarded as having directly either duty or authority in the matter of the archives of the church as a whole. In fact, one may say that for practical purposes the thousands of archives-owning individuals or institutions, public and private, whom I have named or indicated are all autonomous in the matter of their archives. There is no one who can say to them "do this" or "do not do that". You may possibly find in this state of affairs interesting parallels to draw, or distinctions to note, when you compare it with that which is familiar to you in the case of federal, state, county, and other archives in the United States. In any case you cannot fail to realize how it must affect the thoughts and activities of anyone in England who takes the view that all the archives of the nation, without exception, are by their nature related parts of a single whole and that their treatment should be conditioned by that consideration; still more when it becomes his preoccupation to devise means of protecting them not merely against the ordinary dangers which may arise from carelessness or neglect in peace-time but against the instant, abnormal, and unpredictable perils of war.

THE SITUATION UP TO DATE

I must not give the impression that outside the public records no work upon archives has been attempted by the state in England. Apart from a large amount of publication of texts, the old Record Commission of 1800-1837, whose final result was the creation of the Public Record Office, paid some attention in its *Reports* to local as well as national records; and several committees and commissions since then have also issued valuable reports. The Historical Manuscripts Commission, appointed in 1870 and still operating, has not only published many volumes drawn from private archives but also paid some attention to a certain number of those of the ecclesiastical and local categories. A royal commission appointed in 1910 not merely reported upon the present state of local and ecclesiastical archives but made some sweeping recommendations, which have never been implemented, for intervention by the state in this field. Upon two recent occasions, 1924 and 1936, legislation dealing with larger questions has incidentally given the Master of the Rolls and the Public Record Office some connection with particular classes[4] of records outside the national category, and the first of these had the valuable effect of causing the approval by the Master of the Rolls of a number of local repositories as suitable places for the deposit of manorial records which the act had placed under his superintendence — a great stimulation to local interest. Lastly a church measure[5] of 1929 has given to bishops the power — though, alas, not the means — to create diocesan record offices for the reception of parish and other ecclesiastical archives which could not be properly cared for in their original places of custody.

In the period which followed the last war the result of all these pricks to public consciousness began at last to appear in some way other than the publication of texts. Of these there had always been, comparatively speaking, plenty: almost every county had a society devoted more or less to such work. But now there began to manifest itself, here and there and in varying ways, generally under the stimulus of some individual enthusiasm, an apprehension of the fact that conservation and arrangement of the vast masses of surviving documents, even the provision of mere storage facilities for them, might be probems more urgent than the publication of small selections. Public libraries began to make collections of manuscripts and following this to demand assistants specially trained for their custody; and the Library Association and the newly formed School of Librarianship in London made corresponding provision in their curriculum. One county council started an archives department, built a new repository, even added a repairing shop; others followed its example. Deans and chapters raised funds to put their

5. A church measure is the equivalent in ecclesiastical affairs of an act of Parliament.
4. Manorial and tithe records.

records in order; one large diocese succeeded in implementing — and very successfully — the terms of the church measure I have mentioned. And an increasing stream of custodians — parish clergy, city companies, boroughs, even some of the smaller local authorities — sought from time to time the unofficial advice or help of the Public Record Office. Finally in 1932 the British Records Association, an entirely voluntary organization but having the Master of the Rolls for its president and with the support of influential bodies such as the County Councils Association, came into existence with the express object of co-ordinating all this scattered effort; of encouraging those custodians of archives, still comparatively few, who were interested in the technique of archives keeping; and of stimulating the remaining multitude to follow their example. In the following seven years it achieved a remarkable success — much greater than the handful of persons who started it had ventured to expect: increasing its membership four-fold; establishing contacts with the dominions, colonies, and with foreign countries; holding conferences and organizing exhibitions which aroused public interest considerably beyond the bounds of its own membership; initiating the *Year's Work* and other series of technical publications; and in short it came within sight of converting the idea of archives work as a science and a profession into a practical reality.

And at this point the war came.

THE EFFECTS OF WAR

I hope I shall not be thought lacking in a sense of proportion if I say that in the midst of all the dire possibilities with which our minds were naturally obsessed in September, 1939, a few of us could not help thinking with a special pang of its probable effects upon a movement still so young and an organization so imperfect as that I have just sketched. Some of these effects could easily be foreseen, at least in outline, by anyone whose experience went back twenty years and who had a little imagination. In the first place, of course, there was the possibility, so much increased since 1918, of actual destruction of archives by enemy action. Secondly, there was the danger, in some ways more certain, of destruction by our friends; in others words the inevitable call for waste paper in huge quantities for the purposes of munitions, and the efforts of undiscriminating zeal to meet it. And, third, came the less defined but undoubted danger to archives, especially private, semi-public and small local ones, involved in the general re-organization of the community and particularly in the requisitioning of houses, office accommodations, and buildings of all kinds for special war activities.

Only less lamentable than actual destruction was the apprehended discontinuance, if only from motives of economy in labor, of separate archives departments in centers of local government and other places where they had been set up, and the still more certain halt in the process of converting more of such bodies to an active policy in regard to their archives. A corollary to these considerations was of course an end, for an unpredictable period, to our hopes for the development of archival science and the building up in England of a recognized class and profession of archivists. Finally, the British Records Association itself seemed likely to be threatened with temporary eclipse if not with extinction as a result of the call upon all available energies, money and time to meet the more pressing needs of the nation.

ENEMY ACTION

As you will have gathered from the long and generous review of our *Year's Work in Archives* which appeared in THE AMERICAN ARCHIVIST in January, 1943, events have agreeably falsified expectations in some respects. Although there have been many and melancholy losses — one was mentioned in your review and even from our present imperfect knowledge I could cite others not less grievous in every category of archives — there have also been a number of happy and surprising survivals, to mention only three places: in Bristol, in Coventry, and at the Guildhall and other important points in London. Indeed in the case of more than one city company the saving of the muniments has been almost the only consoling feature in the tale of destruction of beautiful and historical things. This applies to at least three of the great companies which in recent years have played host to the British Records Association's annual conference or in other ways assisted its work. In one of these cases, you may have heard the tale already, but it is worth re-telling, the brick-built strong-room was almost all that remained. It was so hot that leather, inside an iron safe within the room itself, was found burned to a cinder — so hot that when, after some days, the company's staff felt obliged to open the door the inrush of fresh air set the contents ablaze. Yet almost all the muniments in that strong room were rescued and almost all are today practically unharmed, although streams of boiling water were added to the last stage of their trials. The documents of another company come to the Record Office from the ruins of a building whose destruction we ourselves had witnessed — it was not two hundred yards away from us — after a long period of immersion in water followed by active fermentation. Our repairing department will not readily forget the long lines of sheets tenderly separated and hung out to dry, nor the smell which accompanied first-aid operations. Yet they also are today hardly any the worse, at least to casual inspection. From the same source a quantity of modern lawyer's papers came to us, more than a year afterwards and still wet; but even these were not, as it proved, irretrievably ruined.

But I must not allow myself to be lured into tales of rescue work or convey the impression that the experience gained in regard to papers drowned or charred — for we have experimented also with that most delicate problem — has not been paid for at a very dear rate, as indeed have a number of other conclusions which may now be added to the stock of archivists' lore. One of these is a most emphatic confirmation of the view that water, not fire, is the great enemy of the archivist. This does not mean that any measure of protection against fire can be diminished. Although the archivist who has protested in times of peace his fear of the danger from a casual spark may perhaps recall in future, with reminiscent amusement, times when he and his repository have stood for an hour or two under a thick shower of sparks, I do not think he will want to relax precautions. On the contrary, the dictum that stacked archives are extremely difficult things for conflagration to destroy, though demonstrably true, rests on two provisos: first, that the materials surrounding them are non-inflammable (it is the wooden uprights of the shelving or the wooden supports of the roof which have done the damage in so many cases), and second, that sufficient staff is present to deal with the fire in its earliest stages.[6] Conviction of the necessity for plentiful fire-watchers is perhaps the knowledge for which London and other cities have paid most dearly. For the archivist fire-guards must always have a special function — that of preventing the necessity for floods of water. Not all the drowned documents have been so fortunate as those I have mentioned above. One of the things we have learned is the incredible speed with which mildew and fermentation may work in favorable circumstances afterwards.

PRECAUTIONS

That last remark may lead to a few words about precaution in general. Naturally precautionary measures had been under discussion officially for some time before the war, although extra-officially it was more difficult to raise such questions. But after 1938, when there were still many who could not believe, until it occurred, that even Germans would go to the length of absolutely indiscriminate air-bombardment, preparation was a practical matter. At the Record Office, and I dare say elsewhere, structural alterations including such matters as facilities for access to all parts of the roof, above and below, and the installation of necessary equipment proved a surprisingly large task; but the possibilities of actually bomb-proof cover narrowed themselves upon investigation to the use of mines or tunnels. Since the quantity of such places was limited, and the installation necessary to make

---

6. At the Public Record Office we have throughout maintained night and day shifts, although the elaborately organized band with which we started has of course been much depleted since.

them suitable for manuscripts elaborate and costly, the archivist, hampered by the bulk of his charges, was at a disadvantage, especially in competition with the more obvious and spectacular value of the contents of museums and galleries. Comparatively few accumulations of archives have in fact found such protection, although there are notable exceptions.

On the other hand the policy of removal from built-up areas and distribution of risk by the use of more than one temporary repository and by the separation of classes which to some extent duplicated each other has been practiced on a large scale by the Public Record Office and preached by the British Records Association. The association has also been able to help in arranging the offer of hospitality by repositories in comparatively safe areas to those less fortunately placed from the point of view either of bombardment or of possible invasion. It is probable however that many custodians have taken this kind of precaution by means of a variety of *ad hoc* arrangements which their special circumstances made possible, If there were a proposal after the war to put a plaque on every country house that has acted as temporary repository for some quantity, large or small, of archives, public or private, I fancy that a large number of plaques would be needed.

At the Public Record Office evacuation had to be preceded by the very difficult business of selection. Ultimately a series of categories was prepared of classes to be successively removed if conditions allowed. The basis of choice was that a class *(a)* had not been printed and *(b)* was intrinsically, *i.e.*, in relation to the whole group of records of which it formed a part, of primary importance. Some concession was made also to the predilections of historians and other students, and to popular or spectacular values. In the end it was unexpectedly found possible, although the process took the best part of three years, to remove the whole of these categories and an extra one, consisting of specimens from classes not evacuated, in about ninety thousand carefully numbered and indexed packages — a weight of about two thousand tons. The buildings in which they have been bestowed include a castle, private mansions, a prison, and a casual ward. I need not tell an audience of archivists what it has meant to carry out these moves and to find manning for the temporary repositories from a small staff already much depleted and charged in addition with the task of defending the London office.

We entertain no illusions as to the future course and potentialities of enemy action. It is possible for instance that another high explosive bomb — you have heard of the first from the press so there is no harm in mentioning it — may do more than demonstrate an unsuspected usefulness in the Gothic towers of the Record Office. Even as I write the enemy is talking much of new terrors in store. We merely record thankfulness mixed with our grief for past losses, and hope for the future. It is the motto of the Cockney in 1940: "Go to bed hopeful and wake up thankful."

MICROPHOTOGRAPHY

A precaution which I have not mentioned but which has been freely used is that of microphotography. Many large business houses had recourse to it in the period immediately preceding the war in order to safeguard their current papers; a service was arranged for solicitors by the Law Society, and so forth. But in addition there have been a number of schemes covering older archives, sometimes on a small, sometimes on a larger scale. I shall only mention three of the latter. The first is that initiated in the United States by which machines installed at the Public Record Office and certain other important centers are making films of great series of documents for deposit in the Library of Congress — a scheme equally beneficial to American students, who can use the films, and to English archivists, who see large classes of their documents given something approaching a double chance of survival. The second is an arrangement by which, at the Public Record Office the same' machine is operated by the staff on duty by night, when raids permit, for the filming of early registers of probate from all courts from the fourteenth to the sixteenth or seventeenth century — a series or rather a quantity of series of records of extreme value which were not included in the American program. The third is a scheme for the filming at various centers of all parish registers. In one large diocese (Lincoln) this has actually been completed along with other work, and the diocesan custodian responsible reports a very great incidental gain in knowledge of the state of parish records in her district. A good deal has also been done in other dioceses.

In this big development in the use of microphotography by archivists we have a positive gain from the war: not only by the making of the films — which, to tell the truth, I think may prove to be of varying value — but by exploration of the limitations as well as the possibilities of the process when applied to archives.[7] In view of the great part which it is, I believe, destined to play in the development of archival work in the future this constitutes a real advance.

PAPER SALVAGE

From precautions against our enemies it is an easy transition to precautions against our friends; the danger in both cases being that of indiscriminate destruction. The word salvage, by the way, has in current usage the initial disadvantage of two exactly opposite meanings: that of "salving" for the national need papers of all sorts, from omnibus tickets (literally) to records, which are presumed to be valueless; and that of saving papers which are not

---

7. Some notes on this subject appear in the current issue (No. 17) of the *Bulletin* of the Technical Section of the British Records Association.

valueless from "salvage." In this instance the course of the war, which has increased the shortage of pulp in unexpected ways, has made the event worse than our anticipations. The necessary campaign for collection of waste has been comprehensively planned, tremendously publicized and carried out as it well could be by a multitude of enthusiasts who in many cases were not very knowledgeable. The result has been to present the British Records Association, which has shouldered the main responsibility for defense, with ever-fresh problems as fresh classes of local, private, and ecclesiastical records presented themselves in the light of new sources of supply to the imagination of the enthusiasts. Some of the attempts to parry these successive attacks are reflected in the series of *B.R.A. Memoranda*, a set of which, with some miscellanea, is annexed to this paper.[8] Apart from publications, broadcasts by the Master of the Rolls, appeals made through local libraries, letters to the newspapers and so forth, the association has worked through an organization of some hundreds of voluntary "referees" all over the country who are prepared to advise salvage officers and proposing contributors to the salvage "drives." You have heard, I think, of this in the review already cited, but I may perhaps record here that the organization is itself a monument of what may be done by mere devotion. It has been carried on, with all the vast correspondence involved, almost entirely by a single person.

What measure of success has been achieved by these various means will probably never be fully known. Even the larger losses will transpire only very slowly, as students here and there find lamentable gaps, after the war. I will not harrow your feelings with relation of the tales — some, I fear, true — which have reached us from time to time, of old established commercial houses which emptied their muniment rooms by the simple process of emptying them, or incumbents who placed the church chest at the disposal of the paper merchant. But that we have prevented quite a considerable amount of destruction is, I think, certain. I will instance only one local authority which was not only dissuaded from a scheme already approved for destroying the whole of the county's old poor law records but converted to the view that it was good policy to preserve a really representative accumulation of every class of them.

8. The annexes, all issued by the British Records Association, are entitled:
    1. *Obsolete Poor Law Records. Brief Hints on Review and Selection for Salvage.* N.d., *1 p.*
    2. *The Safeguarding of Parish Records, a Memorandum.* April, 1942. *2 pp.*
    3. *Records. What Should We Try to Save?* Memo. No. 3. May, 1942, repr. Aug., 1942. *2 pp.*
    4. *Salvage from Solicitors' Offices.* Memo. No. 4. Aug., 1942. 1 p.
    5. *Old Parchments.* Memo. No. 5. Oct., 1942. 1 p.
    6. *First Aid for Damaged Manuscripts.* Memo. No. 6. Dec., 1942. 2 pp.
    7. *Modern Records. What May We Destroy?* Memo. No. 7. March, 1943, reissued April, 1943, new eds. May and June, 1943, reissued July, 1943. 5 pp.

The association's method has been throughout to obtain the concurrence of the salvage authorities in its propaganda, to emphasize the relatively small amount which it was desired to preserve, to rely as much as possible on personal contacts, and to offer its aid not merely in saving but in destroying.[9] There is in fact much work for the archivist to do in the way of encouraging intelligent elimination, as well as preservation. The demand for our latest *Memorandum*, which deals with legitimate destruction in accumulations of modern documents, although it has never been used as a circular it has six editions or issues in as many months, shows the value of this line of approach. The salvage campaign has at this point provided and unexpected but welcome opportunity for the association to spread knowledge and incidentally to improve its own position with the general public.

THE BRITISH RECORDS ASSOCIATION

From the preceding sentence and other indications in these notes you will have gathered that the association has found plenty of special tasks during this War. It has succeeded also, in spite of all preoccupations, in finding people to do them. I may now add that its general work, though naturally much restricted, has not lapsed at any point. Committee work and printing have not ceased — indeed, as you will have gathered, they have found new channels. The annual conference, much shorn, has taken place in London each year — in 1940, to the accompaniment of an air raid, and should be held in 1943 at very much the same time at which these notes will be presented in America. All being well, members will meet in the hall — one of the few which survives uninjured — of a great city company. Propaganda for the maintenance and increase of membership, in peace-time a most important activity because membership means public interest, must obviously cease during war. But membership, although it has decreased,[10] has not done so to anything like the extent anticipated and on the other hand there has been a small but steady flow of new members, which gives me the opportunity to record with gratitude the accession, in a dark hour, of a little band of new members from America — a very heartening gesture. We are also in hopes that the numerous contacts made in connection with the salvage campaign, especially with private and semi-public owners of modern commercial and professional archives, may be turned to account later.

9. The Public Record Office, which by statute controls to a very considerable extent the elimination of papers by public departments, has also been very active during the war in hastening and encouraging the destruction of those papers which are not destined for permanent preservation.
10. Before the war institutional members numbered about three hundred and individual six hundred.

The last remark may introduce the mention of one more point at which our work has drawn unexpected profit from the war. When, to meet the dangers of air bombardment and possible invasion, the whole country was divided into regions under commissioners for civil defence, the association endeavoured to get in touch with these new authorities in view of possible eventualities of all kinds. One result of this was the circulation of a pamphlet of instructions for first aid to damaged manuscrips, since reissued through several channels. An even more important outcome was the preparation, for the information of commissioners and their staff, of the *Regional List* of addresses at which there were or should be accumulations of archives. It was not complete, for it excluded deliberately two of the largest classes — manorial and parish archives — and practically excluded certain others, and in many respects it was very definitely an improvisation. But it was the first attempt ever made at a national register of archives of all categories and as such had an importance which may well go far beyond the immediate occasion which produced it. It may form the basis for more elaborate, perhaps even for official, action in the future.

THE ARCHIVIST IN ENGLAND: FUTURE DEVELOPMENTS

What form will this future action take? The archivist's profession has inevitably been for the last four years in a state of almost suspended development. Not entirely so: There is, for instance, at least one county authority which has actually started a new archives department during the war; and there are signs of stirring in other places. But development of the profession means two things, the provision of new posts and the availability of young people to take them; and both of these have practically ceased for obvious reasons. The School of Librarianship, which provided training, has closed down; and talk of a possible special diploma is in abeyance.

On the other hand we have now advanced so far in optimism as to be thinking of reconstruction and of the unique opportunity it will offer for new developments. This, in our case, could mean, if it occurred at all, only one thing: an increase in public recognition of the value of archives and, by implication, an increase in the amount of work to be done and in the number of people called upon to do it. In other words it would mean the final emergence of that profession, that organized science of archives, which at present, outside the Public Record Office, has so tenuous an existence in England. We are at the moment discussing this possibility and the best way of converting it into a reality. Let me conclude by telling you the lines on which, it seems to me, development might proceed.

They can be summed up in one word, co-operation — co-operation between the state and the local, ecclesiastical, semi-public, and private custodian or owner; co-operation between custodians in small groups formed upon regional[11] or other considerations; co-operation in the planning of work, in the pooling of knowledge, in the actual housing, sometimes, of the archives and making them accessible to students, in the provision of technical facilities, notably for repair work, even in the sharing of the services of ambulatory archivists. I do not think we shall arrive easily at any great measure of centralization. I even hope we shall not, for the idea of unimpaired custody as an ingredient of primary importance in the evidential value of archives is clearly best served by leaving them as far as possible in the hands of their natural custodians. On the other hand it is very obvious that the dangers of neglect, destruction, or dispersal will not be smaller, and there is ground for fearing that they may be very much greater, in the midst of all the changes and chances which the near future may bring, than they have been in the past. Many ·of those thousands of custodians, unless they receive both guidance and help, will fail in their duty through ignorance, carelessness, or sheer lack of means. It is no use to expect the smaller local or ecclesiastical authorities — how much less the ordinary private owners — to install a complete archives establishment, but they may be brought to desire and enabled to secure their share in the benefits of a common organization.

How far in the turmoil of post-war adjustments, of competing claims on public attention and of demands for public economy, it will be possible to realize such hopes as I have indicated, time alone will show. But the fact that they exist and are even being voiced, after four such years as these have been for us, is something for which we may be thankful.

CONCLUSION

And the importance of all this? The justification of so much planning and thought in time of war?

I am not to attempt here an exposition of the value of archives, but if I were asked to define the creed of the archivist in four words I should say "the sanctity of evidence." It is not, primarily at any rate, his business to use or interpret his charges; he need not be interested in their contents — indeed it is in some ways an advantage if he is not, for that detachment preserves him from the temptation to *ex parte* procedure. His training, methods, and rules of

---

11. A singularly encouraging and promising plan is actually under discussion at present by which three county councils, the diocese covering their district and the corresponding chapter, and all the independent boroughs in the same area (with, probably, a large number of smaller units attached) would organize a single record office for their joint needs. Could similar arrangements, *mutatis mutandis*, be produced elsewhere a long step would have been taken towards the solution of a national problem.

conduct are in fact, or should be, such that he can at a pinch make shift to perform his functions faithfully without even understanding the meaning of the documents entrusted to him. His part is simply to conserve intact every scrap of evidence which not only the contents of the documents but their form, makeup, provenance, and position in relation to other documents have to offer. His aim is to provide, without prejudice or after-thought, for all who honestly wish to know, the means of knowledge. Viewed in these aspects the good archivist is the most selfless devotee of truth the modern world produces.

In an age in which untruthfulness is not only increasingly condoned but in certain quarters and by certain powers elevated to the status of a science and prescribed as a rule in the conduct of affairs — in such an age our profession may, I venture to submit, have a part to play the importance of which it would be difficult to exaggerate.

The Protection of Archives
in Italy

Many people must have wondered with a pang, when the fighting reached Sicily, what would happen to the more famous Italian Archives — to the Records of the Medici at Florence or the Norman Kings in Naples and Palermo. For the Archivist, equally concerned with all writings accumulated during the transaction of business or conduct of affairs of any kind, ancient, modern or contemporary, the danger was a double one; and considerable fear was expressed lest the chances of war should lead to destruction and dispersals which would not only mean irreparable loss to the cultural riches of the world but would impede seriously the work of civil reorganization. The War Office accordingly invited the Secretary of the Public Record Office, by permission of the Master of the Rolls, to visit Italy under the auspices of the Allied Control Commission and organize protective measures in concert with the Monuments and Fine Arts section of that Commission: and this was effected during the early months of 1944.

The subsequent posting of two other members of the Record Office staff, seconded from the armed forces to the Monuments section of the Commission, made it possible immediately before the entry into Rome, and afterwards, to keep an Archives' specialist in close touch with each of the advancing armies. It was not possible until later to add a representative from Washington, but a visit from the Director of the President's Library at Hyde Park has kept American Archivists in touch with the situation and ensured co-operation.

The task of protection involved, as a first measure, the preparation of a List covering, specifically or by inference, all classes both lay and ecclesiastical, of Italian Archives; and its issue with suitable instructions as completely and as widely as the organization of Army and Commission made practicable. The Archives to be covered were rich, numerous and highly organized. Besides the *Archivio del Regno* and over 40 *Archivi di Stato* (most of them rich in series inherited from the Kingdoms, Lordships and Republics of earlier periods) there are over 800 townships having ancient Archives; Dioceses and Chapters show a comparable wealth; Notarial Archives add more than 100 large and numerous small Repositories to the total; and modern legislation has created in the District Offices of Land and other Registration (the *Catasto*, and so forth), of the Law, Taxation and the *Stato Civile*, and of the ordinary Local Authorities in Province, *Compartimento* and Commune, well regulated Archive Centres of real importance; and then there are the Private accumulations.

It was not difficult to predict the dangers which threatened accumulations so numerous, so scattered, and so susceptible; nor has the prediction lacked confirmation by the event. On the other hand there is some ground for relief. Deliberate destruction by the enemy, such as that of the Angevin Archives at Naples, burned senselessly and without excuse in September 1943, has been (it is only just to say) comparatively small up to date: nor have large quantities been carried off; though some obviously beautiful or valuable things, such as the painted binding-boards (the *Tavolette di Biccherna*) at Siena, have had narrow escapes. The modern Archives of Ministries at Rome have naturally been largely evacuated either by the Germans or by Fascist co-operators, but what remained included some surprises; from the vast *Archivio Ordinario* of Mussolini, found in order and *in situ*, to the Air Ministry documents discovered at the bottom of a well. The larger modern local Archives seem also, up to date, comparatively immune from destruction, though frequently in great confusion.

Of damage from bomb and shell there is a long and sad tale, though a policy of evacuation has probably saved much, as at Livorno and Pisa. Total or considerable destruction in the *Archivi di Stato* at Foggia, Pizzofalcone and Pistoia, in Cathedral Archives at Benevento and elsewhere, in the *Archivio Notarile* at Frosinone, in the Parochial Churches destroyed at Naples — these are some examples of the price we pay for air support and artillery prep- aration, by whichever side they are practised. It is perhaps more profitable to dwell on what has had the fortune to survive or escape bombardment. Sicilian Archives have emerged comparatively undamaged, and so have *Archivi di Stato* in Southern Italy other than those mentioned; and at Foggia the valuable *Archivi della Dogana delle Pecore* survived a direct hit; the priceless *Archivio di Stato* at Florence, after being in great danger, escaped with negligible damage to the Documents; at Rome, Orvieto, Perugia, Assisi, Lucca, Arezzo, Siena and, most recently, Ravenna it has been possible to report all Archives safe. Moreover, where there has not been fire, demolition of a building has not always meant destruction of its contents. Archives are in some ways singularly resistant, and manuscripts exhumed intact from the ruins of the *Colombaria* at Florence, the *Archivi di Stato* at Pistoia and the *Biblioteca Comunale* at Tivoli, may suggest hopes for the *Archivio Comunale* at Viterbo, for Cathedral Archives at Livorno and even for the *tertia anula* of

Archives (the rest had gone to Rome) buried under the rubble at Monte Cassino.

The period of active hostilities past, come the dangers from civil population and occupying troops. Looting by civilians is always liable to occur, as it did at Palermo, before civil government is restored and while custodians are scattered and doors and windows missing; and where there is not looting there may be indiscriminate destruction, when an uneasy consciousness that Records contain names (especially the Records of the Police or the Tax-gatherer) suggests the remedy of fire. We have perhaps to thank the severity of an opposite clause in the Italian penal code for the fact that occasions of this sort seem to have been so far comparatively few. Occupying troops may do much damage, if not by destruction by dispersal (which is nearly as bad), in mere ignorance. This is particularly liable to occur to modern Archives which do not in their outward aspect suggest great importance (especially if already disordered by the enemy) and which are perhaps housed in eligible quarters in a place and at a time where quarters are urgently needed and difficult to find.

To meet such dangers or palliate their results the Archives or Monuments Officers, however active in personal survey, have had to rely largely on co-operation first with the officers of advanced Intelligence and other formations, then with those of Military Government or Control Commission, and ultimately with Italian Officials. In these later stages comes the final difficulty of civil disorganization and the not unnatural apathy of minor officials whose whole world has crashed about their ears. It may be necessary to suggest with some insistence that pending the replacement of windows snow need not be allowed to lie on the top of volumes; that the leaking lavatory in the Prefect's office should be repaired as a work of urgency in view of the presence of Archives underneath; that while the roof is missing early registers on the top floor should be transferred to the offices below; that if *epurazione* has banished the Archivist the keeper of the Museum might temporarily carry on; even that scattered papers can be picked up from the floor and wet ones hung out to dry. The examples are taken at random from a dozen towns in Southern Italy and Sicily.

The task of taking stock, of getting in reports and of reorganizing in something more than piecemeal fashion, was greatly facilitated, once Rome was reached, by the existence in Italy of an admirable organization under which the Minister and Director at the capital, working through a system of regional Superintendents and Heads of *Archivi di Stato*, can control and activate Officials and even Owners of a large proportion of the country's Archives. To set this machinery in motion again was now a major objective and accorded with the Commission's general policy of using, wherever possible, existing organizations. Fortunately the task proved comparatively simple, for most of the Archivists were at their posts or prepared to return to them; only communications were lacking and these the Archives Officers were able to suggest or supply. Most important of all, the Head of the Italian Archives' Service had stayed in Rome and was both able and anxious to co-operate in every way. By November the system was so far restored that all questions of policy and personnel were being decided at Rome by the appropriate agencies; and even at Florence the Superintendent was communicating with the local authorities in his area through Italian channels. It is perhaps not too much to hope that from the present reorganization may result a general survey of Italian Archives as they stand at the conclusion of the war. This would be a really valuable piece of constructive scholarship, particularly if, by collaboration with the Vatican Authorities (with whom also the Archives' Officers have been in touch), it could be made to include Ecclesiastical Archives; the administration of which is independent of the State. In any case something has been done to repair the mischief of War in this field; and present relations with Italian Archivists recall those between Bonaini and his English correspondents nearly a hundred years ago.

The English Archivist:
A New Profession

THE SCOPE OF THIS LECTURE

While I admit to great pleasure at having been invited to deliver this Lecture — for the occasion of it is the inauguration of a project which has been much in my mind for many years — I must confess also that I have approached it with considerable trepidation: a trepidation that has not been lessened by the kind terms in which it, and I, have been introduced by the Provost and the Master of the Rolls to this Assembly.[1] Apart from a natural anxiety as to whether I could and should do justice to a large subject which I was convinced was of very real importance (and of my conviction upon that point, at least, I hope I shall leave you in no doubt) I was perplexed about my title. I should have liked, if the dignity of a Public Lecture would have allowed me to use the vernacular, to announce it under the title 'Why all this Fuss about Archives?' for it is that which must be in the minds of some of my Audience; and it is that simple question — or the series of simple questions which may be summarized in that form — which I mean to propound and, so far as time allows, to answer.

A DEFINITION

In the first place we need to be clear on points of terminology. The Archivist is easy to define — he is the person who looks after Archives. But what are Archives? Summarizing in a few words ideas expressed at more length in definitions put forward at various times in many places — Belgium, France, Holland, Italy, this Country and the United States — we may say that

1. At this Lecture the Provost of the College took the chair and the Lecturer was introduced by the Right Honourable the Master of the Rolls (Lord Greene). The Lecture was delivered from notes but is here set out as nearly as possible in the form in which it was given; with the addition only of some extra illustrative matter.

Archives[2] are the Documents accumulated by a natural process in the course of the Conduct of Affairs of any kind, Public or Private, at any date; and preserved thereafter for Reference, in their own Custody, by the persons responsible for the Affairs in question or their successors. I must stress, to begin, three points in that definition.

First, it is to be noted that Archives are an actual part of the activities which gave them birth, material evidences surviving in the form of writing. When the Ship Money of 1636 had been demanded, and talked about, and collected (so far as it was collected) and spent; when the disturbances aroused by its exaction, and the Revolution which followed, and the Execution of King Charles which followed that, had ceased to be actualities; when all those things had receded into the past, to become a debating ground for Historians and Economists; there still remained the Documents in the Case (the *Accounts*, for instance, of the Tax Collectors) to tell us, so far as they survive, what as a matter of fact occurred.

The other two points I wish to stress are that Archives may be of any date and result from activities of any kind. Between the earliest *Pipe Roll*, compiled in 1131, and the Accounts compiled in the Treasury in 1947 — however much they may differ in shape, colour, size, material, language, writing and arithmetical method; though the one used wooden tallies and an *abacus* whereas the other relies, I understand, on algebraical formulae of taxability — between these two there is, in respect of their quality as Archives, no difference. When William de Burstall took over in 1377 the historic site in Chancery Lane the Records in his keeping were in essence the same as those which the Master of the Rolls has in his charge and superintendence there to-day or may have transferred to the Repository to-morrow; though the earlier Master would certainly have viewed with concern, if he could have foreseen them, the quantity and the variety of Documents for which his successor is responsible.

In the same way the Quality of Archives is not dependent on the grade of activity which produces them. Every Private Individual or Private Enterprise; every Professional, Charitable or Social Institution; every Industrial Concern, Public Utility Company or Trading Corporation; every Parish, Diocese, Council, Board, Borough, Local or National Authority — all, in so far as they apply writing to the purposes of administration or business, produce potentially Archives: though it is true that some may produce them as Monsieur Jourdain produced prose, *sans le savoir*. The National Register of Archives or the British Records Association, whose interest is in Archives as such, must deal indifferently with any type or date of Document and any

2. Or '*Records*': the words are practically interchangeable in this Country: but '*Archives*' is generally preferable because '*Records*' can be used in a narrower sense.

category of Owner or Custodian; flitting, if necessary, from the twelfth to the twentieth century, ranging from the Church to the Chamber of Commerce, in the course of a morning.

What, then is this special quality or nature which is common to all Archives, independent of their age or provenance? I must ask your indulgence if I pursue the question in a little more detail; for on it depend the functions and duties which we assign to our Archivist and the knowledge and abilities we shall require in him.

'DOCUMENTS' AND 'ARCHIVES'

As an interpolation we may remark that this word 'Document' is in our day applied to many things besides the results of pen and ink upon paper or parchment. Even if we exclude 'Enclosures' and 'Annexures,' whose number and variety are limited only by considerations of space and volume (for there is nothing except practical convenience to prevent an Elephant being at least an Annexure), the list is a long one: including potentially not only reproductions of writing by any mechanical means — especially Photography — upon any kind of material, but even substitutes for it. Quite recently the Master of the Rolls has had to give a ruling on the status not only of Photographic Material but of Sound Recordings acumulated in Government Departments; and only a few days since I was inspecting copper plates — those used in the manufacture of Charts — which are undoubtedly part of the Archives of the Hydrographic Department of the Admiralty.

This apart, what we have to say under the present heading may be put very briefly in the statement that while all Archives are Documents, not all Documents are Archives: or, even more briefly, that Archives are Documents, with a qualification.

THE GROWTH AND ARTICULATION OF ARCHIVES

What is this qualification? It is indicated, I suggest, in two words of our Definition — 'accumulate naturally.' Archives are not collected: I wish the word 'Collection' could be banished from the Archivist's vocabulary, if only to establish that important fact. They are not there, or they should not be, because someone brought them together with the idea that they would be useful to Students of the future, or prove a point or illustrate a theory. They came together, and reached their final arrangement, by a natural process: are a growth; almost, you might say, as much an organism as a tree or an animal. They have consequently a structure, an articulation and a natural relationship between parts, which are essential to their significance: a single document out of a Group of Archives is no more to be taken as expressing in and by itself all it has to tell us than would a single bone separated from the skeleton of an extinct and unknown animal. Archive quality only survives unimpaired so long as this natural form and relationship are maintained.

THE IMPORTANCE OF RELATIONSHIP

We may push this point a little further: for the dependence of Archives on natural relationships manifests itself in more than one fashion. There is first their relation to the activity which produced them or the connexion, it may even be the physical fact of the place, in which they were preserved. When the Allies entered Rome in 1944 the Archives Officer who followed on the heels of the first parties found, and was just in time to stop, a large quantity of Archives being thrown out of the window of a building which a certain important element proposed to occupy. Among the rescued files (I inspected them a few weeks later) were a quantity which contained multigraphed Situation Reports — a type of document, judging them by their face value, of comparatively little importance and anyhow repeated almost certainly in other files elsewhere. Their significance lay in their connexion with the building in which they were found, which proved to contain the *Archivio Ordinario* of Mussolini; and this fact alone gave the key to certain markings with blue chalk which were presently discovered in them: they were, in all probability, the copies specially marked for the information of the Duce; possibly by his own hand. Had the proposed defenestration been accomplished this signficance would have been lost.

A second point of relationship is that between the individual Documents in a single accumulation. It is this point which is so often missed when an ancient accumulation of Archives is broken up in the Sale Room; or when misplaced zeal (it is not uncommon in Private Archives and has happened in the early days of most larger Repositories) brings together in a single artificial collection, because of their similar form or their usefulness for a particular kind of research, Documents taken from a number of separate Archive Classes. The artificial class of *Pergamene* and the *Sezione Diplomatica* in most Italian State Archives, the *Trésor des Chartes* at Paris in the Archives Nationales and our own *Special Collections* at the Record Office are examples of the irreparable damage which may be done in this way. To illustrate this important point by the simplest of examples, one has only to think of the chain of significance which is broken when an enclosure is removed from its enclosing letter: it may mean in extreme cases the falsification of both Documents. Yet errors even so obvious (it would seem) as that are frequently made when the individual Documents in Archives are looked at solely as individual Documents.

Finally there is what we might term an external relationship — a kind of cousinship — which exists, potentially, between Documents in independent Archive Groups.[3] When a Secretary of State in London sends instructions or information to an Agent in Edinburgh the result may be an original at one end and an entry, in identical terms, in a Register at the other; or conceived in the terms of modern typescript, a 'top copy' in one place and a 'carbon' in the other. Their preservation in the Group to which they naturally belong gives it each its distinctive significance: but the relationship between the two is an important factor in the value and interpretation of both.

This question of Archive quality is a fascinating one to an Archivist but time is limited: and the mention of interpretation may serve to remind us of another and a very important topic arising from our definition. We have said much of the nature of Archives and its dependence on the circumstances of their preservation, but nothing so far of how or why they come to be preserved.

THE USES AND USERS OF ARCHIVES

Archives normally pass through three phases. In the first they are the current Files (to use modern phraseology) which may be needed at any moment for reference: the Archive at this stage has not as a rule attained its full stature — the Document is written but is not yet placed. In the second phase the Files may still be wanted on occasion, but for the purposes of precedent and the historical background of the work of the Office rather than for current reference: they are relegated morally (physically, too, if their volume is very large) to a kind of Limbo where they lie half-forgotten and sometimes — for storage space and staff are expensive things — wholly neglected. Finally, if they survive, they reach the third stage; in which their value for the purposes of Research is recognized and becomes the governing factor in their preservation. There is no fixed period for the endurance of the first two phases: it varies with circumstances and in the past the 'Limbo' phase has sometimes lasted for centuries.

Ideally the Archivist, though obviously his intrusions during the first phase must be limited by practical considerations, is concerned with all three: and there is much to be said in some cases — that of the Local Authority, for example — for associating his work fairly closely with that of the Administrative and Executive Sections from which he will, from time to time, receive transfers of Documents. The Public Record Office, which receives transfers from the Departments of Central Administration, has, by

---

3.   In Archives parlance a '*Group*' of Archives is that resulting from the activities of a single autonomous unit of administration. *Classes* are the structural subdivisions within the Group.

the terms of its Acts, some responsibility in regard to their Archives at all three stages: and indeed became acutely conscious of the fact during the War, when a first census of the places in which Public Records in the making were stored produced a total of 399. It is at present actively engaged in securing the provision of a 'Limbo' of rather more suitable character than such places have sometimes had in the past for Departmental Archives which have not yet been actually transferred to its custody.

But it is of the third phase that most people think when they speak of Records; the phase in which they have become available for study: and we may remark at this stage a definite change in the angle of approach to them. They begin to be consulted again — perhaps freely — but the purpose for which they are used is not once in a hundred times (and it would probably be safe to name a much higher figure than that) the purpose for which they were orginally compiled and preserved. The Master of the Revels to James I compiles an Account to vouch his expenditure in that Office; the Audit Office passes it and puts it away for reference; and the Scholar two or three centuries later finds it of supreme importance because it gives him a chronology for the reproduction of Shakespeare's *'Comedy of Errors'* and other plays — a matter as to which its Custodians, the Audit Office, were completely indifferent.

This last is a point which I should like to emphasize: because it is the indifference of the Official Custodian to the interests in which his documents come to be used which gives to Archives properly preserved one of their outstanding characteristics — their unbiased quality: there is no questioning the impartiality of a witness who knows nothing of the point, nor of its importance, which his evidence will be used to establish; who made his statement in a totally difference connexion.

THE IMPORTANCE OF CUSTODY

This brings me to the last word in our Definition upon which we have to comment. We have said something already in illustration of the importance of the place of custody; we come now to the importance of the mere fact: for the impartial quality which we have seen in Archives, being due to the circumstance of their preservation in the custody of persons not concerned with the interests which they eventually serve, is dependent on there being a reasonable presumption that this custody has been continuous and undisturbed during the second and third phases of their existence. The rather spectacular example which I gave above was selected because it illustrates this point: actually the most important of the *Revels Accounts* are known to have been out of the custody of the Audit Office for some time; worse still, to have been in the hands of one who not only edited them for the

Shakespeare Society in 1842 but produced them from his own custody, and tried to sell them as his own property, in 1868; and who — worst of all — was a friend of that arch-fabricator of Shakespearean matter, John Payne Collier. The effect may be judged from the fact that up to date a dozen or more of books and articles have been devoted to maintaining the views *(a)* that Peter Cunningham did, and *(b)* that he did not, forge, with or without the assistance of Collier, the whole or some part of the documents in question.

So much for the elements in our definition and their implications: the nature of those Documents which our Archivist is to conserve. I pass to a brief consideration of the quantity of Records which have in fact survived in this Country and the variety and scope of the Interests which may use them.

THE QUANTITIES

The answer to this question might be given in one adjective, used in its strictest sense — Incalculable: but we must attempt something a little less removed from definition. It is difficult; because, in the first place, very few people have occasion to deal with the larger numbers or apprehend their meaning. Many years ago I used to tell Students that the Public Records (they are more numerous now) must include, at a conservative estimate, not less than thirty million separate Documents. Finding them unmoved by that figure I would add that this meant that, at the optimistic rate of thirty documents a day, it would take them a million days to examine the whole; but even this left them cold: it was not till I pointed out that, provided they made holiday only on alternate Sundays, they might hope to complete the supposed task in three thousand years, that they began to show an alarmed interest. And these were only the Public Records; the results of Central Administration, and that before the effects of modern methods — of the Typewriter, the Camera, the Card Index and so forth — had time really to manifest themselves. You must think in addition, if you wish to get some idea of the total which confronts us, of the 11,000 Ancient Parishes of England, each having potentially *Registers* dating from the Ordinance of 1538 or a little later, not to mention the documents accumulated in subsequent centuries during which they were the ultimate units of Civil Administration in this Country; think of the 20,000 or so of Manors which are known to have some part of their ancient *Court Rolls* surviving; think (but perhaps Lord Greene would prefer not to think of them, for they constitute a distinct problem of administration) of the valuable *Tithe* Records from about 15,000 Districts which recent legislation has placed in the charge and superintendence of the Master of the Rolls; think of files piling up in any large Commercial or Industrial Undertaking; think, if you will, of the British Broadcasting

Corporation to whose Records the News Bulletin alone must add about a hundred scripts every day.

Undoubtedly 'Incalculable' is the adjective.

THE UNIVERSALITY OF INTEREST

Finally, I must say something of the more-than-variety of scope which Archives offer to Research. If you reflect upon the range covered by Administration of all kinds, public or private, you will realize that, in conditions in which writing is applied freely to the conduct of affairs, there is literally no person and no subject of human interest that may not find illustration in surviving Records. For four centuries (to take only one example) it has been practically impossible, at least highly abnormal, for a man to be born or die in England without a Public Authority taking cognizance of the fact: and between these two major events lie all the possibilities of life — Taxation, the Police Court, Marriage, Business Operations, Politics, Public Service, the Church, the Land, the Law — and all the unpredictable accidents which may bring a man or a thing or a thought into contact with one or more of them; to leave, if it so happen, an impression upon their Archives.

It is, of course, in their third phase particularly that Archives offer this scope to human interest; and anyone who has presided over the Students in a place where considerable research on Documents is carried on must recall plentiful examples of unusual inquiries prosecuted with success in unlikely places. I recollect, for example, the Professor from Eastern France who looked for, and found, in the *Wardrobe Accounts* of Edward III evidence not of the French Wars or of their reactions in the Court of an English King, but on a point of pathology — 'touching for the King's Evil': I recollect the *Court Books* of a Surrey town being cited not to illustrate some stage in the development of Borough Custom but to satisfy the curiosity of the M.C.C. in regard to the early history of Cricket. How surprised a medieval Bishop of Winchester would have been to know the use Lord Beveridge would one day make of his *Pipe Rolls* for establishing points in the history of prices: and how much more than surprised countless Parish Clerks and Clerks of the Peace in the peccant eighteenth century if they could have foreseen the researches of Mr and Mrs Sidney Webb.

I have cited spectacular examples but the inexhaustible possibilities of Archives are perhaps seen best of all in the opportunities they afford for the large-scale study of small matters. History in our time is apt to concern itself with people rather than with individuals and with conditions rather than things. It is the faring of ordinary people, our opposite numbers in the past, that we need to study for the enlightenment of our own conduct to-day; the people the total of whose lives made up the life of the fourteenth or the eighteenth century just as the total of ours makes up the life of the twentieth: and for such study Archives — and, very often, Archives alone — supply the material.

MODERN ATTENTION TO ARCHIVES

With the gradual perception of these facts has come the modern attitude to Archives. It has taken a long time. We began to awake to the profit of exploiting old Documents for the correction or enlargement of our ideas upon points of history and antiquities so early as the sixteenth and seventeenth centuries: but even men like Archbishop Parker, Lambard, Dugdale and Rymer worked in limited fields and with a limited vision of their possibilities. It was not till the nineteenth and twentieth centuries that the wealth hidden in Local and Private Archives began to be appreciated; that scholars such as Maitland, Tout and the Webbs introduced us to research upon Legal, Administrative, Social and Economic History; and that we arrived finally at a full appreciation of modern as well as ancient Documents and a realization of the fact that the Current Files of to-day are the Archives of to-morrow. This last stage of all, indeed, we can hardly be said to have attained generally even now: for the treatment of modern documentary material in Enemy Countries by Intelligence Services both Military and Civil during and after the last War gave melancholy evidence that 'to-day' — and a very short-sighted to-day at that — is still the limit of many people's imagination.

ENTER AN ARCHIVIST

The later stages of our awakening to the value of Archives have been marked by the gradual emergence of a new point of view — that of the person interested not so much in the contents of Archives and their exploitation as in the earlier and more instant problem of their preservation and in the technical process of arrangement, care and conservation which follow. I must say a few words of the elements which have combined to produce this situation; for the character who now comes upon the scene is the Archivist.

More than fifty years ago a small body of enthusiasts was sufficiently alive to the dangers of dispersal and destruction to which Local and Private Archives were exposed in this Country to be drafting already proposals for protective legislation; and that was followed by a Departmental Committee in 1901 and later (1910-1919) a Royal Commission. None of these resulted in any active measures, but their proposals all implied the creation of a class of persons specially trained to look after the Local Repositories which they wished to set up. Meanwhile the Local Archaeological and Record Societies, hitherto devoted almost entirely to Publication, had begun to be seriously perturbed by the increasing threat to Records of local interest (notably the Family Muniments no longer required for the practical purposes of 'Title'), to debate the problem of finding Repository space for these unfortunates, and in one or two cases actually to set up Muniment Rooms of their own. The Libraries did better, and Historians and Archivists alike owe them a lasting debt; for they not only provided storage and custody in numerous instances, and almost as a matter of general policy, at a time when no other Authorities were willing to come forward, but also gave a most valuable lead by including a section of 'Palaeography and Archives' in the ordinary *Curricula* of their Diploma Courses and Summer Schools. It is now as much as twenty-five years since I gave my first Lectures in these subjects for Sir John Ballinger at Aberystwyth and here in the School of Librarianship.

The movement thus begun received a considerable stimulus after 1924 when, the Manorial Records being placed, by an Amendment to the Law of Property Act of 1922, in the charge and superintendence of the Master of the Rolls, Lord Hanworth proceeded to 'recognize' as places suitable for the deposit of such Records, existing Muniment Rooms and Libraries in almost every County: and the local interest thus engaged was stimulated still further in 1929 when the British Record Society started a movement for the rescue of unwanted Documents of all kinds — but particularly *Deeds* — and their bestowal in places where Students could utilize them. The idea of Local Muniment Rooms thus became firmly established, but there was still one element missing — that of some material reward for those who might choose to specialize professionally as Archivists. The British Records Association, which came into existence in 1932 with the object of co-ordinating the various interests that from different angles approach the Archive field, has more than once been asked if something could not be done to organize Archive work as a profession: and more than once replied that it was useless to plan a diploma course for Archivists until there was some reasonable prospect of a succession of posts for them to fill. That we have now felt justified in proposing such a course is due to the last development I have to record: a development started by the pioneer work of the late G.H. Fowler in Bedfordshire after the first World War, when he persuaded the County Council to institute the machinery of County Records Committee, properly equipped and fitted Muniment Rooms and trained Staff (he trained it himself and practically made one of it, *en amateur*, for years) — the organization, in short which gradually, as its utility and efficiency were demonstrated, has been adopted by more and more Counties and occasionally by other bodies.

With this recognition by Local Authorities of Archive Work and Workers as a regular, if modest, part of their establishment the Profession of Archivist may be said to have arrived: and the course now instituted at University College with the continued collaboration of the Librarians marks its inauguration in London.

THE NEW PROFESSION AND ITS TRAINING

We are to create then a body of Men and Women particularly qualified to undertake the Conservation of Archives; badged and certificated Archivists: and the question arises — What are we to teach them? Like all good Professionals they themselves will add continually to their knowledge and abilities so long as they remain in practice: indeed this is peculiarly their case because of the enormous quantities of the Documents with which they may have to deal, every one of them *ex hypothesi* unique in some sense: I have published (if I may instance my own case) three books and a number of articles on English Hand-Writings and examined, in the course of a long official career, more Documents than I should care to compute, yet I seldom look with attention at a new one of any age and size without finding some noteworthy fresh feature in the script. But, clinical experience apart, what are the attainments necessary for the Complete Archivist? The subjects of Study are naturally related specifically to the functions he may be called on to perform, and these arise directly from those outstanding characteristics of Archives of which we have already spoken: to recapitulate — the facts that they are *Material Evidences* surviving in the form of writing; that they may be of *any* Date and result from *any kind of Administrative Activity*; that they have always to be approached from the point of view of their *Relationship* to the activity which produced them and to each other; that their mere *Conservation* (physical and moral) is always the primary and very generally (owing to past neglect) the most urgent consideration; that *'Custody'* is the *differentia* between the plain Document and the Archive; that the *Quantity* of Archives surviving in England is incalculable; and that their potential *Uses in Research* are unlimited and beyond prediction.

Let us see how these work out in terms of Functions and Subjects for Study.

'MATERIAL EVIDENCES'

I have put this characteristic at the head of my list because although it can hardly be called a *subject* it is very much a *condition* of the Archivist's studies: affecting both the way in which they are taught to him and his application of them later in practice. Archives, we have seen, are 'the documents in the case,' part of the facts: but we have also seen that they may, and generally do,

furnish evidence later upon matters which have nothing to do with the
original 'case'; and that it is this evidence which, perhaps after the lapse of
many years, when it attracts the eye of Research, may give to a Document
supreme importance in the estimation of Scholars. The Archivist has clearly
the delicate task of making sure that all the evidential value of his documents,
including perhaps some which is not yet perceived or perceptible by himself
or others, is preserved unimpaired while the document is in his keeping. A
difficult condition to attach to anyone's activities: but the fact remains that
all the operations which he may undertake — arrangement, repair, make-up
and provision of accessibility for study — must be subject to it. The way in
which that may affect the practical application by the Archivist of the
knowledge and experience he has gained in training is perhaps most readily
perceived if we seek an instance on the side of the technical processes. Take,
for example, that of Book-binding — one of the Studies we shall presently
commend to his attention. Mechanically speaking there is no difference
between the re-binding of a volume of Records and that of any other book
made of like materials and reduced by time, decay and so forth to the same
state: both, so far as the Binder is concerned, present the same problems, to
be settled in the same way. Actually the Archivist-Bookbinder has continually to devise means of retaining some feature in an old binding which by
ordinary standards might be discarded as valueless or even objectionable:
doing, as our Chief Binder once expressed it to me, "things which would
surprise them in the shops." He may, for instance, have to refrain from
pressing his sheets before re-sewing because it would endanger the evidence
of a margin made by folding before the original binding was put on. There
will probably be no indication that these creased margins will ever be of
importance (though I could cite at least one occasion when they were); but
they are there, part of the evidence, and must be preserved.

The same line of approach will be found appropriate to every operation the
Archivist has to perform even up to the preparation of a text for publication.

HANDWRITINGS, LANGUAGES AND FORM

To do all that is necessary for his Archives their Custodian must be able to
read and understand them; and since our Definition allows them to be of any
kind and any date this means that the Complete Archivist must in the first
place have more than a little knowledge of *Palaeography*. It is true that he may
practically confine himself to what are known as the 'English Court Hands'
(that is to say the hands used in this Country for Business purposes as
distinct from the 'Text' of Literary and Liturgical writings), the history and
development of which are more or less self-contained; and to the period

between the twelfth century, when writing in England began to be applied with some freedom to the purposes of Administration, and the mid-eighteenth, when the Court Hands were finally abolished or merged in the modern. He will find this, however, a quite sufficient task: for within his limits he must be able not only to read but to read well. Ideally he should be able (being an ideal he will never attain it, but it should be his aim) to read all Court Hands with as much ease, given certain other qualifications of which we may say a word later, as he does the letters that come to him by the morning post: and in the hey-day of the Writing Masters (the sixteenth and seventeenth centuries) there were seven distinct varieties of writing in simultaneous use in this Country; not counting 'Text,' 'Roman' and 'Italic' and omitting sub-divisions. I must only add that the amount of time which the Learner can profitably give to practice in transcription has literally no limit.

Of *Languages* he will need, for the purpose of English Archives, three. First there is *Medieval Latin*, developing peculiarities and a progressive degradation through a long period which ended only with its abolition as an official language in 1733. *French*, in the Anglo-Norman variety, again has its accruing peculiarities but in a limited field (for our Archivist need have little to do with the literary side) and during a shorter period: it makes its official appearance in the thirteenth century in some of the newer and less conventional series of Royal Documents (those under the Privy Seal, for example, as opposed to the Great Seal) and is gradually ousted by English in the fifteenth. Its curious survival well into the seventeenth century as a special *patois* of the Lawyers in their notes and memoranda he may probably neglect; though he cannot altogether omit some study of the earlier Legal French of the '*Year Books*' — a language which still awaits its Dictionary. Finally he has the *English*, again without too much regard to literary niceties but in all its larger developments from the fifteenth century onwards. *Anglo-Saxon* is not essential, though a bowing acquaintance is worth while: the Archivist will be lucky who has practical occasion for it.

The third of the Archivist's subjects under this heading is that generally known as *Diplomatic*, which studies the forms of wording as Palaeography studies the forms of letters: which tells us, for instance, that if in a Charter Henry II styles himself 'King of the English' that charter is of the year 1172 or earlier; whereas if he is 'by the grace of God King of the English' it is of 1172 or later. Since a considerable part of the period to be covered is an age of formalism, in which a man could lose his suit in the King's Court by using a wrong phrase and the scope of Administration of all kinds was extended by the extension of Formularies, it is clear that Diplomatic (if the Archivist is to understand what he reads, or indeed to read it with any certainty) must have a prominent place in our curriculum: though I think we may relieve pressure by observing that some of its exponents have gone unnecessarily far in adding to the technicalities of the contemporary Precedent Books the extra complexities of an artificial modern nomenclature. The Archivist cannot do without a knowledge of what Mr. Perker meant when he talked about the 'casa' (the Writ which was the first stage in Mr. Pickwick's progress to the Fleet Prison) but he may at a pinch dispense with such niceties of modern classification as the 'Letter Missive.' On the other hand we have also to note that Diplomatic, in the hands of its best-known professors, has been too rigidly confined to one category of forms — those of the Medieval Letter, whose peculiarities it first investigated: there is, for instance, a 'Diplomatic' of the forms used in Accounting of which the books at present tell us little; that of Private Deeds (which means, incidentally, the early History of Conveyancing) cries out for attention; and even the Diplomatic of Royal Letters has yet to be pursued into its very interesting later stages, when (to take one example) the development of new forms in the Royal Letter Patent marked, or rather made, the development of the Law of Patent Inventions. In such cases as these, but particularly in the matter of Form in Local and Private Records, our Student-Archivist needs to be not merely piloted through known soundings but launched upon a voyage of personal exploration.

But even if the aspiring Archivist could learn by rote all the formal phrases that ever were used in English Archives he would still not have reached the end of his necessary preparations. It is not enough to have discovered that 'casa' is really 'ca. sa.' and means *capias ad satisfaciendum* — he must know further, if he is to understand it, something of the relation of that Writ not only to the other Documents in Mr. Pickwick's case (the *habeas corpus*, for instance, which followed and the process which preceded it) but also to the whole machinery of Legal Administration which produced and applied them: and the like must be said of any other 'diplomatic' form you might choose to cite. Diplomatic, in short, and for that matter the Palaeography of the Court Hands too, and the Latin, French and English Languages so far as concerns their use in Archives, are only sections of the larger subject now generally known as *Administrative History*.

ADMINISTRATIVE RELATIONS

Clearly our Student-Archivist must devote a considerable part of his time to this section of his work. We may lay down for him, as a minimum requirement, in addition to a sufficient background knowledge of General History, the fullest possible acquaintance with the structure, machinery and development of English Administration and Archives in all grades and at all periods. But what exactly does that mean?

The subject apart from the special aspects I have just mentioned is a new one. The British Records Association and one or two other Authorities have worked out within five great headings or Categories of Administration ('Public, Central'; 'Public, Local'; 'Semi-Public'; 'Private'; and 'Ecclesiastical') a classification which is now generally accepted: but there is at present no text-book for the whole subject; and though the effort of a few Scholars like the late Professor Tout and Miss B.H. Putnam, and a few outstanding volumes among the publications of Local and other Record-printing Societies, have cleared the ground at certain points (even, in a few cases, got it well under cultivation) to a very large extent the field awaits the labourer. What course, apart from mastering the general lay-out, are we to recommend for our Student?

Training at this point is not vocational and we must begin by emphasizing the educational value of a close study of all the more authoritative and definitive works which have appeared in this connection (it is not for me to catalogue them here but they are not at present impossibly numerous); without any consideration of whether the Student's own work is likely to be concerned with the particular period, institution or type of Document with which they deal. The reason for this is that there is a certain angle of approach to Archives, a point of view, which our Student has not merely to accept as a maxim enunciated in lectures but to apprehend and make his own in a fashion that can only be achieved by familiarity with the experiences of others *in consimili casu*. He will find that these experiences bring him back always to the same point — the relation of Archives to each other and to the office machinery which produced them. I have remarked already at an earlier point in this lecture that Archives cannot be cared for, arranged, studied, valued, used intelligently without reference to this inter-relation. But the fact is so important that even at the risk of overweighting this section of my subject I will venture to elaborate it with a little further illustration. I will take my examples from two old and familiar series of Records: the 'Tallies' — the hazel sticks, written, notched and split, with which the Receipt Department of the Exchequer for more than seven centuries acknowledged the payments made to it — and the 'Receipt Rolls' on which the Tallies were registered as they issued. Equally good examples could be drawn from almost any branch of Administration but I take leave to choose my old friends.

In the first place, then, the Archivist will find that, to be sure of its significance, he has to consider the relationship of a document not only to its contemporaries but to its predecessors, and often its successors, in the same class: and this may mean a long historical journey in the case of any but the most modern. Development in almost all grades of English Administration and Archives was continuous and unbroken from their earliest appearance down to the reforms of the nineteenth century: when for the first time the introduction of new machinery meant the destruction of the old. Before that, though new Offices had taken over the medieval functions of (for example) the Great and Privy Seals, though the real work of auditing had departed from the Pipe Office, though the Sheriff in his County Court had been all but superseded by the Justices of the Peace in Quarter Sessions, this had not meant that the earlier institutions ceased to operate: it had been the practice merely to add the new, to set it beside the old. As a result we find an extraordinarily large number of things in English Administration and Archives which are being done in the sixteenth, seventeenth, eighteenth century (and even later) by what are essentially the same means as were employed in the fourteenth, the thirteenth and even the twelfth. It is true that Time has often so overlaid their original simplicity with procedural complexities, so surrounded them with supplementary processes, so altered even their outward form, that it may be difficult to recognize them. Having read in the twelfth century *Dialogus de Scaccario* that Tallies should measure in length the distance between your fore-finger and thumb you might well be surprised to find one at the Bank of England which measures 8 ft. 6 ins.: you should certainly be more than surprised (having fixed your mind firmly on the fact that the Exchequer Tally acknowledged money paid in) to find Mr. Pepys alluding casually to it as a means by which large sums were paid out. The answer to both these riddles (which were still riddles not so many years ago) lies in a distant past. The first was answered comparatively easily once a few medieval Tallies had been found (the majority were burned, with the Houses of Parliament, in 1834) to bridge the gap between the twelfth century and the eighteenth. The second, with scores of other perplexities which assail the Student who plunges into Financial Records of the later centuries in this Country, is being solved gradually as minute research upon the Receipt Rolls of the medieval period reveals the Exchequer Officials exploiting, at first tentatively and then as a regular practice, with all the necessary apparatus of new phraseology, supplementary Records, discounting facilities and the rest, the great discovery that a receipt for revenue one has not yet received can be used as an instrument for paying one's debts.

The tangle which must obviously result between the separate Records of Receipt and of Issue in these circumstances furnishes incidentally as good an instance as we need look for of a second kind of administrative relationship — not, this time, between documents of different date in the same class but between distinct classes of the same date. Moreover, anyone who cares to follow the transactions of Mr. Pepys or any other spending Official (as he must do if he is to have a full understanding of them) into the Records of Treasury, Audit Office, King's Remembrancer and Pipe Office, as well as those of the Receipt, will find that he has had a very sufficient example of a third — the potential relationship between Documents in distinct *Groups*:

and, to complete the picture, further aids to comprehension may be sought, outside Official Archives, in the Private Muniments, if they have survived, of Families whose Ancestors held posts in or had dealings with the Exchequer: those of the Fanshawe Family have, in fact, already made contribution.

The same classes may give us good examples of one more line of research in Administrative Relationships and that perhaps the most difficult of all: I mean the tracing of the effects of Office Organization upon Record Form. The most common way in which this operates is the employment of forms and conventions which the Clerk who uses them does not trouble to explain because they are his ordinary office practice, a matter of common knowledge to himself and his colleagues: but we have also to reckon with the effect of office arrangements of other kinds — those of Staff for instance — upon Records. This last is particularly well seen in our Records from the Receipt Department: which begin as a single series in the twelfth and early thirteenth centuries; become well established triplicate series, both for Receipt and Issue, in the late thirteenth and fourteenth (flirting for a short while with the idea of quadruplication); die away into single series, or even nothing, in the fifteenth; revive in the sixteenth; and are reformed as double series under a new staff organization late in the same century, to continue in that form down to the nineteenth: at which stage an attempt was made to force the earlier series — single, triplicate and quadruplicate — into the duplicate mould; with results which may be imagined.

Resisting the temptation to discuss the interesting question how far the words duplicate and triplicate, which I have used for convenience, can in fact be applied with accuracy to Archives, which are *ex hypothesi* unique, I will single out, in conclusion, from a number of conventions of the type I have described which might be cited from these Records one — the dot in the left-hand margin — which for a long time would have defied explanation if it had not altogether escaped observation. This dot does in fact differentiate one out of the three rolls of the triplicate period from the other two: but it does much more; for in its presence, if I am not wrong, and still more in its occasional unexplained absences, lies the solution of more than one question bearing on the significance of the whole roll at different periods.

It will be seen that we have again, and to an even greater extent than in the case of Diplomatic, a study which is in the making: one in which the Student must be prepared himself to push much further than lectures or book-learning will take him. I shall have to suggest later that the Archivist may upon occasion turn Historian and it is in this branch of the Historical services (which is crying for recruits) that he may most properly enlist. His results will have a two-fold value: for elucidation of the Administrative History which lies behind a series of Records previously unworked not only adds to the stock of known facts but provides a piece of indispensable equipment for the researches of others who, in whatever interest, may desire later to exploit the same documents. It should not be too much to hope that the work of Archivists trained in this School may presently do a great deal to accelerate the progress of these essential explorations, especially in the fields of Local, Semi-Public and Private Administration.

CONSERVATION

I turn to the more strictly vocational side of our work. To be able to read and understand his documents is an essential preliminary to any practical work the Archivist may have to undertake; and the right angle of approach a necessary condition to his undertaking it: but, these apart, his primary task is their physical well-being. What is the knowledge and what are the abilities we must require in him, or endeavour to give him in his training? To tell the truth we need for our Archivist something of a Jack-of-all-trades. He must be skilled in Sorting, Arranging and Listing and in the mechanical processes connected with them; neat-handed by nature or training; more than a little of a Bookbinder and Repairer, with a touch of some of the allied crafts; a good deal of a Photographer; something of a Fireman; and a little of an Architect, Builder, Chemist, Engineer, Entomologist and Mycologist.

Of *Chemistry* (with special reference to the Materials of Records) and of *Entomology* and *Mycology* (with special reference to their decay or destruction) he will have enough if he is able to talk and listen intelligently, has studied where and how to find the appropriate books or make the necessary contacts and, above all, knows the points at which Archive requirements may compel a modification in the ordinary methods of the professional Scientist. To take a single example of what I mean by the last proviso — all Scientists tend to be experimental, to rely on Laboratory Tests and to interpret the word 'permanent' in a limited sense. The Archivist cannot afford to do so; for the two reasons that his charges are unique and that they are generally so numerous, and include so many cases requiring treatment, that he must be able, when he has dealt with an individual document or class from the point of view of repair, make-up or whatever the process may be, to put it away without further anxiety and proceed with the next on his list: Documents in a

Documents in a big Repository cannot even count on individual inspection at regular intervals. The recently-invented process of Repair by Lamination, that is by laying a document between sheets of acetate foil and welding the three together, offers a good example of the two attitudes of mind. The process is popular with Scientists because it is new and uses modern materials, is economical of money and labour, and is worked largely by machine. The Archivist should, to my mind, reply to these allurements (has replied in one or two cases) that the material has not yet stood the one test which he can accept — that of time — and that no one has suggested what plan of action will be feasible supposing that it does after all go wrong. It is not unknown for one generation of Scientists to prove a theory to their satisfaction and the next to disprove it.

On the side of the *Architect, Builder, Engineer* and *Fireman* we have a clear course. What the Archivist requires in the way of Accommodation, Storage, Equipment, Safe Custody, Ventilation, Fire and Flood Precautions, Heating and Lighting has been worked out in his own books but for the most part has not yet reached the Professions concerned. It will be his task to make the necessary liaisons and, in particular, to join in solving the interesting problem of providing for his requirements in various types of building the larger part of which is to be devoted, or has already been devoted, to quite different purposes: and his training must fit him for this. He should also know enough of the practice of other Countries — the variations introduced by such considerations as white ants or a dry climate — to give his English ideas flexibility.

The other crafts or branches of knowledge I have named are in a somewhat different category; being those which will or may be in daily use in any Repository. Of the methods and technique of *Listing, Sorting and Arranging* our Student must learn all he can: and (once more) he must be imbued — in this case by means of a course of practical work — with a knowledge of the difference which results from the fact that the objects to be submitted to the processes of Arrangement, Listing and the rest are Archives: natural accumulations and not artificial collections.

Book-binding, Repair and *Photography* also demand, besides instruction in theory, a measure of practical training sufficient to make the Student himself a fair executant: because even if he is not called upon to practise them personally he has to direct the Craftsmen who do, and this cannot be done on a basis of theory alone. Of the way in which, here also, the Archive element produce specialities of practice I have already spoken: but it may perhaps be added that photographic work is affected equally with the others; and that the relation of director and executant in all these matters is governed by the fact that the former can, and does, read the document. To Photography by the way, and especially *Microphotography*, the modern Archivist must devote considerable attention because its developed use will certainly affect Archive Policy on many sides: for instance on that of Publication.

CUSTODY

The maintenance of Custody is, we have seen, one of the most important functions of the Archivist, because without it his charges may cease to be Archives. It is not an easy function because in an age which has become interested in exploiting Archives for its own purposes and (what is more) in exploiting them almost as soon as they have ceased to be current papers — he has to try and reproduce the conditions of preservation which obtained when, apart from their use for office reference, no one was interested in them at all: and when in consequence, though there might be greater dangers from neglect or accident, the risk of careless or deliberate disarrangement, garbling, suppression and the like in the interests of exploiting agencies practically did not exist. For himself this means a kind of self-denying ordinance. The ideal would be an Archivist who should have sufficient intelligence to discharge his other functions but not enough to make him interested himself in what I may call the exploitable value of his documents: but since this is practically impossible we can only say that it is his duty to see that any such interest on his own part is subordinated to the strictest observation of the most careful rules of conduct in regard to the arrangement of documents, the suppression or removal of even the smallest part of one, the making of any notes or marks upon them and in short any action which could in any way modify the evidential state in which he received them.

That for himself. So far as concerns the subordinate members of his Staff, the Students who are allowed to handle the documents, or any other persons who for any reason are admitted to the Repository, he has to establish by the regulations he imposes and the supervision he exercises a reasonable presumption that there has been no opportunity for any malpractices. He can be no respecter of persons in this matter; the rule must be absolute — *No Un-supervised Access*. In one of the great houses which was offered to the Public Record Office as a War-time Repository, the Owner (the late Duke of Rutland) wishing to remain resident we solved the difficulty by appointing him temporarily a member of our Staff; and this was not a meaningless gesture on either side.

For the training of the Archivist in this matter we can only prescribe the formulation of detailed Rules to cover every situation in which he is likely to find himself. The Keys System, Night Watching, Emergency Precautions of all kinds, Production Methods, Search Room Regulations, Rules for Repairers and Photographers — all these must be discussed in detail and all subject to the one over-riding necessity.

FACILITIES FOR STUDY

The Archivist's functions are not limited to preventing improper access to his Documents: on the contrary, the use of Archives by Students is in a sense his own *raison d'être* and it is his business, once he has made sure of their safe custody and also made sufficient provision for their physical well-being, to see to it that access to them is made as easy as possible. This implies in the first place an extension of the activities of Arranging, Numbering and Listing which we have already assigned to him. Indexes will be needed for many classes and also Descriptive Lists — the latter particularly necessary things in an age of Microphotography because they may enable the Student who wishes to work at a distance to curtail the amount of waste photography which is inevitable if he has to order blindly. It may also be part of the Archivist's duties (if he is fortunate enough to have the necessary time available) to prepare Texts or Calendars of certain series of his Records for Publication.

For all these activities his training must prepare him: but Indexing, Listing and Editing are not the sole facilities for Students which will be required of him. He will find in practice, if his Search Room is much frequented, that he will be expected to act as general guide and adviser; that all the really knotty problems will be submitted to him even by Students engaged in the most specialized enquiries. What qualification, besides intelligence and good nature, must we require in him for that? Since we have said that the quantity of topics of human interest which may find illustration in Archives is unlimited the reply might be in one word, 'Omniscience': and (*credite experto*) it is little less that is at times demanded from the Official in charge of a large Repository. Our present purpose, however, being practical it must suffice to say that he should have a close and up-to-date acquaintance with the trend of all the more important Studies which depend for their progress upon documentary work: that is to say that he must be strong on the bibliographical side of Research — well up in what has been done and is doing: that he must be particularly knowledgeable in the matter of Reference Books of every kind: and that his training must teach him how to attain, and keep, such qualifications.

That, brings me to the end of the simple questions which I began by propounding: but they in turn give rise to three more:

the first — In the present situation of English Archives, is the fully trained Archivist our only requirement?
the second — How far does the distinction go between Archivist and Historian?
and finally the third — What are the inducements to an Archivist's career?

ARCHIVISTS, TRAINED AND UN-TRAINED

The answer to the first is, of course, 'No.' We have been speaking of the Complete Archivist, of the training he must undergo and the qualification he must display to merit that title: but you have only to think of some of the quantities I mentioned earlier in this Lecture — the 11,000 Parishes for instance — to see that the wildest enthusiast could not contemplate the provision of a fully trained Archivist for even one in every hundred of the existing smaller Accumulations in England; nor would such accumulations provide full-time work for him.

Much might be said upon this topic: some people, for instance, have dreamed of great concentrations of Local and Private Archives into a few large Regional Repositories; others, while desiring the large Local Repositories should take over such of the smaller accumulations as their Owners or Custodians cannot or will not fittingly provide for, maintain that the best Custodian is the natural Custodian and have no wish to see him abolished. Whatever the merits on either side of this controversy, it seems certain that for many years existing conditions will to some extent continue: indeed, remembering the way in which new accumulations are constantly forming as a result of the activities of modern Institutions, we may safely say that they can never entirely cease. Who then is to supply the expert knowledge required in the small cases?

We must not let down the qualifications demanded of the full-time professional Archivist who is to take charge of an important Repository: we cannot admit, even if his Repository contains only modern Documents (for instance those of a Colony) that he can afford to lack the depth of knowledge which a full training supplies. Three dimensions must always be better than two and it is an undoubted fact that whereas a man trained on medieval Archives adapts his knowledge and experience with little difficulty to serve him in dealing with a modern accumulation the reverse is not the case. Even in the interests of his own career, the Archivist should be able to pass from one appointment to another of different type.

On the other hand there is emphatically in present conditions, and I hope there always will be, room for the Amateur, and in large numbers. The great problem of Parish Records, for example, will be halfway towards a solution when Incumbents generally begin to realize that a little study will tell them most of what they need to know about the mere conservation of the Documents in their Parish Chests and a little labour enable them to implement the knowledge: and I would add one more to the functions of the Archivist in a large Local Repository by saying that it is his duty to aid such realization and to offer his advice and help to all Owners or Custodians of small accumulations in the District. He will find his own Repository benefit, for it will lead incidentally to much valuable material being deposited in his charge.

I would like also to express the hope that our School will always find a place for the part-time student — the Local Official or other enthusiast whose Archives do not need and cannot claim the whole of his time; but who can find enough to undertake their listing or repair or photographing and wishes to acquire, within those limits, something of a professional technique.

ARCHIVIST AND HISTORIAN

As to the relations of the Custodian and the Exploiter of Archives — I have already supplied half the answer to this question when I said that the needs of Research constituted the *raison d'être* of the Archivist. The idea (which has sometimes been suggested) of a fundamental antagonism between the two is absurd. The ideal Library was once defined by a distinguished Librarian as one which no Reader ever entered; and similarly we may sigh for a Repository from which no Document need ever be 'produced': it would simplify enormously, for example, the problem of dealing with mildew at the Public Record Office if we had no Search Department. But the Archivist is well aware that this particular ideal is one not even to be striven for: and the Historian on his side knows, or ought to know, that any restrictions imposed by the Archivist are in the general interest of Scholars as a whole. To a certain extent, as we have seen, the Archivist must himself turn Historian in at least one field — that of Administrative History — and it would be hard if he were cut off from occasional excursions into others. He will almost certainly make from time to time interesting discoveries and must sometimes be allowed the pleasure of following them up, in off hours, himself. The appropriate motto seems to be, if I may vary the metaphor, "Thou shalt not muzzle the ox that treadeth out the corn": we must allow him (one has allowed oneself in one's time) a few mouthfuls; while reminding him that his primary duty is to tread; and hoping that he will not, in the process, tread on any, or many, toes.

WHY AN ARCHIVIST?

I approach my concluding question with diffidence: because having given up to now, to the best of my ability, only the facts of the case I turn at this point to opinion: I may go so far as to call it conviction but it is a personal view.

The Archivist's career, as I have tried to outline it, is one of service. He exists in order to make other people's work possible, unknown people for the most part and working very possibly on lines equally unknown to him: some of them perhaps in the quite distant future and upon lines as yet unpredictable. His Creed, the Sanctity of Evidence; his Task, the Conservation of every scrap of Evidence attaching to the Documents committed to his charge; his Aim, to provide, without prejudice or afterthought, for all who wish to know the Means of Knowledge. Apart from the material reward of a modest livelihood, and the lure of interesting work, what inducement to this career can we hold out?

I think myself it lies in the fact that the good Archivist is perhaps the most selfless devotee of Truth the modern world produces.. That form of devotion has not been common of late years: in fact there has been a strong tendency in the opposite direction and it is because of that tendency that we stand where we do to-day. Without the deliberate perversion of Truth, the elevation of Untruth to the position of a Science, if not a Faith — without that selection and presentation and representation and misrepresentation of Facts which began with Advertisement and culminated (if indeed it has yet culminated) in the *Reichspropaganda-amt* — without these the European War as we have known it could not have been launched. I am not so foolish as to claim for the work I have endeavoured to describe to you the quality of a panacea against the evils from which we are all suffering: but the men and women who take it up may, I think, tell themselves that at least in their Profession the world has found one answer to the Propagandist.

Guide to the Records in the National Archives: United States Government Printing Office, Washington, 1948.

Faced with this very solid work — 700 pages, close packed with information — the task of a Reviewer must be primarily, perhaps almost entirely, to admire and congratulate. To comment in detail on the material for research here disclosed would need far too much space and to attempt any critcism (supposing there to be room for criticism) of its completeness and comprehensive would be dangerous for anyone not intimately acquainted with the complex machinery of American Public Administration. Only fifteen years ago — it seems almost incredible — the first Archives were being gathered into a brand new National Repository at Washington: and only five years later a *Guide* had appeared which gave the world news of an estimated 200,000 cubic feet of Archives, a total already equivalent to, if not larger than, the whole accumulation brought together by our own Public Record Office in a century and with the help of several more centuries behind that. Now here is a new *Guide* superseding that of 1940 and telling us of a total which has swelled to an estimated 800,000 cubic feet: including, besides uncounted millions of the more normal papers, "more that half a million Maps, almost 30,000,000 running feet of motion picture films, more than a million items of still pictures, and approximately a quater of a million disks or other sound-recording units".

Certainly, in face of such figures and such an astonishing body of achievement, admiration (almost one might say awe) and congratulation must be the dominant note: and we offer both sincerely and unreservedly. But perhaps, having paid that obvious tribute, a Reviewer who happens to be also an opposite number, and contemplating himself in another country a work something similar to this, may permit himself to glance through it with an eye still focussed to smaller quantities and different conditions. Any variations of treatment which emerge must be taken as stated or implied rather by way of rumination than criticism.

It is perhaps hardly necessary to say that we are speaking here only of

Federal Archives — the Archivist of the United States has not to deal with those of individual States. We may begin by noting that "the records in the National Archives embrace by far the greater part of the Government's records that are of sufficient value to merit continued preservation": but that these do not include "those of the General Accounting Office and its predecessors, dating from as early as the American Revolution and the records of most of the Federal courts": on the other hand they do include large numbers of Records of a date later than 1925. The short Introduction to the *Guide* aims mainly at facilitating its use; supplying terminological and other explanations to some of which we may recur later. It is emphatic in pointing out that "this Guide presents only the most general view of the records of the National Archives": reinforcing this modest warning with the statistical fact (apposite statistics are very much in evidence throughout the work) that "a thousand cubic feet of records, on an average are covered by about four-fifths of a page of description". A short note about the way in which students may use the Archives concludes the Introduction and we note (with admiration again) the bounteous provision of divisional as well as general Search Rooms. Brief particulars are also given about "processed finding aids" (here and elsewhere one marks the divergence of our two languages) and the like; and we observe with interest that "the National Archives has discontinued its earlier efforts to develop a 'dictionary' catalog of the records in its custody". Apart from these (perhaps it is as well that temptations to break the tenth Commandment should not be too many) the administration of the National Archives is not described: we do not hear anything of the Building, the magnificent Technical Equipment, or the numbers of the Staff who carry on the formidable tasks indicated. The *Guide*, in fact, addresses itself to the Historian or other exploiter of Archives rather than to the Archivist or the general reader. Much of the technical information is, I know, available elsewhere: but I will risk confessing that I was left wondering (and this is a question which does, I think, concern the exploiting student) whether the Washington Repository perhaps contains (as our own Public Record Office did in its earlier stages) a certain proportion of material which will later be eliminated as not sufficiently important to justify permanent preservation; and what the method of elimination will be.

The body of the *Guide* plus the first Appendix gives us an account — including administrative background, covering dates, quantity (generally in linear but sometimes in cubic feet), occasional references to printed works, and general description of their nature and contents — of the Records contained in each 247 Record Groups. Description of the larger Groups is broken by sub-headings of various kinds, such as "General Records", "Records of potash investigations", "Decimal files", "Job folders" and so forth: but as yet there is little indication of what we know as "Classes" within the Groups, still less of the numbers of pieces. This is probably what is meant by the Archivist when he says in his Introduction that "the task of analysing, arranging, inventorying, listing, and otherwise establishing completely adequate control over the records . . . is far from complete". As to the meaning of the term "Record Group" (which, it appears, has changed since 1940) I cannot do better again than to quote the Introduction: "Determination of what records constitute a record group" it tells us "is made by the National Archives after careful consideration of a number of factors, among which both provenance and convenience are especially important." It also tells us of "collective" Record Groups which bring together "the records of a number of relatively small and short-lived agencies that have a functional or administrative relationship": and that "under appropriate circumstances a body of collected records may constitute a record group".[1] The numbering of the Record Groups has no significance other than chronological, following simply the order in which new numbers have been assigned to accruing Archive Groups. Thus the eighty or ninety feet of Documents in R.G. 81 (Records of the United States Tariff Commission) bear no particular relation to the 7,000 or 8,000 feet of General Records of the Navy which precede them in R.G. 80 or to the one News Reel and two Sound Recordings which at present constitute R.G. 82: and on the other hand it is to be observed that R.G. 80 is only one of fifteen Groups containing Naval Records, with numbers ranging from R.G. 19 to R.G. 181. To meet the difficulty which the Student might experience in finding his way, even with the aid of the Index, Appendix B supplies a list of Record Groups classified under 23 headings: sometimes administrative (such as the Departments of the Navy just quoted), sometimes descriptive, such as "World War I: emergency agencies".

Remain two Appendices. Of the "Regulations for the Use of Records" little need be said — they cover a very familiar ground — except that in general they seem to imply rather more discretion for the Archivist in the application of *ad hoc* procedure: though there must be another sigh of envy as one reads of the facilities in the matter of hours and other things such as typing and proof reading and the viewing and hearing of picture and sound recordings: and thinks of what they mean in terms of Staff and Space. Appendix B, "Restriction on the Use of Records", prompts rather similar reflections and is particularly interesting. Besides giving the Archivist discretionary power to "withhold records from examination" and "decline to divulge information obtained from them" whenever he thinks that "the consequences of use will be in violation of law, in disregard of the

---

1. Such an artificial Group has been built up, we notice, in an attempt to replace the Records of the War Department lost by fire and other causes in 1800 and 1814.

rights of individuals as respects the privacy of their personal lives, obstructive of the proper functioning of the Government, or detrimental to national security", it sets our nearly 200 separate orders governing the Access of Students to the Archives described in the Guide: some of them repetitive but a large proportion very much *ad hoc* in their prescription of dates or subjects which are to be closed to the student in the case of a particular Group.

A very notable work, interesting and stimulating both by what it tells us and by what it permits us to infer.

Private Archives

MONSIEUR LE PRESIDENT,
MESDAMES, MESSIEURS,

Je voudrais tout d'abord vous donner quelques explications personnelles.

Lorsque mes collègues du Comité exécutif m'ont fait l'honneur de me demander d'ouvrir la discussion au nom de mon pays sur ce sujet, j'ai répondu que, malheureusement, j'étais extrêmement occupé en Angleterre à l'heure actuelle, et que je n'étais pas tout à fait sûr de pouvoir faire un travail avant la date limite donnée pour la parution de ces documents. J'ai dit cependant que je ferais de mon mieux et, il y a quelques semaines, j'ai envoyé un rapport. Malheureusement ce rapport n'a pu vous être distribué et je ne peux pas me contenter de commenter brièvement une communication qui n'est pas entre vos mains.

Je vais vous épargner sa lecture intégrale et vous lire les remarques préliminaires concernant l'examen des réponses au questionnaire qui nous ont été envoyées par les différents pays; je vous donnerai ensuite le résumé de mes remarques personnelles, c'est-à-dire ce que nous, au Royaume Uni, faisons en matière d'archives privées.

Comme conclusion, je vous lirai une ou deux pages de mon rapport.

Observation préliminaire: En jetant un coup d'oeil sur les réponses faites par les différents pays au questionnaire, dont je n'avais pas eu connaissance avant qu'il fût publié, je trouve, si je puis permettre de le dire, une certaine confusion dans les idées. Je vais donc essayer d'éclaircir le terrain avant d'aller plus loin.

Je pense qu'il est particulièrement important, lors de cette première occasion que nous avons de nous réunir en tant qu'archivistes pour discuter d'affaires d'archives, que nous ayons une définition aussi claire que possible de la nature et des limites des problèmes que nous avons à débattre: que nous ne devrions pas empiéter sur le domaine de l'historien ou de l'économiste ou de tout autre chercheur.

Les historiens du monde doivent se rencontrer ici, à Paris, la semaine prochaine: économistes, bibliothécaires, etc . . . tous ont leur organisation qui leur est propre, leur point de vue qui leur est propre et leurs propres conférences: Dans chacune de leurs activités, nous avons un intérêt fraternal, mais pas d'intérêt direct.

Nous avons notre point de vue propre et notre organisation international propre. Faisons donc extrêmement attention, lors de nos premières réunions, de ne pas donner à ceux qui sont moins bien informés que nous l'occasion de dire: Comment les archivistes ont-ils des intérêts aussi différents de ceux des historiens, des économistes, etc . . . Pourquoi ont-ils besoin d'une organisation séparée et distincte?

Le titre donné au sujet que nous discutons a conduit à cette mauvaise interprétation. En effet, faire la distinction entre les différentes classes d'archives, en appeler certaines économiques est, pour l'archiviste, incorrect, parce qu'il n'existe aucun type d'archive qui ne puisse être utilisé à des fins purement économiques.

Ce qui était dans l'esprit de ceux qui ont élaboré ce programme était très certainement ce qui était dans mon esprit et dans celui des archivistes anglais que, de tous les documents qui intéressent l'histoire économique et sociale, aucun n'était plus en danger que ceux sur lesquels l'Etat n'exerce que peu ou pas de contrôle, en particulier, en ce qui concerne les archives les plus modernes, soit parce qu'elles sont récentes, soit que les gens qui ne connaissent rien à l'affaire les considèrent absolument sans valeur pour cette raison même, soit parce que leur masse est absolument formidable. Ces dernières sont les plus susceptibles d'être détruites à notre époque.

Un autre point de vue qui ne me semble pas pouvoir être admis par les archivistes est que certains fonds d'archives, soit parce qu'ils sont très anciens ou trés récents, soit parce qu'ils proviennent d'une forme spéciale d'activité, soit parce qu'ils présentent un intérêt particulier pour certaines catégories de chercheurs doivent être, pour ces raisons, considérés comme d'une nature différente des autres fonds et en conséquence être traités différemment.

Les documents courants dans les bureaux à l'heure actuelle sont les archives de demain. Ils prendront la suite des archives constituées il y a des siècles. Les archives de la Banque de Rome ou de la Banque d'Angleterre, à l'heure actuelle, ne sont absolument pas différentes en qualité de celles des Banques d'autrefois bien que, du point de vue extérieur, elles puissent avoir certaines différences. Cette différence provient de la qualité des matériaux, de nouvelles formes de comptes, etc . . . qui, naturellement, demandent un traitement physique extérieur différent, mais elles ont les mêmes caractéristiques essentielles et requiérent le même traitement.

La même remarque peut d'ailleurs être faite en ce qui concerne la différence existant entre les archives du fait de leur date, de leur origine, de leur fonction, etc . . .

Pour l'archiviste il n'y a qu'une différence purement extérieure, purement physique entre les archives de la Banque d'Angleterre, par exemple, et les archives de la *British Broadcasting Corporation.*

De la nature même des archives decoulent donc les principes sur lesquels le traitement doit être basé. J'irai même plus loin, et je dirai que distinguer en appelant archives économiques, comme apparemment certains l'ont fait, les archives d'industries particuliéres dans l'état moderne, est réellement une injure pour les économistes et les historiens économistes eux-mêmes. Bien que certains d'entre eux aient pu céder à une mode, à une passion passagère pour une recherche particulière, ou qu'ils alien pu céder également à une ligne de moindre résistance, ils n'admettraient certainement pas que leur étude ne s'en tienne strictement qu'à une certaine date ou à un certain aspect d'enquête.

Deux des économistes les plus représentatifs en Angleterre, á notre époque, Lord Beveridge, d'une part, et permettez-moi de les classer en un seul, M. et Mme. Webb, ont basé une grande partie de leurs travaux sur des archives d'une antiquité tout à fait respectable.

Revenant aux réponses que j'ai examinées, certains semblent avoir inter-prété la question posée comme étant une question de publication. Je dois dire qu'il n'y a naturellement aucune objection à ce qu'un archiviste agisse en tant qu'éditeur une fois qu'il a accompli pleinement sa fonction primordiale et principale, la conservation des archives qui lui sont données à garder. Mais d'après mon expérience, je dois dire qu'il est extrêmement rare de voir un archiviste qui ait pu atteindre ce but enviable: je vais même jusqu'à suggérer que ceux à qui l'on remet la tâche de prendre en main les archives modernes, étant donné les tâches d'élimination, de classement, etc . . . qu'ils doivent accomplir, auraient beaucoup de chance s'ils pouvaient faire autre chose que de faciliter la recherche des autres.

En second lieu, il me semble avoir observé également une certaine confusion entre les lois qui obligent les banques, les compagnies d'as-surances, les compagnies industrielles, etc . . . dans l'intérêt de leurs clients, à faire des archives d'un certain genre et à les garder pendant un certain temps, et les lois qui règlementent la conservation des archives dans l'intérêt des chercheurs.

C'est évidemment aux lois de cette seconde catégorie que nous, qui sommes les archivistes officiels, devons notre existence. Nous dépendons d'elles pour nous procurer un moyen d'obtenir les fonds nécessaires et les lieux nécessaires á notre travail.

Vous avez d'autres lois qui en créant des institutions créent, en même temps, des archives pour l'avenir. Nous ne sommes intéressés à celles-ci que dans la mesure où elles expliquent la signification de nos documents et nous aident à les arranger en tant qu'archivistes. Notre tâche n'est pas de dire aux gens quelles sortes d'archives ils devraient constituer, bien que nous puissions prendre un intérêt intelligent à la facon dont ils doivent travailler, étant donné que cela peut faciliter plus tard notre propre tâche qui est, je le répète, une simple tâche de conservation.

Je vais maintenant vous mentionner simplement les différentes remarques que j'aurais voulu faire sur le rapport que j'espérais que vous auriez entre les mains.

1. Division des Archives anglaises.
2. Contrôle public.
3. Autres influences.
4. Travail des bibliothèques publiques.
5. Essais de proposition entre 1891 et 1919.
6. *British Records Association*.
7. Autorités locales fonctionnant en tant que dépôts d'archives.

Sous ce titre, j'entends toutes les autorités municipales ou départementales qui ont des dépôts d'archives.

8. Plan pour une reconstruction d'après-guerre avec, comme sous-titre: Registre National des Archives.

Enfin, j'aimerais vous parler, bien que ce soit peut-être un peu optimiste de mentionner ce sujet, de la législation que l'on propose d'appliquer à cette fin. Puis, je vous apporterai quelques conclusions.

Je ne vous parlerai pas en détail de la division des Archives anglaises, étant donné qu'elles suivent les catégories mentionnées dans le Guide International d'Archives, à savoir: publiques centrales, publiques locales, demi-publiques on demi-privées; archives ecclésiastiques.

Je passerai tout de suite au contrôle public. Avec une seule grande exception, celle des Archives resultant de dispositions testamentaires, y compris celles qui ont été transférées d'anciennes cours ecclésiastiques, qui sont contrôlées par le Président de la Probate Division de la Cour Suprême, le seul contrôle public concernant la conservation des archives anglaises est celui exercé par le Maitre des Rôles et le Public Record Office, en vertu des Record Office Acts comprenant une loi de 1838 complétée par une ordonnance de 1852 et par deux lois de 1877 et 1898, ces deux dernières concernant l'elimination des papiers inutiles.

La tendance de la législation moderne à socialiser certaines industries, pour accroître en fait le contrôle public sur leur action, devrait certainement aboutir à nous donner la charge d'une accumulation de documents et, très certainement, dans l'avenir, à nous forcer à apporter certains changements à leur sujet. Mais, jusqu'à présent, on a dit que les nouveaux bureaux de contrôle ne sont pas des sections du gouvernement central, et par conséquent, ne sont pas sujets, en matière d'archives, à la juridiction qui préside aux Archives publiques, c'est-à-dire la juridiction du Maître des Rôles.

Pour terminer ce chapitre, je vous dirai qu'en 1929 une mesure ayant force de loi a été prise par l'Eglise d'Angleterre et a donné aux Evêques le pouvoir de créer, à leur volonté, des dépôts diocésains d'archives pour recevoir en particulier les archives de chaque paroisse. Evidemment, la question principale était de savoir d'où viendraient les moyens financiers. Ceci n'ayant pas été réglé, la loi existe, mais c'est tout ce que l'on peut en dire.

En ce qui concerne le British Records Association, je tiens à dire que la base de sa création a été une contribution volontaire en vue de coordonner le travail de tous ceux qui s'intéressaient à ce travail. Le succès en a été très grand. Nous avons environ 1,000 membres, dont 300 sont des Institutions, le reste constituant des membres individuels. Nous avons même pu persuader toutes les autorités locales d'adhérer comme membres de cette association et nous avons également pu les persuader de créer des services d'archives, à tel point que nous avons dû ouvrir, á Londres, une Ecole chargée de former un personnel compétent.

En ce qui concerne les archives locales, jusqu'à maintenant il n'y a aucune obligation légale, pour les autorités locales, de garder leurs archives et de faire certains dépôts spéciaux à cet effet. En essayant de faire une certaine pression sur ces autorités locales et en leur demandant en même temps d'agir d'une façon volontaire, nous sommes arrivés, dans 50% des cas, au résultat désiré.

Lorsque vint la guerre, on s'apercut que l'Angleterre ne possédait pas une liste complète du Fonds d'Archives. La British Records Association entreprit d'en faire une, et ce travail a servi de base au *National Register of Archives*.

Au sujet des plans de reconstruction d'après-guerre, nous avons deux plans:

1. Le *National Register of Archives* dont je vous ai parlé ces listes faites durant la guerre. Ceci est en cours d'exécution actuellement. Il y a un Bureau créé à cet effet, qui, d'ailleurs, fait partie de mon propre Bureau. Nous avons le personnel nécessaire et nous avons pu arriver à persuader les possesseurs d'archives de nous donner des renseignements au sujet des fonds qu'ils détenaient. Ceci ne pouvait être fait que sur la base d'une contribution volontaire. Nous avons reçu beaucoup de rapports, environ 3.000.

2. La législation proposée. Il s'agit de la création d'une autorité centrale dont les pouvoirs s'étendraient à toutes les catégories d'archives autres que celles qui sont déjà couvertes par les Public Record Office Acts.

Les attributions de cet organisme seraient de deux sortes: tout d'abord, il devrait, inspecter et conseiller les autorités locales et également inspecter et conseiller certaines autres institutions locales et privées.

Ce nouvel organisme devrait également faire une certaine distinction entre les fonds d'archives qui ont une valeur nationale, et ceux qui sont importants simplement du point de vue de l'historiographie locale, ou autres questions de ce genre.

On est d'accord pour considérer que le gardien naturel d'un fond d'archives est la personne ou l'institution chez lesquels ces archives se sont formées sous la double condition que ceux-ci soient en mesure d'en assurer la conservation et l'accès aux chercheurs.

J'en arrive maintenant á mes conclusions.

Le problème des archives économiques ou industrielles, ou d'autres archives caractérisées, doit être considéré comme étant une partie d'un problème général de la conservation des archives.

De même, il est impossible de différencier les archives anciennes et les archives modernes. Il se peut en effet que certaines grandes catégories d'archives modernes meritent et reçoivent un traitement physique extérieur un peu spécial, mais ceci n'est pas dû au fait qu'elles sont modernes.

De plus, on peut ajouter qu'il y a encore beaucoup à faire pour faire comprendre au public ce fait que les archives modernes doivent être aussi importantes que les archives anciennes et qu'en fait, un jour, elles seront elles-mêmes anciennes.

Le problème est également d'arriver à disposer de ces archives. Vous avez à ce sujet-là la question du lieu où l'on peut mettre de grands dépôts d'archives. Il faut savoir si ces archives sont considérées comme étant d'un intérêt national véritable ou si, au contraire, elles ne sont que d'un intérêt local. De cette question, seule une autorité centrale peut décider.

Par efforts volontaires, on est arrivé à faire beaucoup de choses dans ce domaine; mais il faut attendre une autre législation pour arriver vraiment à une solution satisfaisante.

Cette législation, qui réglementerait la conservation des archives, ne doit pas être confondue avec les lois qui décident que telle catégorie de documents d'administrations, qu'elles soient privées ou publiques, doit être conservée.

Le problème principal est d'arriver à conserver les archives de manière satisfaisante; une fois ce problème résolu, il y aura encore des questions de détail qui sont également importantes et qui devront être élucidées par cette autorité centrale. Il y a, par exemple, le criterium d'élimination des documents qui ne sont pas jugés dignes d'une conservation permanente.

Cette dernière tâche est extrêmement difficile, peut-être la plus difficile de toutes mais c'est celle que nous autres archivistes, nous avons à remplir. Elle pourrait constituer à mon avis, la base d'un rapport qui serait fait par un comité créé par le Conseil qui vient d'être nouvellement fondé.

Pour autant que toutes les législations puissent sembler satisfaisantes, on peut se rendre compte qu'il y aura toujours place pour le travail amateur en matiére d'archives. Tout d'abord, pour arriver à reconnaître les archives qui seront ensuite l'objet de l'attention de l'autorité centrale qui sera créée, il est certain que nous dépendrons toujours des renseignements que, localement, on possède en matière d'archives, et que l'on voudra bien nous transmettre.

C'est là un travail qui demande intelligence et savoir-faire. Nous avons souligné ce fait lorsque nous avons demandé des aides pour notre travail concernant le *National Register*. Cependant, ceux-ci ne demandent pas une formation spéciale, même lorsque les documents sont anciens.

Si l'on considère le nombre de fonds d'archives qui existent dans les différentes catégories d'archives, qu'elles soient anciennes ou modernes, il est clair qu'il doit toujours y avoir de grandes quantités d'archives qui nécessitent un certain traitement particulier souvent technique, mais que l'on ne peut pas espérer pouvoir inclure dans les dépôts où il y a des archivistes bien formés.

Par conséquent, il semble que notre tâche, á nous archivistes, soit, d'une part, d'attirer l'attention publique sur ces questions et, d'autre part, de demander des contributions volontaires pour ce travail, d'essayer de localiser les archives d'importance et de répandre, parmi les personnes de bonne volonté, un certain élément de connaissance de la technique des archives.

Archive Developments in England 1925-1950

INTRODUCTORY

Reflecting upon the occasion to be celebrated by the publication of this volume — the twenty-five years during which Monsignor Mercati has been Prefect of the Vatican Archives — it is not perhaps unnatural for one who, in another Country, has also spent those years in the service of Archives to let his thoughts turn to the events which have occurred during that time within his own experience and under his own observation. Such was, at any rate, my case: and since it happens that our English Archives have during that same period undergone certain trials and changes, and been the occasion of certain movements and proceedings which, to an Archivist at least, are not without importance and interest, it has seemed to me that I could not do better than offer to Monsignor Mercati some account of what, while he was working with so much distinction at the Vatican, his English Colleagues were attempting to achieve under very different conditions and with very different material but with the same ultimate aims.

THE DIVISIONS OF ENGLISH ARCHIVES

We are accustomed to think of the whole body of surviving Archives in this Country as falling into two great divisions — the Civil and the Ecclesiastical. Those of the first we divide into four categories — "Public Central" (the Archives of the Central Government in all periods); "Public, Local" (those of the bodies — Counties, Boroughs and the like — which control, more or less autonomously, public affairs of a more regional character)[1]; "Private" (the

---

1. There are at present 63 County Councils in England and Wales, 424 independent Cities and Boroughs of which a large proportion are ancient, 1,047 Rural or Urban District Councils and approximately 7,300 Civil Parishes.

Archives both of Institutions and of Individuals conducting their own affairs for their own satisfaction or profit); and "Semi-Public" (a division lying between "Local" and "Private") comprising those Institutions whose affairs are conducted by them for their own satisfaction or profit but are of a nature — for example, those of a Company owning a railroad or canal or those of an Educational or Charitable Foundation — which gives them a public character.

The Archives of the Church (*Ecclesia Anglicana*) fall similarly into categories following administrative divisions — we have those of the two Provinces of Canterbury and York, those of the Dioceses, old and new (there are at present 43), those of 103 Archdeaconries and those of Parishes (the ancient ones numbering about 11,000 and including the Archives of much secular as well as ecclesiastical administration in the past). To these must be added the Archives of more or less independent bodies (notably the Capitular) and those of Semi-Public or Private Bodies and Societies of a religious character. We must add also those of other Communions not forming part of *Ecclesia Anglicana*, including powerful Non-Conformist bodies of which some have Archives of a respectable antiquity. The Archives of Religious Houses, so far as they survived, became, of course, scattered in lay hands in the sixteenth century except where they coincided, or were joined with, those of Capitular or Diocesan Bodies; and it may be well to add for the benefit of the foreign Reader that so far as temporalities are concerned even the Archives which survived to modern times in Ecclesiastical Custody have passed in theory and often in fact to the semi-secular body now known as the 'Church (formerly the 'Ecclesiastical') Commissioners', which since the nineteenth century has administered Ecclesiastical Property. On the other hand the Archives of Benevolent Institutions (Hospitals, Schools etc.) formerly administered ecclesiastically, though the administration itself has likewise passed from the Church — in this case to the body of 'Charity Commissioners' or to other purely lay institutions — generally survive in the custody of their original owners; some Colleges, Hospitals etc. preserving still very ancient and valuable accumulations.

Archives resulting from Jurisdiction *in spiritualibus* remain in the custody of the Church, with one very large exception: the Archives of Testamentary Jurisdiction ('Probate') which (again in the nineteenth century) passed, with the jurisdiction itself into the control of a Division of the Supreme Court of Judicature[2].

---

2. Jurisdiction in Matrimonial Causes also passed into lay control but in this case the Archives were not transferred.

STATUTORY PROVISION FOR CONSERVATION

'The Public Records'[3]

At the beginning of the period of which we are speaking only the first of the Categories I have mentioned — true, it is the greatest and most important of them — was the subject of comprehensive statutory provision: and indeed the same is true today though (as we shall see) efforts are at present being made to alter this condition. The Public Record Office Acts of 1838-1898 placed practically all the Archives of all Departments and Ministries of the Central Government in the "charge and superintendence" of the Master of the Rolls; an Official who, though the developments of five centuries had made him a Judge, remained in theory what he had been in origin — the *custos* charged with the care of the Archives accumulating in one division of Public Administration the 'Rolls' of the Royal Chancery: and the site chosen for the 'Public Record Office' thus created was that upon which he and his predecessors had for more than 450 years conducted their original Archive-keeping functions in Chancery Lane.

Other Categories

If I say that all the other Categories I have named remain almost untouched by Statutory regulation I must not be taken as meaning that Legislation has not affected the making of Archives in this as in other Countries. On the contrary in almost all periods, and increasingly in our own, numerous Statutes have resulted in, or even actually prescribed, the making and keeping of this or that variety of Archive. Many forms, for instance, of the *Deeds* by which Title to Landed Property was established, and the preservation of the *Deeds* themselves among Family Muniments, result directly from Legislation; Acts of Parliament (particularly of the eighteenth century) dealing with a variety of subjects which ranges from the Transportation of Convicted Criminals to Licences for the use of Hair-Powder or for the production of Theatrical Representations, from Assessment for Land Tax to Certificates of Places of Worship, have left their mark upon County and Parish Archives in the shape of a score of well-known classes of Documents; and, to take a modern example, the Acts governing the formation and conduct of Commercial and Industrial Companies of all kinds prescribe very strictly certain Records which must be kept (and are kept in monstrous quantities) either by the Companies themselves or by Public Authorities to whom they are periodically submitted. But all this Legislation is concerned solely with the making and keeping of Records essential for the proper transaction of the affairs concerned: it has no interest in them after their

---

3. The words "Records" and "Archives" are used in English almost indifferently.

usefulness for that purpose has ceased — in their subsequent preservation for
the purposes of Research. For example, of the three types of Archives, we
have just mentioned the *Deeds*, so far from benefitting, have in fact been
affected adversely by Legislation of the nineteenth century which made their
production no longer necessary for the proving of 'title' and thus indirectly
doomed large quantities of them to destruction: the Documents which we
described as accumulated locally in consequence of eighteenth-century
legislation have survived in varying proportions, or not survived at all, in the
various Counties; their preservation or destruction being entirely within the
discretion of the individual County Authority: and as for the older documents accumulated by 'Companies' in their own keeping, preservation has
been (one might almost say) a matter of chance while the Companies
survived; destruction, if the Companies ceased to operate, the strongest of
probabilities; and preservation or destruction alike matters in which the Law
(save in special cases) has taken no interest.

DEVELOPMENTS BEFORE 1925

An almost complete absence, then, of Legislative sanctions affecting the
conservation of any Archives save those of Central Government has been and
is still the condition facing those who individually or collectively interest
themselves in securing the better preservation and availability of this part of
our national heritage. That interest had begun to manifest itself so early as
the date of the 'Record Commissions' of 1801-1836, the immediate predecessors of the Public Record Office; for their Reports deal occasionally
with some of the Local and Ecclesiastical Categories we have mentioned; it
appears in the work of the Historical MSS. Commission[4] which since 1870
has reported upon a very large number of Archives in the hands of Private
Owners and Custodians, including the Ecclesiastical; and it is seen again in
the foundation both centrally and in almost every County, during the last
century of 'Record Societies' — bodies devoted to the printing of Documents
of importance for the history of their locality or for some other special field of
Research. But most of these were concerned by the terms of their constitution, or by their own subsequent development, with the exploitation
rather than the conservation of Local and Private Archives, though from
time to time they might make recommendations on the subject. A body of
private persons interested in the matter went further in 1891 and again in
1898, for they actually drafted proposals for an Act which should impose new

---

4.   For the work of this Commission up to date see its *Reports*, especially the most recent, the
     Twenty-Second Report (1946), and R.A. Roberts' brief account in the S.P.C.K. *'Helps for
     Students of History, No. 23'* (1920). An Analytical Survey and Key to its Reports is in course
     of preparation.

statutory controls: but support, presumably, was not sufficient and the matter dropped: nor did the Report of a Departmental Committee[5], which followed in 1902, result in legislation; nor that of the Royal Commission (1910) on Public Records[6].

The credit of initiating, upon a purely voluntary basis, some practical measures for the fundamental need of conservation must go largely to the Public Libraries; a number of which became active during the first twenty years of our century, or even earlier, in offering a home to Private Archives valuable for the purposes of Local History in their region[7], and even in a few cases had upon their staff persons specially trained for this purpose. Finally before 1925 the late Dr. G.H. Fowler in Bedfordshire and one or two other enthusiasts elsewhere had begun to persuade their local Councils or other Authorities to add to their existing organization an Archives Section, with an Advisory Committee and a modest provision of technical staff and equipment, for the dual purpose of conserving their own Archives and giving a home to other Local and Private Accumulations which were in danger of destruction or dispersal. All these activities were stimulated in 1924 by an Amendment to the 'Law of Property' Act of 1922, under which the Records of the ancient Manorial Courts in private custody, now valueless for practical purposes and therefore in danger of destruction, were placed in the charge and superintendence of the Master of the Rolls; who proceeded to 'approve' local Repositories as places in which such Records might be deposited in case of need. Developments from these beginnings will be the subject of most of the following sections of this Article.

SINCE 1925

A very long tale might be told under this heading: for I believe that English Students of the future will look back with gratitude to the years we are now reviewing as the period in which the nature and importance of Archive evidences and their relation to the progress of knowledge and the conduct of life became generally recognised and something was done to assure their systematic preservation. But this is not the place for a detailed history of the development of Archive-consciousness in England, and I must be content to comment briefly on a dozen happenings which seem to me of outstanding significance.

5. This Committee, appointed by the Treasury in 1899, was under the chairmanship first of Bishop Creighton and, after his death, of Lord Bryce.
6. 'Third Report': 1919.
7. A few County Archaeological Societies performed a similar service.

LEGISLATION AFFECTING COURT ROLLS AND TITHE APPORTIONMENTS

I have grouped these two together because on these two occasions Parliament widened the statutory powers of the Master of the Rolls and the Public Record Office, which had not previously been altered since the Record Office Act of 1838 and the complementary Order in Council of 1852: placing deliberately in the 'charge and superintendence'[8], of the Master of the Rolls first, as we have already noted, in 1924, the Records of Manorial Courts, up to that time the property and in the custody of private persons, and then, in 1936[9], the *Copies of the Instruments of Apportionment of Tithe* deposited under the Tithe Acts in the custody of Diocesan Registrars and Parish Incumbents. These were startling innovations for they not only implied[10] official liaison (not otherwise provided) between the Public Record Office and Local Authorities but also asserted in effect the propriety of State intervention for the safeguarding of Local, Private and even Ecclesiastical Archives purely in the interests of Research. Records of 12,997 Manors, of any date from the thirteenth to the nineteenth century, have now been registered at the Public Record Office; which is constantly called upon to deal with questions of their custody.

THE CHURCH MEASURE[11] OF 1929

The special purpose of this measure (which followed upon a valuable Report[12] from a Commission of the Church Assembly) was to provide for the better keeping of *Parish Registers*: but the Parish in England was for many centuries the unit of Civil as well as Ecclesiastical Administration and the contents of a 'Parish Chest' should, and often do, include quantities of Archives dealing with an almost infinite diversity of topics; from recruiting for the Militia to 'beating the bounds'[13], from the Parish Stocks for the punishment of local Malefactors to the Parish School for the education of local Youth. The existence of all these Records, already somewhat precarious, had been further endangered by the Act[14] which separated the Civil

---

8. The phrase is the same as that used to describe his powers in the Act of 1838.
9. By Sect. 36 (2) in the Tithe Act, 1936.
10. The only category of Public Records previously allowed to remain in Local Custody were the *Quarter Sessions Records* in the keeping of the Clerk of the Peace, the Local Official with whom they originated.
11. A 'Church Measure', promoted by the Church Assembly, is the Ecclesiastical equivalent of an Act of Parliament.
12. '*Report of the Commission on Parish Records*' (1927).
13. A periodical ceremony for settling the precise territorial boundaries of the Parish.
14. The Local Government Act of 1894, repeated in that of 1933.

from the Ecclesiastical function and provided only a rather nebulous scheme for distribution of the Archives between the old and the new authorities. For this state of affairs the Measure of 1929 provided admirably while at the same time making a great step forward by asserting, as it did in effect, the duty of the Church as well as lay bodies to preserve ancient Archives for purposes other than mere administrative convenience: it empowered Bishops to erect new Diocesan Record Offices and to order the bestowal in them of Parish Records which could not be safely kept by their natural custodians. Unfortunately the measure had one great weakness — it made no suggestion as to the source from which Bishops were to draw the funds necessary for this purpose — and has been in consequence largely (though, as we shall see, not entirely) ineffectual.

THE BRITISH RECORDS ASSOCIATION

This Association came into existence after one or two tentative efforts and much preliminary discussion in 1932. Its aim was to combine in co-operative effort Owners or Custodians of Archives of all kinds, whether individual or corporate, and all Persons or Bodies interested in Archive work from any angle but notably from that of mere conservation — an aspect of the work which had tended (as always to be neglected in favour of the more obvious interests of publication. The principal objects set before it were in particular the salving of Private Muniments and other Archives in danger of dispersal or destruction (especially from Solicitors' Offices, in cases where their value for practical purposes had ceased) and their distribution to suitable local Repositories where they could be made available for Students; and "to arouse public interest in, and to create a sound public opinion on matters affecting" Archive Conservation in this Country.

Upon the detailed development of this work there is not space to dwell: it is set out in a Report[15] published on the occasion of the retirement of the first two Joint Secretaries in 1947. The most remarkable point was the way in which the Association had gained a support which far exceeded the best hopes of its Founders. The Membership reached was roughly 1000, of whom over 300 were Institutions — Custodians or Owners of Archives of all kinds — including all major Local Authorities (the County Councils) without exception, a large number of Public Libraries and a representative proportion of Colleges, Schools, Hospitals, Learned Societies and other categories; with even a few of the great modern Commercial and Industrial Corporations. To the surprise and delight of the Association's responsible

15.   *'The British Records Association, 1932-1947'* (1948), by the present writer.

Officers the distractions of the War did not result in an appreciable diminution of this public support nor stop entirely any of its activities: indeed that of its 'Records Preservation Section'[16] was increased; for it became necessary to add to the work in hand an active campaign (with only a very few devoted persons to conduct it) against indiscreet and unnecessary destruction of Archives in the interests of Paper 'Salvage' for war purposes.

It is no exaggeration to say that some results, direct or indirect, of the foundation of this Association — which works upon a basis almost entirely voluntary — may be seen in all the important developments we shall have to note in the following sections.

COUNTY RECORD OFFICES

Among the most important achievements of the British Records Association must be reckoned the fact that whereas at the time of its foundation only one or two of the County Councils had organised Archive Departments, equipped to serve the purposes of Research, such Departments exist now in nearly 40 out of a total of 62 Councils. One of the Association's first tasks was to secure the adhesion as Institutional Members of every one of such Councils in England and Wales, not to mention a considerable number of the Cities and Boroughs which exercise independently within their own boundaries the functions of Local Government otherwise in the hands of the County Councils. The Public Libraries[17] (as has already been stated) were among the earliest public bodies to undertake the safeguarding and housing of Private and Semi-Public Archives which were in danger of dispersal or destruction; and since most of these are maintained by the great Boroughs or Cities, of whose own more ancient Archives they have also in some cases the custody, it may be said that as pioneers in local Archive work the Boroughs take first place. But the Counties are, of course, far larger in their scope and power than any save the largest Cities and are moreover the ancient and natural divisions of the Country; and though their Councils date only from

16. Up to 1947 this activity had resulted in the saving of large and small quantities of Documents from some 700 sources and their distribution to 230 Government Departments, National Institutions, Local Repositories, Libraries, Colleges and other Institutions and Societies: practically all by the efforts of voluntary helpers, notably the founder of this Section, the late Miss Ethel Stokes.

17. The great National Libraries also do much to help the work of preservation, though being not only Libraries but Libraries whose interests are National, not Local, they are constantly assailed by the temptation to reserve their precious space not only for the more important accumulations but even the more important Documents in a single Group of Archives: a line of policy which it is difficult to reconcile with strict Archive principle. The National Library of Wales is an exception, for its policy for many years has been to act as a National Record Office also for the Principality: even to the exclusion in some cases of the County interest.

the late nineteenth century they are in practice closely associated with the ancient bodies of Justices of the Peace, who formerly carried out, in addition to their judicial duties, the administrative functions which the Councils now exercise: indeed the offices of 'Clerk of the County Council' and 'Clerk of the Peace' are still almost invariably combined in a single person; and a single Repository houses not only the modern Archives of the Council but also the most important ancient ones (extending back in some cases to the sixteenth century) of 'Quarter Sessions'[18]. In consequence all plans for a statutory regulation of Local Archive Conservation, however much they may differ in detail, have always contemplated that a large part of the work should be assigned to these bodies.

Actually it will be seen from what we have said that this state of affairs has to a large extent been brought about without legislation by a process of propaganda and the gradual infiltration into County Councils of an appreciation of the practical and cultural importance of Archive Conservation. Though in most cases equipment and staff are still on a modest scale it is wonderful how far in late years that process has gone and how much enthusiasm has gradually been evoked: so that Legislation, if it comes (a matter to be mentioned again below), will be in a majority of cases largely a matter of preaching to the converted, confirmation and encouragement of a policy already adopted and work already in hand. There is even some advantage in the present state, for the Counties have every freedom to adjust the details of organisation to local conditions. The result is seen in the wide and healthy variety of ways in which the work has been extended beyond the initial arrangements for proper care of the Archives naturally accumulating in their custody. Nearly all open their Repositories for the reception of *Manorial Records*, being 'recognised' by the Master of the Rolls for that purpose: and in addition are prepared to receive the non-manorial but closely related *Muniments of Title*: indeed many are active in searching for Records of this kind which they may add to their store. Nor are these the only local developments of Archival activity. In at least two cases where an ancient County is divided between more than one modern Council, these have re-united themselves, or are in process of doing so, for Archive purposes; sometimes, too, County and Borough are coming together; sometimes even Ecclesiastical and Lay Authorities are combining. In more than one instance the County has volunteered to supply for the Bishop that Diocesan Record Office which, as we saw above, he has been since 1929 empowered, but not able, to institute for the better preservation of *Parish Records*. In many cases other Documents of Ecclesiastical origin — the *Tithe Apportionments* already mentioned — are going in the same direction under

18.   Strictly, Quarter Sessions Records are 'Public Records' within the meaning of the Record Office Acts: but in practice they have been left locally in the charge of the Clerk.

order of the Master of the Rolls. Finally (and perhaps most notable of all) by a recent change of policy the President of the Probate Division of the High Court has begun to order the transfer from District Registries to County Record Offices of suitable sections of the older *Probate Records* taken from ecclesiastical custody in 1857. Thus these ancient Archives of the Church, though they do not go back to Church custody, will at least be rejoining some of their old associates as well as being brought into useful contiguity with all kinds of other Archives, Public and Private, belonging to the same region.

There is nothing more encouraging for those interested in Archive work in general in this Country than to see the way in which Quarter Sessions and modern County Records are thus forming the nucleus for Local Repositories whose Archives will represent every variety of activity within their region; the comprehensiveness with which, though their means and equipment can be only gradually and modestly built up, they are endeavouring to supply the Listing, Repair, Photographic and other services associated with good Archive work; the growing appreciation by students of the provision thus made for them and the growing recognition by other Sections of the Councils of a practical and valuable relation between ancient Archives and modern administration; and, last but not least, the effect of all this in the creation of a body of Professional Archivists in this Country.

THE ENGLISH ARCHIVIST

This large increase in the number of establishments having occasion to employ one or more technical experts upon Archive work has brought in its train another striking development, the creation of what is for England a new Profession. While the Public Record Office remained the only institution which experienced that need there was no opening for University or other courses or any academic diploma of proficiency: my Department preferring (as indeed it still does) to take new entrants to its higher posts direct from the University and give them all their training *in situ* and, *mutatis mutandis*, providing similarly for the recruitment of its technical and clerical assistants in lower grades. The Libraries, it is true, taking up (as we have noted) a measure of Archive work, had seen to it that their new entrants should have if they chose a measure also of technical training in that subject: those who obtain their professional qualification from the examinations of the powerful Library Association have for many years been able to take "Palaeography and Archives" as one of their subjects; and when a School of Librarianship was started in the University of London after the first World War the subject was made compulsory, though, being only one of many, its scope was naturally elementary. As Local Authorities began, in the fashion we have described, to institute Archive Departments there began also to be a demand for staff qualified by some recognised diploma or degree to take charge of them; and the British Records Association had been pressed more than once to create itself the machinery for producing them. This was at first too large an undertaking, and the prospect of employment for Students when their training was completed still too precarious, to command more than a theoretic approval: but by the time we reached the Reconstruction period towards the end of the late War circumstances were more propitious. It was felt that the attempt might reasonably be made; plans were drawn up; the University of London was approached; and as a result the School of Librarianship re-appeared as "the School of Librarianship and Archive Administration", with separate diplomas for each of those subjects. This new diploma sends out into the world men and women who have had, in addition to an University degree with honours, a year's training in English Palaeography and special aspects of History and Languages and in Archive Administration[19] concluding with a reasonably advanced examination followed by another year's practical work in an approved Repository. Output is still not large — the School passes out perhaps ten or a dozen Students every year — but the number of Repositories requiring their services is enough[20], and the demand increasing sufficiently, to make it fairly certain that they will obtain employment at an adequate salary with adequate prospects of promotion (by transfer from one County to another if necessary) and a fair likelihood, if all goes well, of conditions improving year by year as the new profession grows in age and size. A modest beginning but I think a real achievement, and already the demand for our training and our Students begins to come from other places besides the Local Authorities: the last Student to be placed went to Jamaica; and Students have attended the School's courses (as indeed they did those of its predecessor) from even more remote places. A similar course, but with a special bias towards the needs and interests of Local History, has been established in the University of Liverpool and there seems no reason others should not accrue if times become better and the demand grows and widens: for there are signs that the great Commercial and Industrial Bodies and other Institutions besides the Local Authorities begin to see the practical value of a trained Archive service for their work. We have always emphasised the relation of the Archivist to practical affairs as well as to research.

19. The present writer, having been responsible for planning the original elementary course after the first World War, had the privilege of delivering, after the second, an Inaugural Lecture for the new Diploma Course in 1947. This (published under the title '*The English Archivist: a new Profession*') gives some idea of the aims and curriculum of the Course.

20. In the three years from 1948 to 1950 thirteen diplomaed Students went to posts in County or Municipal Record Offices and another six to Public Libraries; two to local Record Societies; and one each to the British Records Association itself, to the Historical MSS. Commission and to an University, a Colonial Government, an ancient and important Commercial Body (the Hudson Bay Company) and a Hospital.

REPAIR WORK IN LOCAL
AND PRIVATE ARCHIVES

Parallel with the problem of producing a supply of trained Archivists, capable of reading, understanding, arranging, administering and, if necessary, editing English Archives of any kind or date, has always been that of providing a sufficiency of technical operatives for the lower but very important grades of the work and notably that of Repairing. The difficulty of arranging for this side of the care of Archives in private and semi-public custody or ownership, and of those in Local and Ecclesiastical Repositories, was one of the first matters[21], raised by members of the British Records Association in their Annual Conference; and the matter has only increased in urgency with the increasing number of organized County Record Offices: the amount to be done being enormous and the places where it can be done very few. The British Museum, the National Library of Wales and one or two other large Libraries do their best to help: and the Public Record Office, which has a fairly large Staff of Repairers not only allows them to undertake private work out of office hours but is able also from time to time to let Students from the School come for short periods of instruction[22]. But neither these facilities (though the aggregate of work done in this way in recent years is large)[23] nor the encouragement of local Custodians to take up the simpler forms of Repair themselves *en amateur* met, it was felt, or would meet in the future[24], urgent needs: and when the plan for a School and Diploma of Archive Administration was put forward as a Recontruction measure by the Association at the end of the War proposals for a Repair Centre went with it. The aim was to serve three objects; giving by means of a short course a sufficient measure of training and experience to Archivists to enable them if they wished to carry out simple repairs themselves and in any case to supervise intelligently the work of others; training at more length technical assistants who would make repairing their sole employment; and incidentally carrying out a certain amount of actual repairing work in the process of instruction. The difficulty was to find in post-war London a place where this could be done and it is only within recent months that the first course has

---

21. See a paper by the present writer on *'Repair Work for Amateurs'*, with notes of Demonstrations given at the Public Record Office, in the *'Proceedings'* of the British Records Association for 1936.

22. It has also in a few instances taken Students for Instruction for a longer period: see for example the notes by L. Herman Smith published in the *'American Archivist'*, vol. I, pp. 1-22 (1938).

23. Institutions and Societies for whom Repair work has been carried out include The Royal Society, The Guildhall, Guy's Hospital, several City Companies, most of the Diocesan and County Record Offices and many Parishes.

24. The Record Office has in fact at the time of writing a long waiting-list of Repairs required by Local Authorities and others.

been initiated by arrangement with the London County Council. It is hoped, however, that if it is successful similar centres may come into being in various parts of the Country: the mass of work waiting to be done is certainly enough to guarantee them employment.

The special problem of Repair Binding is even more difficult: being complicated by the facts that it requires a preliminary training of some years; that few apprentices are found willing to take it up; that the great Binding Shops no longer turn out work, or workers, of the kind we need, which has been almost entirely superseded in this Country by machine-sewing and cloth casing; and that hand sewing and the other processes of 'forwarding', formerly underpaid, command now a price which makes good binding an expensive luxury. Whether these difficulties will be overcome remains to be seen, but at least the problem has been recognised and is under discussion: certainly the total quantity of ancient bindings needing highly skilled work for their restoration in Ecclesiastical Repositories alone is now known to be such as would justify the setting up of centres for this also at more than one place, if really qualified Instructors and other requirements could be provided.

But I am allowing a favourite interest to carry me away.

FIRST STEPS TOWARDS
A NATIONAL AUTHORITY

A more ambitious project fathered by the British Records Association in its post-War plans was to secure Legislation which should take some account of Archives in all categories, Public, Local, Semi-Public, Private and Ecclesiastical, consolidating and widening on an official basis the local organisation already secured in part by voluntary effort. Could it, with the added prestige it had so successfully acquired in ten years for Archive work, succeed where so many others had failed during the preceding century? It could at least try. The immediate *causa movens* was the fear felt by many that conditions following the War — financial stringency, the break-up of large estates, the disappearance of ancient corporations or their absorption by larger and newer bodies, and so forth — would result in great losses among Private Archives owing to export for sale beyond seas, dispersal in the sale-room in England or mere disappearance. A Committee, appointed by the Association to report upon this and the question of an official co-ordination of the work of Local Archive Repositories, recommended to the Annual Conference held in 1943 the promotion of Legislation which would set up a single Central Public Authority having certain restrictive powers over all the more important Archives not covered by the Record Office Acts and at the same time exercising the functions of an Archive Inspectorate: it rec-ommended also, as an indispensable preliminary to such work, the preparation of a National Register of Archives. The Conference accepted these recommendations and passed the Report to its President, the Master of the Rolls, who is also Chairman of the Historical MSS. Commission, with the request that he would take steps towards their implementation.

THE NATIONAL REGISTER OF ARCHIVES

The second of the two recommendations was of course much the simpler though the work involved could be seen to be large and has proved to be enormous. In a curious way the needs of the War themselves had prepared the way for it; for when it was found possible to direct the attention of the Military and other Authorities to the propriety of safe-guarding Archives, in all the Countries involved in the military operations, from the moral and physical dangers of War it was discovered that the natural reaction of these Authorities — the demand for a List of the objects to be safe-guarded — could not immediately be satisfied. Apparently no European Country had ever attempted to produce a single comprehensive List of its Archive accumulations in all categories: and by a curious chance the present writer, too old to undertake any save defensive work in warfare, found himself in the first instance preparing a List of English Archives for the guidance of Regional Commissioners for Civil Defence in England and them undertaking similar tasks first in Italy[25] for the guidance of the Allied Control Commission and later, before their invasion, for Western Germany and Austria.

The English List (a mere outline, of course, prepared in great haste and containing only a couple of thousand entries) became in 1945 the nucleus for what promises to be the work of a permanent organisation. Treasury sanction was obtained for the addition of a new wing (as it were) to the work of the existing Historical MSS. Commission, with a modest staff and equipment housed in the Record Office and working under a special Directorate of which the Deputy Keeper is Chairman. The staff has grown, though still within modest limits, and the work (which must obviously depend ultimately for its information on the voluntary efforts of local enthusiasts) has taken the form of organising, as a starting point, large Public Meetings in every County, to which all persons of local importance are invited. This is followed by the creation of Local Executive Committees, generally in close liaison with the County Authority; which in some cases even furnishes the

25.   An accout of the work in Italy has been published ('*Italian Archives during the War and at its close*' by Hilary Jenkinson and H.E. Bell) but the German Lists were printed only for distribution to the Armies. In both cases the subsequent work of rehabilitating the native Archive Services was carried on by Archives Officers attached to the active forces.

Secretary. So far 36 County Meetings have been held (in addition to numerous Public Meetings for smaller areas) and 37 County Committees have been organised: and the Reports which have come into Headquarters for registration in the Central Index amount to over 3,500. A most encouraging amount of local enthusiasm has been evoked and Local Helpers now have an annual Conference in London.

THE PILGRIM TRUST
AND A SURVEY OF ECCLESIASTICAL ARCHIVES

I must interpolate here some brief notice of a piece of work, contemporary with and parallel to that of the National Register of Archives but independently conducted under entirely different auspices: and in doing so record the grateful thanks of one among many Archivists to a Foundation which is perhaps little known outside this Country. The Pilgrim Trust was established during the troublous times which followed the first World War by a great American Friend of the British People, Edward Harkness, to meet some of the more urgent needs of the United Kingdom and to promote her further well-being. The Trustees' present objective is "to preserve and restore the national heritage of things and places of historic value and beauty, to make them more widely accessible to the people, and to stimulate greater public appreciation of them", and they have many times shown themselves much in sympathy with Archive work: particularly at the point where financial questions cause most difficulty — in connexion with the conservation of Ecclesiastical Archives — though they have by no means confined their support to that side[26]. They have made possible, for instance, by very substantial grants, new Archive Establishments on a large scale at Lincoln and Westminster and are doing the same at the moment at Durham and York.

After the last War the Trustees, upon a representation made to them that the amount of such aid urgently needed in many Dioceses was very great, so great that it might be necessary to establish a priority of importance, decided to have made for their own information, but with the concurrence and support of the Archbishops, a Survey, to be based on personal visits by competent investigators, of the present state of Ecclesiastical Archives at all

26. They gave, to take only three examples, invaluable financial aid to the British Records Association in the first three years of its existence; paid for the microphotography of all *Probate Registers* down to 1600 (1700 in the case of the Prerogative Courts) as a measure of security during the late War; and upon a sudden emergency enabled the present writer to secure for the Public Record Office (which has no resources for such acquisitions) a Document of altogether exceptional Public Interest — one of the three signed and sealed copies of the Articles for a proposed Treaty of Union between England and Scotland in 1604 — which was threatened with the perils of the Sale Room.

levels down to Archdeaconries from every point of view: their Survival, Location, Custodians, State of Repair, Security, and Accessibility to Students. This Survey, completed only a few months ago, has occupied two Investigators, working with an Advisory Committee, for some three years: and the result, a Monumental Report, will be presented to the Trustees and to the Archbishop of Canterbury about the time when these remarks are printing. It is much to be hoped that it may be found possible later to publish it, with any necessary modifications: but in any case the work has been done, a very remarkable achievement, and will certainly not be without results: and such of the information compiled as is germane will be available for the information of the National Register of Archives.

THE MASTER OF THE ROLLS' ARCHIVES COMMITTEE

Returning to the other and larger side of the proposals submitted to and forwarded by the British Records Association in 1943 I cannot say very much since the matter is still, disappointingly, *sub judice*. The then Master of the Rolls, Lord Greene, appointed a Committee representative of all the interests involved, to report upon the possibilities; and it was upon a representation of this Committee that the National Register of Archives was called into being. Upon the larger question of a Central Authority, to be established by Statue, which should have the dual charge of inspecting and co-ordinating the Archive work of Local Authorities and of preventing the loss, destruction or disperal of Archives in Private or Semi-Public Ownership of Custody, the Committee produced a Report which did not differ in essentials from that of the British Records Association; and a continuing Committee was then appointed to base upon this instructions to Parliamentary Counsel for the drawing-up of a Bill. It was understood that even in these times of much Legislation it might be possible to secure the passage of such a Bill provided it could be shown to be non-controversial and here lay the difficulty. In principle, even though the restriction of existing rights — the right, for instance, to sell in the open market Family Muniments which chanced to have pecuniary value — must be an inevitable accompaniment of any efficient Measure, all persons of good will and intelligence were prepared to agree that subject to compensation Documents known to be of National value should be protected; they agreed also that there must be a system of Local Repositories, adequately co-ordinated and supervised; and were not, on the other hand, prepared to deny that Institutions already functioning successfully should not be too hastily discarded but rather absorbed into a general scheme which should be sufficiently elastic to allow of local conditions dictating in detail local arrangements. I think also that most if not all were prepared to accept the view, taken strongly by all members of the

Committee, that the Proper Custodian of Archives is the Natural Custodian and that he should not be deprived of that position save in cases where he is unable or unwilling to ensure safety and accessibility; and then only in the way of direction to a Public Repository where his Documents may be deposited. No one with knowledge of the subject desires Expropriation for its own sake. The difficulty has been to secure, as between the diverging points of view of Archivists and Research-Workers, the Professor of History and the Registrar, Private Owners and Official Custodians and Local Authorities of diverse kinds and conflicting interests, the necessary guarantee of unity in support of proposals which all of them, no doubt, would, if the task were theirs, formulate differently. A good deal of opposition and a number of contradictory proposals have been disposed of but meanwhile time has been wasted and hope deferred. One can only trust that in spite of this some statutory control will at last eventuate: for valuable and extensive as is the work voluntary effort has produced in the last twenty-five years it is partial and unofficial; and the time has surely come for measures for the care of Archives to be made a matter of general application and of national supervision.

THE PUBLIC RECORD OFFICE

Introductory

In the last place, as in duty bound, I must say something of developments witnessed in my own Department during these twenty-five years. Of the nature of our work and the way in which it arises from the terms of the Act of 1838 I need not here speak in detail since the '*Introduction*', published in 1949, to a new '*Guide*' gave an historical *résumé* of its various sections — of the system of Elimination and Conservation, Transfer to the Record Office and theory of Custody; of the growth of the present Buildings and gradual disappearance of their predecessors in Chancery Lane and elsewhere; of our methods of Storage and Packing, Numbering, Listing and Checking; of the Repairing Section and its technique, partly original and partly based on the practice of other Countries including Italy; of Production to Students and General Public in the Search Rooms an Museum; and of Publications by way of List. Calendar and Transcript amounting now to something like nine hundred volumes. In all these services the last quarter century has seen considerable changes, adoption of new ideas and modifications of old ones, rejection of *ad hoc* and experimental practices or their reduction to rule: but all can be traced back to the interpretation by the Master of the Rolls and Deputy Keeper of 1838, and their successors, of the duties laid upon them by the Statue and can be seen in gradual development in the annual '*Reports of the Deputy Keeper*,. There have been introduced, however, in recent years certain changes or novelties of adminstration or policy which are of a more revolutionary kind; and of four of these I will venture to speak at a little more length.

The Provincial Repository

The intention of the Act was certainly to assemble in one place the Archives then scattered over a large number of unsuitable Repositories: and for nearly a hundred years the struggle was first to obtain a new Building and then to bring home to those responsible for finance and building the fact that Archives accrue and their accommodation consequently requires periodic enlargement: demand for a new block coming each time as a fresh shock and producing a fresh, animated and lengthy exchange of views. The last addition to the present building had been made in 1896 and by the time of the first War (1914) it was becoming clear not only that another was due but also that the site, though enlarged recently by the purchase of some adjoining land, might eventually become insufficient. This last was perhaps rather a long-term view, not envisaged very generally, but the need for further storage-space, made instant by the vast documentary accumulations of the War, and coupled with the obvious impossibility of obtaining more buildings in Chancery Lane within any reasonable period after it, led to the acceptance as a provisional measure of external accommodation in the shape of a disused Gaol at Cambridge: and when after some years this had to be surrendered in 1929 the principle of a Repository outside London for Archives which, though transferred to the charge of the Record Office, had not yet been thrown open to public inspection was formally accepted. The new place of refuge was again an ancient Gaol, this time at Canterbury, and during the next ten years it was converted to an admirable Repository and its administration reduced to a satisfactory system. Unfortunately the second World War necessitated its evacuation and the Department never regained it. At the moment of writing, after a distressing period of temporary premises, the problem of finding a permanent successor to Canterbury (and one of larger size, for even in 1939 Canterbury was becoming uncomfortably full) seems to have been solved: but the old simple distinction between Chancery Lane, containing all that is open to public inspection, and the Provincial Repository, containing all that is not, can no longer be maintained. A new system will have to be worked out for division of Classes between the two and it is not improbable that a Provincial Establishment, more elaborately organised than Canterbury, may house sub-sections of the Photographic and Repairing services, and possibly of the Search Rooms, all of which are limited in their work at present by constriction of space in Chancery Lane. These are considerable developments, and the beginning perhaps of others.

In any case the Provincial Repository, though it can only postpone the enlargement of Headquarters, has become a permanent feature.

Limbo

Shortage of space at Chancery Lane had for years led perforce to the discouragement of large further transfers of modern Records from the various

Departments of Central Government; and this in turn was producing an alarming tendency in Ministries to take matters into their own hands and seek 'temporary' accommodation for the masses of papers no longer required for current work which embarrassed them by their bulk, without going through the troublesome process of putting these in order for transfer to the Public Record Office. There was real danger of a recurrence of precisely the state of affairs which the Record Office Act had been designed to end: and, to crown this, came the War with its inevitable consequence of existing Offices split up and scattered (it was calculated in 1940 that 'Public Records' were spread over 399 places) of new Offices brought into being, and of official papers monstrously multiplied. Considering these conditions towards the end of the War we could not but take the view that the Record Office must no longer confine its attention to classes of Documents put in order for permanent preservation and formally transferred to us but must concern itself also in future with Documents in all Departments of the Central Government before they reached that stage: for there was no doubt that, by the terms of our Act, all (whether or no we had accepted physical charge) were technically in the "charge and superintendence" of the Master of the Rolls. In other words, we had not only to provide for an extension of accommodation which would allow us to encourage formal transfers but somehow to arrange for some kind of superintendence by the Record Office before the Documents actually came, or were ready to come, into our hands.

The answer devised to this problem in 1943 was the scheme which has become known semi-officially as 'Limbo'. The plan was that the Ministry of Works, which would in any case be called upon to provide the accommodation necessary for any Ministry which desired to disembarras itself of a superfluity of obsolete Archives, should provide a single large building, or group of buildings, which should be available for Archives of this kind from any Ministry and for the staff from that Ministry working upon them; but of which the Record Office should undertake the general supervision. Unexpectedly it was found possible to provide temporary quarters sufficient to make a beginning of implementing this scheme very soon after the War; and it was duly put in action, giving the Record Office an opportunity such as it had never had before for liaison with Departments in regard to the preliminary handling of what will one day become Archives in its custody. At the moment of writing the problem of a permanent building has almost been settled and the Record Office thus enters on a new stage in its career in which it will have three establishments — its headquarters still in Chancery Lane, on a site connected traditionally with Archive conservation, for six centuries: a Provincial Repository for its over-flow; and a 'Limbo' from which will emerge from time to time accruals of Documents "considered worthy of permanent preservation", and set in order to join those previouly transferred.

The 'Summary' and a System
of Reference

This idea of a complete "Summary Inventory" of everything the Office contains is not a new one: it was actively entertained between 1861 and 1867 but was abandoned, probably on account of an overwhelming influx of Documents, and replaced by the well-known series of less detailed printed '*Guides*' by Thomas, Bird and Giuseppi. But with the gradual working-out, after the completion of the building as it stands in 1896, of a system of packing its 140 Strong-Rooms and 35 miles of shelving, some kind of a Directory to and Check-List of their contents became necessary for the use of the Staff. The present '*Summary*' on 366 large type-script pages is the ultimate outcome of this, linked closely with the comprehensive application of a scheme, originally partial and experimental, for the uniform labelling and numbering of all 'pieces' (that is of all volumes, boxes, files or parcels which figure as individual units on the shelves) with an abbreviated reference consisting of three parts: first a letter or letters for the title of the 'Group' (F.O. for example representing the *Foreign Office* Group), then a number (in scarlet on the label) representing the 'Class' (F.O. 43 for example is the class of *General Correspondence* with *Italian States*) and finally (black on the label) the number of the 'Piece' within the class. The advantages of course are first the saving of time in writing; second the fact that no matter in what strong-room or on what shelf F.O. 43/5 is placed it is always F.O. 43/5; and third the fact that it can be produced or replaced under that reference by persons who know nothing of Foreign Office Records or of Research. The Summary gives under each of these numerical Class References, and also (for the numerical order of Classes is not always the same as the alphabetical) under their descriptive titles, the number of 'pieces' that Class contains and their covering dates; while a final blank column can be used for any information (for instance the State of Repair) of which it may be desired to have a 'summary' statement, but is generally filled (in the standard copies used by the Staff) by a manuscript note of the Strong Room in which each Class is to be found. The Number and Date are also entered up afresh in these copies as accruals or other changes occur.

The maintenance of the 'Summary' once established has proved an easy, though laborious, matter. The penultimate stage in its development came when, in the War, it was found perfectly possible to prepare a Special Edition in which was accurately noted the precise location of every "piece" in the 88,000 large packages distributed over seven temporary Repositories as well as those which remained in Chancery Lane. The ultimate stage has been reached within the last few months when it was judged that the 'Summary' had now attained a sufficiently stable form for copies to be offered as gifts to our correspondents in other National Archives (which will receive also from time to time Addenda and Corrigenda) for the use of Students. Other National Archives are thus kept informed of the state of our Accumulations. An alphabetical Index of the Class titles in all Groups is at present under revision.

Photography and Publication

Though Photographic Reproduction of all kinds has of course been practised for the convenience of Students for many years the Public Record Office, less fortunate than its opposite numbers in some other Countries, has not had its own organisation for this purpose until recently. Before the late War photographs for facsimile reproduction and other purposes were taken by visiting professionally; for the process generally known to us as "photostat" (the making of reversed negatives on sensitised paper) we had had for many years equipment but it was operated again by imported experts; and microphotography had penetrated only in the form of small portable cameras operated by Students for themselves. The second and third of these processes we were more or less obliged to take up with our own operatives during the War for the purposes respectively of making official copies without clerical aid and of 'filming' important series as an insurance against possible destruction: and we have since established a Section reasonably equipped (though not with the enviable completeness of our friends in America) for photographic work of all normal kinds; and are only embarrassed by its popularity with the Student Public.

I mention this belated conversion not for any small interest it may have in itself but because of the change of policy to which it seems to me inevitably to lead. To meet the needs of the Student who could not conveniently come long distances to read in our Sarch Rooms the prescribed treatment in the past has been the publication of texts or full abstracts of documentary series; and the Record Office has during the last century produced itself some hundreds of volumes and assisted individual Scholars or printing Societies to publish a considerable further number. But though it must have been obvious to many for a long time that this was not solving the difficulty — for all our efforts had made a real impression on the Records of only one of the three great divisions of medieval Administration, the Executive[27]; and though the *Domestic State Papers* of the sixteenth and seventeenth centuries had fared well publication of the *Foreign* progressed with maddening slowness and later Departmental (Ministerial) Records remained untouched — though it might seem clear that another solution must be sought, no one had come forward officially or extra-officially with any proposals. The advent of Micro-photography,

---

27. With only trifling exceptions Official Publication has so far not touched the seven or eight great series of Accounting Records in the Record Office dating from the twelfth and thirteenth centuries: and has no more than begun upon the Legal.

enormously quicker and cheaper than older photograhic processes, though it cannot accomplish, in the case of older Archives, the miracles claimed for it by some enthusiasts, should alter, it seems to us, both the policy and the method of our proceedings in this matter. The preparation in large quantities of Descriptive Lists and Indexes (not necessarily printed: in typescript they might themselves be microphotographed) might be a very efficient aid to the distant Student in choosing the most advantageous and least expensive way of ordering microfilm for his work.

Though it should not, and I hope will not, affect the amount of our Editorial Work in the future (for Publication in printed form will still be necessary in some cases) Microphotographic processes should have a considerable influence on its direction and method: and their adoption therefore at the Record Office on something like an adequate scale may be regarded, I think, as an event of importance in our annals.

CONCLUSION

At the close of this account of developments in English Archives during the last twenty-five years I find myself wondering whether the results achieved will be regarded as encouraging? or the reverse? An English Archivist's answer to that question will naturally vary with his mood between optimism and pessimism: he may even find himself wondering at times whether he is not, anyhow, making a great ado about matters which are of small moment. This last I do not believe: because I am convinced — if I may venture to labour a point I endeavoured to make in the Inaugural Lecture cited above — that the Archivist has a part to play in the modern world which is by no means merely academic and by no means unimportant. That being so, and as one Archivist speaking to others, whose problems, in whatever national guise they may appear, are fundamentally the same as his own, I shall make no apology for my chronicle of our doings in England: for them even the small details of our success or failure are worth some discussion — they "point a moral" even if they do not "adorn a tale".

The Principles and Practice of Archive Repair Work in England[1]

INTRODUCTORY

Repairs of this kind have until very recently been practised on a considerable scale chiefly in one place in this Country — the Public Record Office in London. Though we must not be taken as under-rating the important work done at some of the Great Libraries — notably the British Museum, and the National Library of Wales at Aberystwyth — such work has naturally been only a part of more comprehensive operations (especially at the British Museum) and on the other hand does not, on the purely documentary side, involve the problems of sheer Bulk, Custody and the like which confront the Archivist; nor offer the same opportunities of gathering experience to an unlimited extent in the treatment of certain materials such as parchment and sealing-wax. I shall therefore confine myself in this article to dealing with the art of Repair as it has taken shape at the Public Record Office (not without some acknowledged debts to our colleagues in Foreign Archives) during the past thirty years; and as it is now developing on the same model in Local Repositories of Archives, especially those maintained by the County Councils and a few of the great Cities. I need hardly add an expression of the hope that this article may elicit similar statements of theory and practice from other Countries which may usefully be compared with ours.

THE REPAIRING SECTION AT THE PUBLIC RECORD OFFICE

At the Public Record Office, which has a total Establishment in all grades of approximately 180 (though at present it is depleted by 25 below that

1. I have received considerable help in the planning of this article from my Colleague Mr. R.H. Ellis, the Assistant Keeper at present in charge of Repairs at the Public Record Office; and Miss Gifford has given me assistance in its compilation.

standard) the work of Repair and Book-Binding is carried on by 26 men, including one Superintendent of Binding and Repairs ('Foreman Craftsman'), a Foreman, and Deputy Foreman. These were supplemented for many years by a varying number of *Professional Binders* sent in from the Stationery Office, whose work, under the superintendence of the Department's own Chief Binder will be described below; but this has been (for the time at least) discontinued recently and the Department includes at present only one trained Binder — the Superintendent himself.

The Repairers formed originally part of the general staff of Messengers, etc., and were liable to be called off to other work; but from about 1895 this ceased and they became a regular and separate section; though for many years it formed part of a single grade which included also the sections of Attendants in the Search Rooms and in the Repository, and transfer or promotion from one section to another was not infrequent. The Repairing Section was re-organised under an Assistant Keeper (the present writer) in 1922, at which time a Survey was made of the State of Repair of all Classes in the Repository, and soon afterwards work on Seals (including their moulding and the making of reproductions) was added to its repertoire[2]: at all times it has been concerned with questions of Make-up, Labelling and Numeration, though as much of that work as possible is delegated to less skilled hands: and when, during and after the War, Photographic Work of all kinds was taken up officially the Repairing Section, which had previously been charged only with the supervision of unofficial photographers, provided the staff for those operations also. Re-organization, however, within the last year has divided this multiple Grade into three — *Binding and Repairs* (including Seals), *Photography*, and *Repository* and *Search Rooms*.

Detailed *Registration* of all Repair work undertaken has been regular since 1882 and since 1922 an Index to this Register has been kept: by means of which, in combination with a system of dated labels, it is now possible to trace the repair-history of any given Document in a few minutes.

The supervision of all work by an Assistant Keeper is a feature upon which we lay much stress, because in so many cases the measures taken both in Binding and in Repair must depend, in our judgment, on ability to read and understand the Document. He is responsible also for assigning priorities to the work — a delicate task in view of the masses of Documents awaiting treatment; for weighing, when necessary, the merits of alternative methods of treatment; for reconciling the claims of an exact reproduction of original form with those of efficiency, of convenience for photography and so forth; and in brief for all matters of policy.

2. The Record Office system is based, with some modifications, on examination of the methods in use at Brussels, Paris and Stockholm. See the article by the present writer in *Antiquaries' Journal* for 1924 entitled *Some Notes on the Preservation, Moulding and Casting of Seals.*

Some *Statistics* of work done in recent years may be of interest. Between 1922 and 1949, when Part I of the new Guide was published, there had been repaired 66,000 Documents (almost all consisting of many leaves or membranes) and 21,000 seals. This volume of work has been maintained and indeed increased. Since 1949 there have been repaired over 20,000 individual membranes of parchment and over 50,000 leaves of paper, without counting such other operations as Binding, Filing, Cleaning and Flattening, Seal Repair and Moulding of Seals.

PRINCIPLES AND METHODS

These have been dealt with on more than one occasion in print and we may therefore pass lightly here. A principle upon which we have for many years insisted is that in the case of Documents which are Archives any physical element which is present (small or large, beautiful or the reverse, obviously important or by ordinary standards negligible), from the materials in which a volume is bound down to the needle-holes through which it is sewn, is *evidential* and must be neither destroyed nor obscured in Repair. The Methods and Materials of Repair are based on this: the aim being so far as possible to add nothing and take nothing away; and where that is not feasible·(particularly in the case of the new materials which must unavoidably be added to strengthen or make good) to use, with as few exceptions as may be, fresh material of the same character and quality as the original and at the same time to distinguish (if necessary by annexing written notes[3] the new from the old. The first thing the Archivist Repairer has to learn is that he must not (as he would like to do) make his work invisible; the Seal Repairer, for instance, works with a wax of the same constituents but of a different colour.

Details of the way in which these principles are translated into practical methods or dealing with Paper, Parchment and Wax; the employment of Parchment Size, especially in connexion with the first of these, and the intrusion of alien materials, particularly flour-paste as an adhesive, silk gauze (one of our borrowings from the experience of our Foreign Colleagues[4]) and linen backings — all these have been described in print more than once[5] and must be left with no more than a reference. At most I may allow

---

3. These written Notes we regard as most important, particularly in the case of Bindings: two specimens are given in an Appendix to the present article.
4. It was based many years ago on procedure at the Vatican; but we use flour paste.
5. See in particular the account of our methods published in the first number (January 1938) of *The American Archivist* by an American worker, Mr. Herman Smith, who joined our Repairing Staff for a period of training in 1935-36; by the present writer in *Manual of Archive Administration* (Second edition, 1937), in articles published by the British Records Association (notably in *Proceedings* I), and in *Antiquaries' Journal*, IV (1924); and more

myself perhaps to mention four of our most characteristic processes — 'framing' which consists in pasting a new sheet of paper over the whole of a Document of that material and immediately tearing away its centre so as to expose the writing and leave only a narrow edging of new paper; the process we call 'backing and filling', applicable to either parchment or paper, by which the new material is added in two thin layers instead of one thicker; our special method of hardening Moulds of Seals and taking impressions in wax (not casts) from them; and the fashion of sewing the sheets of a volume to doubled guards which, doubled again, are sewn in the ordinary way to binding slips, an invaluable way of securing that, no matter where the volume is opened, every scrap of the exposed pages shall lie flat and visible to the reader or camera. These are small matters: but certain larger aspects of the work, or conditions now affecting it, may claim more individual attention.

ANCIENT VERSUS MODERN

The Public Record Office is the Repository not only of the most ancient but also of the most modern Archives resulting from the activities of all Departments of the Central Government: from the *Domesday Book* of William the Conqueror to Forestry Commission Records of 1949. We must hope it will always remain so, for from every point of view (not only that of Repair) practice in regard to the later is (we hold) most efficient when it is rooted in experience gained from treatment of the earlier; especially in this Country, where administrative development has been so continuous and unbroken. On a smaller scale the same remark applies to our Local Archives which now combine in many cases the custody of ancient Archives of many categories — Private Muniments; Seigneurial, Testamentary, Diocesan, Capitular and Parish Archives; and the Records of the Quarter Sessions of Justices of the Peace — with the care and conservation of Administrative Documents accruing in the Offices of County Councils since 1889.

Naturally, having thus contrived a double debt to pay we sometimes find the charge not without its embarrassments: in particular we have to undertake the difficult task of holding the balance of limited resources fairly as between the more obvious appeal of ancient Documents and the needs of intrusive and preponderant modern ones. Worse still, we have to face the problems of enormous bulk, inferior materials and inefficient fastenings in the innumerable files of loose papers produced by modern administration and modern office methods.

recently by Roger Ellis in *The Principles of Archive Repair* (London School of Printing and Graphic Arts; 1951).

To a considerable extent these last are matters the settlement of which should be sought at a stage earlier than that at which the Documents reach the Archivist: what is needed is a reform in the methods and materials employed by the Offices in which they originate, a matter to which I may recur later. Pending that, we have in late years devoted a good deal of attention to palliating their worst defects — inadequate containers, which mean progressive deterioration of the papers, and insufficient attachments which may mean disorder or loss and, in any case, make checking difficult.

'BINDING' AND 'FILING'

We have begun by discarding (in view of the bulk to be dealt with) the expensive method of *Binding* in the strict sense of that word, save where a Document consisted from the first of a bound volume, such as a book for the registration of *Accounts* or *Minutes*, supplied blank and subsequently written up: here the binding is a part of the quality of the Archive and must be preserved. In the case of loose papers (or what were originally loose papers; for the same method is applied to those bound up in dilapidated volumes) we have adopted for many years one of the varieties of ('guarding'[6] if necessary and) *Filing* in hinged covers (now also in use in America, I believe, under the name of 'post-binding'[7]) which are described in one of the works already cited[8].

BOXES AND 'FOLDERS'

Even the above methods we can only hope to adopt for a small proportion of the multitudinous bundles of loose or loosely filed papers accumulated in modern Government Departments: for most of these we have been obliged to concentrate on a measure of security represented by a system[9] of manilla folders to contain small sections of the papers (if possible some fixed number to a section), boxes of approved pattern to contain the folders and a check-list of the contents of each box pasted inside its lid. More than a hundred thousand of these boxes have been put in service at the Record Office since they were first adopted, about twenty years ago: and the system has been copied in many places. The durability of the boxes, however, has unfortunately been found to vary considerably and their present form and

6. I.e. the addition of an artificial margin of extra paper.
7. The American variety, however, involves a more elaborate type of cover with spring attachments of metal.
8. See *Archive Administration*, p. 58.
9. Also described in *Archive Administration*, pp. 58-60, and App. III (d).

material must, to a certain extent, still be regarded as experimental. For countries where the attacks of insects are to be feared we have recommended recently the treatment of the boxes (not their contents) with corrosive sublimate or some other insecticide.

THE PROBLEM OF BINDERS

Concentration on the Loose Paper problem has not prevented our dealing to a considerable extent with Archives requiring, for the reasons described above, true binding. Here we are faced with a new problem: for not only are the processes expensive but it is also becoming very difficult to find trained[10] 'Binders' able and willing to undertake them. For the re-binding of modern books it is generally possible to provide, the methods required being for the most part only slight modifications of those practised in a good Bindery: though the modern tendency to train young 'Binders' in little more than 'casing'[11], and that with a large proportion of machine work, produces increasing difficulty. We mostly use the 'spring back' style; with 'split boards', a whole cover of linen buckram (modern leathers being unreliable), 'blocked' head-and-tail-bands, formed in the buckram, and (for heavy volumes) 'shoes' of hide-vellum rivetted on with brass tacks. For work of this kind (as has already been noted) we had for many years Binders supplied by the Stationery Office working under the superintendence of our own *Chief Binder* and in this way between 1922 and 1949 dealt with something like 50,000 re-bindings during the period named above. Even here, owing to our special conditions, special difficulties arose and *ad hoc* devices had to be invented and applied in the case (e.g.) of volumes weighing in their original state fifty pounds or more, and requiring to be split without re-sewing, or volumes whose sewing was still good but required a style of binding which the binder of today is not trained to execute.

But when we come to the older bindings our troubles are much more pronounced: for here a training of the old-fashioned kind (before the days of machinery) is an essential preliminary and to find an executive with that qualification is not easy: the plain truth being that the Public and the

10. Our Repairers we train ourselves: but a Book-binder is a member of a Trades Union and must have passed through an apprenticeship of seven years.

11. We call 'casing' the process by which the sides and back, with their cover, are made separately and clapped, in one piece, on to the sewn sheets. The whole process can now be done, if a sufficient number of uniform volumes makes it worth while, by machinery. 'Binding' as a title we reserve for the operation in which the boards are attached to the bound sheets, the back formed, and the cover put on, in a succession of separate processes, all necessitating hand-work.

Libraries can in general no longer afford to pay for first-class hand-work and consequently very few men learn to do it. Moreover in the case of the older bindings *ad hoc* methods — the modification of the ordinary procedure of the binding-shop to suit an individual case — are no longer required exceptionally; they are the Rule. In addition the Archivist is bound by the conditions of his work to push this requirement much further than the Librarian: the Librarian confronted with a bad form of binding or material has the comparatively simple task of substituting a good one: but for the Archivist form and material, good or bad, are evidential and must somehow, within the limits of security, be preserved — he has to reconcile the claims of mere conservation with those of efficiency.

THE PROBLEM OF BINDINGS

The History of the Binder's craft (that is the history not of book decoration but of the work which lies within or behind the covers) has yet to be written: and it is not generally realised how many and experimental were the processes through which that craft passed, especially in the hands of local and even amateur executants, before it reached the development we know. Work of this character, continuing experimental down to a very late date, is what we normally find in our Archives; and it is largely from the Archives of Europe, not its Libraries, that the History we have spoken of, if it is ever written, will be derived. The bindings of fine MSS. preserved in great Libraries shew us, as a rule, magnificence of materials and decorative 'finishing' executed by the best craftsmen but little variety in the 'forwarding' — the constructional methods. It is this variety of construction which gives the work of repair-binding in Archives at once its chief difficulty and its fascination; each case being liable to present an individual problem requiring special treatment. We have on view at the moment of writing at the Record Office a selection of no more than 29 examples of such work: but even so small a number includes the problems of dilapidated casings in hair-vellum from Bordeaux with unusual head-and-tail bands; of flapped covers with straps and clasps, or brass bosses and corners, or a label on the back board, to remind us of the period when books did not stand on a shelf but lay on a ledge; of volumes in cases of whole hide, with sides unstiffened; of a volume made up by someone who was perhaps a Saddler — certainly not a Binder — and who had his own ideas on the subject of sewing; of another — early ancestor of the modern hollow back — which has been cased in vellum and then covered with leather; of yet other examples in which either the whole sewn volume or individual gatherings of the sheets are fastened with sewing or thongs or 'tackets' direct to a vellum or limp leather cover; and of one in which the whole of the sewing fell off in one piece, the back of the sheets being completely rotted by damp: with several examples of those too weighty volumes that have had their binding slips or their wooden boards or their glued backs broken through constructional weaknesses which one can see generation after generation striving to overcome by the use of new materials or new methods. It is only proper to add in this place that the Public Record Office has had, for the development of this phase of its work, the services for over thirty years of an exceptionally qualified Chief Binder.

'PRIVATE' REPAIRS

The task of helping Private and Local Custodians or Owners of Archives suffering from the same troubles as our own has long been an unofficial part of our work. For the last thirty years the Repairing and Binding Staff of the Public Record Office have been allowed to undertake private work, out of office hours but under a scheme organised and supervised officially: and as a result a very large amount has been done for the Archives of numerous Counties and Towns, Dioceses, Chapters and Parishes, of Colleges, Schools, Hospitals and other Semi-Public Institutions, and of many Private Bodies and Individuals. The main justification for this is its obvious public utility; but it has also had the advantage not infrequently of giving the Craftsmen employed experience of new forms (this applies particularly to local bindings) and of new conditions such as the effect of fire and of long immersion in water, of which considerable new knowledge accrued during the late War. Another direction in which the Department is able to help in this matter has opened up considerably in the last few years with the increasing interest of Local Authorities in establishing properly organized Archives Sections in the County Offices, the consequent demand for trained Archivists, and the initiation in the University of London[12] of a Diploma Course in Archive Administration; some parts of which are directed, extra-officially, by senior members of the Public Record Office Staff. This Course includes demonstrations at the Record Office and a considerable number of Students from the Course, and from Local Archive Repositories, have been allowed from time to time to send short periods in actual work with the Staff. We have also had occasionally 'Learners' for longer periods from other countries in the British Commonwealth.

NEW DEVELOPMENTS

At the moment the trouble is that these various services have become too popular: so that there is a long waiting list of Documents for Repair and the

12. There is also a course of the same kind at Liverpool.

demand for instruction is more than we can meet. Since there seems no likelihood of an immediate or serious abatement of this very desirable movement (which is fostered also by other contemporary activities such as those of the British Records Association, the National Register of Archives and the recent Survey of Ecclesiastical Archives made for the Pilgrim Trust), and since the amount of work to be done is (we now know) practically unlimited, it is hoped that the result may be the setting up on a modest scale of the long-desired Local Repair Centres for instruction in, and perhaps execution of, Repairs to Local and Private Archives; and in fact a beginning has been made in the shape of a course organised at the County Council School of Printing and Graphic Arts in London.

Several Local Repositories[13] have also started, as we have mentioned above, or are proposing to start, small Repair Sections of their own; and since all this work has originated from the Public Record Office there is a satisfactory homogeneity of method. It is perhaps not too much even to hope that the movement thus launched may do something to solve the worst difficulty of all; which is, as we have indicated, that of maintaining the knowledge and practice of true Binding by a reasonable number of skilled Craftsmen. That alone can make good Repair Binding possible.

FUTURE REQUIREMENTS

Apart from the developments indicated in the last paragraph it is easy to predict some of the new repairing needs of the present which will have to be met by new devices in the future but not so easy to say what form those devices will take: because to a large extent they must depend on the Scientist and the Scientist either has not yet invented the necessary processes or has supplied processes and materials the permanence of which, and their effect upon the materials to which they are applied, have yet to be established by the only absolutely reliable test — their behaviour during a long period under the ordinary conditions of conservation. For example, two of the replies which he makes to certain of the problems we submit to him are 'Conditioned Air' and 'Thymol Vapour': but it has yet to be established that the 'conditioning' of air does not destroy elements which (in our Climate — for we are speaking only of England) and under normal non-morbid conditions are positively beneficial to the animal and vegetable fibres in Documents; and Thymol Vapour has been known to dissolve in a disastrous way that animal size which is an essential constituent not only in Vellum and Parchment but also in nearly all Western Papers till near the

13. For example, those of the Counties of Bedford, Essex, Glamorgan, Hertford, Leicester, Surrey, West Sussex, Somerset and Wiltshire.

end of the nineteenth century. So far as Repair is concerned the problems of the future may be summarised in the Statement that whereas the Documents preserved in Archives down to — say — 1880 are of materials of proved durability those of a subsequent date contain, first, an increasingly large proportion of paper of (at best) dubious and (at worst) definitely impermanent quality, so that, however carefully conserved, they will, we may be sure, presently require treatment; and second, a number of entirely new materials (such as cinematographic films and prints from photographic negatives) of the behaviour of which under the test of years we know practically very little.

Perhaps at this point we shall be thought to lack enterprise. That we or our successors will have to deal with the troubles we have just indicated we are well aware: but the amount of needed repair work bequeathed to us from the past is so large that at present we feel justified in concentrating our limited resources upon them and in regard to the new problems holding our hand; doing little more at this point than to observe and, so far as we can, experiment and, of course, to improve 'make up' by the devices already described. It is very possible that some years hence we may be able to agree that sheets of transparent cellulose acetate material appear to stand the test of time without deterioration either to themselves or to Documents sandwiched between them. Meanwhile we are very grateful to our Colleagues in America (who have not, as we have, the excuse of fragmentary Documents and Seals of medieval date clamouring for treatment) for making on a large scale what we regard as a most interesting experiment by which we hope presently to profit.

LABORATORY WORK

The foregoing remarks must not, of course, be taken as meaning that we never resort to Laboratory Experiment: but since our normal problems, though very large, are comparatively simple and few in number, we have not experienced so far the need for a Laboratory of our own in the same way as the British Museum with its much more complex interests. From time to time some special trouble arises and is dealt with by *ad hoc* methods: the necessity, for example, of examining into the incidence and control of Mildew led to the Imperial College of Science undertaking on our behalf a series of experiments lasting for two years: and we not infrequently appeal to various scientific institutions for information on individual points. In chemical matters we usually have recourse either to the Laboratory of the Government Chemist (which conduced for us many years ago an analysis of medieval Sealing Waxes and is our usual helper in such matters) or to the British Museum Laboratory: the discovery that *Borkhausenia Pseudospretella* (*vulgariter*, the clothes-moth) might on occasion attack Admiralty Records took us naturally for a remedy to the Research Department of the Natural History Museum, and the activities of various wood-mining insects to that of Forest Products in the Department of Scientific and Industrial Research; and burned Documents during the war conducted us to the Police Laboratory at Hendon[14]. For advice in regard to the materials we ourselves use our first recourse is to the Stationery Office, upon whose specification (for example) our Repairing Paper is made specially for us. For the larger problems of wholesale deterioration in modern materials — particularly Paper — we are, as I have already noted, watching with interest the proceedings of our colleagues in American Archives: but some examination into this and kindred questions on an extended scale, with perhaps special reference to our own climatic and other conditions, will undoubtly become an unavoidable necessity before long: it is complicated, as my concluding paragraphs may indicate, by administrative problems.

CONCLUSION

This Article has dealt, if only by implication, with what may perhaps without too much magniloquence be called our national policy in regard to Archive Repair as it stands at present: for although I have been describing policy and practice at the Public Record Office circumstances have made these, as I have indicated, the model for Local Centres which are gradually coming into existence. I will venture in conclusion to emphasize and perhaps expand slightly a few special points.

In the first place, here as in other branches of Archive work the overriding consideration is the sheer bulk of the accumulations with which we are faced: a bulk so great in the case of urgently needed Repair — I mean Repair which is essential for the mere well-being of the Document — that one despairs at times of devising any reasonable solution of our difficulties[15]. It affects the organisation of Repair Work at every point — in the choice between alternative methods, in the assignment of proirity of treatment to

---

14. An interesting parallel to the first experiments in France in the use of ultra-violet rays with ancient MSS; which, if I remember right, took place at the *Sureté*.
15. I have cited often but may venture perhaps to use once more the case of the 21,000 bound volumes in the one class of Admiralty *Logs*, all decayed, with which, among other problems, our survey of Needed Repairs confronted us. In that instance a solution was found because it fortunately appeared that these consisted of a much larger number of small Documents which, on technical grounds, never should have been made up into large volumes at all: these units therefore could properly be resolved into their component parts and boxed — a not impossible task nearly half of which has now been accomplished.

this or that class[16], in the proportion of Staff allocated to Repair Work.

This question of Staff Allocation is one of some general interest. At the Public Record Office we have out of the total establishment available for all purposes — from Administrative and Editorial work to Cleaning and Porterage — about 14 per cent, engaged on Binding and Repairs; and the actual number of Repairers has not increased in proportion to other Staff increases, which again have not kept pace in recent years with the increasing bulk of the Documents in our charge. In an Archives Department situated as we are, that is to say combining the care of unique and invaluable early material with that of modern accruals — and that is the case normally of all important Repositories, Civil and Ecclesiastical, in this Country, though of course none of them have a Repair problem comparing in size with ours — I believe that the assignment of this proportion of the total staff (one in seven) to Repairs, though it may seem large, represents actually a minimum requirement. In small Repositories the proportion would even be higher; because out of a Staff of five or six one should certainly be a trained Repairer: but perhaps, when local organisation has gone further something may be done (particularly in the matter of Binding) by several neighbouring Repositories clubbing their resources for this purpose. On the other hand the danger as well as the inconvenience of transporting fragile Documents from place to place must be borne in mind[17].

The consideration of Bulk lies also behind our insistence as a matter of policy on permanence in both the methods and the materials used in Repair: we cannot, we feel, afford either the temporary[18] or the experimental. The Owner or Custodian of a small number of Manuscripts — or even a tolerably large Museum — may say we will try such and such methods, watch the results carefully and, if necessary, take further steps. We, having to deal with Documents not by hundreds or thousands but by millions necessarily conduct our work somewhat differently: our aim is —

16. Another often cited case which I will venture to use once more is that of the *Plea Rolls* of the Courts of Law and particularly the Court of Common Pleas — piles of large parchment membranes fastened together at the head to the number of as many as 500 in a single 'Roll' — of which we possess over 5,000. To repair one of these may take two skilled men several months with a heavy expenditure for material: but they are important and the work would have been put in hand long ago if the Rolls now marked 'Unfit for Production' were only a few. Unfortunately they number over 300.
17. These questions of transport and fragility are particularly troubling those interested in the Archives of the West Indian Islands at the present time.
18. The exception to this is furnished of course by boxes and wrapping materials which — short of an expenditure that is generally out of the question — must be regarded as things which will need to be replaced after a varying but probably not very long period of years.

must be — to handle a set of Documents in repair in such a fashion that no special watching or further steps will be necessary — that they may be regarded as finally disposed of and our Repairers be free to attack the next in an unending series of tasks. For the same reason we should prefer, and do try, to take up whole series for repair rather than to deal piece-meal with single Documents: but unfortunately individual casualties and urgent cases are always with us.

Finally I should perhaps say a little more in defence of our policy of concentrating our efforts, so far as actual Repair is concerned[19], on our older classes. It is not that we do not recognize, and anticipate with great apprehension, the problems accumulating rapidly, for us or our successors, in the monstrous series of Loose Papers accruing from modern administrative organisation. If we hold our hand for the time in respect of these it is because in the first place attention to the older Classes is, on the lowest count, of equal importance; secondly because modern Archive forms and inferior modern materials (especially the latter) will call for new methods of treatment the efficacy of which (even if they have been formulated in the Laboratory) has still to be submitted to the only final and decisive test — that of time: and finally because some parts of the remedy in the case of modern papers lies as I have hinted, in action which might be taken by the Administrator who creates the Documents rather than by the Archivist and such action is still a possible subject for negotiation.

We have very recently succeeded in giving effect to a plan for a new 'Intermediate' Repository for modern Archives before they are in a state to be transferred finally to the Public Record Office: administered by a small section of our Staff charged with the duty of personal liaison with Ministries and other Public Departments, whose own Staff may continue to work upon the Documents deposited there. This Repository has only been active for six years and its installation is anything but complete: but already it contains 249,292 foot-run of Documents from twenty-one Departments and Staff from thirteen Offices are at work there on Elimination and other tasks. In a few years, if all goes well, this increased liaison between the beginning and the end, the Administrator and the Archivist, may have changed the face of the problem of modern 'Departmental' Archives, though problems of quality and bulk will always be with us.

19. That is, not counting the large operations of boxing, etc., which, as already described, are also undertaken or supervised by the Repairing Staff.

APPENDIX

Examples of Notes Annexed to Repaired Volumes[20]

Exchequer, King's Remembrancer Miscellaneous Books, Series I (E. 164) 4

This volume has been preserved with its original sewing and binding: but one board was cracked at the lacing-holes, the sewing-bands themselves were broken on the front side, the outer cover was much torn and all of the brass furniture, except one D, was missing.

In the present repair the fractured board has been taken off and mended; the severed portions of the sewing-bands have been replaced with new leather sewn on to the old bands; the board has then been laced on afresh and a new back and patchings of natural-coloured African Goat-skin, native tanned, applied to the old inner cover. A portion of the old white sheepskin from the original back is preserved separately.

The outer cover (the lining of which was of white-tawed sheep skin stained red) has been repaired with natural and red African Goat. When found it was stuck down to the inner cover but this was probably due to accident and it has now been left loose except where it is pierced by the fastenings of the clasps and bosses.

All the brass work except the one piece mentioned above is new. The front end-sheet is also new and is left unfastened on one edge of the board to shew the old leather.

Binder: T.E. Hassell.
September 1938

BRISTOL: TOLZEY COURT ACTIONS, 1632, 1633

This volume was originally sewn on five slips of hazel wood with a longer strip of white-tawed leather wrapped around each; and laced into vellum cases by means of these leather strips. The sheets, after being framed in new paper by the Repairing Staff of the Public Record Office, have now been resewn in the same way on to new hazel slips and strips of native tanned African goat and re-laced by means of the latter into the cases; which have been repaired with new vellum. The new head bands (sewn in hemp over two further leather lacing strips) are also reproductions of the originals. The new leather tie is of African goat. The Boards are new.

---

20. The first (a Record Office Volume) is signed and dated by the Assistant Keeper in charge of Repairs, the second (a Local Archive, repaired extra-officially) bears also the name of the Binder.

All the sheets have had to be heavily repaired in the top left-hand corner, thus producing a slight swell in the back of the volume at that point.

It will be noted that there are remains (now mounted up on larger guards) of a number of leaves which have at some time been cut out from the beginning of this volume: probably they contained an Index, now missing.

Binder: T.E. Hassell.
August 1937.

Jewish History and Archives

Presidential Address delivered before the
Jewish Historical Society of England,
3rd November, 1953.

It is the privilege of age to be, within reason, not merely reminiscent but even autobiographical: and though I hope I shall not tax your patience long with the autobiography I must begin by claiming your indulgence for some exercise of that privilege. When I was invited to take office as President of this Society I was in two minds whether I could accept the invitation: not, you will readily conceive, because I failed to appreciate the very great honour it did me, for I am, I believe, only the third non-Jewish President in sixty years, and I was both touched and grateful that members of the Council thought me worthy of such a distinction. I hesitated because I felt honestly doubtful whether I could contribute anything in the way of a Presidential Address which would satisfy either you to hear or me to deliver. The names of past Presidents, some whom I have known a little personally and more whom I have known well by reputation, occurred to me — Lucien Wolf, Israel Abrahams, H.S.Q. Henriques, Gustave Tuck and Philip Guedalla, to name only a few no longer with us whom I have actually been privileged to meet during the long period in which I have been able to maintain some occasional contact with the affairs of the Society. I thought of the quality and variety of the topics they had discussed and of the weight of expert knowledge of Jewish affairs in the present as well as Jewish History in the past with which they had spoken; and I hesitated to take a place in such company. It is true that in the early days of my connexion with Records, and at a date when research in documents was not so common a practice as it has since become, I was tempted to see myself as one of the historians of the English Jewries of the thirteenth century. The remarkable Anglo-Jewish Historical Exhibition of 1887 was then a comparatively recent achievement — two of the colleagues whom I first met when I joined the Record Office (Charles Trice Martin and Hubert Hall) had contributed to it — and one of the first books which gave me some idea of what might be done by patient gleaning in the astonishing series of English Records to which I was then being introduced was Joseph Jacobs' *'Jews of Angevin England'*. My first official tasks of any importance had led me to the discovery of some exclusively Jewish Records (*Receipt Rolls* and *Tallies*) which were new, and that in a relationship with like records of a non-Jewish character which made me, as it still makes me, think that accepted views of the nature and functions of the medieval *Scaccarium Judeorum* might need some revision; even though they had been held by such scholars as Jacobs and Charles Gross. It is true also, that, greatly daring, I ventured to express these views in the *'Transactions'* of this Society in 1912 and that I sought confirmation of them in the preparation of a volume of *'Jewish Plea Rolls'* which the help and encouragement of that kindest and most patient editors, Israel Abrahams, enabled me to produce, after many delays, in 1929. But there, I am afraid, with only very occasional subsequent incursions, my intrusion into the field of Jewish History ended and although my interest has by no means ceased, and the possibilities of the documents which aroused it (in spite of the work of other writers such as Herbert Loewe, Michael Adler and Canon Stokes) have not yet been exhausted, any idea I might have had of figuring modestly as an historian of the medieval English Jewry has lapsed.

I have ventured to be so far personal because this lapse of mine was not confined to Jewish History: I had in fact begun to follow a line which neither I nor I think anyone else had up to then considered as an independent one — the line of the archivist; the person not primarily occupied himself in research but concerned with the conservation and accessibility of documents in the interest of other people, perhaps in the distant future, who may, possibly for purposes quite unknown to him, have occasion to use them. The development of this new profession in England, which I believe to be a matter of profound importance for many branches of Research but pre-eminently for the Historical, has now been my main preoccupation, both officially and extra-officially, for many years: and if I finally decided to accept the honour which brings me here tonight it was because I thought that though no longer a practising historian who could signalise his accession to office as your President by communicating to you the latest results of his personal researches, it might be useful if, speaking definitely as an archivist, I described some features of that development which might be new to you and considered, or invited you to consider, their relation to the special problems of Jewish Historiography in general; and the work of the Jewish Historical Society of England in particular.

You will see that this means that I must seek your further indulgence for a general review (I shall make it as brief as possible) of certain developments in historical writing, and the use of Archives, in this country which have occurred mostly within my own official memory and well within the life-time of this Society. Perhaps after all it will not need so much apology if we remember, what is indeed the text of my Address, that the history of the Jewish People in England, though it is a part of Jewish history as a whole, is also a part of English history.

In the first place, then, what do we mean by the word "Archives"? We mean by it the pieces of writing of all kinds, from formal registers to small notes, which accumulate naturally in the course of the conduct of affairs of any kind at any time; and are preserved by the person or body concerned or their successors. Please observe (it is important) that we prescribe for the "affairs" no limit of date or character. They may be your affairs or mine or those of a Church or an Empire; may have been conducted yesterday or in the thirteenth century. The original reason for the preservation of such documents is, of course, that they may be wanted for reference: their preservation after that possibility has passed has not infrequently resulted from mere inertia: and the discovery that when their original usefulness had ceased they might serve the purposes of scholarship was the beginning of new schools of History in the seventeenth and eighteenth centuries.

At first, attention was naturally confined almost entirely to the archives of very important persons or bodies: and even among these only the more august and the earlier series attracted much attention — *Domesday Book*, for example; the great medieval *Enrolments* of the Chancery; *State Papers* of the Tudors; *Bishops' Registers*, perhaps, and the *Cartularies* of famous Monasteries: Original Accounts (even the medieval), when I first entered the Record Office, were only just beginning to be much thought of; and modern Departmental Records were if not poor, certainly unpopular relations. Moreover, the use made of Records was direct: they were of value because they, being the 'Documents in the Case,' enabled the modern historian to correct or amplify the *ex parte* or incomplete statements made by his predecessors about the events which produced them. Treaties, for instance, were subjects of recognised historical interest, but knowledge of their terms was inadequate till Rymer set out to print for us from the contemporary records accumulated in the course of treaty-making their actual texts. But the use of Archives soon went much further than this. There began the development which has revealed to us the value of Archives for the indirect and incidental information which they may convey upon an infinite variety of topics which were certainly not in the minds of their compilers. An accountant (to take a hackneyed example) sets out to justify to his Auditor his expenditure of so many pounds, shillings and pence: and two centuries later learned men are wrangling over the value of that item in his accounts for the dating of one of Shakespeare's plays.

It is this use of the information profusely but casually supplied by any great series of archives which has made possible in modern times the extension of research into entirely new fields, such as those of Economic, Social and Administrative History; and that in turn has led to the extension also of our interest in Archives far beyond the few great and imposing classes which still made a horizon for most people at the time when this Society's activities began. We have not, of course, ceased to be interested in great men and outstanding events, but we are also, and perhaps rather more, interested in movements and conditions; that is to say, in the things which affected the smaller people, our own opposite numbers in the past — the people whose lives and doings made up collectively the life of the thirteenth or the seventeenth century as ours are making up that of the twentieth. As a corollary, we have to take a good deal of interest in the humbler, but very voluminous, series of archives — the *Taxation or Manorial or Parish Accounts*; the *Court Rolls* and the vast series of *Deeds* concerning small properties; the Wills of minor people and Inventories of their goods; the Apprenticeship Records; the Proceedings before local justices and countless other series — from which the desired information may be drawn.

This change in the direction of historical effort resulted first in a great increase of publication of an unofficial kind: the latter part of the nineteenth and the beginning of the present century saw the establishment of numerous societies, largely regional in outlook but some of the type of the Pipe Roll Society, the Selden Society and our own; devoted wholly or in part to the publication of records in some particular interest. It is true that they for the most part confined themselves still to the more outstanding and early classes of Archives; but at the same time people began to be conscious that the lesser Archives, especially those in private custody, ought at least to be preserved and were in fact (owing to various causes upon which I must not here dilate) in grave danger of dispersal or destruction; and presently a few bodies, notably the Public Libraries, made a beginning by finding house-room for unwanted documents which might supplement their collections of material for local history. At the same time Local and Ecclesiastical Authorities were being urged to spend more effort on the care of their own Archives and in a few cases were beginning to do so. By 1930 some scores of volumes were being published every year in this way and a definite movement was taking shape to locate and preserve documents of historical value which were no longer needed by their natural owners or custodians. In addition it was beginning to be realised that the conservation of archives might require qualifications which neither the historian nor even the librarian would normally possess: so that some of the large libraries were looking for staff specially trained for the purpose; and both the Library Association and the School of Librarianship in the University of London had gone so far as to include Archive Administration in their syllabuses.

At this point there came into existence the British Records Association: concerned first to continue and enlarge an organisation already in existence for the rescue of private archives and their distribution to institutions where their permanent preservation and accessibility to students could be guaranteed; secondly to co-ordinate the work which was being done for archives by all manner of societies and other bodies; and thirdly, and generally, to foster a body of sound public opinion upon all matters concerning the preservation and use of archives and, though perhaps few even of its founder members realised this, to create a new point of view and a new profession in this country. In all these matters it has, in spite of an intervening war, been successful beyond expectation. The work of its Records Preservation section has never ceased and after twenty years of successful struggle, during which it has dealt with something like half a million documents, it has just received, from the Pilgrim Trust, the means of inaugurating an intensified campaign for the rescue of private archives, now, since the War, more than ever endangered not only through ignorance of their value but on account of pressure on space, increased cost of staff, the breaking up of large estates, abandonment of great houses and disappearance or re-organisation of old establishments of every kind. It has a membership of over a thousand, including all the county councils: it has been responsible for a considerable amount of technical publication, including a new journal — 'Archives'; for persuading or encouraging a large proportion of the counties to establish Archives departments properly equipped and staffed not only to look after their own Records but also to give a home to others, private, local and even ecclesiastical, which were in danger; and for planning, to meet the new need for trained archivists, a special school and diploma course in the University of London. Finally it has proposed successfully the official creation of a National Register of Archives.

The function of this last-named institution is to take the first steps — that is location and registration — in the preservation of Local, Ecclesiastical and Private Archives. Analysis and registration are accomplished by a small staff sited at the Public Record Office; but for the primary supply of information it must necessarily depend on Local Knowledge and Local Effort: and its first task has been to organise in the counties — a large proportion of which have now been covered — bodies of voluntary helpers who submit upon an approved system reports of the existence and nature of bodies of archives of every description. Except to rule out the frivolous and ephemeral, no distinction is made as to date or kind: Ancient and Modern; Public, Semi-public or Private; Lay or Ecclesiastical; Official or Personal; Commercial, Industrial, Professional or Institutional: all are *pabulum* for the Register. Inevitably the Registry Staff do much in addition in the way of advice, inspections, co-operation with the British Records Association for the rescue of accumulations in actual danger of destruction or dispersal, and communication to students of information concerning new material for their researches.

There remain to be mentioned one new question which is obsessing some of us to an increasing extent and one new development which transcends the boundaries of country. The question is — how far is the old specific of publication, as it has been understood up to date, sufficient to meet the needs of students in view of the vast extension in bulk and date of the archives we now present as worthy of their attention? My first predecessor at the Record Office — that distinguished Jewish scholar Sir Francis Palgrave — had no qualms: he looked into the future, as Maitland put it, "down along vistas of imperial folios" and was satisfied: so also were his contemporaries and those who came after him until very recent times, not only at the Public Record Office but in those other publishing bodies I have mentioned; and the result has been our enrichment by some thousands of valuable volumes. But the disquieting truth is that publication has only touched the border of the field which it started, a couple of centuries ago, to make accessible, and meanwhile that field, by the addition to it of new classes not previously much esteemed, and still more by reason of vast and growing accruals of modern Archives, and their growing popularity with students has grown to even more embarrassing dimensions. Clearly as a formula for providing that accessibility which it is part of the archivist's business to provide, 'Publication' is obsolete. Modern facilities for travel and modern devices such as microphotography, making personal access to the originals more possible, are offering us new means of dealing with the problem, but it is by no means solved. For the moment, however, the question of how we shall in future deal editorially with our Archives is submerged in the larger problems of finding out what and where our Archives are; and how we may ensure their preservation.

Finally I have to chronicle the birth of a new international outlook upon the work of the archivist. I will say no more of this at present than that the recognition of certain elements in that work as common to all nations and therefore susceptible of international handling began in conferences twenty years ago under the auspices of the Comité International de Coopération Intéllectuelle, a committee of the League of Nations, and has become since the last war an accomplished fact. An International Council for Archives is now in existence and acts as one of the advisory bodies to the institution known as UNESCO, which has recognised archive studies as an independent element in the "Educational, Scientific and Cultural" interests that it is commissioned to serve.

I have selected here for your consideration, if I may summarise, five major developments: (1.) the widening (an enormous widening) of the scope of interest in archives to include low as well as high and modern as well as ancient; (2.) realisation of the present day danger to archives, especially private ones, not only of neglect but of actual destruction or dispersal, and measures taken to meet this; (3.) distinction between the functions of the historian, for whom archives are a source to be exploited for his particular purpose, and the archivist, whose business it is to conserve and make them available for any purposes; (4.) recognition of the inadequacy of straight publication as a specific accessibility for study; and (5.) the international point of view.

Now how do these developments affect in particular Jewish Historiography and the work of the Society?

May I take first as the most obvious, that question of the publication of texts or calendars and its insufficiency by itself as a means of making Archives accessible to students: should that affect the policy pursued by the Society up to date? So far as concerns the medieval records I think the answer is No. I have always held, and I think most medievalists would agree, that up to at least an advanced date in the thirteenth century available material as a whole is relatively so small, and the Archives which survive are so packed with detailed allusion to persons, places and topics, that at least all the principal series are worth publication in the form of full indexed texts or calendars, if only to serve as general reference books for the period — a kind of medieval encyclopaedia — and, fortunately or unfortunately, the purely Jewish classes surviving to us up to 1290 are sufficiently limited to make complete publication a realisable ideal. It is no light task; indeed it is formidable: also one would like to see it proceeding at a faster rate; and I think means might be found to shorten the form of presentation in some cases without omitting any of the facts: but it seems to me feasible within a predictable time and eminently worthwhile. In saying this I am thinking not only of the Jewish *Plea* or, as I prefer to call them, *Memoranda Rolls* but of the Jewish *Receipt Rolls*. Known survivals of *Tallies* and *Starrs* you have already dealt with. Outside these series there are not likely to be found now for the medieval period more than stray documents, nor many as important as the curious record of Jewish complaints, parallel with those of Christians, against the Poitevin officials of Henry III in 1234 which were published by Mr. Michael Adler some years ago. Such occasional *trouvailles* can be dealt with in published notes as they come to hand.

In the work I have just been describing we are spared at least one problem: the material is already located. Apart from the financial question, the difficulty is that of finding suitable editors and it is considerable: but even in these times there is still a proportion of young students who are capable and desirous of pursuing their graduate studies in the medieval field; and I cannot believe it impossible that occasional Jewish students should be stimulated into following the same path. They could not have a more obvious ground for exercising themselves in research not only to their own profit but to that of the Community. When we come to our next period — that between 1290 and 1656 — the lay-out is quite different. Apart from the *Accounts* of the House of Converts in Chancery Lane, which the work of Mr. Adler and others have made so familiar, there are for obvious reasons no series of exclusively Jewish Records made in this country. It is true, as was long ago pointed out by the first President of this Society, that in the centuries following the Expulsion there must have been a considerable penetration of Jews into England in various guises or capacities; true also that the reconstruction of single episodes in this period, such as the metamorphosis of Edward Brandon, Convert, into Edward Brampton, Knight, a prominent figure in the later fifteenth century and mixed up somehow with the affair of Perkin Warbeck, is a fascinating possibility; especially perhaps (a matter to be touched upon later) with some help from foreign sources. But it is not possible to predict for ourselves or prescribe for others specific tasks in research of this kind: they must wait on the appearance of some new fact casually revealed which starts a train of deliberate investigation. The same applies to the period immediately following the Cromwellian. The Jew in England, though still subject to disabilities, was no longer so situated that references to his activities will be found only or mainly in special classes devoted to Jewish affairs. He may appear like any of his English contemporaries in almost any type of record; that is to say not only in such series as the *State Papers* but also in all those minor Archive classes which now, as we have seen, claim almost equally the attention of historians. I had a curious example of this very recently in a casual note, in the Quarterly Report of a county archivist, of the emergence during the sorting of some exceedingly miscellaneous files of documents belonging to a certain diocese of a petition addressed to the Bishop in English and Hebrew, about 1675, by a person described as "Jacob Son of Dr. Samuel", who was or had been Clerk to Menasseh ben Israel.

It is to be observed that the time of which we are speaking is that in which certain categories of local Archives first begin to be plentiful — those of Quarter Sessions, for instance, and of the Parish (do not forget that there are about 11,000 ancient parishes in England) which were to be for the next two centuries not only legal and ecclesiastical organisations but the centre and the executive unit respectively of local government of every kind all over the country and therefore the points at which the lives of ordinary people were most likely to impinge on official records. I will not dwell on this because frankly, such discoveries as that which I instanced just now are dependent on either good luck or good indexing: and the archivist can do little to help the Jewish, or any other, historian unless and until — and I am afraid that is a far day — he has the resources for making his lists and indexes on a scale which few if any archive establishments can at present afford. The best that can be said is that the historian can himself do something to ease the situation. For its starting point — for finding as it were the point of impact of the topic in which one is interested upon any given body of archives — research of the kind we are now considering depends very largely on regional or personal connexions: and from this point of view I welcome the suggestions made, I think, by my immediate predecessor in office in a paper read some years ago in which he advocated a much increased attention to Jewish Genealogy in this country and to the history of local congregations. We must also welcome the work undertaken at various times in regard to individual Jewish personalities or to groups of them such as that which Mr. Wilfred Samuel has given us in his study of Jewish underwriters at Lloyd's; and finally and particularly we must welcome the volume on '*Anglo-Jewish Notabilities*' published for us by the Society in 1949 — an invaluable work of reference to be followed I hope, as is the way of invaluable works of reference, by many supplements. Research of this kind contrives "a double debt to pay", for not only is it interesting in itself but it furnishes tools for the opening up of other resources.

But I am anticipating a little or rather have allowed my thoughts to slide from the late seventeenth century into the more modern period upon which I had meant to dwell separately. We reach with the eighteenth and nineteenth centuries the largest and most unexplored tract of the whole vast field of English Archives. On the other hand so far as Jewish History is concerned we come back here to a state in which we have once more a certain amount of information available in categories of Archives exclusively Jewish — and Jewish this time in their compilation as well as their content; Archives which give us accordingly a specific problem to solve and, I shall submit, a specific duty to perform.

There are two major categories of such Archives. The first is that of Jewish institutional records — the Archives of synagogues, schools, charities and societies of all kinds, including certain set types of Registers, Minutes, Accounts and so forth which began now to be kept regularly and series of which may with good fortune survive for our enlightenment. Archives of the Western Synagogue, to take only one example, were extant — I am afraid we must use the past tense for many were destroyed during the War — from about 1750. The use made by Dr. Roth of those and the Archives of the United Synagogue and like material, especially in his books on the Great Synagogue and on Provincial Jewry has demonstrated how fruitful such Archives may be: and the same may be said of Dr. Lionel Barnett's '*Bevis Marks Records*' and Mr. Hyamson's '*The Sephardim of England.*' But I think those authors would agree with me that we have here exceptional cases. I believe I am right in saying that at present — apart from a few such exceptions — no one knows to what extent Archives of these classes have survived: and I hope you will not think me too much of an alarmist if I add that experience elsewhere leaves me in little doubt that this may mean considerable danger. Here then is room for much valuable work. It is archivist's rather than historian's work, because it is concerned only with safeguarding the material, not necessarily with its immediate exploitation, but it is fundamental, urgent and something that anyone historically minded may undertake with little technical training or equipment. I suggest to you that so far as the Modern Records of Jewry in England are concerned our first need (and I do not think the object should prove unattainable) is a complete Survey which shall take account of all the Jewish institutions in this country that from the eighteenth century — or the seventeenth if you will — down to the present day may have produced, or are producing, Archives. We need the Survey to go further and verify what Archives do in fact survive, where, and in what condition: and we need it to go further still if possible and list the individual pieces. Other work in connexion with such matters as repair, the elimination of what is valueless, and perhaps even custody and housing may follow. Those, however, are matters which in some cases involve questions of policy and require anyhow technical treatment — matters for the full-time archivist — and I shall therefore not attempt to deal with them here. But upon one point let us be quite clear — until we know what there is we can neither safeguard it nor use it. Such a Survey as I have suggested is of course closely related to the task of the National Register of Archives: a task (let me underline this) which would be impossible without the aid of numerous historians turned archivists. That aid, as I have indicated, is organised upon a regional basis; but there are some institutions which transcend regional divisions and of these the Jewish People is emphatically one. I should like to think that an effort by Jewish historians (who alone are competent to do it effectively) to take this first step for the safety of modern Jewish Archives in England might be integrated with our national effort to secure the safety of archives in this country as a whole.

The remarks I have just been making apply equally to the second category of modern Jewish archives to which I referred — that of Private Family and Business or Professional Archives. Indeed the need for a comprehensive Survey, as an essential first step towards practical measures for conservation, is perhaps even more urgent here; because preservation of documents of this nature depending on personal and individual considerations they are in even more danger of destruction or dispersal through carelessness or any of the other circumstances which I mentioned when speaking of the work of the British Records Association. Yet they are potentially both valuable and numerous. Dr. Roth — if I may cite him once more — in the admirable address which he entitled '*The Challenge to Jewish History*' gave very sufficient indication of the way in which Jewish personalities of importance emerged in every walk of life after the Resettlement in England. I suggest that this indication might be followed by systematic research into the possible existence still of documentary survivals from their activities and from the activities of many others, particularly those engaged in commerce or industry. The late Sir John Clapham referred on the occasion of this Society's Jubilee celebrations, to indications of Jewish material which he had found among the Archives of the Bank of England

and I notice that this has been followed by an article by an Officer of the Bank, Mr. Giuseppi. Valuable indications indeed, but how much might their value be increased if we had the private Archives of the persons concerned to supplement them. The subject is much too large for detailed treatment here, but to take only one example, the London Chamber of Commerce published some years ago a list of nearly 1,400 firms in London alone which had been in existence for more than a hundred years, including many of twice that age. I have often wondered — and the National Register of Archives, when it has time, will have to inquire — how many of those have preserved their Archives: and I add for your consideration the further speculation — how many were Jewish, and what contribution their archives, if preserved, and the archives of others like them, might make to Jewish History?

You will have perceived the point of view which, very diffidently, I am venturing to commend to your consideration. No one who has examined, as I have been doing lately, the Catalogue of and Index to the published papers of this Society which we owe to the devotion of Mr. Hyamson — and may I in passing pay my tribute to the value of that laborious piece of work, which I hope it may presently be possible to make generally available for study — no one who has realised the richness and variety of information which this one subject, the History of the Jewish people in England, has already drawn from casual approaches to the great mass of English Archives, could wish to divert into other channels any part of the energy necessary to continue the flow of such contributions to knowledge. The names of many of the writers alone including some from outside the Society — such as my own tutelary deity F.W. Maitland; my old friend Charles Sayle, expert on incunabula; and Sir John Clapham, the distinguished economist; with others still living — authorities upon subjects primarily non-Jewish, are evidence of the way in which the Jewish vein, running across other strata of Research, produces from time to time such an outcrop as that to which Maitland gave the characteristic sub-title of 'An Apostasy at Common Law'; or that which a more modern lawyer (I am sure he will not mind being bracketed with Maitland) has called Jewish Causes Célèbres. Long may the Society's publications continue to attract such contributions. On the other hand the initial safe-guarding of archives must always have a certain claim to priority over their exploitation, however great the charms of the latter: and I must (if my experience such as it has been, is to be of any service to you) insist, even at the risk of being repetitive, upon the dangers to which Jewish in common with non-Jewish archives of the types I have mentioned, are subject under modern conditions; on their potential quantity and value; and on the possibility for persons of good-will, alive to the interest and importance of historical evidences and having the essential qualifications of a knowledge of Jewish affairs, to make an invaluable contribution to the safeguarding of this part of our inheritance of historical material. The compilation and publication of such a Survey as I have indicated is, as I have said, only a first step: but that step once taken I should have little fear but that practical measures would follow where necessary: at least they would be possible; which at present they are not.

I come finally to one more of the developments — the most recent — which I mentioned in the first part of this paper: that of the International Point of View. As a rule international organisation has for me, I confess, a certain suspect quality inasmuch as it is an artificial creation rather than a natural growth: and if there is one outstanding characteristic in Archives it is that they are, as I began by saying, accumulations due to natural causes. But the Jewish people furnishes in this, as in other matters, an exceptional case. Its History and Archives in England have a double character: for while they are in one sense part of the History and Archives of this country, in another sense they are units in a whole composed of elements drawn from half the nations of the world. In stating this point of view I am, of course, saying nothing new. It is expressed — and with much more eloquence — in the very first paper (contributed by a distinguished foreign visitor) which figured in the volume brought together by the Exhibition of 1887: and you will find it exemplified in many of the articles in this Society's '*Transactions*'; where the story which has its starting point in English or Anglo-Jewish archives is supplemented or concluded from those of Portugal or Holland or Hamburg. Indeed the '*Transactions*' go further in illustration of it. For a mere glance at the titles shews Anglo-Jewish historians devoting whole articles to Jewish archives and history in Jamaica and the Canaries, Malta and Canada, Dublin, Spain and South Africa. It would seem then that the ground is already prepared for the suggestion (indeed I believe it has already been made tentatively) of a Survey in which this Society might play a prominent part and the scope of which should go far beyond what I have suggested. The first effort at international treatment of Archives produced a '*Guide International des Archives*' and the second has in contemplation a new edition of it. How necessary such work may be I can testify from my personal experiences when, during the late War, I tried to frame measures for the protection of Archives against the hazards threatened by friend or foe first in this country and then in Italy, Austria and Germany; and, as a preliminary, endeavoured to construct Lists which should answer the question put to me by the Powers with whom I had to deal, who were prone to ask, not unnaturally — Where are these Archives? I am bound to add that I found particular difficulty in respect of the Jewish items.

It is tempting to indulge the thought that parallel, or perhaps preliminary, to a new general '*Guide International*' there might be compiled, in rather more detail, a Guide to Jewish Archives all over the world; and that members of this Society might be the means of starting the movement to provide it. I hope I shall not be thought unsympathetic — I am not — to this idea if, with an eye perhaps upon my own more restricted proposition, I make the obvious remark that setting one's own house in order is the time-honoured preliminary to larger operations, but indeed the two are very closely related: it may even be found that they are inseparable.

I have spoken throughout, as I said I would, in the character of an Archivist addressing Historians. But I have gone further, for I have suggested that for those interested in Jewish History in this country, except for the earliest period, the most urgent work at present is themselves to turn archivist for the location, and if necessary conservation, of material which is essential for an orderly and systematic scheme of research and which may be, if that operation is not undertaken, not only neglected but lost. But there is one thing more that I should particularly like to say to this audience by way of conclusion. It is a thing I have said twice already, once in inaugurating the new School of Archives at our old friend, University College, and once to an international meeting at The Hague: but I should like to repeat it here.

Archives, we have seen, are the documents in the case; the things which, if properly preserved and properly used, will tell us what as a matter of fact occurred, because they are themselves part of the facts: and the archivist's business is not himself to research upon or make deductions from them but merely to preserve them in their integrity and make them accessible. His Creed, the Sanctity of Evidence: his Task, the preservation of everything, physical or moral, which is evidential in the documents committed to his charge: his Aim, without prejudice or afterthought to make available, for all who wish to know, the means of knowldge. Seen in this light the good archivist is almost as selfless a devotee of Truth as it is possible to imagine. That is a form of devotion which has been common in the world of late years. Indeed our times have witnessed the erection of its very opposite almost into a creed, certainly into a science: and upon the skilled suppression or fabrication of evidence, upon the disregard or misrepresentation of facts, has been based all that is most hateful and perverted (how hateful and how perverted I need not tell you) in the history of Europe during our lifetime. I am not, of course, presenting to you the work of the archivist as a political or social panacea. But it has importance — and if I am not wrong will have more — in modern life not only because it ministers to those who wish to undertake research, but because in its methods and its ideals the World may find one answer to the menace of the Propagandist.

The Future of Archives in England

*Presidential Address to the
Society of Archivists,
15th December, 1955.*

The present occasion (if I may be personal for a moment) comes very near to coinciding with the fiftieth anniversary of my first entry into a Record Office — into *the* Record Office, I may say; for at that time it had, I think, no competitors for the title. For me therefore it is almost inevitably an occasion either for retrospect or for anticipation; and of the two I prefer anticipation. Looking back, though it may be interesting for the looker, is apt to be boring for his audience: they have to have so much explained to them — to be reminded, for instance, that fifty years ago motor transport as a general means of conveyance for Records or other commodities not only did not exist but had not been thought of; that ordinary people (including the present witness) had seldom if ever used a telephone or thought of writing with anything except their hand and a pen;[1] and that the word 'Archives', if it had occurred to anyone to employ it, would have been dredged from the depths of a Dictionary, with perhaps a quotation from Charles Lamb or Mrs Howitt adhering to it but with little else to explain its significance. On the other hand, having spent fifty years (barring the interruptions due to a couple of Wars) almost entirely upon Record Work of one kind or another, I find it interesting to speculate upon the novelties of experience which await my successors: and they too may perhaps think it not unprofitable to look forward from the standpoint of the present (even a little from that of the past) and induce some kind of prevision of what is in store for them in future years.

What then is, in the most general terms, the question that suggests itself? I suppose it is the question whether in the future our conception of Archives, and arising from that our conception of the part Archivists are to play in the work of the world — whether these are to alter. Basically, I

---

1. The Record Office possessed, I believe, one typewriting machine, but the Secretary's official letters were written normally by his own hand or that of a clerk.

think they are not. I see from the review in '*Archives*' of a little book in 561 pages on '*Archivkunde*' recently published in Germany that a Manual of my own is "beginning to show signs of age; experience, practice and archive-theory are overtaking" it. I am to some extent consoled by observing that my book shares that disability with the work of Fruin and Casanova: but while admitting that practice and experience can hardly have failed to advance quite far (perhaps even so far as to overtake me!) in a period of over thirty years I find myself wondering whether, if what I said about Archive Theory (that is about the fundamentals of Archives and Archive-keeping) was true in 1922, it is not true still.

There are, of course, people who say in effect 'The whole position in regard to Archives — both their material character and their importance — is changing and will continue to change. Archives began with the discovery that if a sufficient number of people could read and write the bounds of administrative activity might be enormously extended by the substitution of written for oral communications: the implementing of that discovery went on for centuries and with it went the development of Archives. But now development is proceeding in the reverse direction: equipped with telephones, motor-cars and aeroplanes we are getting back to the oral, substituting it for written communication. Moreover, Writing itself, when it is used, thanks to stenography and typewriters and photographic reproduction and the rest, is quite a different thing from what it used to be. Surely all these considerations must make it necessary to revise our views about the nature and treatment of Archives?'

People who say that forget, I think, that the mere manufacture of documents is only one element in the creation of Archives: another and a much more potent one is their preservation for reference; that is to say their substitution not merely for the spoken word but for the fallible and destructible memory of the people who took part in whatever the transactions may have been that gave rise to them. *Recordari* still means, as it meant in the twelfth century, to remember. So long as memory is a necessary part of the conduct of affairs so long will it be necessary to put that memory into a material form, and so long as that is necessary so long will you have Archives; whether they take the form of writing on paper or parchment or palm-leaves by hand or that of steel tape (shall we say) engraved by mechanical means with microscopic grooves which enable you to reproduce at will the voices of men who forget or have been themselves forgotten. No one denies that the technical problems of the Archivist, and the equipment required for dealing with them, have changed, will change in our own day, and must be expected to go on changing; the steel tape will require quite different conditions for its storage and use from those appropriate to paper. But the principles on which the Archivist must base his treatment of these new problems and new materials remain, I submit, unaltered because Archives will still be, as they have always been, the Documents in the Case: requiring, before we can be sure that we have their significance correctly, a full knowledge of their administrative background, but entailing, for the Archivist, no primary duties other than those he has always had — the duties of *Conserving the Evidence* and of *Communicating it to the Student Public*; with anything in the way of special technique which the material and nature of the Evidence, and the circumstances of the Public's enquiries, may render necessary.

I may perhaps be allowed (it is indeed the main theme of my Address) to come back to this later, if only by way of peroration. For the moment I turn to a consideration in more detail of some of the changes which our own age is witnessing or which may be readily and reasonably predicted. In doing so I shall assume, if you will allow me, that you are all potentially, as many of you are in fact, so closely connected with the active conduct of affairs that you must be prepared to receive more or less regular accruals of Documents no longer required for current business: and in describing the changes which these may entail in your existing procedure and equipment shall not, for the moment, consider the question how those changes are to be effected.

The most obvious are those which are and will be resulting from the vast increase in bulk, and decrease in quality, of many of the existing classes of Archives: with which we may couple changes in the form of well-known classes (*Ledgers*, to take a sad example) which retain their old titles but not their old character; largely as a result of mechanisation. Apart from accentuating, so far as it may be considered to affect the Archivist, the importance of the all-but-insoluble problem of Elimination, these changes will induce in time, if they have not already done so, modifications in every section of your work. In the Repository there will probably be alterations in your established system of make-up, packing and racking; and there will certainly be recurrent demands for more space. In the Repairing Room new methods will be necessary to enable you not only to deal with quantities hitherto unthought of but also to defeat the menace of that sheeted sawdust which now so often passes for paper: something like the American system of lamination (mistrusted hitherto — perhaps unjustly — in this country) will certainly have to be considered — indeed it is urgent that this matter should be the subject of fresh investigation:[2] and later perhaps (who knows?) you may have to add to the qualifications of your operatives devices borrowed from the metal-worker or the cinema industry. In Search Rooms the time may not be far off when space and equipment must be

2. In this connexion the work of Mr. W.J. Barrow, of Richmond, Va., may be commended to the attention of any who have not already studied it. I am glad to hear from him that he is about to publish a book on the subject.

provided not only for the use of microphotographs but also for the examination (has not Bernard Shaw predicted it?) of pictorial and sound recordings in the shape of discs, strips and reels of strange materials; and allied to
these requirements is the immediate need for photographic equipment
which will enable all Repositories to cater in modern fashion for that
familiar (and rather tiresome) client, the 'student at a distance'. Already,
when I left the Public Record Office, the photographic Staff, though it had
been in existence for less than ten years, had swelled to the proportion of
nearly ten per cent of the total personnel.

That last remark raises in turn the whole question of the effect of modern
quantities and modern types of Document upon the policy of Publication.
Clearly the old methods of providing by means of printed Transcripts,
Calendars and so forth for the needs of the Student who could not or would
not make personal search — the method which in the case of the Public
Records has proved inadequate to deal in reasonable time even with the
relatively small survivals of medieval material[3] — must be far more insufficient when confronted with the sheer quantity of modern Archives. We are
driven more and more to look for, and content ourselves with, methods of
'making public' which will rely much less on printing; giving the Student
no more in that form (save in exceptional cases) than will enable him to
embark economically and intelligently on the task of personal examination,
with such additional aids as Photography and other mechanical devices can
now supply.

Altogether, you will say, an ambitious programme: and please do not
think I am unaware of that fact, and of the difficulties (financial ones, for
example) that must be overcome before such developments as I have
sketched can be realised, because in a short address I merely summarise
uncompromisingly the new duties and new fashions that lie ahead of you.
When I say that the same process of patient endeavour which has brought
you so far will be required to carry you so much further it is with a strong
conviction that that endeavour, and that patience, will be forthcoming.

But we are verging here upon major problems; and the first of them —
from which indeed the others all stem — is a question not merely of
numbers but of relative numbers: I mean the growing preponderance of
Modern over Ancient Archives. We are faced — you will be faced, if I am
not wrong — not only with the technical problems I have just described as
resulting from the spate of modern Documents and development of modern
techniques but with problems of policy resulting from the fact that the pro-

3. Sixty years of work and something like two hundred large volumes have not quite finished
    dealing with the medieval Enrolments and a few other classes of the Chancery; have
    barely touched the six great series of the Exchequer (not to mention important subsidi-
    aries); and have only begun on the vast Records of the Courts of Law.

portion of Modern to Ancient is constantly changing, to the disadvantage of the Ancient. The numbers of these last — though we are all doing our best to increase the tale of those known and cared for — are in a sense static, whereas those of the Modern are continually increasing: and (what is more) a like ratio is to be observed in the numbers of Students using the one or the other. When I entered the Record Office the intrusion of comparatively modern Documents from Public Departments had of course begun — it began in fact in the early nineteenth century as soon as it came to be known that there was now a place where such things could be dumped — but they were little regarded: to say that a Student was working in the Search Rooms was to assume, with only a few well-marked exceptions, that the documents to be produced to him or her were, at the latest, of the seventeenth or very early eighteenth centuries. I need hardly say that the position now is very different and since such influences as the London School of Economics and Ph.D. degrees in all the Universities began to make themselves felt the number of Students who, for their researches, choose the primrose path that is not embarrassed by the initial obstacles of Court Hand, Latin and the like has grown enormously while that of the medievalists has sensibly declined.

You may say that from the point of view of the Archivist, whose business it is (as I have myself so often insisted) to minister to the researches of others rather than to conduct, or even suggest, them himself, this tendency (however regrettable) is not a matter of great moment: but we are threatened by two other results of this unwieldy growth of Modern Archives which touch us more nearly. The first is the suggestion that the care of the Modern ought to be divorced from that of Ancient Records. This is not altogether a new idea — I heard it advocated many years ago as a solution of the housing problem of the Public Record Office — but recently it has been sometimes advanced as a serious theory of Archive Organisation; with special reference to the alarm which began to be felt at high levels (not before it was time) about the monstrous accumulations of paper in Public Departments and to the Report of Sir James Grigg's Committee on that subject recently presented to Parliament by the Chancellor of the Exchequer. Any proposals which may ensue would of course affect directly only the Public Records: but accepted theories touching the conduct of these are bound to have ultimately (it is natural and proper that they should) some repercussion at the level of Local Government; and the question is therefore one upon which all Archivists should have clear views. I ought not, within the limits which I have set myself for this Address, to attempt to influence your opinions by expression of my own: but there are two or three permissible and even desirable observations to be made which are of a factual nature. I will make them as briefly as possible.

In the first place, then, in any case where a single Authority is the natural custodian of Ancient Archives and also the regular producer of Modern ones it would almost certainly be found uneconomical to administer the two separately, because that would mean doubling staff and accommodation in certain sections. Secondly, it would be inconvenient for Students, whose period of research would frequently transcend any artificially fixed boundary between old and new. Also since presumably any Authority which adopted the plan would fix its own date for the division, and since in addition many Authorities having Archives of a like standing but not large enough to make action imperative would not adopt it at all, there would be confusion as to where Archives of certain types were to be found in any given case. A third objection, and perhaps the most serious though it is not easy to express in few words, is that the plan not only imposes upon natural accumulations of Archives purely artificial (i.e. unnatural) divisions but also involves breaches of that continuity which is one of the most precious attributes of English Administration and Archives, Central, Local and Private alike. Even if the actual breaking of long continuous series were barred there would still be a breach when modern series were separated (as could hardly be avoided) from their predecessors in function under the same Authority. Imagine (to take an obvious example) the deterioration in the Public Records as Archives of the Central Government, if the Records of the Chancery, the Privy Seal Office, the Secretaries of State and Modern Departments, successive holders of the chief executive control, were sundered. It would be almost as disastrous as lopping off a fine tree a few feet from its roots: and that remark is not merely sentimental; for in numerous cases the significance of the later Records in a long series (such as those of the Exchequer or the Justices of the Peace) can only be appreciated by a scholar who is familiar with the earlier ones in the same series, or even in a different series, out of which they have developed; nor, *per contra*, are there wanting cases where the key to what has puzzled us in the earlier is to be found in the later.

I am afraid I have rather extended myself over these points of danger: but there is a final and a very serious one which must not be omitted — the potential danger to the professional standards of the Archivist; for (to speak quite frankly) there will be a tendency (no one who has had experience of dealing with Finance Divisions over questions of Staff can doubt it) to employ for the administration of Modern Archives, if that is made a separate affair, persons of a lower educational grade, or, at least, persons not qualified by special training to act as Archivists.

That last remark brings me to one more branch — the last, I think — of what I have to say about the changes which the future may hold for you: the possibility of changes in what I must call, for lack of a better word, the set-up of the Archivist's profession. I have said much of the dangers and embarrassments arising from that modern multiplication of Archives the prospect of which — more than the prospect, the fact; for it is already in being — we all view with some dismay: but what of the multiplication of Archivists, which is (we must all agree) a consummation devoutly to be wished?

I have spoken of the danger of the un-trained Archivist: but we have to face the fact that what are in effect Archive Repositories (though they may not themselves realise it) number, if we include such items as the Church Chest, or, at the other end of a long scale, the strong-room of an Industrial or Commercial or Professional Body, many thousands; or, taking only the more important, many hundreds. What is to be the provision of Archive Service for these? In many cases they do not want, or cannot afford, or have not work for an individual Archivist: yet their Archives should certainly have the benefit of skilled organisation; and the case cannot always be met by offers on the part of larger Repositories to take over their older Documents when these are no longer wanted for current work. Even if we leave aside this awkward problem and consider only the case of the really large modern organisations which may be converted (as indeed a few have been) to the view that their establishment should include a trained Archivist we have still to consider the question how that Archivist should be trained. There is, of course, no reason that they should not have one trained to deal with Documents of all periods even though their own are purely modern: indeed it would be a very good thing both for them and for us if they did. But there will be cases — probably many cases — in which, while agreeing that their Archivist should have high educational qualifications, they will press, and not without reason, in view of the very nature of their Archives, for persons whose earlier academic training has been in Science rather than in the Humanities: and for such our present system of Graduate training for Archive work has little room. I am aware that we approach here a problem, or series of problems, of considerable difficulty: but there is no doubt that it will have to be faced. There are in fact signs already of a demand for Archivists with a knowledge of such subjects as Metallurgical Chemistry comparable to your own knowledge of Latin and History; and even a suggestion of the way in which the further requirements of such Students might be met in the tentative proposals which have been made for the setting up, parallel with the existing Diploma Courses in Librarianship and Archives, of a third intended for the training of Information Officers, especially those of large Industrial and Commercial Concerns. If a suitable measure of Archive Science were included in that training our desire that persons charged with the care of Archives of that kind should be properly qualified might be fulfilled. On the other hand it is easy to see troubles arising from the importation of such a new element into the Archivist's profession.

I must not on the present occasion attempt to deal with this complex problem in more detail: but it will arise — is arising already — and who, we may wonder, is going to set about solving it? As you know there have been in preparation, since 1943, proposals for Legislation which, among other things, would set up a National Council of Archives; and it would be an obvious and early task for such a body. But I fear we must face the fact that the prospects of our Bill are at the moment not good: and, failing the Bill, what can — what ought — to be done? The interests involved are directly interests of members of this Society: but the Society, though the progress it has made in a very short time is truly remarkable, is not as yet strong enough to shoulder by itself such a responsibility; nor is it in some respects suitable that it should do so: and indeed in securing for existing Repositories some of improvements in staff and equipment (not to mention conditions of employment) which are implicit in what I said earlier of the changes produced by the increasing bulk of modern accruals, and in exploring all kinds of technical matters such as the policy to be pursued in elimination, the possibility of common action in the Listing of Maps or Seals, and in general the establishment of stronger relations between Repository and Repository — in such tasks as these it will have for many years to come very sufficient employment. Yet the future welfare not so much of Archivists as individuals but of the Archivists' Profession is deeply concerned in the matter and I cannot conceive this Society being blind to that fact or failing in any effort it can usefully make. Moreover you have powerful allies: the National Register of Archives has also in a very short time achieved a wonderful success — greater than is generally realised — and its unofficial parent, the British Records Association, in a longer, but still remarkably brief, space of time, has carried the work of peaceful penetration for the ideas of its founders much further than they themselves ventured to hope when they founded it. If you need only take the fact, which I ventured to stress in the Catalogue of that Exhibition at Grocers' Hall to which so many of you contributed, of the creation within that same short period, without any legislative or official encouragement, of properly equipped and staffed Archive Repositories in a large majority of the Counties of England and Wales, in a considerable number of other units of Local Government (not forgetting the great Libraries) and in various Academic institutions.[4]

Twenty years ago I remember G.H. Fowler, the founder of that first County Archive organisation at Bedford which has been the model of so many others, lamenting to me that he 'had not founded a school'. I wish he could have lived to see how wrong was his prediction as to the result of his own work in his own field: but I think he would have joined me in

4. Even while I was writing this I received a letter from one of the older Universities speaking of the satisfactory development and increasing use of 'The University Department of Archives'.

projecting further extensions of that field. For I believe that if close co-operation between our Society, the Society of Practising Archivists, and the two bodies I have named, the National Register and the Records Association, can be secured (and I welcome very heartily — as the Master of the Rolls did at the Records Association's Conference — the steps that have been taken towards that end during the past year), and if those three can be reinforced by further co-operation with the great Commercial, Industrial and Professional Bodies who at present stand to a large extent outside our orbit but whose Archives engage so frequently the attention of modern Students — if that can be achieved we may go forward (with or without statutory recognition) towards a new goal: the goal of an Archive Service for this country not only complete within its present cadre but extending to all the fields in which human effort produces Records that can be used for the furtherance of human knowledge.

I have tried elsewhere to put into a few words a clear and simple conception of what it is the Archivist's public service to do: a kind of Philosophy of Archives hammered out first while I was waiting for bombs to fall on Chancery Lane in 1940. Perhaps you will allow me in concluding this Address to use the words once more though they have now seen print three times — first in a war-time article in the *Contemporary Review*, then in an Inaugural Address for the Diploma Course in Archives at University College, and last at The Hague when I used them in winding up a discussion in which speakers from various countries gave various views about the training of the Archivist. On that occasion I was told that a distinguished foreign Archivist remarked that what I had said made unnecessary what had gone before. I quote that not (please believe) because it tickled my vanity but because I believe it to be true and the words in question to be applicable to all manner of Archives, past, present and to come. I said, then, that *the Creed of the Archivist was the Sanctity of Evidence; his Task, the Preservation in the Documents committed to his charge of everything that was Evidential; his Aim, without prejudice or afterthought, to make available for all who wished to know the Means of Knowledge.* You may find better wording: but if you can adopt that Creed, accept that Task, achieve that Aim, then I may wish you, with complete confidence that the wish will come true (whatever the Archives which Fate may send you), Success in this new Profession of ours, for which you have already done so much and may do so much more; Good Fun (why not?) with Good Fortune; Good Luck and Good Hunting.

Archivists and Printers

Presidential Address delivered at the Society's Annual General Meeting at Guildhall, London, on 29th November, 1956

It happens that from several different angles — that of the Local Archae-ological Society; that of the Local Record-printing Society, which is a different if only because it is a public, not a private, body — from several angles I have been concerned lately with the same question: the question whether the institutions I have mentioned should continue the policy of printing and publishing by which they have so long been guided (in some cases for more than a century); with the further question how (supposing the answer to the first question to be 'yes') they should set about it in view of the enormously enhanced cost of printing. This financial consideration is of course the one which affects most immediately the Private Societies, who see no possibility of raising the subscriptions on which they exist in a fashion that would come anywhere near to keeping pace with the con-tinually mounting costs. But there are considerations other than the financial which (it has for some time seemed to me) are germane to any review of a century-old Publication Policy and which are of common interest to all the institutions I have named. These considerations I have recently endeavoured to summarise in a Memorandum for the information of a Committee of the Historical Manuscripts Commission; and it has seemed to me that I might do worse on the present occasion than to repeat that summary, with a few modifications, in order to look at the problem from yet one more viewpoint — that of the Professional Archivist.

Here then is the situation as I see it.

At various times during the last century and more the question has arisen of giving, so far as possible, to 'Students at a Distance' the same advantages in relation to some body or bodies of Records as those enjoyed by Students who were able to visit and use them *in situ*. In the case of the Public Records it came up, as a continuation of the policy which had produced the

imperial folios of its predecessor the Record Commission,[1] so soon as the
Record Office Act was passed in 1838;[2] in the case of the large accumulations in the hands of great Families or great Institutions, Lay and Ecclesiastical, it arose automatically with the creation of the Historical
Manuscripts Commission in 1869; in the case not of one particular category
of Archives but of one category of Students (those interested in some special
branch of Historical or Archaeological inquiry — Church History, Legal
History and, especially, Local History) it was responsible for the foundation
of dozens of Private Societies devoted to those studies; and in particular the
County Record Societies.

In every case the answer to this question of the 'Student at a Distance'
was the same — publish, print (that is to say) volumes containing texts or
elaborate 'calendars' which would practically make a visit to the Archives
concerned and their consultation in the original unnecessary. As a result
about 750 volumes have been published by the Public Record Office, 200
by the Commission and many hundreds (indeed the total must run far into
four figures) by the Private Societies. This work was made possible by two
conditions. In the first place printing was cheap: so cheap for example, that
at the cost of a subscription of no more than ten shillings a Society of no
more than 150 or 200 members could print a volume of respectable dimensions every year. Secondly, there existed in most cases a considerable body
of persons who had the necessary knowledge and the necessary leisure to
undertake the work of editing for a small fee or, more often, gratuitously.

But the enthusiasts who started these various series either did not
consider or wildly underestimated in most cases the bulk of documents to
be dealt with. The Public Record Office, after more than sixty years' work
and the production of over 200 large volumes has barely completed publication of the medieval portion only of one set of classes — the Enrolments
of the Chancery — has scarcely touched the no less important medieval
Records of the Exchequer and has no more than begun publication of the
priceless series of medieval Legal Records. Private Societies dealing with
(e.g.) Sessions Records are finding that after prolonged effort they have
made available only the Records of a few years from classes which cover
centuries; and only a few such Societies have touched this important
category of Records at all, though it exists, of course, in all Counties. The
Historical Manuscripts Commission, in spite of its 200 volumes, has

1. There were of course earlier official printings than these but they were by Special
   Committees set up for the publication of specific Records — *Domesday, the Lords' and
   Commons' Journals, the Parliament Rolls* and *State Papers.*
2. The earliest printing of Lists and Calendars by the Public Record Office was in
   Appendices to the Annual *Report of the Deputy Keeper:* this inconvenient method was discontinued in favour of the well-known series of '*Calendars*' and '*Lists and Indexes*' in the last
   quarter of last century.

attacked only a small proportion of Family Muniments of first class importance and finds itself deploring the slow progress of those it has in hand. The
more eminent accumulations of Ecclesiastical Archives (saving always the
Bishops' Registers, where the Canterbury and York Society has a comparatively finite task) offer still (as the Pilgrim Trust's Report recently demonstrated) little help by way of print to the exploration of very large survivals.

Besides realising this discouraging position of affairs those interested in
this form of public work (for it is public work, and important) are confronted by three difficulties of modern growth. The first is that the stock of
available Editors is shrinking. There may be as large a number as formerly
(in fact it is almost certainly larger) of persons who have or could acquire
the necessary competence: but the number of those who under modern
conditions can or will undertake the work as a voluntary and unpaid service
is unquestionably smaller. More serious still, in spite of doubled subscriptions the costs of printing have become or are becoming prohibitive to all
bodies save those subsidised out of public funds;[3] and even in the case of
those so favoured (the Record Office, for instance, and the Historical
Manuscripts Commission) is severely restricting possible output. Finally all
are faced with the prospect of having added to a task already beyond their
powers a demand for work upon the huge and growing mass of modern
accruals, the use of which is desired in these days of economic and social
research by a much larger number of Students than had recourse formerly
to earlier series: Ph.D. degrees, the London School of Economics and other
modern developments have worked a great change.

Any hope of a solution of these difficulties must lie, I suggest, in a review
of our opinions and policy. We must still, I submit, contemplate publication after the old fashion, but it must be upon a carefully restricted basis.
A newly discovered *Cartulary* of some Religious House whose muniments
were believed to have perished; series of Records belonging to a period for
which few other authorities exist; small survivals of important classes which
have almost entirely disappeared (such as the unique fourteenth-century
Sheriff's Roll for Bedfordshire and Buckinghamshire published by G.H.
Fowler, or the scanty remains of medieval Rolls of Justices of the Peace in a
few Counties, discovery and publication of which we owe to the energy of
Miss B.H. Putnam); Records which, once printed and indexed, would serve
unquestionably as Reference Books for Research of every kind — Documents of this calibre, but few others, would be obvious candidates for the
privilege of full publication. For the rest we have to take into account, I

---

3. Lately there has come news that some aid for struggling Societies may be forthcoming
   from Public Funds administered by the British Academy. But I think it may be assumed
   that such aid cannot be on a scale which would bring the publications of such Societies
   back permanently to anything like their earlier proportions.

submit, three great changes which have materially altered the position and the claims of the 'Student at a Distance'.

In the first place owing to the much widened scope of Research, and in particular its extension to modern Documents, the would-be Student is no longer compelled to look to the Records in a limited number of Repositories as the only sources from which he can draw material: in a large number of cases he may find it near home in the shape of modern series not formerly taken into account. More important still, he may find, again near home, Repositories now available' which were not formerly open to him: for example, though the County and other Local Repositories in England have only come into existence, or only opened their doors to Students, during the last ten or twenty years they are already dealing with a flow of Record Workers (particularly Students reading for higher degrees) which is very considerable. The same thing is being reported from places outside this country; to take only one obvious example, the Central African Archives serving the two Rhodesias and Nyasaland: and it may be safely assumed that the Dominions will to an increasing extent meet the demands of their own Students from their own National Archives.

Even if it be contended that the effect of this additional supply of Documents locally is discounted by the enormous increase in the number of Students — that the quantity of Students who need 'distant' Records, and our responsibility to make these available for them, are not materially reduced — there are still two great changes to recognise which definitely alter the situation. To begin with the Student, however distant his location in miles, can now, in almost all cases, come at any Documents he requires with an expenditure of time which (in comparison with the seriousness of the voyage twenty or thirty years ago) is negligible: and on the financial side much is now done at this stage to assist him. Secondly, if even so Mahomet still finds it difficult to come to the mountain, the mountain itself is no longer immovable: it can go to him in the shape of photographic reproductions with a speed, and in quantities, and at a price, which are truly revolutionary.

In these circumstances I think that our responsibility may reasonably be limited to making it easy by our publications for the Student to find his way direct to what will serve his purpose without undue waste of his available time, if he comes personally to the Documents, or of his available money for photographic reproductions if he chooses that method. In other words we have to contemplate, if we are to meet the situation as it now presents itself satisfactorily, a much increased publication of *Guides* and *Descriptive Lists*: we may even have to contemplate the extension of the word 'Publication'[4]

---

4. It is important to have this point quite clear. I am not proposing the sale of typed copies in lieu of printed ones and in like numbers: this unpleasing and clumsy device would do little,

to cover the preparation of some of these works in typescript and the organisation of machinery by which they can, on demand, be conveyed to individual Students in the form of photographic copies.

Two objections may be made to these conclusions. First such a change in policy as I have indicated means admittedly that we throw back upon the Student the responsibility of doing his own work: of undertaking the labour of reading his MSS. in manuscript and even (if we push this method far enough back) that of learning first to read strange scripts. We recognise that we can no longer undertake to spoon-feed him to the same extent as in the past. But a certain number of those responsible for directing Students, I know (and a considerable proportion of them, I believe), would accept the view that this would be, by and large, a good thing for the Student and therefore for Scholarship. Admittedly also we cease, except so far as is indicated in what I have said of a restricted publication of Texts and Calendars, to cater for anyone except the Student: we do not provide for the General Reader. That sounds very regrettable: but I cannot feel that in view of what we have seen of the vastness of the field and the practical impossibility of covering it in the old way this objection can be treated very seriously. Actually it is, I think, more than doubtful whether apart from the specialists, for whom we should in fact continue to cater, the publications that have been named command a very considerable reading public: and we have been careful to maintain the desirability of full publication, after the old fashion, in the case of documents uniquely important or interesting.

And now what is the moral? What is the part in all this of the Archivist? Some of you may very well say — 'There is no need to preach to us about the propriety of putting from us the temptation (and as we all know it is a temptation; and a natural one) to spend our energy in editing and publishing a few of our documents and of concentrating instead, so far as our resources allow, on the preparation of means of reference to all our charges: because that is exactly what we are doing — what in fact the limitations of our staff and of our finances compel us to do.' No one could agree more than I — there may even have been occasions when I have made myself unpopular by the vigour with which I did agree — that the primary duty of Archivists is not the publication of large volumes drawn from a few Records and it does not seem likely that staff or finances (though we must all hope for an upward tendency in both) will expand in the near future to an extent

we are told, to effect economy. What I am suggesting is that from a carefully typed exemplar of any List made and preserved for use in the Repository copies (probably in the form of micro-photographs) should be supplied to individual students on demand at something like cost price. I do not think the procedure could be applied to anything except Lists: but to have these available would enormously help, in the first stages of his research, a student who was proposing to study the Documents themselves in the form of photographs.

that will enable us to contemplate, save in exceptional cases, any change in that point of view. But that does not by any means end the matter. If, speaking in another capacity, I have been so fortunate as to secure your agreement in my summary of the present situation in regard to printed volumes, and of possible means of escape from present difficulties, may I now as a member, or ex-member, of your Profession suggest that the Archivist has here an important part to play? In the first place he has to put forward convincingly, whenever opportunity offers, to his Committee or his Council the views just propounded: perhaps even to combat occasionally a natural tendency to expend their resources in staff and money on such obvious and tangible achievements as the publication of a handsome volume to the detriment of the routine work of the Repository There is also the task of working out the means by which students in general — not merely the students of a particular region — may be made aware of the existence at this or that Repository of particular Lists and the means (microphotographic or other) by which they may gain access to them. There seems to be occasion here for the fixing of a policy — perhaps even the arrangement of joint action — by a general consultation between Archivists; and very possibly co-operation with the British Records Association or the National Register of Archives.

The mention of microphotography brings to mind another matter of considerable importance in Archive Economy at the present day — the provision of photographic equipment and the staff to work it: an essential element, in my opinion, in the solution of the problems we have been discussing. I hesitate to say that all Local Repositories should press, as a matter of urgency, for the acquisition of this equipment (if they have not got it) because such a provision is usually justified on the financial side by evidence that it will pay its way; and in some cases it would be difficult to state a probability of that with complete conviction. On the other hand it is true I believe in this case to say that supply for once creates demand (we had in fact experience of that at the Public Record Office when we started a photographic section):[5] and moreover the use of microphotography is not confined to communications with students; it has an important part to play in the exchange of Lists and Facsimiles between Repositories in cases where the interest of a document, or documentary class, transcends the ordinary regional boundaries. In any case microphotographic equipment and its use in the ways I have tried to outline are emphatically ideals to be kept in mind.

Finally I come back to those problems of the Record-publishing Societies and must say something of the possibility, and to my mind desirability, of a

---

5. Within a few years of its institution it was possible to say that the work of this Section now absorbed ten per cent of the whole staff of the Department.

much increased co-operation between them and the Archive Services now maintained by Local Authorities; in particular those of the Counties: Services which for the most part were not in existence when the Societies began their work and framed their policies.

I am not unaware of the valuable work for Local History already done since then in some, in fact I think I might say in many, cases by joint action of the Local Authority and the Local Record Society: I have every reason to remember it in the case of my own Record Society of Surrey, which has had assistance in publication not only from the County Council (on half a dozen occasions) but from at least three Boroughs.[6] But what I have in mind is a deliberate policy. Local Authorities, and particularly County Councils, have tended more and more, as we all know, in recent years to accept responsibility for the due conservation not only of their own Records and those of Quarter Sessions but of Manorial and Tithe Records and of Muniments of Title and other accumulations of Private, Family and Business Records; in a smaller, but increasing, number of instances their hospitality extends to Ecclesiastical Records — Diocesan, Parish and even Capitular Archives; and (latest development of all) they may take over the care of Records from District Probate Registries. They are thus making themselves, without the aid of any Statute, and in varying ways according to local conditions, what every enthusiast who has endeavoured since 1891 to frame a Local Record Office Act has tried to create — a chain of Provincial Repositories which should house the Archives of every kind of Public and Private Administration that has functioned locally; Archives of the most diverse provenance but interrelated (often very closely, as in the case of Parish and Quarter Sessions Records before County Councils came into existence) by the fact of regional functioning. This means that they serve as a focus for Research in Records of many kinds — in extreme (or should we say ideal?) circumstances of almost every kind outside the Public Records contemplated by the Record Office Acts: and that in turn means a very large proportion of the Documents which the private Record Societies desire to publish for the benefit of Local and other Historians.

Here then we have in any given County two bodies both interested in Record Publication, though perhaps after a fashion more carefully though out and restricted (as I have suggested) than formerly. One of them — the private Record Society — is capable still of producing a certain amount of voluntary editorial effort and has in its membership a small but useful nucleus of regular puchasers by subscription, but is unable, owing to increasing costs of printing, to publish with anything like the regularity and frequency at which they originally aimed and which subscribers (especially

---

6.   I have taken the example which came most naturally to my mind: but quite a number might of course be cited from other Counties.

if they are Libraries) are quite naturally and reasonably apt to demand. On the other hand we have the County Record Offices with their professional Archivists anxious also to undertake publication, but prevented in most cases by the fact that a limited staff has already upon its hands more work of what I have called a primary kind than is sufficient to give it ample occupation. Is it not time that this community of interest was recognised on both sides as a regular basis for planned work? that co-operation should become something more than an occasional and unpredictable piece of good fortune?

Upon that question perhaps I might cease to ride my hobby: but, as I have said, I speak at this point in two capacities; not only as an Archivist of fifty years standing but as a Publisher of Documents in the interests of Local History over a period almost equally long; so perhaps you will indulge me with a few moments more in which to make clearer at one or two points what I mean; and, still more, what I do not.

I am *not* proposing the establishment of any rigid line dividing up the field of work upon Local Records between the Repository maintained at public cost for the Conservation of such Records and the Society privately financed for the purpose of their publication. I do *not* mean that the Local Authority should be invited merely to subsidise the Society; or to finance the issue of volumes of (shall we say?) *Feet of Fines* in which it can have no more than an academic interest. I am *not* suggesting, on the other hand, that the Society should forgo the publication of such volumes from time to time when it has accumulated the necessary funds. I do *not* feel that Archivists employed by a Local Authority should be expected to spend official time upon editorial work (however important) for a Society unless such work is for some reason important also to the Authority; though it might well be (it has happened not infrequently) that if their personal interest were engaged they should offer their own skilled service, in their own time, as any one else might, either in the capacity of Editor of some particular volume or to fill an honorary office as Secretary or General Editor, with great benefit to the Society and not without advantage to themselves.

But I do suggest that there are a number of publications which it is equally to the interest of the Societies and of County and other Local Repositories to see produced; and that it is (may I say?) common sense that they should concentrate on increasing the frequency of publications of that kind by joint effort. If you ask for example I would reply immediately (to name only one) that I personally shall never feel that this matter has been placed on a proper footing till the preparation and publication of Guides to all categories of Local and Private Archives in every County — all without exception, whether they are in public custody or not[7] — has become the

7. Where they are not we have obviously a case for the assistance of volunteer workers from

accepted policy alike of Local Record Societies and Local Archive Repositories.[8] In special cases an expansion of this or that section of a Guide into a Descriptive List, or even into a Calendar or Text, may be considered worthy of printed form: but I think that in the Guides alone you have a sufficiently ambitious programme, in most Counties, for some years; and you are not to forget the case of Accruals.

I believe that if Archivists, and the Local Authorities for whom they work, in concert with their Local Record Societies (and not forgetting to keep in touch with the Historical Manuscripts Commission) can decide upon a programme of such work they may presently find that the difficulties of our time have opened the way (as difficulties sometimes do) to an actual improvement — an improvement we may hope in the quantity, certainly in the efficiency, of this form of service to Scholarship.

the Society; though I do not suggest that the services of such workers might not on occasion be useful to the Archivist even in his own Repository.

8.   Actually I must not suggest that this is an entirely new idea; for an attempt to achieve something like a series of this kind was made many years ago by the Surrey Record Society acting in co-operation with the Surrey County Council, though no formal declaration of a policy was made at the time.

Modern Archives. Some Reflections

on

T.R. Schellenberg: *Modern Archives: Principals and Techniques*
Melborne: F.W. Cheshire (1956). XV. 248

This book is the fruit of lectures and speeches delivered, and seminars held, in very varying circles — from Rotary Clubs to Royal Institutes of Public Administration and a gathering of Senior Administrative Officers of the Commonwealth — during a visit of the Author on a Fulbright Lectureship to Australia in 1954: and the National Librarian at Canberra, Mr. H.L. White, writes a commendatory Foreword. In spite of its title, which suggests a more general scope, the book is really a description of Archive Practice and Principles as they are exemplified in the National Archives at Washington and no one could be better qualified for this task than the Author, who is Director of Archive Organisation there.

Ex America semper aliquid novi: and though our Author is careful to assure us in his Preface that he does not believe American handling of modern Public Records to be necessarily better than that of other people — that it is merely different — it is difficult to escape an uneasy feeling that if the authorities of the National Archives have adopted plans different from our own in dealing with the problems familiar to us all — Elimination, Repair, Listing and the rest — it must be because they consider those plans an improvement on ours. Actually, however, a nervous European after careful study of the two procedures, as set out by Dr. Schellenberg in parallel, will come, I think, to the conclusion·that in a comforting number of cases where only questions of Technique are involved there is really not so much difference between them — only the (very interesting) variety induced by comparatively superficial causes such as climatic conditions, preponderance on one side or the other of a particular type of material or documentary form, comparative bulk, or the fuller facilities for experiment and for the employment of new equipment enjoyed (how we envy them!) by a younger generation. We may therefore concentrate in the present notice on the differences of principle which our Author sets out for us, again with European parallels and contrasts, the compilation of which must have cost him much labour.[1] Two are particularly important. The first is his thesis that the documents resulting from the activities of Public Administration should be regarded as having a different quality according as they have or have not been consigned to permanent preservation in an 'archival institution' — a view which has, it seems to me, some surprising corollaries. The second, not perhaps so explicitly stated but implied, I think, throughout, is that 'modern' Archives (what exactly constitutes modernity, especially in the case of an accumulation which in virtue of mere continuity may be said to be both old and young, is not quite clear) that modern Archives can and should be dealt with separately; on different principles from those which guide us in the treatment of ancient ones.

To take the first of these. Dr. Schellenberg emphasises his demarcation by distinguishing official documents before they have passed to permanent preservation away from their office of origin, as *Records* and after that apotheosis as *Archives*.[2] "Admittedly," he says (p. 14) "the first, or primary reason why most records are preserved is to accomplish the purpose for which they were created and accumulated:" but "they must be preserved for another reason to be archives, and this reason is a cultural one." He goes on (p. 16) to define the two separately, Archives being "those records of any public or private institution which are adjudged worthy of permanent preservation for reference and research purposes and which have been deposited or have been selected for deposit in an archival institution".

Three comments occur to me. First, we require to be quite clear what is meant by 'selection'. In a sense we may say that every document which is preserved has been subject to it at some stage (or even some stages) in its

1. So much that it was only to be expected that some inaccuracies or lack of clarity should creep in from time to time. For instance Dr. Schellenberg quotes (p. 12) in a not very literal translation Casanova's definition of Archives as "the orderly accumulation of documents which were *created* in the course of its activity by an institution or an individual and which are *preserved*" (the italics are mine) "for the accomplishment of its political, legal or cultural purposes by such an institution or individual": but on the next page this has been portmanteaued into a statement that the documents are *created* in order to accomplish the cultural purposes; which Casanova certainly neither said nor meant. To take another example — after being puzzled by the statement (p. 181) that our English conception of the Archive Group "is applicable only to dead records (past accumulations to which no more records will be added or records of dead agencies)" I was still more bewildered to find our Author (pp. 202, 203) describing at some length two Groups in the Public Record Office (*Admiralty* and *Colonial Office*) which are obviously quite alive and regularly receive accruals.
2. It is not easy to imagine with equanimity the introduction of this distinction into England; where the two words are practically synonyms and most of our Archives are preserved in Record Offices! The attribution to the present writer (p. 13) of a use of the words in 1922 in the sense now given to them by Dr. Schellenberg is of course a slip; justifying no more than a mild remonstrance.

early career when for administrative reasons it was consigned to the file as an alternative to the waste-paper basket. But that is not the sense with which we are here concerned: Dr. Schellenberg is speaking of a selection for preservation made because some one has decided that the document may have value for purposes other than those for which it was compiled. My second comment is that though at this point Dr. Schellenberg pauses for a moment[3] to say that his definition may be applied to documents accumulated by "churches, business houses, associations, and unions, and even private families" he has not, I think, considered anywhere whether such application is, as a matter of fact, feasible: and some of us in this country could assure him from experience that in many cases it is not and that large quantities of documents of some importance would be excluded by his definition from consideration as Archives.

A still more serious objection lies, for me, in the frankly arbitrary nature of this definition. Up to now definitions, in America[4] as well as Europe, have generally come as it were from within — been based simply on an analysis of the nature of documents used in administration; which is why there is no difficulty in applying them to Archives of all categories. Here we are told (pp. 15 and 16) that "the modern archivist" must "re-define archives in a manner more suited to his own requirements"; and that since "his major problem . . . is to select archives for permanent preservation . . . the element in its definition, though it may reasonably affect its treatment.

The necessity for decreasing by selection of some kind the intolerable quantity of documents accumulated by modern administration is very well known to all of us who have had the responsibility for preserving modern as well as ancient Archives, but it is known as a disagreeable necessity: disagreeable because we know also that there can be no absolutely safe criterion for Elimination. Experience in our own generation has shown that very often two equally qualified historians or economists will differ in their judgement of what must be kept or may be destroyed; and experience drawn from a knowledge of what has happened in the past establishes a strong probability that some future generation will decide that both were wrong. To make the fact that Archives have been subject to selection of this kind an essential part of Archive quality is to mask the sad conclusion that our generation is bringing Archives a long step nearer to the status of those artificial 'Collections' to which Dr. Schellenberg a little later (p. 19) assigns, in agreement with me, an inferior quality as evidence; and that in doing so it surrenders one of the most valuable Archive Characteristics —

3. It is one of the very few places in this book in which documents of these categories are mentioned at all: and the do not figure in the Index.
4. For instance that put forward by the late Charles M. Andrews which is quoted, along with my own, in the *'Third Annual Report of the Archivist of the United States'*.

their impartiality. That is a fact which, if I am right, should never be masked: on the contrary it should be continually in the mind of the Archivist: informing the manner in which he carries out, when he must, the act of selection and restraining him from that act whenever it can be avoided.

I have taken so much space in criticising one point of view which seemed to me dangerous that I must cut short anything I might say about the second — the possibility or desirability of dissociating our treatment of modern from that of ancient Archives: and besides I am not sure that I may not have exaggerated the distance to which Dr. Schellenberg is prepared to pursue this theory. I shall only suggest therefore that pushed to its logical conclusion it is like asking a botanist, or a practical gardener, to deal with a plant without reference to its roots; or trying to describe a landscape which one has seen only, in two dimensions, from the air. But I must venture to add that my own experience, extending now over a longish period of years, and over Archives of most of the major categories, has been that students who were to take charge of modern Archives were better, not worse, qualified for that task by being trained in those of earlier date.

Lest I should seem to have neglected the 'Techniques' of Dr. Schellenberg's title too much in favour of the 'Principles' let me say in conclusion, varying slightly my initial remark, that as an exposition of present practice in the largest Modern Archives in the world it is not only authoritative but of great interest to Archivists everywhere.

Archives and the Science and Study of Diplomatic

Presidential Address (not delivered)
to the Society of Archivists,
1957.

I have often — perhaps you will say quite often enough — emphasized the fact that for the Archivist anything in the nature of elaborate publication (I mean the publication of Texts or full Calendars) must come second to the less attractive but essential tasks incidental to mere conservation: that is to say the tasks of location, reception, sorting, listing, repair, make-up, and packing; followed in due course by the preparation and publication of summary Guides. (Blame my advancing years if momentarily I preach to the converted: not so long ago the converted were few; and outside our own ranks they are still not numerous.) Latterly, too, I have had occasion, both before this Society and elsewhere (for instance to the Historical MSS. Commission), to dwell on certain modern changes, developments and inventions which, in this matter of publication, are (or, as I think, should be) moving us away from the point of view of our predecessors in the nineteenth century; who did so much to start the great advance towards better conservation and wider use of records, but who could not, naturally, foresee the wonders, or horrors, of our time.

The first of these changes is the much increased knowledge we now possess of the bulk of the records which our ancestors set out so courageously to tackle, by way of imperial folios and large, stout quartos in green cloth cases, for the benefit of a personage called 'the Student at a Distance'.[1] It is merely a matter of simple arithmetic now to discern that valuable as such volumes are, and important as is the result achieved by the publication (e.g.) of the Chancery Enrolments, now (after some sixty years) nearing completion, they have failed, and had in fact no chance of success, as a solution to the problem of making available to that distant student even a reasonable selection from the most important medieval classes among the Public Records.

1. It was, I think, Sir Thomas Hardy who coined this appellation.

A second aspect of change is the discovery that difficult as is the problem I have sketched it is only a small part of one much larger if you add to the classes of ancient records in the Public Record Office of which our ancestors took cognisance those of which they did not — the previously neglected classes such as *Port Books* to the importance of which modern Economists and the students of Administrative History have introduced us. If we add further to these the Local, Private and Ecclesiastical series outside the Public Records (as we must, knowing what we now do of the close relation between the national and local, public and private, lay and ecclesiastical components in the one great body of surviving English Archives) the total to be faced becomes fantastic: and when going yet further (as again, we must) we include in the body of material to be made available substantial sections of the post-medieval its enormity literally defies description.

Nor is this all, for yet another development of our times immediately suggests itself. If the requirements and conditions of modern research have enlarged enormously the fields in which it is conducted they have also multiplied many times, with their new degrees and new collegiate foundations, the number of students engaged in it; all of them with individual needs to be satisfied in the way of material.[2]

It seems almost superfluous to add a fifth development — a very unwelcome one — to the tale: but it is painfully well known to those of us who still try to keep alive the work of the Publishing Bodies. The cost of printing has increased out of all proportion to the amount of material which we would like to print and for which, even in these hard times, we could still find competent (and unpaid) editors.

I am not maintaining that the publication of series of archives, whether out of public funds or by the efforts of Record Societies or other unofficial bodies, or by private individuals — that all this type of work should be given up as hopeless. I sincerely trust it will not. Nor am I suggesting that the Archivist, busy as he must be with his own specialized tasks, may not on occasion take an active part in such work with great profit to the work, to the student public and to himself: as President of a Record Society which is fortunate enough to have one Professional Archivist as its Honorary Secretary and another as its Honorary Editor I should be both ungrateful and unconvincing if I took any such postition. But I am saying that *for the Archivist* publication in the old grand manner has ceased to be a formula for the discharge of one recognized part of his professional duties — that of making his archives, as nearly as possible, available as well to distant student as to those who can frequent his

---

2. I have sometimes thought it might be beneficial to all concerned if we could have a short moratorium of publication and aspiring graduates be compelled to find a subject by reading a few of the hundreds of volumes of *Close Rolls, State Papers* and the rest which are already in print. But this, it seems, is not feasible.

search room. For this purpose publication by printing must cease to be a panacea. We must, to a considerable extent, turn our attention to satisfying the needs of the individual rather than any general body of readers, and must use, to attain that end, the camera[3] instead of the printing press; reserving the latter for the production of work which is unquestionably of general use for reference purposes — Lists and Guides which will enable any student to decide the classes that he may most profitably search (whether by personal inspection or through the medium of reproductions); and, in more exceptional cases, whole documents which by their nature are not merely of intrinsic interest but serve as aids to the elucidation of others.

This brings me — after, I fear, a rather long exordium — to the problem to which I thought I might venture to call your attention on the present occasion: the problem of Selection; of securing (an important, even an urgent, matter in view of those difficulties of labour and expense to which I have referred) the best possible use of our resources for Record Publication. As a whole the question is, of course, too wide to be discussed here. Indeed, its solution involves, if I am not wrong, an interchange of views between publishing bodies, and an organization of co-operative work between them, on a large scale. But there is one criterion for publication, one interest which (as it seems to me) ought to have a strong claim on the attention of all publishing bodies; and one aspect of it that I think might be of special concern to Archivists. That interest is in one word *Diplomatic* or, to give it the spelling under which it first made its bow to English scholars, *Diplomatique*. This title was given a few years ago by a member of this Society[4] to the study of documentary form in one particular category of English Archives, those of Quarter Sessions; which was a considerable extension of the original narrow sense of the term.[5] I wish to extend it yet further and to suggest that in that extended sense the study might offer an opportunity for active publishing work of a kind particularly suited to professional archivists.

I am tempted at this point to claim the privilege of age and become for a short space reminiscent and even autobiographical: because in one way and another, as apostle sometimes and sometimes as heretic, I have been a good deal mixed up with the attempts of this science of Diplomatic, during the last fifty years, to push itself in academic society in England. As a small piece of historiography the tale is not uninteresting for it covers first a general

---

3. No doubt at some future date the camera may in its turn be superseded by some other mechanical device: but for the moment microphotography offers the best means of 'publishing' to the individual student the documents which he (and perhaps no other) needs for the purpose of research.
4. Mr. J.H. Hodson in a paper published in 1951 in No. 8 of the *Bulletin of the Society of Local Archivists*.
5. As used by its early exponents it applied only to original *diplomata* issued by authority.

recognition (rather a vague recognition) of the subject as a subject, and not merely an incident[6] or an eccentricity, and then the stages in development of a new idea, that of a deliberate training of students for research in Records; which was first given practical form by Maitland at Cambridge (when he presided over that famous class of 'two faithful women and William Cunningham'), was carried on by Hubert Hall in a class held at the London School of Economics, and blossomed finally (still under Hall) into a Readership at King's College, to which the present writer succeeded. It covers also the birth of a new department of English History — that of the History of Administration; and the inception[7] and completion of Tout's great work, *Chapers in the Administrative History of Medieval England* (the first volume appeared in 1920) which was so largely responsible for that development, with all the other works on the same subject which have followed. Further, it covers a gradual realization that to be of any use to the students of archives the science of Diplomatic must be made to apply potentially to a field much wider that the first syllables of its name imply and supplemented by, or subordinated to, studies of the organization which produced the documents quite independent of their form and writing; and, if I may be personal for a moment, it covers my own conversion to the view on which I based my first lectures for the Maitland Memorial Fund at Cambridge in 1911[8] and by which I was guided in all the courses that I gave or instituted thereafter for Historians, Librarians and, finally, Archivists in London. That view, which owed much to my first teacher at the Public Record Office, C.G. Crump, and to the experience gained in compiling the work on *Court Hand* in which I was privileged to co-operate with my colleague Charles Johnson, was first formally stated in a paper read[9] to the

6. I am not, of course, suggesting that nothing of the kind had been done in this country: to name only one example, brilliant work had been done upon the form of Royal Charters and other Letters under the Great Seal by Sir Thomas Hardy in the eighteen-thirties: but neither he nor his later followers such as R.W. Eyton and J.H. Round thought of giving a special title to this section of their labours and certainly none of them thought of themselves as providing examination questions for graduates.

7. I believe I might claim to have been present at this inception, for I was presiding in the Search Room when Tout, having undertaken to review the *'Etudes de Diplomatique Anglaise'* by Eugène Déprez, came to take a look at some of the *Privy Seal* class upon which Déprez had worked. His own *Chapters*, which resulted, were intended originally to deal simply with the Privy Seal and its Records.

8. The subject assigned to me was 'Palaeography and Diplomatique' and a very distinguished Historian, who was one of the Managers of the Fund, came to see me about my plans. As he rose to go he turned to me suddenly and said, 'By the way, what is Diplomatique?' To which I replied that I did not intend to lecture about it to any great extent. The Managers were always very good in letting me work out this introductory course to a new subject on my own lines.

9. The very small but very select audience included Reginald Lane Poole, Editor of the *English Historical Review*, and his son, afterwards President of St. John's; Tout himself, I think; Charles Homer Haskins of Harvard; Bodley's Librarian, F. Madan, and my colleagues C.G. Crump and Charles Johnson.

International Congress of Historical Studies in 1913 and published two years later. In it I suggested that so far as preparation for studying records was concerned "the importance of Palaeographical Science is at present over-rated, while that of the History of Administration is dangerously undervalued," and that "the methods of the Conventional *Diplomatique* and Palaeography, invented to deal with early and sparse documents, break down when applied to the large mass of Records".

I have ventured to quote these passages, which will no doubt seem extremely commonplace to you, for that very reason: because in 1913 they were regarded in many quarters[10] as rank heresy; indeed at least one reviewer publicly mourned over me as a promising young scholar who had gone astray. Actually, of course, all I had done was to put Palaeography and Diplomatic in what seemed, and seems to me their proper place as important sections, but (so far as archives are concerned) sections only, of the larger study of Administrative History. If, however, I still say that administrative history is in general[11] all-important for elucidating the meaning of records, I would also say that no description of an administrative department (save in the case of the most modern) can be complete without a description (probably including specimens) of the forms of document it produced and the way in which they were written (including probably facsimiles).

It will be seen that I have adopted here the extension for the meaning and implication of the word 'Diplomatic' to which I referred above: but I would go further and say that in the case of a considerable number of the documentary types, early and late, with which members of this Society have to deal, we might allow the term to cover not merely the precise verbal conventions employed but the general form and arrangements of the document: for example, in *Manorial Accounts* the headings of the various sections and the order in which they occur. Indeed, in regard to many classes this is most important because of its bearing on the very interesting question of the documentary forms used in local and private administration, and the way in which, at an early date, certain conventions apparently become common in use in all or nearly all parts of the country. I was particularly struck with this when dealing with *Private Tallies* and noting the surprising way in which some hundreds of these primitive

---

10. Not in all. So great a man as Sir Frederick Pollock, for instance, I was proud to find, agreed with me, remarking aptly that "an English lawyer who is ever so little a medievalist will recognize *heredibus vel assignatis suis* or *warrantizabimus contra omnes homines* in an English charter long before a trained palaeographer who sees such an instrument for the first time and knows nothing of English conveyancing".

11. Not invariably. In the case of Common Law Records the wording of the initiating Writ governs so large a part of the procedure that administrative history and diplomatic alike consist for the moment in a knowledge of the '*Reguistrum Omnium Brevium*'.

documents, drawn from divers sources, were found to resemble each other in the minutest details of notching and writing: a similar comparative study, if it could be pursued sufficiently far and widely, of conveyancing documents locally drawn would probably produce like results, and the same might be said of sealing practices. In all these cases 'diplomatic' evidence of a sort promotes intriguing speculation in regard to the underlying administrative organization and the extent to which it may affect our evaluation of the document. I must not wander farther down a fascinating by-way but there is one more, slightly different aspect of the same subject on which I would like to touch — the adaptation of a single documentary convention to different purposes, and the effects which this may have on its form and wording. For example, most of us have had to deal at some time with the archives of Local Courts and have seen something of the possible variations in this form of Record resulting from variety of function: but a really wide study, if it could be made in a sufficient number of the Public Repositories in which regular series of these records are now to be found would produce undoubtedly many new facts and perhaps some surprises, in regard to their development and functions.[12]

This brings me at last to my main proposition which I will state very shortly. At various times I have made, and subsequently abandoned, plans for something in the nature of a corpus of information which should serve as an Introduction, or perhaps even a Formulary, for students anxious to study this or that variety of local or private archives. Lately, with the happy multiplication of County and Borough archives (and archivists) each having in charge at least some examples of all the better known categories of local and private muniments, I have wondered whether the thing is now so impossible. Would it not be very valuable, and might it not be feasible, taking one or a few of the best known categories — *Deeds* for example (down to a certain, not too late, year), *Account Rolls* of various types (not forgetting the comparatively rare and most valuable Building Accounts), early examples of *Private Correspondence, Surveys,* or perhaps some class or classes of later date, civil or ecclesiastical — to collect first from repositories information as to their holdings? Might we not envisage, once that was done, the transcription, editing and printing by co-operative effort of a sufficiently representative selection of examples in each category to serve as a Formulary of Records of that class? And might not the members of this Society thus aim to produce from their own resources over a number of years, chapter by chapter, a manual and formulary of the chief classes of Private Archives in England?

12. My own latest surprise was the account of surviving Rolls of a Wreck Court in the possession of the Abbey of Leiston in Suffolk contributed by Mr. Schofield to the volume of '*Studies*' presented to me last year.

The Problems of Nomenclature in Archives

Presidential Address to the
Society of Archivists,
27th November, 1958.

Looking back on Addresses I have been privileged to give in previous years on the occasion of your Annual General Meeting I have been wondering whether I may have been at times a thought too didactic. I hope, and on the whole believe, I have not; for even in a period of rapid development — and developments in Archive principles and practice have been, after long stagnation, very rapid in recent years in this country — even in such circumstances the remarks of one who is, in virtue of mere seniority, *echo* if not *laudator temporis acti* may have their uses: in the way of enabling or provoking members of a later generation to formulate their own conclusions on more correct lines. I am accordingly venturing in the present instance to lay before you what have been for some years my own views upon a matter which is obviously not without importance. We are all finding it necessary to talk and write in more and more detail about technical problems arising in the course of our professional work; and to do that efficiently we must clearly have, so far as possible, an agreed vocabulary of technical terms. I am not thinking here so much of the nomenclature of modern machinery: the technicalities, for example, of Microphotography (though, by the way, I believe internationally there is still some undesirable confusion between Microphotography and Photomicrography) may be left to adjust themselves to a common level without our aid, because the Archivist's is only one of the numerous professions which employ that and other photographic processes. My concern is with those technicalities which relate almost or quite exclusively to Archives: and at certain points we Archivists have not, I shall submit, attained all the community of practice which is to be desired. How far, then, and by what means is it possible to improve our professional equipment in this respect?

The convenience of uniformity, and plans to secure it, may be and have been urged from two points of view, the national and the international: let us take the second of these aspects first. Any suggestion for dealing with this *desideratum* must inevitably take the form of a proposal to publish something in the nature of an International Dictionary of Archive Terminology; and proposals of this kind are in fact not new. One was put forward at the first Committee of *Experts Archivistes* summoned about 1933 by the *Institut International de Coopération Intellectuelle*, a sub-section of the League of Nations and predecessor of the present UNESCO. On that occasion I found myself to my confusion presiding over a meeting which included Casanova from Italy, Fruin from Holland, the then *Archiviste de France*, Henri Courteault, and other distinguished continental Archivists and which had as well the active assistance of Henri Bonnet, at that time Director of I.I.C.I. and later French Ambassador at Washington. The proposal was then politely but firmly pigeon-holed; partly because a proposed *Guide International des Archives* (a volume of which subsequently appeared) was obviously enough for the moment to absorb all our energies and resources, but also I think because some of us considered that an International Dictionary of this scope was not merely an ambitious but practically an unfeasible proposition. Recently, as you will be aware, a similar proposal to that conveyed through I.I.C.I. twenty-five years ago has been put forward through UNESCO: but though our little world, the *piccolo mondo del Archivista*, is admitted very different in 1958 from what it was in 1933 I remain impenitently of the same opinion.

I had better perhaps mention in defence of my intransigence a few of the difficulties which seemed, and seem, to make any really useful work of this kind unrealisable.

(i.) *The difficulty — indeed impossibility — of finding literal translations for the technicalities of one country's Archives in the language of another.* The compiler of a Dictionary of Commercial Terms in seven languages — one lies before me as I write — may have some hope of success because a large proportion of the objects, practices, occurrences or institutions which are essential or at least familiar elements in the commercial life of one country are equally so in that of another; though even here it is surprising how often he will find that a single word in one language may have varying shades of meaning which can only be expressed by the use of several quite different words in another.[1] But difficulty in the case of Archives goes much further, because peculiarities of form in these in any given country result from the peculiarities of institutions that do not exist elsewhere; and consequently the names which distinguish them cannot be translated — they must be described and explained, often at considerable length. We discovered this even in editing

---

1. It is only fair to interpolate here that the trouble is of course far less as between the languages (French, Italian, Spanish, Portuguese) most closely connected with the Latin.

the *Guide International*,[2] which dealt as little as possible with minute detail: but in our imagined work (which, you will observe, is assuming the character and dimensions of an Encyclopaedia rather than a Dictionary or Word List) the trouble will be magnified. That brings me to a fresh point.

(ii,) *The difficulty of knowing where to stop.* Few books, it will be agreed, are more irritating than the Reference Book which is not, within clearly defined limits, complete, so that one can know what one may reasonably expect to find in it: and such, I submit, would be a Word List which because (for example) its compiler happened to be deeply versed in the peculiarities of English Legal Records (an improbable supposition, perhaps, but not impossible) should present the reader with a fine array of technical terms drawn from that source only to disappoint him when he looked for a parallel completeness of terminology peculiar to Accounting or, shall we say (to be modern), to Treaty-making. I have chosen the Legal example because, frankly, that is the field in which I have failed most egregiously to find a stopping place when I have tried to envisage such a work as we are discussing and to define its limitations from the point of view of English Archives. Even the most general, and generally, used, words and terms — 'Plea Roll', 'Writ', 'Summons', 'Court Leet' and 'Court Baron', 'Assise', 'Coroner' 'Inquest', 'Indictment', 'Nisi Prius', 'Oyer and Terminer', 'Year Book', 'Reading', 'Court Hand', and the like — will involve something much longer than translation (which in fact some of them defy) to make them intelligible to the Continental, or indeed to the non-Lawyer anywhere. Moreover, these examples touch only the fringe of the problem: but of that more, perhaps, later.

(iii.) A third difficulty, supposing the second settled, is that of *finding Editors or Compilers competent to deal with Archive technicalities as they appear in each of the major languages of Europe.* It would be a large task; for in England, and I think in other countries, there is no single work in which all that is wanted is to be found. Much probably (but the amount is dependent on the settlement of my second problem — the stopping point) would have to be culled from Legal and other specialised Dictionaries and even Treatises.[3] A certain amount is common knowledge among Archivists but nowhere else — few people, I fancy, outside our own profession (and perhaps not everyone within it) could define and explain what the English may mean when

2. I recollect the surprise of Fruin when, in discussing the Dutch draft, I ventured to say that it was no good talking to me of *Polder*, because I did not know what that word signified: also my relief on discovering that other members of our Editorial Committee were in the same shameful state of ignorance.

3. I cannot see the English Section failing to include at least the titles of the better known Writs which occur so continually in Legal Records and even outside them: but where, if we started to levy a contribution from the *'Registrum Omnium Brevium,'* should we stop?

they talk of a Roll — what, if any, resemblance a *Plea Roll* bears to a *Patent Roll* and how far either resemble a *Pipe Roll* or any of the three a *Sessions Roll*.

(iv.) Finally there is the difficulty of deciding on a *single governing or co-ordinating language* under which information internationally collected could be set out. Frankly, for the reasons already stated in another connexion, I believe this to be not so much difficult as impossible. The obvious parallel — to compare small things with great — is the vast project for an international re-edition of Ducange which has settled down at present into national compilations of material. But there is this great difference, that the Ducange material, if these national compilations can be completed and brought together, can and will take the form of a series of articles upon the words, alphabetically arranged, which form the vocabulary of a single language — *Media et infima Latinitas*. Our Archive technicalities would not fit into any such framework.

So we come back to the first of the two points of view which I mentioned, the National: the attempt to secure the greatest possible measure of uniformity in the nomenclature of English Archives and of the methods and instruments we use in dealing with them; simply for our own English convenience. I do so rather regretfully, being myself by disposition an individualist: but there are now so many of us engaged upon the task of conserving Archives — not to mention research in them — that in the general interest it is no longer possible to let everyone make his own rules and follow his own fancy even in so comparatively small a matter as this. Individuality is all very well (provided it does not take the form of eccentricity) when one person is talking or writing of an entirely new subject: but it may become a nuisance and a darkener of counsel when the person who insists upon it is only one of a number labouring in the same field from whose otherwise uniform procedure he arbitrarily dissociates himself. I am not inviting you to join me in attacking a state of wild disorder among English Archivists: such a state does not, of course, exist. But I do venture to suggest that there are not a few cases where more uniformity than appears in our practice at present would be advantageous. May I instance some of these?

There is initially of course the case of what I may call *General Nomenclature*. Are we all as careful as we might be in distinguishing by our use of them the meanings we attach to such words as *Manuscripts* and *Documents*, *Groups*, *Classes* and *Series*, *Enclosures* and *Annexures*, *Deposits* and *Transfers*? or marking a difference between natural *Accumulations* and artificial *Collections*? Are we flirting (I hope not) with Dr. Schellenberg and his arbitrary distinction between *Records* and *Archives*? I will pass lightly over this last because I have said my say about it in a review published in your *Journal*. But the other queries I have just voiced are not so unimportant as might be supposed: because these distinctions of name are, or should be, the outward and visible signs of differences of nature which are vital and which are very far still from being generally recognised; especially by the Owners or Custodians of the modern Archives of Commerce, Industry, Scientific Investigation and a host more of those large public and private activities which compile nowadays such alarmingly vast quantities of papers and have so alarmingly small an idea of what to do with them afterwards.

A small but not unimportant pendent to the above remarks is that we seem still somewhat undecided as to *the names we shall give to the printed or manuscript or typescript means of reference we provide* for Students of our Archives — the 'Lists', 'Descriptive Lists', 'Calendars',[4] 'Texts', 'Translations' and 'Editions'; the 'Inventories', the 'Summaries' and the 'Repertories'; the 'Indexes' (of more than one kind); the 'Catalogues'; and the 'Guides'. It is disconcerting for Librarians and other readers — our Consumer Public, in fact — to find two publications by two Archivists dealing in exactly the same way with two similar manuscripts labelled with different descriptions; or conversely two quite different treatments given the same label: nor is it very good for our own work. I have no more than a natural penchant for my own published interpretation of those various methods of treatment: but they are, or should be, quite distinctive and it would surely be a good thing if all English Archivists could agree to a standardised employment of them.

Then there is the case where 'Nomenclature' becomes almost identical with 'Classification' — the case of *Short Titles* or *Code References*. There are now in any large Repository so many Groups and Classes, and in particular there has been and is such a glorious flow of accessions from private and semi-public sources, that for everyone's convenience they must be given not only titles but short references consisting as a rule of letters and/or numbers distinguished in some way from the numbers assigned to individual pieces. The Public Record Office led the way in adopting such a system thirty years ago, it was advocated by Dr. Fowler in his treatise published by the County Councils Association, and most Local Repositories have, I think, adopted some plan of the kind almost from their earliest days. Here some individuality in regard to the precise form adopted has been inevitable and it has, of course, gone much too far by now for any suggestion of change. Had all Local Authorities, as the result of an Act of Parliament, started to organise Repositories at the same time an uniform system might possibly have been laid down: and though the existing variations are, no doubt,

4. An âpposite footnote is supplied as these remarks go to Press by an article in the *Times* (20 December, 1958) on the volume of Banks' Letters published by the British Museum. "It is", says the writer, 'a "calendar", which in this technical sense means a listing with a summary of the purport of each letter, together with a note of its present location," This may be an accepted, or acceptable, modern definition: but, if it is, then some hundreds of volumes published from the Public Records by the Stationery Office during the last seventy years or so have been wrongly entitled 'Calendars'.

largely superficial some occasional puzzlements would certainly have been avoided. That perhaps is of no great consequence: but there is one point more worth stressing in this connexion. These short, or code, references (their total, throughout the Local Repositories of England must now amount to a very high figure) are admirable for office purposes — for the Student demanding and the Archivist producing a document in the Search Room — but by no means so admirable as references in a publication. I still recollect the remonstrance of that great Editor, Reginald Lane Poole, when someone (I hope it was not I) wrote *E.401* as a substitute for *Public Record Office, Exchequer of Receipt, Receipt Rolls* in a footnote to an article for the '*English Historical Review*': the one, he pointed out coldly, told him a great deal, the other nothing. I adopted then and have followed ever since the rule that a code reference may be used in publication where a single class has to be cited repeatedly, but only if it is accompanied, at least on its first appearance, by the full title of the Group and Class. Archivists cannot of course enforce this rule upon Historians and Economists (a stiff-necked generation) but they may 'still' (as the Chinese history book said of Girls) 'set an example'.

I turn to another matter of rather wider scope — the question of uniformity in the use of *Terms descriptive of either the Nature or the Shape, Form, Material or other physical elements of Documents*. May I illustrate in a series of questions (it is only illustration, not an attempt at complete exposition) the kind of matters in regard to which we might with advantage, as it seems to me, have an agreed policy? Let us take first two great (I hardly know what to call them: certainly not groups or classes) — two great divisions or categories of Records very familiar to most of us: the *Manorial Records* and the *Deeds*; which in large or small quantities occur in almost every type of English Repository or Muniment Room save those whose contents are exclusively modern.

The Public Record Office (unfortunately) assembled many years ago its vast holdings of *Manorial Records* in three great 'Special Collections' under the titles of *Court Rolls, Ministers' Accounts* and *Rentals and Surveys*, and, as you know, in so far as these titles suggest uniformity either of content or origin they are extremely fallacious. Should we then in our Local Repositories be content with these descriptions? or create, at any rate for our lists, subdivisions according to the nature of the documents, the officials whose work they record or any other criterion? and if we do so distinguish varieties how far should we go? and by what titles distinguish them? and would it not be scholarly and desirable, if the policy is to be adopted, that it should be adopted by agreement in all major Repositories? or at least that where it was adopted the titles to be employed should be uniform?

The like question might be propounded in the case of those huge congeries of Documents of quite distinct kinds known collectively as *Deeds*:

and probably in the case of other documentary types of general occurrence. It will be noticed that the question of a common nomenclature is here becoming associated (as was in fact inevitable) with the larger one of a common policy in regard to the method of describing documents[5] in any form of reference work we may propose to compile for the benefit of our Students. That, though closely related, is another story: but we may perhaps have occasion to recur on it briefly in concluding this survey.

Another series of questions which occurs to me arises in connexion with certain *Named Varieties of Document* which are not peculiar to any one branch or variety of Administration but may occur in all categories of Records and at widely separated dates: to take a few at random — 'Controlment', 'Entry Book', 'Register', 'Journal' (which has at least three meanings), 'Ledger' (which has certainly two), 'Day Book', 'Cartulary', 'Minutes', 'Enrolment', 'File'. Your own experience in County, Borough, Ecclesiastical and Private Muniments will readily add many others. Can we say that we have mastered, and express in our own practice, the correct and exact significance of each of these? that we are in a position, without danger of misleading our readers, to apply any one of these names to a document even when the original writer did not put it into a heading or the contemporary binder letter it on the back of a volume? ('The back of a volume', by the way, has two possible meanings.)

Then there is the question of the *Varieties of Materials and Make-up* in Archives. Can we, and do we, name these correctly? or are we liable (for instance) to refer to a Casing (or even a modern version of the File) as 'Bound'? Do we distinguish (a very difficult task, by the way, at times) Vellum from Parchment? Have we accepted, and do we use, the Public Record Office system of names (the only complete one, I think, in print at present)[6] for the varieties of Seals and their attachments? or persist in the employment of a French terminology? or perhaps (but here I am trespassing again on another field) cut the difficulty by doing nothing? Are we very clear about the terminology of Maps, Plans and Elevations?

As I read through my draft for this Address I was assailed more than once by the fear that since I began with the case for and against any scheme for an International Word List of Archive Technicalities you might be disappointed to find that I did not go on to propose, or repel, the suggestion that some active steps might be taken for the publication of such a

---

5. A common scheme for the description of *Deeds* was in fact recommended in a brochure published some years ago by the British Records Association: which even went so far as to make available for its members stocks of printed Index Cards of approved pattern. Unfortunately the mischances of War destroyed the stocks and stopped any operation of the Scheme.

6. The proposed brochure on Seals to be prepared for the British Records Association may of course qualify this.

work upon a purely national basis. Perhaps, too, you might be finding my insistence on a number of small points of regularity or irregularity a little trivial; hardly worthy of the occasion. Apart from the fact that some of the difficulties I have formulated in connexion with any international scheme (though not the greatest — that of language) must apply also in the case of a national one, and therefore need not be re-stated, my reply to the first of those misgivings on my own part, or criticisms on yours, is that we cannot set out to list the technical words and phrases commonly employed by English Archivists until they are commonly employed. As to the triviality of little matters — yes, they are trivial: but it is often the small and apparently unimportant points which, when it comes to the test of practice, give most trouble. "It is the trifles that will wreck you at the harbor mouth". Moreover, a number of small things may on occasion combine to make a large one: and for me at least, as I wrote down that succession of trivialities certain larger conclusions, certain principles, seemed to emerge, directly or by inference, more clearly than before. May I try to embody two of them?

In the first place we need, as it seems to me, not so much a set of rules (which might attain gigantic proportions and still be incomplete or subject to too many exceptions) as some principle, if we can isolate it, upon which rules may be framed: by which every Archivist may be guided in the giving of names or titles to his Archives, to the elements composing them, and even to the means and methods he employs in dealing with them.

That gives us three divisions of the subject. In the first case, that of *Titles for Series or Classes or Categories of Records*, it is comparatively easy, I think, to plan our Archivist's course. If the persons who compiled the Archives in question gave them a title, that title (if we are to avoid hopeless confusion) they must continue to bear. It is true that this may occasionally put the modern Archivist in the awkward position of having to apply in one case a title which elsewhere he uses in a totally different sense — as when (for example) contemporary or at least early and accepted usage insists on a particular *Cartulary* being called a *Ledger*;[7] or the Clerks in two Dioceses give different titles to exactly parallel sets of Registers; or the Master of a Ship refers to his *Log* as a *Journal* regardless of the fact that the super-cargo would appropriate that name to a quite different type of Record. The conscientious Archivist can only, in such cases, have recourse to explanatory annotation. Where the compilers of his series have left no trace of what their own practice was he will have done his best, and will leave no ground for criticism, if he chooses with care for their Records a nomenclature which they themselves might have employed — one for which there is contem-

---

7.   I am citing here an actual case — that of the great Chertsey Cartulary in the Public Record Office; where the use of the word *Leiger* provokes interesting speculations as to the derivation of the word, upon which 'N.E.D.' is conclusive.

porary evidence or precedent. When even this resource fails him (as happens not infrequently after the close of the medieval period, when Archives begin to present themselves in the form of masses of loose papers) all we can do is to bid him choose names — *In-Letters, Out-Letters, Accounts* — which arise naturally from the character of the documents and include no technicality (such as *Entry Book* or *Register* or *File*) if he is not satisfied that its significance cannot be questioned. Finally, the old repairing rule replies even to intitulation — the Archivist must make it clear what he has done: if it is he, not the Record itself, that has supplied its title the fact must be made manifest.

Turning to what I have called the *Elements composing Documents* — not the documents themselves but their Form, Materials, Writing and the like — we shall find ourselves perhaps deriving less assistance from the practice of our ancestors; for the simple reason that it sometimes did not occur to our ancestors to give them distinctive names: ink (for example) was ink, whether it was what we should describe as a true ink — a liquid which stains the fibres of paper or parchment — or a mixture containing gum and carbon and making a surface deposit. If I may venture to use in illustration of the difficulty, which seems to confront us here two cases in which I have myself stood god-father to certain of these documentary 'elements', the question of a nomenclature for the hand-writings used in English Records of the fifteenth and early sixteenth centuries gave no difficulty: for every one of the nine distinct hands which occur I had a name for which there was good contemporary warrant as well as for the collective title which grouped six of them as 'Court Hands'. But when I sought to describe the varieties of Seal and Seal Attachment in the same period I found as a rule no evidence of any contemporary nomenclature at all; or if I did (as when, for example, I was charmed by discovering that a seal-tag was a *pendiculum* it was only to find soon after some other contemporary calling the same thing by another name, my *pendiculum* becoming a *label* or *lambeau*. The seal nomenclature which I have proposed in the Record Office *'Guide'* is in consequence frankly modern;[8] though, as in the case of modern documents mentioned above, it may claim, I hope and believe, to be based strictly on the nature of the materials or the method of their employment; not on any personal fancy.

---

8 It is an enlargement of suggestions made many years ago in the Report of a Committee of the Anglo-American Conference of Historians which was published in the first number of the *'Bulletin'* of the Institute of Historical Research. The same Report, and another published in No. 7 of the *'Bulletin'*, also defined some, though not all, of the different forms which, as I have suggested above, may be taken by printed or manuscript compilations serving as means of reference to Records. These Reports have not, I think, received as much attention as they deserve.

The conclusion implicit in that last sentence is that failing any aid from precedent the Archivist will not go wrong if he bases his practice in nomenclature as strictly as possible on the nature of his documents or of their materials, or, we may add (not to omit my third division), of the means and methods he employs in dealing with them; and it seems, when one puts it into words, so simple, so obvious, that I almost hesitate to propound it to you as the principle for which we have been looking. Yet does it not in fact furnish us with all we need? giving us a simple but a secure (because natural) foundation on which to base any detailed rules that we may find it necessary to draw up from time to time to meet the special cases which occur in the course of our work? Perhaps we may best estimate what it covers by noting what it excludes. It rules out absolutely what I may call the external approach to Archives — the arbitrary naming or description of documents or documentary classes or materials (and with naming go only too often classification, handling and treatment) not with the object of expressing what is in them but in order to suit the convenience of some specially vocal section of the student public, or to support a theory, or just to save trouble, or perhaps even (worst of all) simply to be modern and different. Can you not all from your own experience or your knowledge of Archive History think of cases where one or other of these things has, in Agarde's phrase, brought rack to Records? I can think of plenty.

I am conscious that I may here have expressed ill something which I feel very strongly — the attitude of mind which in my view should distinguish the Archivist, whose position in regard to his charges is stable, from the Exploiters of Archives (I mean nothing derogatory by that phrase) whose point of view changes, of necessity, from generation to generation, and even from School to School. But I must not enlarge further on that tempting theme; for I have one more conclusion to offer for your consideration.

The general situation of Archives in England, as it stands at present, has been reached by almost imperceptible stages in a curious but typically English fashion. The Central Government has resisted for seventy years or more all suggestions that it should pay from public funds for the conservation of any Archives except its own or enforce that duty upon other bodies by legislation. But actually by what can best be described as a process of peaceful penetration Local Authorities have gradually been converted to the view that it should be one of their functions not only to conserve in an approved fashion the Archives accumulated as a result of their own and their predecessors' activities but to provide also accommodation and care side by side with these for other categories of Local Archives (Public and semi-Public, even Ecclesiastical and Private) which may be regarded as regionally or administratively related to them. I must apologise if, for convenience, I have ventured in those few lines to summarise a piece of English Administrative History which is very well known to you and add that the same forces which have brought about that development have created a new Profession in this country — your own Profession, that of the trained Archivist. The point I wished to reach is that the adoption, now almost unanimous, by Local Authorities of this new attitude to Archives has produced (or should produce) a change not perhaps quite so widely recognised in the point of view from which we look at these new Local Repositories and at the various categories of Archives preserved in them. *De jure* the Repositories are all independent institutions and the Quarter Sessions or County Council or Diocesan or other categories of Archives which they contain independent and individual accumulations: nor am I suggesting that this independence and individuality have been or (failing some future legislative rearrangement) will be surrendered. But *de facto* the Repositories are units in what is, though not officially provided, sanctioned or controlled, a single piece of national organisation for the care of Local Archives: and the Archives of any given category — Quarter Sessions or Diocesan or what you will — preserved in any one Repository to be regarded similarly as one unit in the whole body of Archives of that category distributed in Repositories all over the country.

You will see of course why I have laboured to emphasise the new point of view which, as it seems to me, may properly be taken at the stage we have now reached[9] in the perfection of a national system of Local Archive Conservation; and its relation to all that I have been saying about the desirability of an increased uniformity in our treatment of Local Archives. While the Records of Quarter Sessions preserved at Chichester or Taunton were still regarded as Records of Sussex and Somerset — only that and nothing more — the case for an agreed treatment of them in the matter of nomenclature, or anything else, might possibly be regarded as weak: let Taunton and Chichester settle these matters for themselves, individually. But suppose these Records and their brethren from all the other County and Borough Repositories all brought together as a single group — could any diversity of treatment then be defended[10]? And have we not reached a point when they and other great categories similarly distributed may be morally though not physically unified?

So to the last question of all. If a greater uniformity of practice as between our now numerous Local Repositories is to be attempted how are we to set about it? How is the problem to be approached; the various initial steps — careful, tentative and above all not too ambitious — to be planned?

9. 'Reached' is perhaps the wrong word if it suggests that this stage or state has been deliberately worked out by any person or authority. It has not of course: like Topsy it has not been made — it has growed.
10. There was actually a scheme at one time for assembling them all in the Public Record Office.

the information as to existing rules or practices to be collected? There are various interested bodies whose co-operation and advice may be sought (notably the British Records Association and the Historical MSS. Commission) but in the absence of any external controlling Authority who is to start the movement from within?

Seals in Administration

A PLEA FOR SYSTEMATIC STUDY.

By the wording of the title I have chosen for this brief contribution to the volume of articles offered to an old friend and honoured colleague I have suggested that in my view there is something not altogether satisfactory, something incomplete, in the present state of Sigillographic Studies. That is not because I am unaware that in my own and other Countries there has by now been published a very large quantity of books, articles and notes dealing with some point, or some series of points, of sigillographic interest: in England alone the number of such studies, large and small, must reach far into four figures. Nor is it because I wish to call the attention of the new President of the International Council for Archives to the fact that this subject has not as yet commended itself for discussion at a Meeting of that body. Actually, though I think such a discussion could undoubtedly be made entertaining, and might possibly elicit from certain Countries information which (in England at any rate) is at present lacking, I do not think there is much hope of any active intervention at an international level which could be productive of useful results. Any attempt, for example, at a complete Bibliography[1] of the subject would involve the organisation of co-operative work by a band of experts drawn from many Countries; and even if this could be achieved the resultant compilation, however narrowly restricted its description of individual titles, however carefully classified its contents, would be so large that its sheer bulk would discourage consultation.

1. Madame Tourneur Nicodème published many years ago a Bibliography international in scope and has in hand, I understand, a much enlarged revision which will doubtless be of great value; but such a work must of necessity be a selection, reflecting to some extent the personality of the compiler; and I submit that anything in the nature of a selection is work for an individual scholar rather than an international body.

What I shall try to do in the present short note is to present afresh for the reader's consideration one or two points of view in regard to Seals[2] — angles of approach to their study — the possibility of which I have already ventured to emphasise in a recent publication[3] and which are, I think, for many Students new ones. Should this by good fortune elicit information about the extent to which study along these lines has gone, or might go, in other Countries it will be both interesting and instructive. Since the points of view I am to advocate are pre-eminently those of the Archivist they may perhaps make some modest appeal also to the attention of members of that profession; now becoming a considerable body in most Countries.

The numerous published studies to which I have referred, apart from certain large and well known works of a more general character[4], have usually followed one or other of certain well recognized lines. Their writers' interest, for example, may have been *Iconographic*; or, stretching that word a little, may have covered the conventional rendering of the achievements or characteristics not only of Saints but of Sovereigns, Popes, Lords, Knights, Ladies, Bishops and other less important *Dignitaries* or *Officials*[5]; or concern with the conventions and subject matter of the Devices on Seals may have carried them into less frequented fields of research such to name only two, as the representation (not uncommon in England in the later medieval period) of *Topographical* features in the Common *Seals of Towns*[6] and (an unexpected but remarkably successful quest carried out some years ago)[7] that of *Ships* and their rigging. Another interest, largely followed at the present time[8], is the *Heraldic*; Seals being, until the beginning of recorded *Visitations* by Heralds in the sixteenth century, a main source of information on this subject. Then there are the articles, or books, dealing in detail (owing to their extreme rarity or beauty) with some particular *form*[9], or

2. The word Seal is used in English either for an impression in wax or other soft material or for the matrix which makes it. I use it in the sense of impression throughout.
3. *A Guide to Seals in the Public Record Office*: 1954.
4. To name only two — Douët D'Arc's *Collections de Sceaux* (1863) and the British Museum's *Catalogue*, compiled by W. de Gray Birch (1882 and later).
5. For a few examples, the late Sir William St. John Hope's articles on the Seals of *English Bishops, Archdeacons* and *Kings of Arms and Heralds* and of course A. B. and Allan Wyon's *Great Seals of England* (1887); Mr. Hunter Blair's work on *Durham Seals* in *Archaeologia Aeliana* over a number of years; and (if I may mention one of my own) my *Great Seals Deputed* in *Archaeologia*, LXXXV.
6. For example St. John Hope again on *Municipal Seals of England and Wales*.
7. See the *Catalogue* compiled (1938) for the Maritime Museum by the late Prof. H.H. Brindley.
8. Especially the compilations now being made for a new edition of J.W. Papworth's *Ordinary of British Armorials* by the Richmond Herald (Mr. Anthony Wagner) and others.
9. For instance, Prof. Pietro Sella's *Le Bolle d'oro dell'Archivio Vaticano* (1934).

some very notable *catena or collection of Seals*[10], or with an *individual discovery* of an impression embodying some novel and remarkable feature[11]; and we must add to these the much more numerous published notes upon impressions not intrinsically so important but again unique (uniqueness is a common feature in seal survivals) and valuable to Topographers and Local Historians on account of the person or institution to whom some particular seal matrix belonged. Finally I must not omit to mention the work of Scholars interested not so much in the impressions in wax or other materials of which we have been speaking as in the much less numerous survivals of the matrices, large and small, from which the impressions were made — from finger-rings to the heavy twin lumps of silver, six inches wide, that constitute a Great Seal — and in the Craftsmen who produced them. This last is a particularly difficult field of research (that is part of its charm) because of the scattered nature of its evidences either in the form of material survivals[12] or of written descriptions (which lurk in the most unexpected places)[13] especially during the early medieval period: and even later, when our best authorities (Accounting Records)[14] begin to be more communicative, we are faced by the difficulty that most of these are, and owing to their immense volume must remain, unpublished and unindexed[15].

10. For a single example, the thirty-six fine Armorial Seals on a Ratification by the three Estates of France of the Treaty of Etaples (1492) and those on other French Ratifications of the same (see the *Catalogue* of an Exhibition of Treaties at the Public Record Office in 1948). The English Ratification, in the Archives Nationales, carries only the Great Seal; an interesting procedural contrast.
11. For example the unique impression of what is apparently a Privy Signet of Charles I on a letter to the Pope discovered by the late Mons. Angelo Mercati in the Vatican — a most intriguing find.
12. A surprising number of medieval matrices are still in use by Colleges, Towns and other corporate bodies; for example those given by William of Wykeham to his foundations at Oxford and Winchester and the fifteenth century double-sided seal of Colchester. On the other hand, I know of practically no survival of matrices out of all the hundreds of Royal Seals (Great Seal, Departmental Seals, Privy Seals and Signets) of which we have surviving impressions.
13. I owe to the kindness of Miss Rose Graham two recent notes of elaborate medieval description of Seals in unlikely places — the *Registers* of Archbishops of York and of Canterbury in the thirteenth or early fourteenth century.
14. The corrected ascription (which I owe to the kindness of Prof. Pietro Sella) of the golden *bulla* (formerly attributed to Cellini) on the Papal Confirmation of the title of *Fidei Defensor* to Henry VIII was based on a record of payment for a *piombo d'oro* to Lautizio di Meo de'Rotelli.
15. The Public Record Office *Calendars* of Treasury Books are a happy exception: they furnish much detail concerning Royal Seals of various kinds made about the end of the seventeenth century by the Roettier family and others. See my article on the Great Seal of James II in *Antiquaries Journal*, XXIII.

I hope that the comparative length at which I have described (though only in summary) the variety of interests which Seals have aroused in Antiquaries in this and other Countries may acquit me of any failure to appreciate the value of such studies and serve as a sufficient *exordium* to what I have to say in the way of comment upon them as a whole. In a sense I have already made this comment by ascribing them to the enthusiasm of Antiquaries rather than Historians or Archivists: but to put it in another way Seals have been, I think, too exclusively treated as Museum specimens — isolated (though numerous) examples of medieval design and decoration, or of the engraver's craft, evidence of heraldic developments, or interesting curiosities connected with particular persons or places — rather than what they primarily are (and what they were in the view of the persons who used them): an essential part of the document to which they were attached and of the administrative machinery which gave that document birth. I do not of course mean that this connexion of Seals with various classes of institutions and officials or other individuals has entirely escaped notice: actually it provides the easiest and most generally used framework for their classification in catalogues[16]. But its effect upon their significance and comparative importance has, I suggest, been too often missed. In the days (and these words cover more than five centuries of European history) when, although writing was being used with increasing frequency for the conduct of affairs at all levels, the vast proportion of the persons concerned could not, or at any rate, did not, themselves write — in those days and in those conditions the Seal was the only means of authenticating a written order or communication; and the person who had custody of the matrix that produced it (if, as frequently occurred, this was not the actual owner) held in consequence a position of primary executive importance and power.

I will venture to illustrate this by tracing very briefly the descent, entirely through Seals and their custodians, of executive power in the Central Government of this Country. It has by now become something of a commonplace among English Historians, largely as a result of the work of the late Professor Tout[17] and one or two others during the last thirty-five years; but it is not perhaps quite so familiar to readers abroad. We start (eleventh and twelfth centuries) with a period in which the Great Seal was apparently

16. For example in the British Museum *Catalogue* and, still more, the Public Record Office *Guide* already cited.
17. *Chapters in the Administrative History of Medieval England* (1920 and later). I should cite also the late Sir Henry Maxwell Lyte's *Historical Notes on the Use of the Great Seal* (1926).

the only one[18] used by the Sovereign for all purposes, from the domestic to the political; and its Keeper — the Chancellor — was the Member of the Royal *Curia* who controlled executive functions. When (thirteenth century) the business and staff of this Official grew so large that it could no longer follow the King there came into existence a smaller Seal — the Privy Seal — with a *Custos* who was a member of that more intimate section of the Royal *entourage*, the Household: to this passed some of the actual executive work — notably that of Foreign Affairs and also purely Household matters — together with the task of activating by Warrants the Great Seal. When the Privy Seal in turn became as the Great Seal had done departmentalised like considerations produced again a similar result — a yet smaller Seal, the Signet. At first there seem to have been several, finger-rings probably, and definitely controlled personally by the Monarch[19], but soon he same tale is told — we find an Official Signet, in the custody of a Secretary, drawn from the inner circle, this time, of the Household, taking over certain direct controls and activities and having the task of activating the Privy Seal as the Privy Seal activated the Great Seal. It is difficult to know how much was carried out under the Signet independently of the routine duty last named at any given moment because no record of its activities was kept (or has survived), at any rate for its earliest period, and we depend for information on casual and rare survivals of originals in Local and Private or even Foreign Archives[20]; which gives special value to such *trouvailles* when they occur: but at some dates (during the War of the Roses for example) this independent use of the Signet was almost certainly greater than has commonly been supposed and unexpected finds might easily modify or correct accepted historical views derived from older and more formal sources.

Seal (and Administrative) History subsequent to the emergence of the Signet went on new lines; for when it became in turn departmentalised the Secretary (or Secretaries), elevated under the Tudors to something like the modern position and powers of Secretaries of State, while retaining control over the Signet Office, established a separate Office and separate Seal. Following this comes a period during which the Sovereign had and on occasions undoubtedly made importance use[21] of yet another Seal, the Privy

---

18. As early as the twelfth century there was a second Great Seal. Later it became the Seal of the Exchequer, the earliest of numerous deputed or departmental Great Seals; but in the beginning it was simply a duplicate made for convenience. It still exists in the nominal custody of the Chancellor of the Exchequer, who is in origin the Chancellor's Deputy for that purpose.

19. Richard II had at least two in use at the same time; another impression of one of these was recently discovered on a letter in the Archives Nationales a valuable clue.

20. A very revealing sequence of letters from Henry VIII to the Pope sealed with the Signet has been noted in the Vatican Archives.

21. The letter of Charles I to the Pope mentioned above is a good example.

Signet; of which much still remains to be learned. Down to our own time Secretaries of State have continued to take office by receiving from the Sovereign three Seals of different sizes; two representing historically those of their two Offices and the third, there is little doubt, the Privy Signet, departmentalised at some period like its predecessors.

I have given these developments of the Royal Seals so much of my space not only because they illustrate clearly the importance attached to the actual custody of Seal Matrices[22] but for two other reasons as well. First, they exemplify admirably certain natural developments which undoubtedly occurred also in other great establishments[23], both civil and ecclesiastical, though at present these have been little traced — are calling in fact for research. Secondly, they demonstrate the importance which may attach to the recording not only of one but of all known examples of a Seal even when it has not any of the obvious qualifications of beauty or rarity to commend it: at any moment the discovery not of one but of a score of examples of the use of — say — the Signet by a Tudor Sovereign[24] may throw a new light on procedure and make possible far-reaching historical inferences; and this leads me to a final remark concerning unimportant Seals.

It is becoming abundantly clear from casually occurring examples[25] that from early in the thirteenth century onwards a much larger section of the population than had hitherto been supposed felt it desirable (though one would have said they had very little occasion for writing in the conduct of their affairs) to possess the means of authenticating documents. What contribution this may make to the working out of a not unimportant

22. It is to be observed that the eclipse of the Great Seal, which has come near to (but not reached) totality in our own day, continued to be partial only for a longer time than the activities of Privy Seal and Signet might lead us to suppose. James II when, in his flight in 1688, he threw the matrices into the Thames was apparently confident that he could thereby paralyse public administration. See the article cited above.

23. The use of both Great Seal and Privy Seal (or *Secretum*) by great Lords and others was apparently a common piece of organisation at an early date. On the *Barons' Letter to the Pope* (1301) in the Public Record Office both types figure and earlier examples than that are not uncommon in Ecclesiastical as well as Lay Administration. Where the Great Seal is single-sided the *Secretum* (kept probably by a second Official) is commonly used as a Counter Seal.

24. An interesting series of impressions of the Signet of Mary came to light recently in an accumulation of Private Archives (the *Losely MSS.*) in a Local Repository. Those of Henry VIII in the Vatican have been already mentioned.

25. A striking example — the Seals (all different) of some fifty very humble persons, Burgesses of two small towns in Lincolnshire in the early thirteenth century — is reproduced in the *Guide to Seals in the Public Record Office*. An almost equally large number of *Free Tenants*, including three Women, engaged in resisting an Inclosure of Common Land on a Middlesex Manor in 1316, appended their Seals to a document now in the Middlesex County Record Office. (See the *Catalogue* of an Exhibition organised by the British Records Association in 1955).

matter, the character and social standing and ideas of the little people —
our own opposite numbers, we might say — in the past, is a question which
can only be solved by the synthesis of a large quantity of accumulated
instances. But that, as well as some of the considerations mentioned above,
points to the necessity (and this is where the Archivist's point of view
becomes prominent) of recording, when the cataloguing of documents is in
progress, at least the existence of all survivals, even the most fragmentary,
of Seals; not only those which seem to the Cataloguer worth while on
iconographic or other grounds, but *all*. The difference which this method
may make was startlingly illustrated by recent experience at the Public
Record Office; when a recension of the Seals in a rich seal-bearing class
(one of the series of *Ancient Deeds*) showed that out of the first thousand
documents only 31 seals had been noted by so good an Antiquary as the
late Sir William St. John Hope, whereas the total number now catalogued
was over 600.

I have referred repeatedly in the present note to practice in this Country
and have drawn my few illustrations largely from English sources: and
undoubtedly the development of Seal practice with us had elements which
were peculiar to our nation owing (among other things) to the very slight
use made here, as compared, for example, with France, Italy or Spain, of
the services of Notaries Public. *Tabellionum usus*, said a Legatine
Constitution in 1237, prescribing the use of Seals by English Ecclesiastics,
in Anglia non habetur. On the other hand I am conscious that many
peculiarities of usage and practice as well as of design and convention, in
our Seals may be parallel to, even associated with, like developments in
other Countries and particularly in France. But the possibility of
comparison will come only when the Cataloguing of Seals has been taken
up much more seriously in this Country, and I think in some others, and
the synthesis of results of which I have spoken achieved first at a national
level. That, however, is in itself an end much to be desired.

Roots

Presidential Address to the
Society of Archivists,
7th December 1960.

INTRODUCTORY

In trying to explain to lay Audiences what Archives are, and why it is important for them (the lay Audiences) that Archives should be preserved, and how it comes that their preservation demands knowledge and conditions different from those required for the preservation of other important things, I have (several times, I am afraid) used the similitude of Trees: pointing out the comparative obviousness of the beauty or use of boughs, leaves, flowers and fruit, all of them visible things, and *per contra* their absolute dependence on the roots, which are not visible nor, in many people's estimation, beautiful or usable. Not perhaps a very profound observation and anyhow I honestly did not propose to labour it on the present occasion; partly because I *have* used it before and partly because I am *not* addressing a lay Audience. But as I grow older, and reflect with the addition of more and more years of experience, and some occasional side glancing at modern doubts and difficulties, I become more and more convinced that the apparent complexity of our jack-of-all-trades profession, with its jumbled elements of History, Palaeography and Mycology, Heraldry and Photography, Medieval Latin, Law and Architecture, Bookkeeping by Double Entry and Book-binding by reputable methods, and an increasing number of other and stranger Crafts and Sciences, can still be resolved quite simply if we attach ourselves firmly to a few primary and unchanging essentials — Root Origins and Root Principles — and let them decide finally what the Archivist may and may not do. I have also seemed to note recently signs here and there that attention to fundamental principles is not invariably fashionable just now. Pondering these things I thought I would like at one more of these Meetings, at which you are good enough to let me give my Presidential hobby-horses an airing, to indulge in some random illustrations of these changes of attitude and of my own impenitent conservatism in regard to them.

DEFINITIONS: OLD AND NEW

Forty years ago, then, I ventured to propound a Definition of Archives or Records: partly because no one else seemed to have thought of doing so, at any rate in England, and partly because I was lecturing to the newly founded School of Librarianship at University College and needed one. (This was, of course, before the days of County Record Offices and Archivists: indeed the word Archives itself was rarely used in this country.) In defence of this act of audacity let me add that I was fortified by discussions with the colleague, C.G. Crump, under whom I first worked at the Record Office: one of many debts which I owe to a very good friend and fine scholar. Now, in 1960, I still believe that the Essentials and First Principles of which I have spoken are expressed or inherent in that Definition: with its insistence on *Natural Accumulation* (as opposed to artificial Collection), *Administrative Basis, Preservation primarily for Office Reference* and *Custody*; and on the *Applicability of this Definition to Documents of all kinds and dates*. For its phraseology I hold no particular brief: alter it if and as you will, provided those five elements remain.

This brings me to the first point upon which I had it in mind to comment — the appearance from time to time of that form of heresy which would offer us not merely a new but an *Artificial and Arbitrary Definition*: one based not on analysis of the thing defined but on such external considerations as convenience, or documentary form, or age. Do you think it unnecessary to dwell on so obvious an error? I cannot share that optimism. Have we not had within the last few years a prominent Archivist propounding in so many words the view that "the modern archivist" needs "to re-define archives in a manner more suited to his own requirements": and has anyone thought what will be the result if Archivists in different countries, accepting Dr. Schellenberg's dictum that "the definition may be modified in each country to fit its particular needs", proceed each to reckon up what documents the distinctive conditions, laws and organisation of his country (and the interests of the more vocal of his country's Historians and Economists) make it convenient for him to label 'Archives'? That it will make an international meeting of Archivists even more suggestive of the Tower of Babel is the smallest of the ensuing evils.

Take again the acceptance of *Documentary Form* as a criterion in Definition; and therefore potentially in Arrangement. The disastrous effect of this upon great classes of the National Archives of France, Italy and England is an old story: but as a source of error the idea is not yet defunct. Only the other day in distinguished company I heard it solemnly maintained that two classes, both preserved in the Public Record Office, had different grades of quality as Public Records because of their diversity of form: one being a class of *Plea Rolls* and one of *Ministers' Accounts*.[1] Diverse? Of course they were diverse, not only in Form but in Content, Writing, Make-up and everything else, except one thing: but that one thing was vital — the fundamental fact that both were there because they had formed part of Central Public Administration. There lay the roots of both trees.

With the third question I mentioned — the possibility of *Age* as a criterion in definition — we come to a more comprehensive matter: the problem, looming larger every year, of the Records our own generation is compiling — their mass, their materials and their deplorable self-consciousness. Of that, if there is time, we may have something to say later: but the mere question of Ancient and Modern (Modern by the way, has a sad habit of becoming Ancient after a while) suggests another of the topics I had it in mind to mention.

THE TIME FACTOR

In considering Date or Age as an element which (apart from its physical effects in the shape of wear, decay and so forth) may affect the work of the Archivist we have to remember that it may operate two ways — call them vertical and horizontal — in the relations it establishes between one Archive or Archive class, and others. On the one hand you have that Archive's relations, in a line above and below it, with its own ancestors and descendants. Those relations are vitally important for all the primary tasks of the Archivist who has charge of it — his Sorting, Arrangement, Listing, even his system of Packing and Make-up. Moreover they give him the necessary key to the significance of his documents: no one (if I may cite an old favourite) could see a continuity between Wooden Tallies of the nineteenth century, three feet or more in length and oddly notched and inscribed (which were all that were known to us when I first entered the Record Office), and the description of Tallies in the *Dialogus de Scaccario* till a find of thirteenth-century examples bridged the gap and incidentally started a whole train of speculations (still in progress) about the Royal Finances in successive centuries. Not that the Archivist indulges in specu-

---

1. To anticipate (though I think it can hardly be necessary) the possible objection that many of these are in origin Private Archives, I must add a reminder that it is by no means unusual or classes of Archives to change, for administrative reasons, from one Group, and even from one Category, to another. Thus (to cite an old example) the Archives of the *African Company* of 1662 became part of those of a new Company in 1672 and both sets were turned over to yet a third body, the *Committee of Merchants trading to Africa*, in 1750: all three were private organisations but when, in 1820, the Nation assumed responsibility for West African affairs their Archives were vested with their Forts and other property, in the Crown and became, *as from that date*, Public Records.

lation — he leaves that to the Historian — but he does want, and need, to know the How and Why and What of his Archives.

On the other hand the Time Factor, working side-ways, will establish the relations of a particular Record, or Record Class, not with predecessors or successors but with contemporaries, possibly in quite other classes. There is obviously some relation of the 'horizontal' kind to be established potentially in the case of two-thirds of the documents that past Administration has bequeathed to us; because you cannot have an original letter preserved by A., the recipient, without the possibility of a copy surviving in the otherwise unrelated Archives of B., the writer. Thus the Archives Nationales at Paris preserve the original Ratification of a Treaty of which a copy has been enrolled by the Protonotary at the Chancery in London: the occurrence recorded by a Village Constable or Church-warden has its sequel in a presentment among the Records of Quarter Sessions: and so on. The possibilities of such relations are unlimited so soon as writing becomes a general practice in the conduct of affairs at all levels.

Now relations of this kind are a necessary subject for study by the Historian or Editor: no one certainly could quarrel with the admirable footnotes, drawn from other classes in England and abroad, with which Mr. Chaplais is enriching the text of his excellent edition of the *Treaty Rolls* for the Public Record Office. But for the Archivist they are by no means so important because they do not or should not affect his practical work: they have for instance (or should have) nothing to do with his Arrangement of his Archives. The danger of their doing so is of course greater in the case of a composite Record Repository, housing not only a number of Groups but a number of Categories of Archives; Categories which, though they may exist harmlessly (even beneficially) side by side must never be coagulated.

Am I here hinting at dangers too familiar and elementary to be feared; errors to which it is not to be thought any properly trained Archivist could possibly succumb? In this presence I must hasten to agree. But what of the future? We are working for, and I hope approaching, a situation where all kinds of Institutions whose vision extends at present to nothing further than current or obsolescent Files will be moved to think a little in terms of permanent Archives; without (I fear) going further in many cases than to detail for the post of Archivist some member of an (archivistically speaking) un-trained staff. May not the tale then be different — disastrously different?

However, I am here approaching once more that subject which I have reserved for a concluding section. May I turn to another of my 'Essentials'; and I am afraid another and even earlier reminiscence.

THE ADMINISTRATIVE BASIS

Forty-five years ago I ventured to propound to a small but select (and scandalised) audience of Historians, and afterwards to a slightly larger number of readers, the view that Palaeography and Diplomatic, in the strict sense in which those studies were understood, did not supply all the preliminary training necessary for students who proposed to embark, as increasing numbers were in fact embarking, upon Research in Records — generally Public Records, because few others were normally open to inspection. For many months I had been deep in the compilation of the work on Court Hands which C.G. Crump and Charles Johnson had planned and which Johnson and I executed; and fresh from the humiliating difficulty experienced in transcribing some of the facsimiles which we ourselves had selected, was able to say with conviction[2] that the Medieval Court Hands with which students would be confronted bristled with abbreviations, all-but-unreadable letter-forms and the like problems which no Palaeographical rules would enable them to solve; that correct reading depended in fact in a majority of cases on knowing in advance what the words to be read probably were, a knowledge which in most cases Diplomatic was as powerless as Palaeography to supply; that neither of these recognised aids to reading would, for example, enable us to extend insertions in the right-hand margin of a fifteenth-century *Receipt Roll*; and that the only sure basis on which to found was familiarity with the Office Routine that lay behind the Written Words. The answer to the despairing question which then arose, "If not Palaeography and Diplomatic what *are* we to teach our students before they come to your Search Room?" was in fact "Administrative History".[3]

But it was not only as a tool enabling Students to read the un-readable that Administrative History was commended. These and the years that followed the First War were the period which saw it raised to the position of a new and important section of History, to be studied for its own sake. Great days in the Round Room when Tout embarked[4] on that study of the *Privy Seal* which, beginning as no more than a review of the work of a French Archivist[5] ended in six volumes that came near to being a general History of Administration in Medieval England; when Bertha Putnam was bringing to life the medieval J.P.; when Miss Mills spent ten years in unravelling the

---

2. A conviction not lessened by experience some years after, with the Later Court Hands.
3. I think it was Crump, not I, who actually made that reply to no less a Medievalist than C.H. Haskins, of Harvard.
4. I believe I was privileged to be present at the embarkation.
5. Eugène Déprez, *Etudes de Diplomatique Anglaise*.

complexities of a single membrane in one *Pipe Roll*,[6] and J.F. Willard planned heroically a cross-section through the available Records of a short
period of the fourteenth century in search of administrative details at all
levels. Many disciples since have followed the trails blazed by these and
other pioneers: but of late I have seemed to discern signs of revolt, of
Historians saying that Administrative History has had a long enough
innings and it is time that some other variety of History went in.

From the point of view of the Historian this position may very possibly
be justified; but those who take it (and I fear one or two have been
Archivists) are liable to make the old mistake of assuming that the point of
view of the Historian must of necessity be that of the Archivist also: and
this assumption in the present case (and in others; for instance that of
Publication) is, I submit, wrong. For the Archivist the study of Administrative History is a matter not of choice but of necessity: he not only needs
it as a background but must from time to time engage himself actively in
extending it for the immediate purposes of his own work; and I do not think
the date up to which this remark applies can be limited. Certainly it may
extend far beyond the medieval, as anyone who has had to deal with the
earlier *Sessions Records* will probably have found; and the largely uncharted
ocean of Borough Records (especially the Legal and Accounting series) will
in due course provide not only a large number of individual fields for
research in this subject but, when sufficient material has accumulated, opportunities for synthesis and comparison. A number of other categories
might be mentioned which probably include types of Archive with forms
peculiar to themselves — clear enough to the man who wrote them but by
no means clear to anyone else.

I will even hazard a guess that the tale might be carried down to our own
time in some cases. Certainly, to judge by modern Records of this kind that
I have seen, those charged with large series of modern Accounting Archives
will find it both valuable and interesting to trace the Rise, Decline and Fall
of that once venerable Record the *Ledger* and its satellites. I am afraid it is
too much to hope that they will restore it to its former usefulness and pride
of place — loose-leaf and code letters have done their work too well.

LEARNING TO READ: THE ESTABLISHED COURSE

Once more I have been trespassing on my own preserves, anticipating
my own concluding remarks: but before I finally reach these there is one
more topic — or perhaps resumption of a topic on which I have already

6. The Surrey membrane for the year 1295. The complexities involved research in other *Pipe
Rolls* extending, backwards and forwards, over nearly 200 years.

dwelt — one more point at which, as it seems to be, we do not altogether or always get at the root of the matter: that of the Reading of Archives. It is different from the other topics on which I have touched, for Writing cannot be said to be an element in any definition of Archives though it and its peculiarities may be closely associated with (indeed form part of) the History of Administration: but I venture to think it is of some moment for it concerns the training of Student Archivists and has been occurring to me in so practical a connexion as the examination of candidates for the Diploma in London University.

When I speak of 'the root of the matter' in this connexion I am not referring to the origin of the Alphabet but to the basic principles from which students may be trained to approach the problem of learning to read English Records of all dates with ease and accuracy. I have no desire to prescribe for our Archivist a course in Roman or Greek Palaeography, not to mention more remote sources. It may be taken as generally accepted that to be a competent reader he need push his studies no further back than to the Caroline Minuscule, and even this only in the late development of it which we find in our earliest Records — *Domesday* and original *Royal Charters*. As a starting point it is very convenient not only because the letter forms are nearly all recognisable by their similarity to the 'Roman' of modern printing but because all the writings in which English Archives will appear from that time onwards can definitely be shown to derive from it through unbroken series of developments. When therefore the teaching of what was rather grandly called 'Palaeography' began in the newly founded School of Librarianship about 1920 the course laid down for it was to begin at the point in the twelfth century when the 'Court Hands' first came to be distinguished from 'Text' and follow them down through all their subsequent growths and variations until they were finally superseded (or practically superseded) by derivatives of the Italic in the eighteenth. It is to be remembered that when this teaching began the students were all Librarians; that it was a growing practice for Public Libraries to give house-room to documents of local interest which were in danger of destruction or dispersal; and that a large proportion of these refugees were *Deeds*, which might be of any date from the twelfth century onwards and written in practically any of the varieties of 'Court Hand': so that the course proposed was justified by practical considerations. It was (and is) justified also as a teaching method in any case because there is no question that any student who has made himself really proficient in reading the small and highly current hands of the thirteenth and fourteenth centuries will have little difficulty in mastering any of their successors; not excluding the 'Secretary' and 'Special Set Hands' of the sixteenth and seventeenth. It had (and has) only one drawback — that students, however hard they try, will never succeed in reading accurately the earlier writings unless they are fairly competent Latinists. For their teachers that has constituted from the first a major problem.

LEARNING TO READ: A COMPROMISE

As a result of that problem it has since been urged that there is a case for allowing students who have not the Latin to start their studies of Court Hands at the point where a large proportion of the documents written in the hand which is most commonly in use (the 'Secretary') are in English. There is something in the suggestion subject to certain provisos; and it is in regard to the two most important of these that I take up my parable.

The first is obvious but not perhaps very easy to comply with: it is that the person concerned should be reasonably certain that he or she will not be called on to read documents of earlier date than (say) the later sixteenth century. The second requires rather more exposition.

The medieval writer of 'Court Hands' — whoever (an uncertain point) were his teachers and whatever the copies set before him — was himself actively involved in the development of new letter forms and styles which was going on all the time. The school-boy of the later Tudor period, on the other hand, came into a world where the old oral teaching was being superseded; where printing was fixing the basic form of letters permanently; where Writing Masters and printed Copy Books abounded; and where he was set to learn for ordinary purposes (he often had to learn others as well) two alphabets whose forms (whatever he might make of them in his private practice later) were more or less standardized. He thus acquired, from printed facsimiles, hand-writings which were being taught at the same time in the same way to thousands of other boys. The modern reader who elects to start from this half-way house between medieval and modern will be (as his prototype was) the poorer for not knowing the quite logical and sensible reasons for a number of things which will strike him as illogical and unintelligible; such as the reason why the original simple form of many capital letters is camouflaged and obscured by meaningless extra strokes and how it comes that the small *e* is apparently written backwards: and there are certain difficulties, such as the very small highly current *Legal* and the oddities of the *Pipe Roll* Hands, with which no Writing Master's Book will help him. But he can, if he will, have an advantage which we can never have in the case of medieval writing — that of approaching the documents he has to read on the same footing of equality with the writers as we have when dealing with the writing of our contemporaries: because he can, if he likes, learn to read in the same way as the seventeenth-century writers learned to write, and from the same models. It is of course a condition that he shall bestow as great pains on learning the letter forms as they did: he might, in fact, do worse than practice writing one or other of the 'Secretary' styles himself. The task is laborious perhaps, but not difficult: and I confess I have little sympathy with the Student (or for that matter the Historian) who makes mistakes in transcription because he has not troubled to learn his alphabets as they are given in the pages of Cocker and a dozen other Masters, earlier or later.

The next stage, so far as writing is concerned, is that in which it ceases completely to be a subject of special study. We come in fact at last to our concluding section or sections, that King Charles' head which has so obstinately intruded prematurely into every point I have endeavoured to make with you up to now: the problem (or rather — for there are many — the problems) of the Archives piling up in our own day.

THOSE MODERN DOCUMENTS

I have taken up (you may think) a great deal of time with repetition of things I had myself said already in some distant past. I can only plead that it was not altogether vain repetition, because my object was deliberately to re-affirm. I repeated in this way my old Definition, re-stating all the Essentials which I believed to be inherent in it: all except one — the *Applicability of the Definition* itself *to Documents of all Kinds and Dates.*

I do not propose to deal in detail with the present situation, because that would be too long a task: but I think I may usefully put up for you a few friendly and tentative nine-pins. To begin, then, I will make bold to say that there is nothing in my old Definition which the nature of Modern Archives need compel me to withdraw or qualify. They *do* in the first instance accumulate naturally; they *are* the result of administrative activities; they *are* preserved primarily for purposes of reference by the persons or institutions that created them. Other preliminary matters, which may be taken as admitted facts, are first their enormous and at present inevitable *Mass* — a greater quantity than any of us conceived even during the War with the Army's monstrous consumption of paper going on under our eyes; then the *Duplication* or *Multiplication* resulting from the facilities offered to lazy or indifferent people by modern machinery; next the dubious quality of most of the *Materials* used; and finally the ultimate necessity for some measure of *Elimination* with the implied intrusion of *Selection*: an old trouble, this last, for some of us have been eliminating (and looking for some criterion for retention) these many years; but not intensified.

With certain problems resulting from these facts we must not attempt to deal now; because they are questions of practice, to be worked out as they arise and varying with circumstances: I mean the problems of Space, Staff, Repair and Make-up and a concomitant — Means as well as Ways.

Remain certain large questions to plague you who have not the one advantage which is mine — that of being old. May I tabulate half-a-dozen, with perhaps here and there a tentative personal comment?

1. *Is this increase of size to be regarded as an evil which will go on, perhaps even grow worse?*
I think myself it will diminish (though how soon cannot be predicted) with the introduction of substitutes for writing — mechanically recorded speech, for example.

2. *Is our trouble only the increased size of existing Archive Sources? What about New Categories of Archives from sources not hitherto archive-producing?*
It is a disturbing thought that we are, in some ways, doing our best to encourage this!

3. *What are to be*
(a) the *Means of Lessening the production of Documents* which will turn into Archives? and/or
(b) the *Criteria for Elimination* from those which are produced?

AN INTERPOLATION

The Grigg Committee on Departmental Records produced in its Report proposals which may seem to some extent applicable to Archives other than those of Central Administration.

(a) It proposed to attack the problem of over-production at the root: attacking, that is, the sections which in large offices have the charges of issuing and of filing; and which in many cases operate (it would seem) without the slightest thought of whether it is necessary even to make, let alone to keep, the mass of papers which modern machinery makes it so easy to produce.

(b) To meet the problem of Elimination the Committee began by accepting definitely the doctrine that a *First Pruning of Current Files* should take place soon enough for necessary knowledge of the circumstances in which they were produced not to have faded from recollection; should be undertaken by responsible staff acquainted with the business covered; and should be based on the primary question whether the documents were or were not necessary for 'Official Reference'.[7]

I do not imagine you will cavil at these common-sense proposals: I cannot because I enunciated them myself many years ago. But the Com-

7. I think that at this point we might usefully give to 'Official Reference' a slightly more precise definition. I have always put it that Preservation should be of such an order that even if a piece of business or a section of organisation had been discontinued for some considerable time surviving files would enable it to be taken up again without difficulty or delay.

mittee goes further by proposing a *Second Pruning* many years later, to be based on the probable or possible value of the documents for secondary purposes, those of research. I incline myself to think (for what my opinion is worth) that, failing substantial diminution in the accruals of written matter in the ways I have suggested as possible, though problematic, in the future, this ultimate intrusion of selection based on the interests of research is inevitable. But note that *none of the pruning processes is made the task of the Archivist*. The business of the Keepers of Archives is still, as Sir Thomas Hardy once put it, to keep them.

RESUMING

4. Are the Records of our own day, or the latest ones beginning at some fixed date, to be separated off from the more ancient, possibly with some specious distinction of title, such as 'Modern' and 'Historical'? (Again you will notice a point coming up which we have already approached.) I have no doubt there will be found persons to support some such proposals. My only comment would be that already made — or inferred — that severance at an arbitrarily fixed date means a severance of vital relations. If the proposal is made on grounds of economy of staff or space, it is one which has been discussed not infrequently in the past in connexion with the Public Records (there actually was, of course, a separate State Paper Office for many years; and within my own recollection there was a proposal to create a separate Record Office for Departmental Records) and the balance was always found to be against it. A far preferable alternative is to divide the actual Repository (the buildings) on grounds purely of convenience in management, but to maintain a single controlling authority.

5. A more reasonable case for severance might be found on other grounds and in view of really novel conditions: the suggestion might well be made that there was a case for separate housing and separate management for the documentary remains of activities which have no roots in the past, products entirely of our own times. It is a large question and I do no more than voice it: but it is not difficult to think of some — many — great and newly established scientific or industrial or even commercial concerns or institutions, or possibly an aggregation of several such institutions of like quality and function, the Archives of which might suitably be treated in this way and not joined to any existing local or even National Archive Organisation. There might be a strong argument, in view of the special nature of the activities which gave birth to these Archives, for a Repository specially equipped and with a Staff having technical knowledge of the activities in question.

6.This leads me to a final question which is to me the most interesting of all — that of the Specialist Staff which may undertake the care of Archives accumulating in such Institutions, or Bodies, or Concerns, as I have imagined; and the relation of them, their work and their training to those of the more ordinary Archive organisations with which we are familiar.

SPECIALISED ARCHIVES AND SPECIALISING ARCHIVISTS

Shall we try for a moment to envisage the needs and nature of an Officer in charge of the Documents accumulating in such an Institution, Body or Concern?

(a) His employers will require him (and he will need) to have had some training, in whatever may be the scientific or other specialised knowledge which they require of their more highly graded staff: he will, in fact, before he becomes an Archivist, have received the education of a Scientist rather than a Humanist.

(b) He will not contemplate changing over at any future date to what we may call ordinary Archive work; and will not, therefore, need or wish to acquire proficiency in many of the studies which are necessities for (e.g.) a County or Borough Archivist: he will not need Palaeography, nor a great deal of History, nor Medieval Latin or French; though he will probably, instead of these last, need some foreign language or languages.

(c) On the other hand it is most desirable that he should be affiliated to the Archivist's profession as practised elsewhere. The documents he will have in charge, though wildly different in content (and different, in some cases, in form) from those normally found in a County or Borough Repository will still be Archives, conforming readily to the standards expressed in our Definition, Archives in quality and to be guided by the same principles and sorted, numbered, listed according to like rules.

(d) Though not enabled by knowledge and training to undertake many of the ordinary tasks performed by 'ordinary' Archivists he should acquire at least background knowledge, some acquaintance with the nature, require- ments and conditions of their work, and may reasonably expect his 'ordinary' colleagues to reciprocate: and there are some branches of study which they might well (I would even venture to say "which they ought") to pursue in common during their period of training.

THE CONCLUSION OF THE MATTER

I must not prolong this Plutarchan examination into the parallel lives of the Specialising and the General Archivist; nor is it our business here to lay down Schedules of Study. But I suggest to you, as a matter of immediate and real importance, that the Specialising Archivist (as I have called him) is coming; that we want him to come and want him to co-operate with us; and that it may be a wise thing to formulate now (or to secure their formulation) the conditions which will make such co-operation possible and fruitful.[8]

8.　The corrected and extensively revised script of this Address, so far as is known Sir Hilary Jenkinson's last completed literary work, was passed by him for press on 29 January 1961, five weeks before his death. The Society in indebted to Mr. Roger H. Ellis for the checking of the proofs.